SOUTHERN BAPTISTS OBSERVED

SOUTHERN BAPTISTS OBSERVED

Multiple Perspectives on a
Changing Denomination

Edited by
Nancy Tatom Ammerman

The University of Tennessee Press • Knoxville

The paper in this book meets the minimum requirements of the
American National Standard for Permanence of Paper for Printed
Library Materials. ∞ The binding materials have been chosen
for strength and durability.

Library of Congress Cataloging in Publication Data

Southern Baptists observed : multiple perspectives on a changing denomination / edited
by Nancy Tatom Ammerman. — 1st ed.
        p.   cm.
    Includes bibliographical references and index.
    ISBN 0-87049-769-3 (cloth: alk. paper)
    ISBN 0-87049-770-7 (pbk.: alk. paper)
    1. Southern Baptist Convention—History—20th century.
2. Baptists—United States—History—1965– . 3. United States—Church history—20th
century. I. Ammerman, Nancy Tatom, 1950– .
BX6462.3.S68   1993
286' .132—dc20   92-18725
                                                     CIP

■ CONTENTS

■ TABLES

■ FIGURE

ACKNOWLEDGMENTS

It has been delightful to work with the people whose chapters make up this volume. But bringing this all together would simply not have been possible without the able assistance of Karen DeNicola, administrative assistant in my office at the Candler School of Theology, Emory University. Karen has kept track of the innumerable details that go into keeping up with sixteen authors, and she has ably formatted the notes and constructed the bibliography. Her scholarship, no less than her clerical skill, has made this volume possible.

■ ABBREVIATIONS

Throughout the text, the following abbreviations are used.

BJCPA	Baptist Joint Committee on Public Affairs
CBF	Cooperative Baptist Fellowship
SBA	Southern Baptist Alliance
SBC	Southern Baptist Convention

CHAPTER 1

OBSERVING SOUTHERN BAPTISTS: AN INTRODUCTION

Nancy T. Ammerman

It was an event too big to miss, this "conservative resurgence" in the Southern Baptist Convention. Even people normally not interested in religion paid attention. As the nation's largest Protestant denomination and the South's dominant religious institution, this group's transformation in the 1980s captured the public eye and caught the attention of scholars.

To people inside the SBC, it was all simply known as "the Controversy." Never before in their history had differences among them run so deep and so wide. For these insiders, the Controversy was a story of pain and disappointment, of anger and despair—or of triumph and vindication, depending on where they stood relative to those differences.

But people outside the Southern Baptist Convention—especially scholars—felt more curiosity than pain. The Controversy was a phenomenon that needed to be explained. How could a once-monolithic, seemingly unstoppable evangelical force such as the SBC come to such a fate? In the "church growth" literature of the 1970s, the SBC was the star.[1] Long after mainline denominations began to decline, the SBC's growth curve seemed to move ever upward. The SBC had been one of Dean Kelley's exemplars of "why conservative churches are growing."[2]

For some scholars the question was, What went wrong? Others raised questions because this conservative movement seemed to occur at the wrong time and place, in the midst of an increasingly progressive and modernized South. If conservative religion endured primarily where education and urbanization had not yet had their liberalizing influences, the Southern Baptist Convention should be in the process of shedding its traditionalism, not buttressing it. Others, however, saw the changes in the South as creating precisely the sort of social environment likely to produce religious upheaval, and some scholars leapt at the chance to test theories about the relationship between social and religious change. Still others simply wanted to watch carefully to see how events unfolded. The opportunity to observe such an organizational take-over—especially a conservative one—is rare, and understanding how a conservative movement managed to organize such a stunning coup occupied some.[3]

The events in the Southern Baptist Convention were both fascinating and vaguely disturbing for scholars. Here were events that challenged long-held theories about the inevitable march of education and science and progress, about the organizational strength of bureaucracies with well-educated elites at their helms, about the proper relationship between religion and politics, and about how "supernatural" explanations of the world were disappearing. For diverse theoretical and personal reasons, dozens of scholars were drawn to the Southern Baptist Convention's Controversy; for each, it was a phenomenon to be explained.

This book is both a collection of those explanations and a look at the enterprise of explaining. It offers an opportunity to examine this event through a number of different disciplinary lenses, to "explain" it from a variety of vantage points. Like the blind men and the elephant, each writer's description is shaped by the particular sense of touch afforded by his or her way of studying.

Historians, for instance, look for the watershed moments that have shaped the world. They want to know when we started doing things this way, how it used to be different, and why the change came about. They look for the signposts—people and events that were formative and had lasting influence—even if almost unnoticed at the time. Journalists, on the other hand, look for the people and events that make news today. Sometimes events are of interest precisely because they are *not* usual or ordinary. Still, the informed journalist also looks for signposts, trying to understand today's events in the light of history and trying to anticipate who future historians will point to as the people who shaped the world.

Social philosophers look at events with a keen eye for the ideas that weave their way through history and the news. How are people building on, or discarding elements of, the intellectual tradition they have inherited? How do they defend their actions? Religious philosophers look for the influence and application of ideas, as well, but ideas specifically related to sacred texts and events. How do people understand the relationship between themselves and the sacred? And how does that understanding change, evolving as new challenges or confirmations occur? Others in religious studies may simply be fascinated with the ways in which people tell the stories of how this world came to be, is now, and will ever be. Each of these scholars wonders how our lives would be different if we were guided by different stories and principles.

Social scientists of all sorts have tended to focus their energies on the various processes out of which social life is made. With increasing precision we can identify the influences of ideology, cultural norms, network connections, and organizational resources. Anthropologists can see long-standing cultural patterns, and they can show how these patterns are transmitted from one generation to the next and how they may reappear in a new guise. Sociologists can trace communication paths and identify the ways in which both cultures and organizations define the limits and opportunities of the people in them. Political scientists focus on the way the structures of power and government define, and are defined by, those limits and opportunities. We all want to know which ideas gain credence and why, which events are meaningful, and whose actions are remembered.

The events, texts, behavior, and people of the Southern Baptist Convention can be read and re-read, then, interpreted and analyzed from any of these perspectives. Although each of this book's authors may tell the story as if his or her version were complete, each also recognizes that that version is only one layer, or only one part of the elephant. Even if modern universities have divided human knowledge into discernible, bounded "fields," human life and human events do not neatly follow the bidding of universities. Still, those "fields" are the ground on which each of us must stand. It is there that we have gained our skills for reading the texts of the world around us.

Each of us also stands within a particular life story, and each life story has intersected with the Southern Baptist Convention in a different way. Some—Barnhart, Hill, Norsworthy, and Farnsley—grew up with the Southern Baptist tradition, but broke with it in various ways. For Hill and Norsworthy, the civil rights movement was the point of exit. Others—Ammerman, Metcalf-Whittaker, Anders, Turner, Knight, Ingram, McSwain, and George—have in one form or another stayed with the tradition. Guth grew up Baptist but was not Southern Baptist until he moved South. Still others—Winston, Rosenberg, Heriot, and Harding—have approached the SBC as outside observers, noticing what others might have missed. Only McSwain works for an institution directly threatened by the take-over, but Turner, Guth, George, and Anders work in Baptist colleges and universities. Knight left his denominational post as an indirect result of the Controversy and founded an independent "moderate" newspaper, for which he serves as publisher.

My place is different now from what it was when I wrote *Baptist Battles* (1990). As I said in the introduction to that book, although I began the research with no partisan alignments, by the end of the writing, I had become convinced that I wanted to support those in the Alliance of Baptists who were trying to create a new future for Baptists no longer at home in the SBC. Since then I have been elected to the SBA's board of directors and have helped to form the Cooperative Baptist Fellowship, a somewhat broader coalition with similar goals. My thoughts on the future are clearly shaped by those commitments as well as by my sociological training.

Although institutional locations and loyalties created both opportunities and constraints, each author's expectations also were shaped by the events of particular times. The youngest of this book's authors were born in the 1960s, whereas the oldest lived through the Great Depression and World War II. Some bring the eyes and ears of men, but their views are complemented by the perspectives of women. Some write as believers, others as agnostics; some write from within the Christian tradition, others from within the Jewish tradition. And all, except Knight and Winston, saw these events from inside the academic world. We may pretend that "objective" observers occupy a privileged position of neutrality, but our own lives have provided us with the vocabulary we use, the passions that motivate us, and the impulse to explain a phenomenon such as this.

Even the terms we use to describe the combatants are shaped by where we stand. Those on the theological right are called *fundamentalists* by their opponents, *conservatives* by their friends. Those on the theological left are called *liberals* by their opponents and *moderates* by their friends. At one point Baptist Press, the denomination's news service, invented *moderate-conservative* and *fundamental-conservative* as compromise terms. In this book we avoid those awkward compromise terms, but each author will describe what happened in terms that suit his or her particular task. Generally, *fundamentalist* describes leaders and activists who sought to stem the tide of liberalism in the denomination. As I argue in *Baptist Battles,* this term has been used historically to describe similar movements that have sought to restore orthodoxy after a period of disruption and change.[4] We will use the term *conservative* to describe the direction in which they wished to move. But conservative also describes the vast majority of Southern Baptists and will sometimes be used for the mainstream. Because so few Southern Baptists are liberal by any standard used outside the denomination, that term will be used rarely here. Those who organized in opposition to fundamentalist activists will generally be called *moderates.* That term, along with *progressive,* will also be used to describe the left wing of Southern Baptist life.

And so, a disrupted denomination, in which even the nomenclature was in dispute, is the object of study undertaken by this group of observers. The initial chapters came from two sessions of the meetings of the Religious Research Association in 1988. Subsequently, I worked with Ray Norsworthy, who was then on sabbatical at Emory, to see what other vantage points might make the book more complete. The views of journalists and historians were added, as were the views of various "insiders." The aim was to allow a diversity of disciplines and viewpoints to inform us.

Each writer found something different to explain. Some sought to explain it all; others found one fascinating facet to explore. Each looked at what happened with his or her particular disciplinary tools at hand, and told a story in ways that both complement and challenge other stories. Together they help us examine these unfolding events more carefully and more completely than any one could do alone.

All of the authors in this volume have had access to the data on the Southern Baptist Convention collected by the Center for Religious Research at Emory (major portions of which are reported in *Baptist Battles*). That information about what happened in the conflict provided background for some, corroboration for others, interesting sidelights or contrasts for others. Most of these authors have collected additional data specific to their own discipline and focus, but the center's survey results form a thread of empirical continuity throughout this collection.

A Preview

We begin our observations in the way that many people first encountered this conflict—through the news. Diane Winston, a journalist who covered the story for papers in North Carolina, Texas, and Maryland, takes us to the scene of the battle. She introduces us to the contestants and re-creates for us the sights and sounds of the conflict. By the end of her essay, we feel as if we have been there, as if we know these people and understand something of how they came to be who they are and why events unfolded as they did.

Historian Samuel Hill is concerned, of course, with where these events came from. He has listened carefully to this denomination's story about itself and has found in it some peculiar ironies. Stories about spectacular growth and all-encompassing programs were the stuff of Southern Baptist bragging a generation ago—a kind of proud centerpiece to the denomination's identity. But here Hill finds the seeds of the conflict to follow. It was a conflict that first appeared—not surprisingly—in the seminaries. There and elsewhere there were ironic, unintended consequences of the organizational decisions made from the 1920s onward.

Social philosopher Arthur Farnsley would not disagree with Hill about the outlines of the story, but he focuses his lens somewhat differently. He wants to know how people make decisions about their collective destiny and how that decision process has changed in the SBC. He looks for the life ex-periences they draw on and for the ideas that shape their sense of how things ought to be done. And he wonders both how Baptists have learned their rules by being Americans and what lessons the SBC has to teach others in the American polity.

The transformation of the SBC into a bureaucracy—beginning in the 1920s—is something Hill, Farnsley, and Norsworthy see as a critical change. In fact, sociologist Ray Norsworthy insists that the conservative resurgence was really an antibureaucratic movement at its heart. It may have protested loudly about "modern" interpretations of the Bible, but it was modern ways of organizing—and the often-secular criteria they embodied—that fundamen-talists in the Southern Baptist Convention sought to reverse.

All three of these interpreters also agree that the 1950s and 1960s were a disruptive period in the life of Southern Baptists. As I have argued, as well, the South was transformed during that period in a variety of ways, and Southern Baptists lost their comfortable symbiotic relationship with a rather stable, predominantly rural and small town, culture. In the midst of such changes, people often begin to look for new ways of telling the most basic and ancient stories about themselves and the world, stories labeled by theologians and historians of religion *cosmology* (stories about beginnings) and *eschatology* (stories about endings). From the discipline of religious studies, Helen Lee Turner takes a look at the way in which the telling of such stories directed change in the SBC. Different groups in the denomination simply began to tell the story of the world differently, and for the conservatives the new story included their own active and triumphant role.

Joe Barnhart also has heard people fighting about their creation stories, but he has listened with the special ears of a philosopher of religion who specializes in understanding the processes by which people understand and interpret sacred texts. He has heard these people talk about "inerrancy" and wonders just what they really mean. He reads between and beneath the lines and uncovers the ambiguities of that word. Barnhart wants to know which rules of interpretation these new conservatives are ready to pursue.

The story conservatives were telling, however, was not just about cosmic realities. It was also about the way they wanted their cultural, political, and social lives to be ordered. The agenda and alliances of the SBC's conservative movement, argues anthropologist Ellen Rosenberg, are a new expression of the old racist and male-dominated patterns of southern society. And they were aided by a conservative administration in Washington that provided states with new means and new rationales for old habits of keeping their poorest citizens—disproportionately African Americans—outside the mainstream.

Whereas Rosenberg saw those patterns as an outsider and an anthropologist trained to see such cultural regularities, Walker Knight saw them from inside the denomination, as editor of *Home Missions* (later renamed *Missions USA*), a magazine that describes the wide variety of ministries in which Baptists in the United States were engaged during the critical years. During the 1960s and 1970s, Knight chronicled a denomination struggling to change. Alongside the conservative effort to preserve racial tradition, there were other courageous individuals, churches, and institutions that sought to find new ways of being Baptist and southern and integrated—efforts often featured in the pages of Knight's magazine. In the 1980s those moderating efforts largely came to a halt, however, stopped in large part by the need to contain the conservative resurgence, but stymied as well by other forces of change.

We now have a plate full of explanations—from racial politics to theology to modernization. Is one of them better than the others? Using the tools of survey and statistical analysis, political scientist James Guth puts a series of explanations to the test. In the process he offers a view of the complex way education has played a key role in shaping a two-party SBC system in which political and religious ideas have intertwined to create loyalty among some and dissidence among others. The status that matters in this system is not so much the measurable advantages social scientists usually look for, but differences in prestige defined by the particular history of this denomination.

It is no accident, of course, that until now women have been nearly invisible in our analysis. This denomination's official story is told almost entirely by men about men. Men have been the presidents and pastors and denominational leaders. From one angle, this looks like a man's fight. But the story is not that simple, say Sarah Frances Anders and Marilyn Metcalf-Whittaker. Women historically have played a variety of roles, and in the 1970s they seemed to be slowly moving into leadership positions in the SBC. Only slightly behind women in other denominations, they also began to move toward the pulpit. And their entry into the ordained ministry—something each Baptist church decides for itself—has placed women at the center of this conflict. They are the symbol of heresy for one side and the symbol of open-mindedness and freedom for the other. These two sociologists ask us to notice these women's lives, noting their importance to the overall conflict.

If women have absorbed much of this conflict into their lives, no less have those who have served Baptists by teaching in denominational colleges. They have had to reexamine the meaning of their vocation, taking new measure of the academic freedom they have or do not have. Sociologist Larry Ingram, with colleagues Robert Thornton and Reneé L. Edwards, asked a sample of Baptist college professors to tell them what they thought about these issues. By looking at what those professors said academic freedom is, and seeing who said they have it and would defend it, these observers are able to see some ironic patterns of accommodation and resistance. Although the colleges are not controlled by national SBC elections as the seminaries are—and most do not have fundamentalist boards of trustees—Ingram and his colleagues find that a fundamentalist presence is felt. Undoubtedly it is this looming threat that accounts for moves by historic Baptist universities—Baylor, Furman, Stetson, and earlier Wake Forest and Richmond—to sever their official connections to state Baptist conventions.

As one moves outward toward the smaller, rural congregations that still make up nearly half of all SBC churches, the terms with which to define the denomination's conflict are much less clear. Jean Heriot, an anthropologist, was in one of those smaller churches when the conflict was at its height. Interestingly, at that time the church changed pastors, bidding farewell to a man whose sympathies were with the fundamentalists and welcoming as interim pastor a man aligned with the moderates. Each pastor had a different version of the denomination's story (and the congregation was thoroughly confused). What is even more interesting, however, is the *way* those stories were told—the differences in the rhetorical styles of the pastors, the contents of the stories, and the cultural framework in which the stories were heard. Here was a place in which the question of who to support in a national denominational fight challenged the cosmic terms in which conflict usually had been framed.

In other places, however, the potential of fundamentalist control was vitally salient. Larry McSwain found himself in just such a place—as a teacher of religion and society, then dean and later provost, at the School of Theology of the denomination's flagship seminary in Louisville. He watched from the inside as moderates tried to organize a resistance movement. Both his social scientist's eye and his role in the conflict have given him a way to see how the denomination has been transformed. He wonders what the unintended consequences of this revolution may be. What new norms are emerging? Is inerrancy really the defining trait at the center of Southern Baptist life? By looking at this as a social movement—and countermovement—McSwain offers some wry reflections about its future.

Timothy George sees the future somewhat differently. By looking at Southern Baptists from the vantage point of the larger evangelical movement, George hopes to see an increasing sense of kinship. He argues that the conflict has been "deeply ideological" and that the beliefs being defended are squarely within the evangelical tradition often shunned by previously insular Baptists in the South. As dean of a new divinity school on a Baptist university campus, George is understandably concerned about theology. He points out that all sides in this controversy were hampered by decades of theological neglect fostered by misreadings of what it meant to be "creedal." Calling for a "holistic orthodoxy," he is hopeful about the changes this conservative resurgence has wrought.

Although ideas have divided Southern Baptists, those divisions are beginning to take tangible form. The organizational shape of the future is the question addressed in my chapter. As a sizable group of Southern Baptists turn their energies away from the attempt to counter fundamentalists and toward new alternatives, they face a bewildering array of choices. The shape of denominational life in America is being transformed, and these Southern Baptist pilgrims have become a part of that transformation. They may form a new denomination in the old form, or they may create some new coalitional form that links them in complex ways with old organizations and traditions and with the thriving para-church sector in American religion.

The Explanations in Perspective

Each of these writers uses the tools of a scholarly discipline to examine a major change in America's religious landscape. Together, they seek to explain what happened and why. What Susan Harding suggests in her concluding essay, however, is that we all have been caught up in our own story—a way of looking at the world given to us by our schooling and our place in the scholarly community. She wonders why we find the Controversy so fascinating and expend so much energy explaining it. Her essay proposes that in our zealous interpretation of fundamentalism, we are defending and advancing a particular version of history, one of almost mythological importance in chartering modern Americans. She reexamines the Scopes trial not to find parallels in current events but as a "fundamentalist origin story" that shapes how scholars and journalists narrate and interpret current events. As an anthropologist, she is interested in the way people produce and enact the central stories of their lives. The SBC presidential battles were major cultural dramas for

Southern Baptists, but they—and stories, essays, books, and conferences about them—were also important cultural dramas for the scholars and journalists who examined them. Changes in how we tell the story of fundamentalism not only reflect changes in the lives of fundamentalists but also changes in the lives of those who tell the story.

This book, then, is both a set of explanations and an exercise in thinking about explaining. We are forced by the many-faceted nature of these essays to confront the layers of reality in which we live, the many ways in which we can tell the story of our lives and of the world around us. And we are forced in the end to reflect on our own activity, to recognize our own roles in creating these stories.

Notes

1. See Dean R. Hoge and David A. Roozen, eds., *Understanding Church Growth and Decline* (New York: Pilgrim, 1979), especially Phillip Jones's "An Examination of the Statistical Growth of the Southern Baptist Convention."
2. Dean M. Kelley, *Why Conservative Churches are Growing* (New York: Harper & Row, 1972).
3. My own *Baptist Battles: Social Change and Religious Conflict in the Southern Baptist Convention* (New Brunswick, N.J.: Rutgers Univ. Press, 1990) is largely a report on this aspect of the event.
4. See Ammerman, *Baptist Battles,* 16-17.

CHAPTER 2

■ THE SOUTHERN BAPTIST STORY
Diane Winston

Prophets are not without honor, except in their own land. That helps explain why Cecil Sherman and Paige Patterson were not the most popular men in the Southern Baptist Convention during the 1980s. Both Patterson and Sherman stumped the countryside, preaching in big city churches and backwater congregations. They railed against different idols, but their message was the same: Something unholy is happening here, something needs to change.

What both hoped to change was the fifteen-million-member Southern Baptist Convention. Once called the Roman Catholic church of the South, the SBC provided the social, cultural, and religious threads that knit together brothers and sisters south of the Mason-Dixon line. The SBC was born in 1845, when Northern Baptists informed their slave-owning cousins that they no longer could serve as foreign missionaries. Southerners maintained that their Bible permitted holding human beings as chattel and, thus, a denomination began.

The fledgling denomination took on the coloring of the region. Its members were wary of centralization, suspicious of creeds, skeptical of higher education. During the Civil War, its preachers trumpeted the South's holy crusade; when Dixie fell, her pastors offered solace in personal salvation. The SBC reflected hallowed southern identity. Because it sanctified individualism as well as conservatism, the denomination tolerated a diversity of biblical interpretation. The men who controlled Baptist educational and evangelistic endeavors put more stock in furthering collective goals than in maintaining creedal purity. The denomination felt like family, which made it possible for the Cecil Shermans of the SBC—those who believed more in discerning God's message than in cleaving to his word—to coexist with diehard fundamentalists such as Paige Patterson.

The mix worked—until the turmoil of the post-World War II era. Suddenly Yankees were moving into magnolia-lined neighborhoods; young ACTEENS and Royal Ambassadors—the denomination's youth groups—trudged off to college, and television sets, automobiles, and fast-food restaurants linked the nation to new dreams of bigger, better, faster, and richer.

At first Baptists were slow to change. The white clapboard church at the country crossroads still brimmed each Sunday with roughhewn believers eager to hear the word of God. They dipped their converts in the river, sang "Amazing Grace," and gave happily to the programs they believed in—evangelistic efforts to bring sinners to Jesus and educational efforts to raise up the clergy.

But it was these very educational efforts that began roiling the surface of Baptist life. Baptists were ambivalent about book learning. Not only could schooling put a preacher at odds with his people but too much learning could lead to questions that chipped away at Bible-believing faith.

History had proved Southern Baptists vigilant in guarding against such doubts. In 1879 a professor at Southern Baptist Theological Seminary in Louisville, Kentucky, began teaching that the Old Testament was derived from a complex oral tradition, and that Moses did not really write the first five books of the Bible. Soon after, he was forced to resign. Almost one hundred years later, in 1961, a professor at Midwestern Baptist Theological Seminary in Kansas City, Missouri, offered similar notions in a book about Genesis. He, too, lost his job.

Throughout the 1970s a critical mass of true believers began wondering what was going on in the denomination's colleges and seminaries. Were young men and women fraternizing too freely? Were the wrong kinds of people invited to lecture and teach? Did textbooks undermine basic biblical beliefs? Paul Pressler, a federal appeals court judge in Houston, says he was galvanized by a late-night call from students at Baylor University in Waco, Texas, asking him to come up and look at their study materials. Pressler, who for years harbored suspicions about the soundness of denominational teachings, was horrified to see school books that questioned the divine origin of Scripture.

Pressler's Houston roots run five generations deep. He is a small, soft-spoken man with a Torquemada-like sensibility: he hates liberals. His aversion developed during his school years in the North. A student at Phillips Exeter Academy in New Hampshire, Pressler was enraged when a Baptist minister told him, "I never understood what you Southerners mean by being saved." His college days at Princeton were no better. Pressler left the North convinced its churches had been emasculated by liberalism; he swore his own denomination would never suffer a similar fate.

For years Pressler nurtured his passion alone. But toward the end of the 1960s, during a trip to New Orleans, Pressler found his match. Paige Patterson, a barrel-chested, red-haired seminary student, was as disgusted with liberalism as the judge. At their first meeting, the two swapped miseries deep into the night. "I was living on campus in a small apartment with my wife and a Siamese cat when a guy knocked on my door around midnight," recalls Patterson, who is now president of Criswell Bible College in Dallas. "He said, 'I am Paul Pressler from Houston and a mutual friend said we should get together.' We went to the Café du Monde for café au lait and doughnuts. We discussed things like my best friend from seminary buying into liberalism and leaving the ministry. We talked about the times conservative beliefs were subject to ridicule, and we talked about what we could do about it."

Back then they could not do much. Patterson was a graduate student and Pressler an unknown lawyer. Still, they kept talking and seeking others who shared their concerns. By the end of the 1970s, they had formulated a strategy. They would target the Baptist theological seminaries—specifically, Southeastern in Wake Forest, North Carolina; Southern in Louisville, Kentucky; and Midwestern in Kansas City, Missouri. They would say the schools had taken a leftward tilt. They would charge that faculties and administrations were unresponsive to conservative criticism. And they would offer a way to force change and save the Baptist schools.

The way was this: The SBC's president, who could be elected to two one-year terms, had appointive powers that determined who sat on trustee boards. If conservatives elected their own man to the presidency for ten years, they could pack boards with their supporters and make policy and personnel changes to suit their beliefs. In the past Baptists had politicked through networks of friendships and associations for the honor of the top post. This was the first time an organized effort with an explicit platform had coalesced.

Patterson and Pressler found at least one man in every state to support the plan. They held their first meeting at the Ramada Inn-Airport in Atlanta in the winter before the 1979 convention. They explained the denomination's constitutional process and how it provided for a course correction. Next they outlined how to get the new course in place. They would alert Baptist people to the dangerous teachings in their seminaries, then explain that the problem could be taken care of by electing conservative men to the SBC's presidency. Pressler and Patterson instructed the men with whom they met in Atlanta to organize their states. The two Texans would be front men for the group, holding public rallies, speaking to the press, and catching flak from the other side.

When Baptist messengers—as convention delegates are called—descended on Houston for their annual convention in June 1979, Pressler and Patterson had done their job. In the months before the meeting, the judge and the pastor had spoken at rallies in fifteen states. Traditionally, seats for the annual Foreign Mission Board report were the hardest to come by; this time, the election for president gathered the peak convention crowd.

The word whispered in corridors was that Memphis pastor Adrian Rogers was the man to beat. For the past two years, Jimmy Allen had held the top post. Allen, a plump, gray-pompadoured denominational stalwart, had felt the rumblings of discontent. He was said to have headed off Rogers earlier by asking friends if they would prefer him or the man from Memphis. Allen made use of contacts and supporters nationwide, the first candidate to openly declare his interest in the top denominational spot. He later tried to differentiate his strategy from what he called the Pressler-Patterson precinct-style political machine. But the Texas twosome disagreed; they said Allen was the first denominational candidate to lobby for office. Few Baptists argued; they doubted Pressler and Patterson had done anything different from Allen. Even fewer understood in 1979 that the Pressler-Patterson coalition had a long-range strategy to reshape the denomination.

What messengers did understand was Adrian Rogers's charisma. His dark good looks, velvet-toned voice, and solid scriptural faith made him the conservatives' darling. The Reverend W. A. Criswell, the fiery fundamentalist patriarch of the First Baptist Church of Dallas, told a cheering crowd of ten thousand conservative preachers in a Houston hall, "We will have a great time here if for no other reason than to elect Adrian Rogers our president." [1]

Rogers insists he did not want to run for the top spot and agreed to do so only after an old family friend implored him. He went up against five candidates and won handily on the first ballot. Amid the huzzahs, Rogers's opponents looked up to see Pressler and friends celebrating in the convention hall's skybox. Afterwards they charged that Pressler and Patterson had run the proceedings from their above-ground perch. The two men denied pulling strings from on high; Patterson added that their preconvention politicking was nothing out of the ordinary. "The moderate element was looking for anything it could to establish an emotional reaction to us," Patterson said of the skybox. "It was more an effort of comfort—a place to eat. . . . Now deciding who to run—that was no departure. That's always how it's been. When I was a kid I'd be in backrooms with my dad [T. R. Patterson, formerly the head of Texas Baptists] when they discussed who ought to run. It was a matter of consensus. But there was always considerable political activity."

That activity continued after Houston. Patterson and Pressler, aware that one election did not a revolution make, continued to press their case. Over time their criticism of the seminaries crystallized as a call for inerrancy—the belief that Scripture is without error. "Inerrancy" became a popular battle cry. It could easily be tested: Either you believed the biblical accounts were real—whether Jonah's survival in the belly of the whale or Jesus rising from the dead—or you did not. Moreover, inerrancy was a difficult charge to assail. Fighting it meant battling against the Bible; and within Baptist life, where Scripture is paramount, opposing the flag, motherhood, and apple pie would have been an easier mission.

Thus even as opponents to Pressler and Patterson's strategy saw what was happening, they seemed unable to do anything about it. Denominational leaders cautioned against organizing, believing that opposing Pressler and Patterson would only harden their positions. Furthermore, what banner could they rally 'round? Charges that a political machine was in the making evoked skepticism in a denomination celebrated for persnickety individualism. Criticism of the Pressler-Patterson crusade rang false: How could anyone disagree with fidelity to the Bible?

In 1980, when the Baptists met in St. Louis, Rogers announced that health problems prevented him from seeking a second term as president. The Pressler-Patterson group picked Bailey Smith, an energetic evangelist from Oklahoma, as their candidate. Five others were nominated, but Smith won on the first ballot. Later in the proceedings, messengers went on record as opposing abortion, except when the mother's life was endangered, and as opposing ratification of the Equal Rights Amendment.

Pressler and Patterson were pleased their candidate was elected and their political stands backed, but their real goal was yet to be achieved. Rogers's trustee appointments were all stalwart inerrantists, but they were just one year's worth of nominations. Now, with Smith's election, there would be at least two rounds of conservative picks.

Three months after St. Louis, Pressler piquantly described his strategy during a rally in Lynchburg, Virginia: "We have been fighting battles without knowing what the war is all about. We have not been effective because we have not gotten to the root of the problem. . . . The lifeblood of the Southern Baptist Convention is the trustees. We need to go for the jugular—we need to go for the trustees."[2]

Before long, "going for the jugular" became synonymous with the Pressler-Patterson strategy. Pressler said he was speaking metaphorically, but the message had already mobilized opposition. It spurred Cecil Sherman, a tall, bespectacled North Carolina pastor, to invite several friends to a meeting in Gatlinburg, Tennessee.

Sherman was the thinking man's preacher. He, too, hailed from solid Texas stock, but unlike his opponents, Sherman did not run from the conundrums of the modern world. For him being a Baptist meant applying biblical principles to each new challenge and finding strength in the synthesis. Sherman spoke slowly, but his measured words found their mark in a ministry to the marginal. He believed in both living out the message of grace and challenging deceit where he found it.

The Gatlinburg Gang, as the seventeen participants at Sherman's meeting were called, represented Southern Baptist strongholds from Texas to Virginia. They called themselves denominational loyalists but, over time, they would be known as moderates—just as the Pressler-Patterson group were dubbed fundamentalists by their opponents, conservatives by their friends. "We decided to go back and put together a network in each state to resist these people," said Sherman, now pastor of a Fort Worth church. "We correctly reasoned if our vision of the Southern Baptist Convention were to prevail these people would have to be defeated."

Cecil Sherman's vision of the Southern Baptist Convention clashed vehemently with Paige Patterson's, and each man's desire to preserve what was best in the denomination turned him into a politician. Their differences began with theology but spilled into world views that diverged on everything from political issues to denominational structure.

For Patterson, the Baptist is first and last a soul winner bound to the irrefutable word of God. God's word supersedes all else—in fact, it shapes all of life. God's word dictates political stands—opposing abortion and the ERA, fighting godless communism and strengthening a Christian America; it clarifies ecclesiastical choices—building larger churches and bringing in more lost souls; it advances theological positions—banning women ministers and opting for evangelism, rather than dialogue, with other religions. Patterson's is a rigorous system demanding adherence to an all-or-nothing faith. It is also an ideology that coincided with the then-reigning sensibility in American life. Like Reaganism it vaunted the triumph of the chosen, as evidenced in outward signs of election: bigger, better, richer.

Cecil Sherman's understanding of Baptist life has fewer sharp edges. The Baptist is bound to the Bible, but each human being is free to interpret Scripture. Denominational life is not undergirded by creed but by freely given cooperation in missions and educational work. Religious life is a rich weave of faith-driven individuals seeking God in their own way. Moderates may not like abortion, but they recognize it may be necessary in some cases. They believe the Baptist way is right, but they will listen to a Jew or Muslim. They can appreciate big and beautiful sanctuaries, but they say teaching believers to live Christian lives is as important as saving souls.

To thousands of Baptists like Cecil Sherman, Paige Patterson represents a dark incarnation of right-wing forces bent on ripping the Southern Baptist Convention from its historic moorings of tolerance for each individual's walk with God. But to just as many believers, Cecil Sherman is a liberal devil, ready to sell the denomination's scriptural soul for an Ivy League degree.

After Gatlinburg, Sherman went back to North Carolina and began organizing his supporters. He hoped to persuade older pastors with influence in their states to find like-minded men and women concerned with the conservative drift. It was hard going. Patterson and Pressler denied they were politically active, and fledgling moderates felt sullied by initiating their own movement.

When the SBC met in Los Angeles the following year, Sherman was dressed down by the denominational leaders whose bailiwicks he wanted to protect. Some scolded him for organizing, others swore he would make a fool of himself when he failed to turn out the vote. But Sherman knew how many ballots his candidate would get; it just would not be enough.

The Los Angeles convention had the makings of a melodrama. The two positions had hardened into opposing sides; for the first time, it was a one-on-one, head-on contest. Reporters predicted a "bloodletting." Big city newspapers flocked to see if SBC President Bailey Smith would make a fool of himself. A few months earlier, at a Republican party rally in Dallas, Smith had triggered a public-relations fiasco by saying God did not hear the prayers of a Jew. Would Smith make any more gaffes, and would messengers reelect him? He would not, and they did, by a sixty-to-forty margin.

Next year in New Orleans, Sherman's network lost again to Jimmy Draper, a Euless, Texas, preacher. Draper, more conciliatory than his two predecessors, proved so popular that when Sherman polled his people in 1983, the majority voted not to run a candidate against him. That decision so infuriated Foy Valentine, the head of the denomination's Christian Life Commission, that he vowed to organize the next convention himself.

Valentine thought his organizer could deliver the numbers, but he was wrong. Charles Stanley, a relative newcomer to Southern Baptist organizational life, easily beat the two moderate candidates. Stanley, who pastored the First Baptist Church of Atlanta, was known through his nationally broadcast television show, but he was not active within the SBC. Still he had the support of Pressler and Patterson, and he was active in the Christian Right political movement through his founding membership in the Moral Majority.

The convention was a new low for many moderates. Conservatives passed resolutions against abortion (except to save the life of the mother), against the teaching of secular humanism in public schools, and against the ordination of women. Resolutions are not binding in Baptist life, but they represent the sense of the convention. A principle tenet of the denomination is individual church autonomy. Churches are voluntarily bound and free to do as they wish—including calling whomever they choose as pastors. The fact that the convention would go on record against women ministers galled many moderates.

Russell Dilday, president of Southwestern Baptist Theological Seminary in Fort Worth—the denomination's largest school—made clear his opposition to the Pressler-Patterson coalition when he preached the convention's sermon. Dilday's harsh words marked the first time an agency head, at least one not on the verge of retirement, criticized the growing conservative movement. "Incredible as it sounds, there is emerging in this denomination, built on the principle of rugged individualism, an incipient Orwellian mentality," Dilday told listeners. "It threatens to drag us down from the high ground to the low lands of suspicion, rumor, criticism, innuendos, guilt by association, and the rest of that demonic family of forced uniformity."[3]

During the convention Dilday and two of his fellow seminary presidents—Roy Honeycutt of Southern and Randall Lolley of Southeastern—decided to speak publicly against the conservatives and to work to elect a candidate of their choice when Baptists met the next year in Dallas. The man they set their sights on was a slow-talking, wisecracking, grandfatherly figure from west Texas. Winfred Moore of the First Baptist Church of Amarillo described his theological beliefs as being "to the right of the Ayatollah," but he had no sympathy for the conservative "take-over" movement he believed was bent on absolute control of the convention:

> In 1983, a Dallas layman came to see me and told me I had not paid
> my dues to the convention. It was almost as if he was preaching to
> me. I had been just pastoring my church, and all the things going on
> in the take-over movement would impact everything I held dear, and I
> would have done nothing to put a stop to that. I agreed to let my
> name be put in nomination as president of the Baptist General Con-
> vention of Texas and when I got into that job and saw what was hap-
> pening in the Southern Baptist Convention, I let myself become a can-
> didate because I didn't think anyone else would do it.

But in the autumn months of 1984, Moore was hardly a lone crusader. Honeycutt, in his fall convocation speech at Southern, decried "unscrupulous and unethical acts by politicians" heading an "independent fundamentalist party." He described a "Dallas war room," at Criswell Bible College, filled with secretly taped speeches and lectures by the seminary faculty. There was no other choice but to declare a "holy war" against the "unholy forces" who were bent on taking control of the convention.

Paige Patterson quickly counterattacked, calling Honeycutt's address "a demonstration of denominational fascism." Patterson said it was Honeycutt's views that threatened to eviscerate the denomination and noted that the alleged "war room" was simply the college archives.[4]

At Southeastern's convocation, Randall Lolley addressed the role of women in the church. His theme, "First at the Cross, Last at the Tomb," was intended to encourage the growing number of women studying at the North Carolina seminary. Meanwhile Dilday was on the road. He defended the conservative record of his school while questioning the motives of the Pressler-Patterson coalition.

Cecil Sherman's network, which had sat out the Kansas City convention, also was gearing up. Strong statewide groups of moderates formed in North Carolina, Virginia, and Georgia. The hope was that the East Coast moderates would combine with home-state support for Winfred Moore and unseat Stanley.

But while moderates lambasted conservative ties to the Christian political Right and independent Baptists such as Jerry Falwell, supporters of the Pressler-Patterson coalition struck back. Some blasted denominational leaders for taking sides in the controversy; others threatened to put their denominational contributions in escrow accounts. Still others said the moderates were balking because their control of the agencies was eroding. "Dr. Honeycutt and others are sore about it because the Convention is not working their way at this time," Patterson said. "They are learning how some of us felt for 25 years."[5]

During the months before Dallas, tension rose to a fever pitch. Moore campaigned extensively, speaking at rallies, church suppers, and ladies' lunches. Stanley traveled less, but his supporters held prayer meetings in his behalf. A new crop of partisan journals crowed over the blatant shortcomings of the opposition, and some pastors even addressed the conflict in their sermons.

The moderates went all out to win Dallas, but conservatives were almost certain they had the numbers. "Dallas represented the biggest all-out effort by the moderates; they unleashed every volley they had," Patterson recalled. "Our hearts had been in our mouth every year up until Dallas but coming off the victory in Kansas City we had more confidence than ever before. By then we knew how to communicate effectively."

That effective communication translated into "prayer" rallies, mass mailings, and political-style newspapers. The political machinery of both sides was so formidable that secular reporters had begun to speculate whether the embattled SBC would split after Dallas. Concerned state leaders called for the formation of a Peace Committee to calm the rolling waters threatening to engulf the denomination.

On 11 June 1985, when the gavel dropped at the Dallas convention, more than 45,400 messengers—twice the number attending previous Southern Baptist meetings and the world's largest assembled democratic body—spilled into over-flow halls at the Civic Center. Temperatures indoors offered little respite from the steamy Texas weather. Not only were messengers forced to wait in long lines for everything from ice cream bars to bathrooms but also they felt the discomfort of wondering whether the brother or sister in the next seat had their mind right—that is, shared their thinking—on the denominational conflict.

Charles Stanley had sought to be a reconciler during his first year as SBC president. He never attacked critics by name and barely campaigned for reelection. During his presidential address, which stressed forgiveness and humility, he described the experience of being "loved into submission" by a former enemy. Just when Stanley's soft words had lulled messengers into believing reconciliation was possible, the news that evangelist Billy Graham was supporting him for president swept the convention hall. Graham, a life-long Southern Baptist and nominal member of Criswell's church, was not in-volved in SBC politics. The suggestion that he had sent a telegram telling Stanley he would vote for him if he were in Dallas was stunning. But Graham's office confirmed he did, indeed, send the message, although he had not ex-pected it to be made public. Friends of Stanley, believing the extra boost would help their man, convinced the Georgia pastor to release the telegram the night before the convention opened.

Whether it was Graham's endorsement, sympathy for the incumbent, or Stanley's television popularity, he beat Moore by 55 to 45 percent. While mod-erates groused in disgust, Moore told reporters he was keenly disappointed. Suddenly Moore felt a tug on his arm; a friend said he was wanted on the platform. "Stanley asked me if I was willing to run as vice-president," Moore recalls. "I thought he was asking me himself, but that was the last thing he was doing."

Moore agreed to run and was elected with a two-thirds majority. Many Baptists believed an eleventh-hour miracle had occurred: the two former foes now held the convention's top spots; could this signal the end of the controversy? On Wednesday morning, June 12, when the Peace Committee was formed to deal with "issues, personalities, and spiritual problems," it seemed as though the denomination was back on track—especially as the committee's twenty members ran the gamut from Cecil Sherman to Adrian Rogers. But the euphoria was short-lived. When a moderate plan surfaced to replace Stanley's nominating committee appointees with state denominational leaders, messengers warred openly on the convention floor. Moderates and conservatives bickered by the microphones and shouted when it was their turn to speak. Cries of "point of order" ricocheted around the room when Stanley tried to control the debate.

When Stanley ruled an entire slate of nominees could not be changed as a group but would have to be debated one by one, he was voted down. The convention adjourned for lunch before the issue was finally decided, and when it reconvened Stanley ruled that the motion for a substitute slate, as well as the motion defeating his ruling, were out of order. When moderates tried to argue, he cut off their microphones. Although some Baptists applauded Stanley's no-nonsense approach, others were appalled by what they perceived to be his hard and arrogant spirit. Some swore never to return to another convention; others renewed their vows to topple the conservatives the next year in Atlanta.

Despite the emergence of the Peace Committee to settle the denominational disputes, the post-Dallas mood was sour. Moderates realized they had lost control of the denomination, and conservatives were embittered by their opponents' refusal to accept the change. Both sides looked forward to Atlanta as the final test of strength. An incumbent would not be running for president, and moderates would be at the center of their East Coast strength.

The year before the Dallas convention was a year characterized, for both sides, by intense but optimistic organizing. The months between Dallas and Atlanta were markedly different. Baptists were coming to terms with the breadth of their antagonism and the depth of their division. An Alabama couple, Robert and Julia Crowder, had filed a suit in federal court claiming their rights were violated during the Dallas convention, because Stanley forbade messengers to vote on an alternative slate of nominees. The Crowders may have hoped to raise public awareness about the conservatives' high-handed style, but many moderates believed their strategy—which named the Southern Baptist Convention itself as a codefendant—backfired.

Meanwhile moderates and conservatives used the secular press, as well as denominational publications, to snipe at one another. Lee Roberts, an Atlanta layman, made headlines when he charged Southern Baptist professors with teaching "spiritual slop." Some months later Roberts wondered publicly if Winfred Moore believed in "truth."[6] For their part, moderates accused their opponents of turning over Southern Baptist resources to the Christian political Right and selling out the convention to the likes of Jerry Falwell.

The Peace Committee cried for a truce, but their calls did little to stop the political sloganeering. Moreover, the committee's initial findings added to the tumult. After visiting the denomination's six seminaries, Peace Committee members reported they had found "significant theological diversity." For example, some faculty believed Adam and Eve were actual people, others viewed them metaphorically. Similarly, some professors regarded biblical miracles as historical, while others considered them parabolic. The seminary presidents cried foul, claiming the Peace Committee had painted a picture of greater diversity than what actually existed. But an overriding sense among committee members had already gelled: Theological diversity was the problem, and their task was to correct it.

By the time Baptist messengers arrived in Charles Stanley's hometown, the stage was set for what the press came to call "the second battle of Atlanta." The night before the convention opened, claques of conservatives and moderates met in hotel rooms around the city to set their strategies. Adrian Rogers would be the conservative candidate; Winfred Moore would carry the moderate standard. Messengers met to pray but also to count heads. Moderates hoped registration would stay under thirty-five thousand; the Southeast was their stronghold, but they knew some of their troops intended to stay home after what happened in Dallas.

Grim-faced messengers climbed the small hill to Atlanta's World Congress Center on the convention's opening day. Gone was the backslapping camaraderie of years past, when preachers were busier swapping stories than attending plenary sessions. Gone was the easy fellowship between brothers and sisters bound to save souls. Gone was the innocence of a denomination that, unlike its northern counterparts, had never fought the twin sirens of secularism and modernism. Southern Baptists were assessing their corporate soul; Atlanta would be the altar call.

This time Charles Stanley had a professional parliamentarian on the platform with him. Before each ruling Stanley sought his advice and relayed the decision. Still his stands were not popular among moderates, whose parliamentary initiatives to modify the president's appointive power were repeatedly squelched. Before the morning session ended, Stanley gave the presidential address. Preaching from the Old Testament, he told forty thousand listeners that they were in sight of the Promised Land and should not compromise their "inalterable convictions" about "the living word of God."[7] He finished to wild applause.

That afternoon, when messengers returned from lunch, two candidates, Adrian Rogers and Winfred Moore, were nominated to succeed Stanley. It took a couple of hours to count the ballots, but when Lee Porter, the convention's veteran vote counter, returned to the platform, a hush fell over thousands of messengers as members of both sides said a final prayer. When Rogers's name was announced, with 54 percent of the vote, the house broke out in song. As rows and rows of flushed white faces roared "Give Me that Old Time Religion," desultory moderates filed out of the hall.

Moderates had reason to feel despondent. The Controversy had lasted seven years, and they had yet to win an election. Worse, their string of losses had begun to take a palpable toll on trustee boards. Many agencies and institutions were either already governed or soon to be governed by a conservative majority. The differences were being felt as the new trustees clamored for more say in personnel and policy decisions.

In the next two years, newly hired executives at denominational institutions were hardline conservatives whose views were quickly put into practice. Richard Land, at the Christian Life Commission, organized his agency as a political force for "traditional values" opposing abortion and pornography. Lewis Drummond, at Southeastern Baptist Theological Seminary, brought inerrantists to the school's faculty. Larry Lewis, at the Home Mission Board, ended stipends to women pastors and forbade appointing divorced or Pentecostal missionaries.

Changes in trustee and staff leadership also affected the institutions' internal strength. The Home Mission Board and the Golden Gate Baptist Theological Seminary, located in Mill Valley, California, experienced budget short-falls. Moderate leaders with conservative boards—including Russell Dilday at Southwestern, Lloyd Elder at the Sunday School Board, and Keith Parks at the Foreign Mission Board—were scolded behind closed doors. More than eighteen members of the Southeastern faculty and staff resigned; 50 percent of its student body left, and concerns about the loss of academic freedom led to accreditation reviews by the Southern Association of Colleges and Schools and the Association of Theological Schools.

From the conservative perspective, the ups and downs were part of the change. The quest for doctrinal purity might cause discomfort, and even financial setbacks, at some institutions, but the denomination would be safe from liberalism.

When messengers prepared for the 1987 convention, many expected the issue of "liberal taint" to be addressed in the final report of the Peace Committee. Many Baptists hoped the committee would say once and for all whether there was a liberal threat to the denomination and, if so, what could be done about it. But the report proved, at the time, anticlimactic. It reiterated the existence of theological diversity within the denomination but affirmed the historical accuracy of Scripture and asserted that "most Baptists" take the conservative position on key contested passages. Although it affirmed the individual freedom to interpret Scripture, it said Southern Baptist agencies should hire only people who believe what most Baptists believe. For moderates the document did little to vindicate their side or to ease the sting of the conservative purge. Conservatives were more pleased; they knew they could use this report to justify their policies in the future. In fact many of them supported a Peace Committee recommendation to continue to monitor adherence to the report for three more years.

After the Atlanta convention, a growing number of moderates began to weigh their options. Many of those in the Old South—Virginia, North Carolina, and Georgia—were weary from nine defeats. Tired of the political activity, they sought refuge in the Southern Baptist Alliance—a new group offering fellowship and organizational alternatives. Members of the alliance were less interested in electing a president than in starting new ventures. They cared less for winning back the denomination than for ministering to those who had been hurt in the fight. "These are moderates who are ready to say,

'Let those guys go,'" said Sherman, explaining the attitude of some alliance members to the conservatives. "But the Alliance is also a hospital for people of ideals who have been damaged. Now they are ready to do something together."

But while the East Coast moderates tended their wounds, a new assertiveness was dawning in the West. Texas moderates, who had been slow to realize the effect of Pressler's and Patterson's success, were worried. Once Winfred Moore had been a lone voice in the prairie; now a growing number of pastors and laity were concerned with the denomination's future. This group, more centrist than their Old South counterparts, began dominating the opposition movement. They networked with the East Coast moderates, established their own newspaper, found organizers, and laid the groundwork for winning back the presidency. They came close in 1988—closer than ever before—but they did not succeed. Nor did they sweep the 1989 convention in Las Vegas.

Cecil Sherman did not attend the Las Vegas convention. He told his congregation he needed a year off. In less than ten years, he had seen changes that belied his understanding of what it meant to be a Baptist. No longer did brothers trust one another's interpretations of the Bible. No longer did separation of church and state mean Baptists would oppose prayer in school. No longer would believers allow the Lord to work in mysterious ways—including calling a woman to preach.

The network Sherman had established almost a decade earlier merged with the Texas Baptist group and hired two paid organizers. For these moderates, the struggle would continue, at least for one more year—one more try against a nonincumbent. For his part Patterson was no less determined. He had come too far to turn back. "Either the conservatives will prevail in 1990—at which point a permanent return to the faith of our fathers will be established—or else the conservatives will not prevail and it will make for another decade of struggle and upheaval," Patterson explained. "Those are the only options."

By Patterson's standards the "faith of our fathers" prevailed when Southern Baptists met in New Orleans in 1990. The Reverend Morris Chapman, a boyishly handsome pastor from Wichita Falls, Texas, stood against the Reverend Daniel Vestal of Dunwoody, Georgia, for SBC president. Both men called

themselves inerrantists, both urged unity, both prayed for missions and evangelism. But Chapman was endorsed by conservatives—now joined by a group
of formerly nonaligned, high-profile pastors—whereas Vestal, who had lost
the election in 1989, was aligned with denominational moderates.

When the messengers gathered—a mere 20,437, opposed to projections
in excess of thirty-five thousand—a grim determination hung in the air. The
rest of the city might let *le bon temps* roll, but Baptists were going to settle the
fate of their fractured convention. The suspense did not last long. When moderates were short on an early vote—they hoped to stop an initiative that
would take money from the Baptist Joint Committee on Public Affairs (BJCPA)
and give funding to a Washington, D.C., presence for the Christian Life Commission—they knew they would need a miracle to win.

Instead they received a death blow. Chapman beat Vestal 58 percent to
42 percent. It was a definitive rout by a nonincumbent. The Patterson and
Pressler crowd crowed. At an invitation-only celebration the next night at the
Café du Monde, the architects of the conservative resurgence received a
plaque honoring their achievement. The plaque, which had been an offhand
suggestion of Pressler's before the convention, commemorated the spot where
the two men had planned their strategy twenty-three years earlier. After
prayers, speeches, and backslapping, the party was capped by participants
singing "Victory in Jesus."

For conservatives the final victory may well rest with Jesus, but the immediate future is in their hands. They must raise the funds, find the leadership, and instill the vision to confront the twenty-first century. That may be
difficult. Already some middle-of-the-road conservatives are distancing themselves from the hard-line, hardball tactics of Pressler and Patterson. Already
conservative-controlled trustee boards are debating how creedal their institutions must be.

Moderates have a different challenge. There is a certain freedom in loss;
the worst is over. Not long after the New Orleans convention, the top staff of
Baptist Press was fired. Within the year Lloyd Elder, head of the Sunday
School Board, resigned under pressure. The Baptist Joint Committee lost its
funding. Southern Seminary trustees voted to accept the Peace Committee
report for faculty guidelines.

Rather than fight such changes, moderates have begun planning alternatives. In May 1991 moderates (including many members of the four-year-old Southern Baptist Alliance) sponsored a gathering in which several thousand participants discussed how they could remain faithful to their understanding of the Southern Baptist heritage. Leaders of this group, called the Cooperative Baptist Fellowship, say they do not want to leave the Southern Baptist Convention, but their organization could provide the foundation for a new denomination. A new Baptist seminary, offspring of the Southern Baptist Alliance, opened in Richmond in 1991, and there is talk of starting other seminaries in Wake Forest, North Carolina, and Waco, Texas. "I do not believe I left the [SBC]," said Vestal, one of the meeting's organizers. "Rather, the [SBC] left me."

Who left whom will be the stuff about which scholars will speculate for years to come. In the meantime observers will note that in a twelve-year span, a small conservative group became a self-assured movement. In the process its leaders changed the course of the nation's largest Protestant denomination and put fundamentalism, a movement nearly invisible for more than five decades, on the national agenda.

Notes

Unless otherwise noted, all quotations in this chapter are from interviews with the author.

1. James C. Hefley, *The Truth in Crisis: The Controversy in the Southern Baptist Convention,* vol. 1 (Dallas: Criterion, 1986), 66.
2. Ibid., 87.
3. Ibid., 107.
4. Ibid., 108.
5. Ibid., 114.
6. James C. Hefley, *The Truth in Crisis: The Controversy in the Southern Baptist Convention,* vol. 2, *Updating the Controversy* (Hannibal, Mo.: Hannibal Books, 1987), 36.
7. Ibid., 67.

CHAPTER 3

THE STORY BEFORE THE STORY: SOUTHERN BAPTISTS SINCE WORLD WAR II

Samuel S. Hill

Describing the Southern Baptist Convention as a "changing denomination" should not lead anyone to suppose that the momentous changes of the 1970s and 1980s happened overnight and without preparation.

Change is as natural as continuity, of course. In the case of the SBC, the decades following World War I witnessed a denomination significantly revised from its earlier nature and character. As a matter of fact, as convulsive as the 1980s were, they do not supersede the 1920s in significance. Different, yes, but not more dramatic; turning in opposite directions, yes, but both periods have been powerfully formative for this massive company of Christians. It is necessary, even if somewhat trite, to observe that the centrifugal force of recent years has been tearing apart an organization that had constructed a formidable institutional unity, most notably in the 1920s. Only something so unified—in program as well as pride, destiny, and cultural identity—could undergo such trauma as sundering forces have done their punishing worst.

Historian Walter B. Shurden captures the curious correlation between the SBC that crystallized in the 1920s and the revolution that began in the late 1970s: "Denominational unity is more important to most Southern Baptists than arguments about the Bible."[1] How accurately those words published in 1978 described the SBC élan until almost the very year they were written. Any keen observer would have said much the same thing during the long season between 1920 and 1975. How unity as the animating force was stood on its head is the story these chapters seek to illuminate.

The period from the modern origins of the SBC in the 1920s to the end of World War II is, indeed, the career of a body unified. Its centripetal nature took shape much earlier, with its founding in 1845. But the realization of that entelechy awaited the period under discussion. A number of projects and agencies that had begun locally, in states, or informally among cooperating colleagues became parts of the denominational structure. (In fact almost all that did not move from independence to integration were soon to die.)[2]

Between 1917 and 1945, several agencies acquired either official status or executive leadership or both: the Baptist Brotherhood in 1926, the Annuity Board in 1918, the Baptist Student Union in 1928, and the Education Commission in the same year. The new Southern Baptist Hospital was built in New Orleans in 1923. In 1917 the first executive secretary was appointed to head the long-influential Sunday School Board. The Executive Committee's first executive secretary-treasurer was elected in 1927.

Accompanying this enlarged and more-centralized organization was the addition of state conventions: Arizona in 1928, California in 1940, and Kansas and Alaska in 1946. Work in Oklahoma and New Mexico was expanding rapidly. And this expansionist philosophy was building toward its grand climax of the 1950s and 1960s.

Taking all this together, we see a religious organization sure of itself, devoted to its mission, and possessing vast resources of funds and personnel for accomplishing its goals. The SBC had come a great distance from incipient centralization. Now it was determined to centralize much more in order to guarantee the development and growth it was committed to: training and mission for all people of all ages and stages—men and women, laity and ordained, the ill and the well, the young and the old—according to a comprehensive vision of education, social ministry, evangelism, and political concerns.

As for the story before the story, things were hardly standing still from 1945 to 1975. Growth in membership and in financial support for myriad causes was astonishing—and was the first subject mentioned by most of the faithful asked to muse on developments during that third of a century. In the year World War II ended, membership stood at 5,865,554. In 1954, having grown by 3.6 percent over the previous year, membership reached 8,169,491; and in 1960 there were 9,731,591 SBC members. By 1975 membership had expanded to 12,735,663, and the number of churches had increased from 26,134 (in 1945) to 34,902. On the financial front, the magnitude of SBC contributions is staggering. Total gifts by members were more than $98 million in 1945 and vaulted to $1,387,339,703 in 1975. Contributions to missions or benevolence causes stretched from just under $2.5 million in 1945 to $237,617,406 in 1975.

By any reckoning, expansion numbers and percentages such as these point to an organization vigorous in its motivation and organized to maximum efficiency in order to carry out its mission. Slogans adopted by the convention and brandished from pulpits and periodicals everywhere afford a clue. "A Million More in Fifty-Four" was a brilliantly crafted clarion call to rally the membership. A memorable motto, if forgettable to the tastes of some, it called for the evangelization of the lost in the "Southland" and America at large. Its phraseology bespoke a spiritual urgency suffused with a marketing tone. The eternal danger lying ahead for all the unsaved was enough to convince the believers to take up the burden of sharing the Good News with that million, and the theological point was only strengthened by the familiar language of business.

The "Million More" slogan rallied the membership to evangelize the lost at a rate congruent with the eternal danger that lay ahead for the unsaved and with the depth of responsibility that rested on the shoulders of believers to share the Good News. The reported number of converts in 1954 came to 396,857, for an SBC total membership of 8,169,491. Many of these converts were the progeny of SBC members, of course, and that year the SBC reported 517,388 "additions by letter," referring to persons who transferred their membership from one congregation to another. It is true that Southern Baptist families moving about and the children of the faithful were "easy" recruits, yet that takes nothing away from the effective outreach activities of a company of Christians committed to the salvation (and church membership) of each person.

That commitment extended as well to the evangelization of the world. Attractive, vigorous appeals were mounted to impel young people to answer the call to mission service, to overseas countries most pointedly. At World War II's end, 519 foreign missionaries were under appointment; by 1975, the cohort had grown to 2,667. More than 2,100 homeland missionaries served the denomination's causes by 1975.

Such astonishing growth to such a staggering size stands as the middle term between the decision made in the 1920s to institutionalize and the severe disruption that took place in the 1980s. A great enterprise launched after World War I grew by incredible proportions after the World War II and was riding high, despite major regional changes, into the 1970s. From the perspective of the furious battles that erupted in the 1980s, pitting "moderates" against "fundamentalists," we do well to ascertain this earlier keen sense of world evangelization through unity.

Since the 1920s this diverse body, informally consensual at best, has been wary of currents and movements that pose a threat to a unity always maintained with a measure of fragility. In his study of the SBC covering the decade of the 1920s, James J. Thompson portrays vividly the SBC's sense of mission, what can only be called its sense of destiny as a unique force in the divine cause. He pictures this cause as a set of stair steps. The top step is labeled The World, pointing to the scope of the task of preaching the Gospel. The next step down is marked America, referring to the singular and auspicious opportunity given this nation for Christianizing all people. The next step is The South: "Here lay the hope of America, for only the South could convert the nation to God." Drawing upon their acute awareness of the South's history, which had produced a "certain depth of soul," Southern Baptists were sure they should and could build a "great Christian civilization in America." Thompson summarizes: "At the base of the strategic steps, supporting the other, lay the step labeled 'Southern Baptist.' Southern Baptists must save the South; the South would convert America; and America would evangelize the world." Denominational spokesmen (such as M. E. Dodd) declared that "the Baptist hour of all the centuries had sounded. . . . As goes America, so goes the world. Largely as goes the South, so goes America. And in the South is the Baptist center of gravity in the world."[3] A sense of destiny so well developed demanded unswerving denominational loyalty, a commitment to unity commensurate with the urgency of the mission of world evangelization.

Having been fired by rhetoric of this kind in the years after World War I, the SBC put in place elaborate institutional agencies for realizing its vision. Some of their efforts were devoted to strengthening existing work among women and men in domestic and overseas missions. In 1925 the Cooperative Program was born, a strategy by which, desirably, all benevolence funds sent by the churches to the convention treasury would be divided among the various denominational operations. This was intended to minimize special appeals, forge a great unity, and promote generous giving. Two years later the Executive Committee (formed in 1917) assumed the responsibility for formulating denominational policy between annual convention meetings and regular financial allocations (in 1987 it managed an income of $337 million). No further flurry of institutional activity occurred until World War II was over, when agencies such as the Radio and Television Commission (a unit that appeals to the get-out-the-message concerns of this constituency), the Baptist Joint Committee on Public Affairs, and the Christian Life Commission were established.

Thus the shape of the denomination's corporate life was molded. With a vision of world evangelization, rooted in regional culture and expressed in expanding and successful organizations, the Southern Baptist Convention set the terms by which the struggles of the next decades would fought.

Struggles in the Seminaries

One way to see how an upheaval affected an organization once dedicated to unity is to look at the tensions and changes in the denomination's theological seminaries. The 1950s witnessed the creation of three new ones—another sign of growth in size and efficiency. Their locations are noteworthy, as well: Golden Gate in the San Francisco Bay area and Southeastern in Wake Forest, North Carolina, in 1951; and Midwestern in Kansas City, Missouri, in 1957. And in 1946 a Bible institute founded in 1917 became the New Orleans Baptist Theological Seminary.

The formation of these seminaries to supplement the operation of the two "ancient" seminaries, Southern in Louisville (1859) and Southwestern in Fort Worth (1906), was to prove extremely significant. Just how significant this expansion in the area of theological education was would become clear in the controversies of the 1960s and, more intensely, in the controversies from the late 1970s forward. All of that turmoil arose from concern over doctrine and theological positions—a shift from the earlier preoccupation with institutional growth and unity. This shift in orientation meant that what was taught in seminary classrooms was acquiring a new, dominating importance.

The seminaries became the lightning rod for many of the tensions experienced by a huge organization living in a social-cultural framework of radical and unprecedented change.

It is essential to view the correlated roles of the theological seminaries and the most influential members of the convention's leadership. Looking at each, and noting their interaction, affords insight into the troubled season from 1957 or 1958 through the 1960s that set the stage for the devastating confrontation that characterized the 1980s.

The first episode involved the internal workings of the "mother seminary" in Louisville in 1958. *Internal* is accurate in that the dispute involved thirteen members of the faculty who opposed the leadership manner of the president and some of his policies. They further resisted the growing influence of the "applied" areas in the curriculum, especially pastoral and clinical psychology. They acknowledged the basic importance of training future ministers in the practical matters of pastoral care and church administration, but they feared the dilution of the classic theological curriculum: ethics, history, biblical studies, and theology. They feared a ministry that "meets the needs of the people" in the context of a denomination that emphasized "religious experience" and promoted church growth with business-derived initiatives. They held their ground against perceived incursions on the venerable—sturdy, "objective," and basic—disciplines. Even more they urged changes in the approaches taken to administrative leadership.

This was a struggle that can now seem either momentous or insignificant. While some alumni and a few others took sides in the Louisville Seminary dispute, the conflict remained largely local. It involved faculty-faculty and faculty-administration differences. Although the conflict of 1958 was intense and resulted in the departure of a dozen members of the faculty, it had little directly to do with the SBC at large or with theological heresy. Yet for all that, it bespoke a denomination and a regional culture at unrest and in transition.

As it turned out, the 1958 internal struggle at the Louisville Seminary was one of two "last hurrahs"—failed efforts of the denomination's schools to embrace openly a more ecumenical and progressive orientation. Actively participating in national Baptist life until 1845 when the convention was organized, Southern Baptists minded their own business throughout the rest of that century. A minor exception was when they became charter constituents of the

Baptist World Alliance in 1905; in this fellowship they mingled with fellow Baptists from other national and world cultures. And in the nineteenth century, a healthy percentage of their seminary professors received graduate training in Europe or in the Northeast. Even those connections eventually disappeared, however, and by the 1920s, SBC insulation was nearly complete.

Ironically, despite that insulation, a cadre of leaders with cosmopolitan vision, if not experience, remained on the Louisville faculty, and some denominational leaders shared a similar outlook. From this elixir emerged a mild dose, hardly a rich compound, of ecumenism in understanding the church and of cosmopolitanism in educational commitment. Few of these faculty members had been trained at Yale, Princeton, Heidelberg, or Oxford, but some had served in World War II, and all had tasted of diets more varied than okra, black-eyed peas, corn bread, and iced tea. The new beginning felt by Americans generally in 1946 and over the next few years prompted a yearning among these Southern Baptist educators. Curiously, the same instincts that helped give rise to the formation of the four new seminaries instilled a sort of liberal—cosmopolitan, really—spirit within convention educators. Theologically "liberal" by any standard description they emphatically were not. But they were open, deprovincialized, progressive, and eager (often also quite able) to carry on dialogue with fellow Christians, Roman Catholics included.

The 1958 Southern Seminary crisis involved, then, several aspects. Near its heart lay aspirations toward the classical tradition in Christian thought—one factor, surely, in the faculty's concern over the role of the practical areas in seminary education. Standing with the giants of the heritage and gleaning depth from their teachings, these scholars gave weight to the theological tradition of the Church catholic, to Augustine, Thomas, Luther and Calvin, and Barth. At the same time, they were responsive to modern, international currents of thought, including world-class biblical scholarship. To take seriously each, the classical and the modern, and to strain to correlate them, entailed a bold venture that permitted them to see their regional tradition in a comparative light. It also invited suspicion and criticism from a parochial constituency.

In pursuing this dream—it was exhilarating for quite a number—they encountered a second kind of obstacle, one quite different from the company of suspicious, critical pastors and laymen of influence. They ran headlong into a certain variety of denominational leadership, men who prized efficiency and diplomacy no less than do managers in a highly successful, profit-driven business. Cadres of this kind had been forming since the 1920s. In the 1950s and 1960s, this approach to leadership became standard, spilling over into the management of educational institutions as well as the Sunday School Board and the missions enterprises. High and low, in large urban churches and small town congregations, and representatively in denominational officialdom, the corporation-executive model of leader came to power. In fact the entire company, in small and large gatherings, moved from a "town meeting" structure of government to the standard "corporation" model.[4]

Leadership so flavored was bound to change the mode of congregational life and even the atmosphere of theological seminaries. It was not so much that the corporation-like officers repudiated the new openness; rather, they did not prize it. They geared everything for growth and efficiency, both of which necessitated the primacy of denominational diplomacy. Older reliance on charismatic leadership gave way to what James T. Baker terms a "form of executive membership."[5]

Open and searching, that is, risk-filled, inquiry cannot flourish under those conditions. Thus a dozen faculty members were dismissed (having thrown down the gauntlet). Paradoxically, a faculty more cosmopolitan in its formal education was assembled over the next decade, but the spirit of hunger and adventure was notably diminished. For one thing, they were a younger lot; for another, the tendency was to invite quieter, less controversial scholars to the faculty.

But the results of that earlier, riskier era were not quite gone. In 1961 an Old Testament teacher at the new Midwestern Seminary, Ralph Elliott, a gentle-natured man nurtured at the Louisville Seminary a decade earlier, wrote a commentary on the book of Genesis for the denomination's Broadman Press. *The Message of Genesis* created a raging storm, one that issued in the recall of Elliott's brief book and, eventually, in his ouster from the seminary faculty.

Elliott said in print little more than many Old Testament professors had been teaching for a long time. Moreover, he presented a mild version of a standard scholarly interpretation of Genesis 1-3 as an option, not ramming it down anyone's throat, and did it with an authentic and attractive piety. Nevertheless, Elliott's commentary on Genesis brought great criticism upon the press, his seminary, and him. The book was recalled and the offending scholar was on his way to an American Baptist Convention pastorate in upstate New York.

Why such consternation and reaction? The idiom of the attack on Elliott was not the language of biblical inerrancy that was to become the battle cry in the 1980s warfare, and Elliott was an avowed believer in biblical authority, taking the infallibility position. But the text he worked with, especially chapters 1 to 3 of Genesis, is volatile stuff on the issue of divine creation—the evolution controversy lay barely in the shadows of this battlefield. More important, however, is the passage in Genesis 3 about the Fall of Man—into sin and eternal condemnation—which seemed to be stripped of its clarity, specificity, and urgency by the Elliott kind of interpretation. Elliott, of course, intended nothing of the kind. But his work was seen as undermining the central message of evangelism, the life-force of the SBC, especially of its numbers-oriented corporate bureaucracy. If all are not sinners eternally condemned, there need be no salvation.

Worst of all it was a denominational agency, the Broadman Press, that was publicizing the fruits of cosmopolitan scholarship, the same kind of biblical interpretation taught at Chicago, Duke, Vanderbilt, Cambridge, and Marburg. This could be viewed by southern churchmen as challenging the Bible's authority; it certainly was not geared toward world evangelization. The controversy might have been little more than a tempest in a teapot had a university press or trade house published Elliott's commentary.

In the wake of the Elliott-Broadman Press dispute, the annual convention of 1963 (in Kansas City, Missouri) adopted a doctrinal statement, the Baptist Faith and Message. This formulation revised slightly the Memphis statement of 1925 (which had been drawn up in the midst of the fundamentalist-modernist controversy). What is important about it is that it was produced at all, that a need for it was perceived. This doctrinal standard was deemed essential for reasserting SBC orthodoxy concerning biblical authority. At the same time, it affirmed Baptist freedom to interpret the Scriptures under the Spirit—"soul competency"—and thus failed to resolve matters indisputably. The SBC had become sensitive to its internal pluralism and eager to defuse tensions in the interest of denominational unity. (These concerns were exacerbated by the civil rights revolution that was destabilizing the conventional regional society at the same time.)

The second of the two "last hurrahs" toward a more ecumenical and progressive orientation occurred during the early history of the Southeastern Baptist Theological Seminary. Located in Wake Forest, North Carolina, Southeastern set out to chart an alternative course. The choice of location was fortuitous for achieving such a goal, because the Carolinas, Virginia, and Maryland have long been known as the most open and progressive, or liberal, states in Southern Baptist territory. This condition owes much to the lingering influence of early English and New England, even Anglican, forms of church life. The seminary was always unmistakably Southern Baptist, yet it celebrated an openness to "foreign" currents of thought in biblical and theological studies that set it apart. Early in its history, some tension developed within its own faculty, not so much on liberal-conservative disputes as on how far to go in modifying traditional Southern Baptist modes by embracing ecumenical Protestant (European and North American) hermeneutics and programs. By the mid-1960s, the high hopes entertained by faculty progressives and pastors in the upper Atlantic seaboard area were dying. Several members of the faculty left for other academic positions, a few of them to public colleges and universities.

Looking back, one wonders how Southeastern managed such a different animation for as long as it did. There are limits to Southern Baptist elasticity, after all. Those limits were to tighten notably in the 1970s and 1980s, but for a "brief, shining moment," about a decade, one of the SBC's theological seminaries thrilled many of its faculty members, students, and supporters with its measured but bold foray into the larger world of Christian scholarship and citizenship. It should accordingly puzzle no one to learn that Southeastern Seminary became the first "hostile take-over" engineered by the fundamentalists after they had consolidated their power in the latter 1980s.

Struggles in the Culture

From the analysis presented so far, one could gain the impression that the ecclesiastical history of the South's largest denomination is recountable in only ecclesiastical terms. That is incorrect, of course. Because the church lives in society and culture and is in many real senses the people who comprise it, a great many other factors contribute to its nature and the flow of its development—most emphatically. The southern cultural roots of the Southern Baptists may be more palpable than, say, the midwestern roots of much American Methodism, but no church has any quarter on the cultural-setting issue.

What else was happening in the South in the thirty years following World War II? Much, to be sure, but nothing holds a candle to the civil rights revolution. From the interracial experience of the war years to the Truman administration's legislation on civil rights in 1948, with the culmination in *Brown v. Board of Education* in 1954, the South's segregated social arrangements were being challenged and overturned. Everything about the South and everyone in the South were affected by these changes. Perhaps those citizens who resisted the alteration of regional ways, clutching to traditional values and customs, felt the changes the most. But those who were advocating the new social arrangements were equally aware of the disruption of the familiar.

The SBC often had not lived with much of a sense of ministry to the region's social structures. It had always expended its major energies in evangelism and building up congregations; in the ethical area, it had typically confined itself to teaching personal and interpersonal moral righteousness. Thus when the desegregation order became the law of the land, the SBC apparently stood to lose little—or figured that it would not have to give away very much. Strictly internally, the civil rights battle did not force any significant changes in policy. Beginning in the late 1940s, however, the SBC's Christian Life Commission (formerly the Social Service Commission) acquired a somewhat enlarged budget and strengthened visibility to carry out moral and ethical ministries. These included concerns for the welfare and education of black people in the region. They were joined by churches and a great many church members who had long been dedicated to the basic care and education of their black neighbors and friends.

Appearances were deceiving, however. That is to say, the civil rights struggles and the dismantling of the old segregated society provoked major perturbations within the SBC, by changing all the ground rules for its members—indeed for all southerners, whites no less than blacks. During the seemingly interminable season of discord that lasted from the late 1940s until the early 1970s, communities were disrupted. Tempers flared, violence was in evidence, and the composition of public schools and the constituency of public facilities changed—in general all values, policies, and cultural conventions (what is taken for granted) came under scrutiny and, inexorably, were revolutionized. The Southern Baptist churches were not often cauldrons of hate or violence, but they were caught up in the concern to maintain order and stability, which was sometimes expressed as stubborn resistance to the enforcement of the law. More often people were anxious, wondering if their treasured ways of life were being wrested from them by "outside agitators" who had no right to intrude. Confusion, uncertainty, puzzlement, fear, and anxiety—these were the standard responses, and sometimes bitterness and resentment accompanied. The newspapers carried reports of a number of attempts by one or a few black people to join white Baptist churches in cities and towns. Feelings always ran deep and sometimes ran high. It was a period of severe distress for an entire region.

The SBC churches did some adjusting and accommodating, and even some reaching out, especially after the early furor subsided. Not infrequently they provided some leadership, through the laity more often, it would seem, than through pastors. And the Christian Life Commission printed relevant materials and offered direct encouragement for Baptist people to confront the law and biblical teachings about human relationships and justice in society.

Perhaps the greatest single mark the civil rights revolution made on the SBC was to divert its attention from its usual business to the task of putting out fires and offering encouragement and some guidance to a beleaguered society. The magnitude of this societal dislocation prevented indifference to it. It was an issue that would not go away, most certainly not of its own accord.

Corollary to the diversion from evangelism and congregation building to wrestling with this momentous social change was the response of the bright young students and pastors from the SBC churches. A sizable number of them, perhaps many thousands, came under conviction over the South's sinful fostering of or compliance with segregation (and, historically, slavery). As they grappled with biblical and theological truth juxtaposed to a regional ethic, they concluded that the SBC (and other churches) had failed. Indeed they accused the churches of continuing to shirk their responsibility to call segregation what it was—sin—and to expend major spiritual resources to rectify a morally indefensible situation.

This resulted in the formation of a progressive—in political respects, liberal—sector among the young leaders, some already in church leadership positions, others showing great promise for the next generation. Nancy Ammerman argues that the SBC lost a cadre of its "best and brightest," referring to them as a "missing generation."[6] There is evidence to support this contention, though the details and exact implications have yet to be delineated. To whatever degree this "missing generation" was—is—a reality, a leadership vacuum emerged, making more feasible a realignment in the proportions of moderates and fundamentalists by the 1980s. It is quite clear that a group of would-have-been SBC leaders were channeled into other denominations, some as ministers, others as laymen. Many others suffered a loss of faith, or a crippling despair concerning the church, owing to the shallowness of its involvement with the major social agenda—moral to its core—that gripped the South between 1955 and 1975.

A concomitant factor in this loss, whatever its size and lineament, was the attractiveness of secularism as a way of looking at reality. As never before, secularism—the practice of the absence of God—lured younger, more cosmopolitan southerners in the 1960s. The opening of the South to larger currents of thought and moral interpretation is the heart of the story of our period. Desegregation prevailed because of forces outside regional life: American law and democratic pressures. This of course takes nothing away from the dedicated and brave black southerners who mounted the crusade and fought it through to victory, without whom no amount of legal reconstruction or democratic pressure could have been effective. Nor does it take lightly the white southerners and Americans from other regions who contributed to the cause, sometimes at great sacrifice. The South's problem was the nation's, and many within the region and outside it devoted themselves to its resolution.

There is a certain irony in the alliance between democratic ideals, which led to a biracial society striving toward equality, and the heightened appearance of secularism in southern life. The former was initiated by Christian men and women of the southern black church—in concert with many other Christians. In turn they were joined by other change-minded Americans acting out of general moral sensibilities and not from specifically Christian springs of action. The southern conservatives of the 1960s had much truth on their side when they warned that to open the windows would be to allow all manner of creatures to fly in. The rest of the nation contributed its racial justice principles to the South, and at the same time let in a much larger percentage of people and ideas that may loosely be termed "secular."

Nothing is gained by imputing blame to Americans from other regions. Blame is simply irrelevant. The South had already begun to experience deprovincialization and was moving apace toward embracing a general "modern" culture. Nevertheless, the myriad changes that accompanied the over-turning of the old segregated structures brought to the South secular ways of looking at things on a scale never experienced before—and quite often with a surprising social tolerance, even acceptance.

The presence of black people in southern society has made it what it is, and has been, for three hundred years. This truism is also a profundity. In the period of our study of the SBC, between 1945 and 1975, the black church succeeded with its commingling of the vertical and horizontal dimensions of religion—Christian salvation and spirituality, the vertical, integrated with the ethic of a Christian calling to social justice, the horizontal. The Christianity of African Americans never has separated the sacred and the secular. On this issue, in contrast, Southern Baptist theology resembles other forms of Euro-American Christianity in distinguishing between "spiritual ministries" and "social ministries" and in ranking them by priority. White Baptists in the South have emphasized the former, expecting that the force of its spiritual power would reveal the divine leading toward ethical causes, and then toward their realization.

One of the reasons for dissatisfaction with SBC churches on the part of a younger breed of reflective southerners has been the churches' disinclination to correlate the spiritual and the social. The other side of that issue is the lure of the social at the expense of the spiritual, a mark of the effectiveness of secular modes of thought.

The Fundamentalist Take-over

Bound with this complex of forces and factors, perhaps as both cause and effect, is the long-standing policy of SBC leaders to avoid taking stands on sensitive issues. Those responsible for producing the literature used in Sunday school, short courses in Bible study, or missions education, or various training enterprises for the young or women or men or families have followed a course in the golden middle. Their policies and strategies have been to enlarge understanding gradually and to stimulate reflection without disturbing. Viewed from this perspective, the "fundamentalist take-over" in the 1980s was rather easily accomplished. The Southern Baptist faithful had never been equipped with tools for vigorous investigation of the meaning of biblical texts or challenged to think theologically. Mostly the study material provided for them was devotional in nature and impact, or it reinforced the denomination's preoccupation with evangelism. Neither did what the people heard from the pulpit alter perceptions much. All of this is curious in that many of the writers of the denomination's literature, when their minds were probed, actually believed in a critical approach to biblical study and were quite capable of theological insight. Similarly many of the pastors, perhaps 40 or 50 percent, had some acquaintance with critical thinking, and when in seminary studying Christian thought were not resistant to or upset by what they heard. Their lack of resistance, of course, may have been the result of the way many seminary teachers have presented their views with extreme caution or couched them in such familiar language as to conceal what they really meant.

Not that the laity knew no more than what they heard at church. Always a company of them has been quite discerning in study and reflection. Some of them have tried to pry loose their pastors from safe, party-line positions. Nevertheless, the orientation has been toward the lowest common denominator or toward not rocking the boat, to view standard behavior censoriously; or, granting the benefit of the doubt, toward doing nothing that would divert or disturb a body dedicated to the evangelization of the world, a task that necessitated unity and unquestioning participation.

When the fundamentalists undertook their crusade in the 1970s and 1980s, they did not need to redirect Southern Baptist thought very seriously. Either the people had no firm positions—being primarily devotional—or they were easily attuned to dogmatic appeals to fortifying their commitment to biblical truth, the evangelistic imperative, and the denomination's indispensable role in the "cause of Christ." The force of this fact seems to be corroborated by the inability of the moderates to formulate and promulgate an equally rationalistic and definitive canon of beliefs. By and large a denomination more program-directed than theologically cultivated, Southern Baptist people are subject to being swayed. And the propensity for precise propositional formulation belongs altogether to the faction well described as fundamentalists.

When the spokesmen of that party refer to their having been out of favor, hence out of power, and dealt with condescendingly by the moderates for many decades, they interpret correctly. Hard-line doctrine, constantly monitored standards of orthodoxy, and a stoutly sectarian spirit have not been the hallmarks of Southern Baptist Convention sessions, seminary classrooms, or congregational fellowship. When those "fundamentalist" traits have been present, the people espousing or embodying them have been viewed as extremists and trouble-makers. Not that this phenomenon is without precedent, however; what is new is the number of SBC churches and members who have rallied 'round the "fundamental" flag. One suspects that more pastors possess the proper credentials for the crusade than do lay people. Moreover, many of them, lay as well as clergy, are better characterized as defenders of traditional ways in a conservative era than as card-carrying fundamentalists. Whatever the exact circumstances, they have made up the majority of voters in annual convention meetings every year since 1979 and have redrawn the SBC map permanently. Their reply to moderates' recent complaints over being left off committees and left out of consultations over SBC business is, in so many words: Now you know how it feels.

Recognizing the success of its fundamentalist strategy tells us one more thing about the SBC between 1945 and 1975, and earlier: political power is a dominant force in the denomination's life and those who hold it assume it is theirs to dispose. Thus those observers who attribute the Southern Baptist "holy war" to politics, to a contest for power, have a point. There is no doubt that gaining and retaining power and, conversely, determining to obtain a share of it after a long season of disenfranchisement, has been a factor in the crisis. Those who have long held it resent yielding it and distrust their successors. Those who have recently claimed it relish possessing it and live with a brash confidence that God's hand is entrusting them with overseeing his vital mission. Just the same a political analysis cannot fully explain the tumultuous developments of the past dozen years.

Deprovincializing the South

"The opening of the South to larger currents of thought and moral interpretation is the heart of the story of our period." By reiterating my assertion, we may be able to see that the crisis in which the Southern Baptist Convention is embroiled is neither new nor a development entirely of its own making. The tug-of-war that has characterized recent SBC life is part and parcel of the modernization process, the reality of plural philosophies, and the deprovincialization of the South. But the crisis also has roots in SBC denominational values, those reflected in programs and strategies, common attitudes toward education, and theological-ethical teachings.

To claim that the SBC is reaping the consequences of its decision in the 1920s to institutionalize its life is going too far. Yet that way of doing business, as a matter of historical fact, renders solid position taking difficult and restricts a body's elasticity. Accordingly, examining where this organization has come from since 1945, and before then to the 1920s, is crucial to understanding the ruptured condition of the SBC.

Notes

1. Walter B. Shurden, "The Problem of Authority in the Southern Baptist Convention," *Review and Expositor* 75, no. 2 (Spring 1978): 220-33.
2. Robert A. Baker, *The Southern Baptist Convention and Its People, 1607-1972* (Nashville, Tenn.: Broadman, 1974), 345.
3. James J. Thompson, *Tried as by Fire: Southern Baptists and the Religious Controversies of the 1920s* (Macon, Ga.: Mercer Univ. Press, 1982), 10-11.
4. For elaboration on these changes in polity, see Arthur Farnsley's chapter in this volume.
5. James T. Baker, "Recent South," in *Encyclopedia of Religion in the South,* ed. Samuel S. Hill (Macon, Ga.: Mercer Univ. Press, 1984), 861-62.
6. Nancy Tatom Ammerman, *Baptist Battles: Social Change and Religious Conflict in the Southern Baptist Convention* (New Brunswick, N.J.: Rutgers Univ. Press, 1990), 143.

CHAPTER 4

"JUDICIOUS CONCENTRATION": DECISION MAKING IN THE SOUTHERN BAPTIST CONVENTION

Arthur E. Farnsley II

Although the Southern Baptist Convention (SBC) is often thought of as a powerful force, many of its individual members would not describe themselves first in terms of their *denominational* affiliation. Southern Baptists are fiercely loyal congregationalists, preferring to think of themselves first as members of particular local churches who cooperate—to whatever degree—with others under the auspices of the SBC. The denominational pride they take in their home and foreign mission programs, their seminaries, and their publishing efforts is matched by their pride in the autonomy of their congregation and their freedom of individual conscience.

Baptists in America are usually independent but seldom isolated. They have traditionally banded together in local associations for the purposes of cooperative benevolent work. In the nineteenth century, many of these associations cooperated in even larger benevolent organizations, such as the General Missionary Convention, the Baptist Home Mission Society, and the Baptist General Tract Society.[1] As their names suggest, these were societies, not denominations. Participation in them was voluntary, regulated only by the consent of the cooperating associations and congregations

The mid-1800s witnessed a schism within these societies. Northern Baptists refused to cooperate with Southern Baptists; specifically, they refused to accept slaveholders as missionaries (though, interestingly, there is little evidence that they refused to accept southern money). Most Baptists in the South, displaying their independence, withdrew to form the Southern Baptist Convention.

The Southern Baptists would still sponsor the same sorts of benevolent enterprises—home missions, foreign missions, Bible and tract distribution societies—but they would now do it under the umbrella of a larger institution. As the convention's first great statesman, W. B. Johnson, put it, "Judicious concentration is of the first moment in all combinations of men for important enterprises." [2] Baptists in the South had determined to concentrate their efforts in an unprecedented way.

The SBC System of Cooperation

To facilitate this concentration of efforts, Southern Baptists developed a system of cooperation. Each cooperating church could designate its funds, whatever percentage of its resources it chose, to the benevolent work it wished to sponsor. [3] Every three years (later two, then one) the cooperating churches would send messengers to a meeting—a convention—at which corporate decisions would be made. It was assumed that men of God, operating under the guidance of Scripture, would be able to clear a path for the fledgling denomination. [4] When differences arose, the messengers sent by the individual churches voted to settle them.

At least that was the system in principle. In practice such an organization presented as many potential problems as it solved. There was no precedent among Baptists for such a unified effort. And, in fact, for the first few decades, the convention's efforts were seldom unified. Local associations challenged the denomination for both power and resources. Ideological differences often led to schisms among groups with no method of maintaining doctrinal control. And the Civil War changed the economic landscape of the South, threatening to cut off the convention's monetary lifeblood.

In addition, to say that the denomination regarded the votes of its messengers as the final source of power and authority fails to account sufficiently for the other potent sources of both. Local pastors could wield great power and authority by virtue of their personal charisma and the prestige accorded their office, despite an official polity that downplayed the assumption of pastoral authority. Moreover, the Scriptures were regarded as the ultimate source of both authority and power—every decision had to be defended in terms of its biblical basis. The messengers had no real authority, even when they exercised considerable power. As their name implies, they were not representatives of their congregations but simply members chosen to attend the conventionwide meetings. They had no authority from their congregations as they went to annual meetings and took none from the convention back home. They spoke and voted simply as Baptist individuals who belonged to particular churches. They assumed that godly men working with Scripture would "reason together" and reach the right decision.

Thus the channels of power and authority were varied and confused. Fortunately for the convention, its problems during the first century never outgrew its resources for dealing with them. When the Landmark movement challenged the whole notion of corporate authority, the convention withstood that pressure by reaffirming its common missionary purpose.[5] It was able to develop educational institutions to undergird its missionary and publishing boards. Although there was some ideological and geographical disagreement about policy, there was a widespread consensus about the convention's goals. At the turn of the century, it would be fair to say that pastoral authority, scriptural authority, and the democratic mechanisms of the annual convention converged sufficiently that disorganizing pressures could be tolerated or repulsed.

Indeed the convention went into a period of almost hyper-organization in the early twentieth century. The formation of the Executive Committee and the Cooperative Program, in 1917 and 1925, respectively, laid the foundation for the growth and modernization that would follow. Although individual churches and associations could still designate funds for specific benevolent work if they wished, it was assumed that the bulk of their giving would be undesignated, to be divided in a budget developed by the Executive Committee.[6] Clearly the central bureaucracy would become a major force in denominational life. The heads of the boards and the members of the Executive Committee assumed more and more power as the organization grew. Messengers meeting for three days a year simply could not direct the denomination as they once did.

Cooperation and Problems of Authority

Because the denomination lacked a sanctioned hierarchy, those in the bureaucracy found themselves wielding enormous power with virtually no corresponding authority. The groundbreaking research into this matter was done by Paul Harrison in his study of the American Baptist churches. Harrison concluded that the reasonable solution was to give messengers representative authority such that decisions in the bureaucracy could be more clearly constrained by corporate votes. That is, if the convention's authority was assumed to come directly from the pews and the bureaucracy's authority was clearly outlined by that mandate, the bureaucracy would have less liberty in deciding how to use funds and develop programs. In short, more authority in the bureaucracy, because official lines could be better controlled, would mean less de facto power.[7]

Such a system would result, however, in a corresponding authority for the convention over the local associations and churches that sent representatives. If those chosen to represent were not merely messengers but carried the authority of their bodies, their corporate decisions would be reciprocally binding on those bodies. Southern Baptists chose, however consciously, to keep absolute local autonomy and to risk the hazards of loosely controlled central power.

Of course that central power did not grow unchecked. Because the local groups were so independent and the tradition of democratic participation was so strong, every move to consolidate power was met with a corresponding step to insure democratic governance. Among these steps was the establishment of trusteeships, through which the convention could exercise more direct control over its many seminaries and boards, and a complicated system of committees responsible for nominating those who would serve on boards.[8] If the messengers meeting at annual conventions could not directly control their various enterprises, they could at least maintain a thorough system for electing, and checking, those who did.

This required, in turn, a reasonable means of providing and limiting participation at the annual meetings. If this was not to be true representation based on population or associational status, what was it to be? As Southern Baptist historian Robert Baker notes, "Almost every year between 1877 and 1917 someone raised the question from the floor of the Convention relative to changing the method of representation."[9] Southern Baptists were aware that their convention was becoming a true denomination with a great deal of central power, but they had trouble settling on the best mechanism for directing that power democratically.

After much tinkering they developed a simple method for allotting messengers: (1) every church that considered itself a cooperating body could send one messenger; (2) for every 250 members or $250 given to the convention's work (a figure derived in the late nineteenth century but still in use), a church could send one more messenger; and (3) there would be a maximum of ten messengers per church.

This system was not then, and is not now, representative. Churches that give $1 million to the convention can send no more messengers than those that give $2,250 (the first messenger is free). Those with ten thousand members can send no more than those with 2,250. It is important to remember, however, that this disproportionality was not regarded as a fault. The messengers were never intended to represent their churches, their communities, or their state and local associations. They were to speak as *Baptists,* and as Baptists they would determine the course the convention and its agencies would follow.

Although the convention was a democracy, it was a democracy organized around the principle of consensus. Baptists would reason together under the guidance of Scripture and set their course accordingly. By the early twentieth century, it was clear that this democracy was representative in the sense that these messengers represented all of their peers corporately and the various boards represented the convention's wishes in concrete programs and actions, but there was no intention to develop a "fair" or "proportionate" method of setting policy.

That numbers, whether money or members, should be so discounted points up three interesting tenets of Southern Baptist life that are often overlooked by outside observers. The first is an insistence on local autonomy that refuses to grant superior status to convention activities. To treat churches as congressional districts, to be apportioned by size or wealth, would be to admit that they are ultimately only constituent elements of a larger whole. Although in one sense this is true, Southern Baptists insist that the local church is a self-standing whole that, of its own volition, cooperates with others to form a different (and larger) unit.

The second tenet is the belief that the truths of Scripture are clearly available to every reader. Such a commonsense view of the Bible lends credibility to the claim that it does not matter how big one's church is, or how much money one gives, or even who goes to the annual meetings. What matters is that God's word clearly directs one's actions and that all agree on what that word is. On one level this creates a unanimity of purpose; on another, it points to an amazing level of spiritual independence in which one does not need a higher authority to insure either salvation or right action.

The third, related, tenet is that if all are able to understand Scripture and each has freedom of conscience both as an individual and as a member of a free, local church, then every Baptist possesses a rough spiritual equality. One's views may be represented by messengers, boards, or seminary teachers, but these people are not above or below, but alongside, one on the spiritual journey. Thus it does not really matter who votes or who holds positions of power so long as God's will is done.

Such a view may seem naïve, and Joe Barnhart's chapter in this volume will show the ways in which growing numbers of Baptists have been unable to sustain such a straightforward trust in everyone's ability to discern the meaning of Scripture. I would contend, however, that in situations of cultural stability it makes a great deal of sense. When consensus is possible, such a model weaves the various threads of formal and informal authority—Scripture, pastoral leadership, individual conscience, bureaucracy, and democratic governance—into a coherent whole. It allows for the widest range of individual, small-group, and large-group participation. It is only from the point of view of radical pluralism and heterogeneity that it seems simplistic.

The Rise and Fall of Cultural Consensus

The South's culture was, of course, not uniformly stable. Not all southerners were Baptist (though Baptists were, and are, the South's most potent religious force). Not all Baptists agreed: the Landmark controversy is one good example of ideological, scriptural differences. But the disagreements tended to be limited to specific issues within a framework accessible to all parties involved. When Landmarkers made their charges of biblical inconsistency, they operated within a biblical frame of reference shared by their opposition. The two sides did disagree, and even split over their contention, but both saw the point the other was making. If the region was not culturally monolithic, it was still aptly referred to, in Samuel Hill's terms, as the "Solid South." [10]

Even the first great fundamentalist controversy in the South was handled as an "intramural" matter. In the 1920s a group of fundamentalists within the convention challenged the status quo. Represented most colorfully, if not most accurately, by Frank Norris of Texas, these fundamentalists charged that the denomination was too centralized, that its seminaries had allowed secular academic thought, including evolution, to infect biblical truths, and that certain denominational leaders were too self-important.[11]

The denomination withstood this attack. The importance of this controversy lies not in the SBC's victory, however, but in the manner in which the conflict was resolved. Fundamentalists were repulsed—shoved aside might be more accurate—because they could not find a large enough opposition. The convention voted to reaffirm its consensus on biblical infallibility and its disapproval of the Darwinian hypothesis; indeed, it developed its first quasi-confession of faith to support its claims of staunch biblical conservatism. By agreeing with Norris and his colleagues in principle, but disagreeing with their confrontational tactics, the convention turned away fundamentalists without needing to defeat them.

This episode underscores the degree of homogeneity within both the convention and the larger South. Biblical conservatism, even inerrancy, was more or less taken for granted. Although there doubtless were secular influences in the seminaries and some degree of the emerging higher criticism, these were simply not forces requiring constant attention. In the Northeast fundamentalism had emerged as a reaction against modernity and secularization. It was a recognizable, identifiable movement that could clearly locate its foes. Inerrantist activists in the South, though they may have felt a kinship with their northern counterparts, had no such modernist opposition. The encroachment of modernity that had prompted the fundamentalist response in the North was simply not a part of the southern experience—at least not yet.[12]

From the 1930s until the late 1950s, the denomination increased in members, money, and institutional bulk. Paced by the efforts of the Sunday School Board (SSB)—which fed the denomination's "consensus" with uniform literature and lesson plans to be used universally—the convention developed an ever-stronger central institutional base, symbolically and actually located in Nashville. Though the denomination is broadly based throughout the South in theory—the Home Mission Board is in Atlanta, the Foreign Mission Board

is in Richmond, and the seminaries are in various places—the location of the
SSB and the Executive Committee in Nashville gives special significance to
that city. When the Historical Commission and several smaller agencies followed the Executive Committee there, and when all of these eventually
moved to a new building adjacent to the SSB, it was clear that the denomination had established an institutional center.

Such centering should come as no surprise. The entire region was feeling the economic pull of its major cities. Industries, and later white-collar
occupations, were drawing both blacks and whites from rural and small-town
settings into urban and suburban centers. By the middle of the century, the
sunbelt cities were among the fastest growing, and thriving, cities in the nation. If the myth of the South was still plantations and sleepy little towns with
tree-lined streets, the fact of the South was, more and more, industry and
commerce in a cosmopolitan setting.

Of course such a change meant massive social dislocation. People from
relatively homogeneous cultural backgrounds now lived with people from
different cultures, including those who were already urban and a fair number
of first-generation immigrants drawn by the economic vitality of the cities.
Social status differences between blacks and whites in the cities could not be
expected to mirror those in rural and small-town settings; the civil rights
movement was soon to change racial "stability" in the South forever.[13] Many
biblical conservatives—"small-f" fundamentalists, if you will—were faced for
the first time with neighbors who did not share their beliefs, including some
who showed open contempt for them and for others who were not even
Christians. They found themselves in a position of having to insist on biblical
certainty, including certainty about their role in the cosmos, not as a matter of
course, but as a matter of personal privilege.

As a response to their new situation, many of these people became
"big-F" Fundamentalists. Ammerman's research has found a marked correlation between moving from rural to urban and suburban settings and what
she calls "self-identified fundamentalism."[14] Many southerners simply were not
willing to exhibit the sort of accommodation their new situation seemed to
demand. They might be willing to tolerate some diversity (or they might not),
but they were not willing to accept or endorse it. As the South became less
solid, as the influences of urbanization, industrialization, and secularization

became more apparent, a true fundamentalist movement arose to challenge those influences.[15]

The end of the solid South meant the end of a homogeneous Southern Baptist Convention, and its institutional establishment—unlike the fundamentalists—was ready to acknowledge that change. The convention would never exhibit the diversity of the region as a whole—people who came to the South for economic reasons did not automatically become Baptists (or even Christians)—but the changing demography of the region demanded a new kind of toleration and inclusion. Baptist institutions gradually softened their stance on racial inclusion (although most remained all white), "new" biblical scholarship, and even abortion. The elite of the denomination—the best educated and often the most wealthy—continued to staff the expanding bureaucracy, moving in step with the "new South."[16] Their policies were often more progressive than the views of the average Baptist in the pew.[17]

The Rise of Partisan Politics

The best example of the difference between the bureaucracy and the average Baptist, and a symbolic turning point for the SBC, was the controversy over the publication in 1961 of Ralph Elliott's commentary on the book of Genesis. Elliott was perceived by the fundamentalists within the SBC as a real enemy threatening their biblical beliefs. A decade later, when the SSB announced a new Broadman Bible commentary again containing controversial interpretations of Genesis and Exodus, the convention voted by more than two to one to have them withdrawn and rewritten from a more conservative viewpoint. When the next year's convention rejected the rewrite, the SSB changed authors for the Genesis section. They maintained, however, that they felt the convention's wishes had been carried out, and they proceeded to sell the original volumes in Britain.

The battle lines were drawn quickly. Fundamentalists, already suspicious of the denomination's large central bureaucracy and of liberalism in its institutions, took these episodes as a challenge to their place within the convention. They were being told, they believed, that the denomination wished to follow a more progressive, moderate course, and that their inerrantist views were no longer welcome. Their leaders found themselves, by their own account, unable to serve on key boards and trusteeships, or on the Executive Committee, even though they might be pastors of large, wealthy churches.[18] They were no longer part of the "consensus" that governed the convention; this was all the more frustrating to them because they believed their views represented those of the majority.

In the aftermath of the second Genesis controversy, several of the fundamentalist leaders chose to organize. Speaking at evangelism rallies and other such meetings of conservatives, these pastors began an informal network opposed to "business as usual" within the SBC. This led to the more formal organization of the Baptist Faith and Message Fellowship and the publication of the *Southern Baptist Journal,* an independent organ for disseminating the inerrantist point of view.

Neither of these channels was immediately successful, but through them the groundwork was laid for future change. Through the fellowship fundamentalist pastors were able to meet with others who were like-minded. Through the *Journal* these same men could promote their ideas, their evangelism conferences, and even their own para-church institutions (such as the independent seminaries that were drawing more and more fundamentalist students).[19]

By the mid-seventies it was evident that these efforts were, by themselves, insufficient. It was not enough to criticize, or occasionally circumvent, the denomination's main channels; the old guard was too firmly entrenched and too certain that the fundamentalists would fade into the shadows as they had in the past. Lasting change in the SBC could be effected only by changing the composition of the denomination's hierarchy.

The Baptist Faith and Message Fellowship gave way to an informal coalition of fundamentalist leaders committed to a more organized political effort. Under the leadership of Paige Patterson and Judge Paul Pressler, the coalition set out to change the course of the denomination from within the hierarchy.[20] They recognized that the key to the process was the election of the president—often considered by rank-and-file members as an honorary post—who would nominate the Committee on Committees and effectively name the trustees who would thus start the bureaucratic ball rolling.

Such a course lacked the emotional appeal of sharply worded resolutions passed overwhelmingly on the convention floor. This course would require patience and tenacity, waiting each year for incumbents to rotate out of their various positions to be replaced by fundamentalists, and waiting again until a fundamentalist majority could be achieved. It also would require "getting out the vote," making sure that fundamentalist sympathizers took advantage of the method of allocating messengers to the greatest extent possible.[21] But if fundamentalists truly *were* a majority within the denomination and at the annual meetings, time was on their side.[22]

It took a decade, but from the election of Adrian Rogers in 1979, the coalition never turned back. They immediately established control of the Committee on Committees and the Committee on Boards, and were then, gradually and persistently, able to appoint trustees sympathetic to their cause. The Executive Committee gradually changed from the old guard to the new, giving authority to those fundamentalists—such as Fred Wolfe and Paul Pressler—who believed they had been ostracized in the past.

These fundamentalist successes set two precedents, one clearly favorable to their cause and one that later might haunt them. They made it clear that candidates from outside the establishment could win elections, because their concerted effort had indeed tapped into a spring of discontent among the denomination's membership. In so doing, however, they made it equally clear that the political arena was the center of the controversy, and that party politics were the appropriate—and successful—response to this new reality.

The fundamentalists' tactics, and the new politicization of the SBC, drew swift and bitter criticism from the former establishment. They accused the fundamentalists of being autocratic and unfair, and berated them for refusing to appoint anyone with a more moderate or progressive point of view. The fundamentalists publicly responded that the convention had made its views on biblical infallibility known, and that they were simply seeking to follow that course; privately many were saying that "what goes around, comes around."[23]

Those from the old establishment, and others opposed to the new coalition and its tactics, quickly learned what the fundamentalists had already discovered: there was no mechanism in the convention for dealing with dissent. The "democratic" system in the SBC was intended to evoke, and formalize, a kind of common consent among its members. It had no constitution, no supreme court, no proportional system of representation to protect the rights of the minority. Southern Baptists had not intended their organization to be political; they did not imagine it as a forum for competing interests. For that reason there were no safeguards for those whose interests were losing ground.

The moderates, those opposing the fundamentalists, were left to consider their options. They could leave, they could try to win back the convention's machinery wholesale in a political coup, or they could seek a more equitable system of representation by trying to reform, and work within, the new political system.

Leaving was a very serious matter. As Ammerman suggests in her chapter in this volume, most Southern Baptists regard their denomination as a family and are reluctant to abandon it. Moreover, they are heavily invested— with emotion and time as well as money—in the convention's various programs. Pulling out altogether would force them to leave behind not only a precious past but also a strong present infrastructure for educational and mission work.

Beyond these denominational reasons, however, lurks a deeper, more ideological commitment. Moderates tend to be both better off and better educated than their fundamentalist siblings. Probably for those reasons, they are heavily invested—if anything, more heavily invested than the fundamentalists—in the American ideals of fairness and justice, those ideals on which democracy is based. Insofar as the fundamentalists "won" by playing within the rules (despite moderate claims that the fundamentalists had used tactics, such as bussing in messengers, that were ungentlemanly if not actually illegal), the process was fair. Insofar as biblical inerrantists truly do constitute a huge majority within the denomination, their hierarchical ascendancy is just. [24] In terms of American ideals of representation, the denomination's change of course simply makes sense.

Redefining the Terms of Membership

Many moderates considered themselves rightful members of the denomination. They wanted the same rights to participate and to lead that were accorded to others in the convention. They were now forced to acknowledge, as many had failed to do before, that other members in the denomination could lead and participate too. Although the former denominational establishment had not denied that fundamentalists were nominal members of the denomination, they had blocked them from positions in the hierarchy, effectively denying them full membership. Moderates could now do little more than attempt to take back for themselves the same full membership fundamentalists had gained.

In that attempt many moderates were forced to recognize and state publicly the new criterion for such full membership: biblical inerrantism. Although the content covered by that label is less certain now than it has ever been, it is certain enough that those who wish to lead in the SBC must position themselves as inerrantists, as all later moderate presidential candidates would do. The old cultural consensus gave way to a literal, textual boundary for membership. Recent debate and party alignment in the convention signal a startling admission, and adjustment, to that fact.

Accordingly, the moderate wing aligned in two distinct groups. The Southern Baptist Alliance was made up of the most progressive elements in the denomination, including those who simply no longer had the desire to fight at annual meetings and those who could not even symbolically or allegorically subscribe to biblical inerrantism.[25] The alliance moved inevitably toward its own programs, its own seminary, and its own internal network for placing pastors. Joining the efforts of the alliance was a new group, the Cooperative Baptist Fellowship (CBF), which also turned away from the battle and toward its own agenda. Very few of the six thousand who attended the 1991 CBF meeting in Atlanta were messengers to the SBC's annual meeting (also in Atlanta) that same year. Although there has not been, as yet, an official split between the CBF and the SBC, points of agreement are getting fewer and farther between.

The second group of the moderate wing, Baptists Committed, was more prepared to stay and fight to defend their sense of justice. Convinced that they were full members, that they were not a minority—most of them are, after all, biblical conservatives—and that they could muster the votes at annual meetings to redirect the convention, they talked of winning back the SBC and accused the fundamentalists of being less than fully cooperative in the denomination's joint programs. Many from this centrist group, particularly the leaders from the former establishment, are now active in the CBF. But given the conservative theological leanings of most members of Baptists Committed, it is reasonable to assume that many of its members will blend, however awkwardly, back into the SBC fold.

No moderate party was ever able to win a presidential election. Their losing electoral activities might, at first glance, even have seemed a bonus for the new elite. By institutionalizing the competing-interest model and reinforcing the dominance of the political arena in the SBC's polity, these new parties legitimized the fundamentalists' victories. In one sense their presence represented a living, breathing opposition that could be used to justify the winner-take-all tactics of the fundamentalist coalition.

In another sense, however, the two living-and-breathing parties made the fundamentalists' reactionary agenda somewhat harder to sustain. It is one thing to say that one's opponents are liberalism, secularism, humanism, and higher criticism;[26] it is quite another to point to real men (and a few women) who pastor large churches and people who are themselves known inerrantists and claim that they are the enemy.[27] Those moderates who established their credentials as full members (inerrantists) also positioned themselves to compete in the new political arena and, perhaps, even in the new establishment.

Once fundamentalists had assumed control and had changed key personnel, they could no longer attack the establishment with such vigor. By the mid-1980s, the opposition similarly had recognized the need to field more conservative candidates who could insist on full participatory rights. They had, in effect, accepted the fundamentalists' new criterion for full membership in the body. As long as some moderates were unwilling to leave and unable to win back the convention wholesale, the fundamentalists were forced to admit that these centrists were indeed members who could join the political process. Such an admission eventually could precipitate a search for a more equitable system of representation.

Can a Competing-Interests Model Survive?

A change in how Southern Baptists think about representation would not be easy to accomplish. For one thing fundamentalists and their sympathizers are in no hurry to accommodate those very persons who not so long ago refused to accommodate them. When a motion to change the messenger selection system came before the Executive Committee in early 1989, the chairman of the subcommittee responsible for it remarked that it was "odd" that moderates should propose such a change now, after one hundred years of the same system. He commented that he favored as "inclusive" a model as possible, reasoning that "the more Baptists we can get together the better."[28] Thus the old consensus model was still operative in his mind, serving as a bulwark, or even a weapon, for those currently in power.

Writing to American Baptists, Paul Harrison warned the establishment in the fifties that

> little is gained by pushing [fundamentalists] aside and awaiting the day when they shall gain sufficient power to reverse the procedure. In the world of secular politics the rights of the opposition are preserved through such institutions as the party system, minority rights, and civil liberties. It is a strong indictment against the Baptists that they have not discovered any means to permit their own minorities a voice in the convention.[29]

The establishment of the SBC did just what Harrison warned against, however, and their present cries of injustice fall on unsympathetic, and suspicious, ears. This is not to say that all hope for democratic reform is lost. Harrison continued, "It has been shown that, in all probability, even if the fundamentalists were to gain control of the national organization, they would find it necessary to be obedient to the organizational imperatives if they wished to remain in power.[30]

There are already signs that the fundamentalists in the SBC are feeling that pressure. Although they certainly have made the boards and agencies more conservative, they have not brought the wholesale changes their most strident supporters might have wished. The "organizational imperatives" Harrison spoke of—the rational, cooperative structures of the denomination—proved very strong.

One example of this struggle between ideological purity and competing-interests democracy was the repeatedly blocked efforts of fundamentalists to change the relationship between the SBC and the Baptist Joint Committee on Public Affairs (BJCPA). The BJCPA is a coalition of Baptist groups committed to preserving religious liberty and the principle of separation between church and state. Its office in Washington, D.C., is headed by James Dunn, an outspoken progressive who, among other things, has opposed prayer in school, belonged to Norman Lear's People for the American Way, and, reportedly, called several visible members of the New Christian Right "crazies."[31] He is, for obvious reasons, unpopular among fundamentalist leaders.

Because the SBC historically has provided the lion's share of the funding, fundamentalist leaders wanted the BJCPA's actions to reflect more closely the denomination's conservative views. Toward that end they first changed the size and composition of the Public Affairs Committee (PAC), the body that represents the SBC on the BJCPA. The PAC was enlarged and heavily weighted with political and religious conservatives. Despite that the BJCPA made few substantive changes.

In addition fundamentalists regularly sought drastic reductions in each year's SBC budget allocation to the BJCPA. But just as regularly, those efforts were defeated by the same messengers who had elected a fundamentalist president. Indeed, a 1989 plan to open an office in Washington that would represent only the SBC, supplanting the BJCPA, was withdrawn from consideration despite its passage by the Executive Committee.[32] A motion from the floor to withdraw half of the BJCPA's funds, in lieu of the new organization, also was soundly defeated. The convention simply was not yet willing to make the change. Old assumptions about organizational commitments and individual freedom formed a bulwark against this assault by the new orthodoxy.

The next assault, however, left that bulwark badly shaken. At the 1990 annual meeting in New Orleans, fundamentalists were able to cut most of the BJCPA's funding. Morris Chapman, widely considered to be the weakest fundamentalist presidential candidate to date, easily defeated moderate inerrantist Daniel Vestal. And soon after the annual meeting, the Executive Committee fired, without publicly disclosed cause, the two longtime establishment leaders of Baptist Press, Al Shackleford and Dan Martin. The 1991 meeting in Atlanta dealt a decisive blow to the SBC's affiliation with the BJCPA. With the moderate leadership sitting out the convention in favor of the CBF meeting, the denomination voted to shift its Washington operations to the Christian Life Commission.

These moves do not necessarily signal the death of democracy in the SBC. They do, however, suggest even stricter limits on participation and toleration, the prerequisites for any genuine two-party system. Because the appeal to democratic decision making *assumes* an open exchange of ideas and the possibility of an honest difference of opinion between members, the most recent changes in the convention probably mean that its membership boundaries will be drawn even tighter. Ideas may be exchanged and differences may be tolerated, but only within a shrinking arena of acceptability.

The fundamentalist majority is faced with the difficult task of balancing its own desire for ideological purity with a denominational tradition of democracy and inclusion. It must approach the former in the context of the latter, or risk losing the support of the great middle of the convention that is remarkably committed to both democracy and biblical correctness. Any group that can exploit a democratic model ill designed to fit the current circumstances, if it cannot change the model once in power, can be exploited by it. Fundamentalists have encountered few democratic constraints thus far, but have not removed the possibility of such constraints in the future.

Initial opposition to the fundamentalists, a sort of liberal/establishment party, was quickly rejected as outside the denomination's mainstream. Its members have withdrawn, formally or informally, into their own organizations. The second opposition party to arise, much more theologically conservative but still steeped in the tradition of democratic toleration and inclusion, fared better in annual elections. Nonetheless the events of 1990—especially the BJCPA failure and the Baptist Press firings—left them disillusioned and defeated. Some of them, as a direct function of their commitment to inclusivity, will likely withdraw.

But that does not mean that some third party, or a fourth, will not arise as an opposition. Most Southern Baptists still hold fast to both biblical infallibility and democratic freedom and toleration. That the combination has proven to be much more heavily weighted toward infallibility than many had thought does not make it any less a combination. As long as both commitments remain, fundamentalists will have to recognize both tenets in their policies or face renewed, albeit increasingly conservative, opposition.

Some fundamentalist overtures have, in fact, hinted at a limited policy of toleration and inclusion. Several fundamentalist leaders indicated to me at the 1989 annual meeting that it was time to reach out, choosing candidates and board members not because they had battle scars and had paid their dues, but because they were clean. Perhaps the most surprising event at the convention was the election of Richard Jackson to the Home Mission Board, marking the first time a presidential candidate from the opposition had received any such nomination since the coalition began its take-over in 1979.

These somewhat more inclusive policies will surely not bring members sympathetic to the new CBF back into the fold. And some fundamentalists have suggested that the extreme right wing of the convention may be alienated by the prospect of any accommodation. Less certain, and therefore more interesting, is the fate of those inerrantists who have been the most recent opposition and part of the great middle of the convention that has often supported the fundamentalist coalition, but with less than full commitment. Some of the defeated opposition will leave, but many will stay. It is unclear how the SBC will align itself, or how much control the current fundamentalist party will retain when the old Left is gone and the first generation of fundamentalist leaders gives way to the next.

In many ways Harrison's vision of the American Baptist churches proved astonishingly prophetic for the SBC. Despite that, Harrison's solution, a more formal system of representation, was not the answer then—nor is it now. Baptists are too firmly committed to pastoral authority and the autonomy of their local churches. If that means turmoil for the convention, so much the worse for the convention.

Harrison's insistence on channels for minority expression and his warning that the winner-take-all distribution of informal authority and de facto power of the bureaucracy would lead to problems were directly on target. Polities that fail to recognize internal changes—whether ideological or demographic—and fail to establish means for dealing with these must pay the price.

That price need not, as the SBC has demonstrated against Harrison's thesis, be paid by a change of formal structure. But its payment will surely involve the recognition that shared values and shared experiences, even within a group as homogeneous as we imagine the SBC to be, are often insufficient to settle the most serious philosophical and methodological debates. Faced with such a standoff, Southern Baptists turned intuitively toward democratic, political mechanisms grounded in freedom, open debate, and individual rights.[33] They may keep the same structure, and they will certainly keep many of the same biblical suppositions, but they have been forced to recognize that their continued coexistence can be swiftly reduced to a question of membership in a common political arena.

Such considerations can be painful. Many Southern Baptists lament the loss of the good old days when annual meetings were uneventful.[34] Their complaints echo those of longtime residents of sunbelt cities, such as Atlanta, who remember when everyone got along and everyone knew his or her place. But in the SBC, as in the South as a whole, pluralism is no longer a pending threat but an established fact. Most outside observers would consider Southern Baptists a fairly homogeneous group. Most Southern Baptists would describe themselves as biblically based, citing the Bible as the source of their division and their hope for reconciliation. That these people would turn to democratic structures based on liberal values to try to resolve their differences says something about their controversy and its potential for resolution.

The commitment to democratic participation, individual freedom, and toleration runs deep in American life, but for some the crosscurrent of religious certainty and absolute truth also is strong. When the two run together, as they have in the SBC, their confluence is noteworthy. For many the SBC may seem an anomaly, a place where modernization and secularization have not yet made the outcome of the conflict inevitable. But the decline of a white Protestant center in American culture, and the growth of religious cultures as diverse as Islam and Hispanic Roman Catholicism, promise to make conflicts between religious and political values even more pressing. How such conflicts have been addressed, and with what results, are questions of practical concern. As the SBC struggles to decide just how judicious its current concentration of political and theological power is, its balancing act merits everyone's ongoing attention.

Notes

1. Robert A. Baker, *The Southern Baptist Convention and Its People, 1607-1972* (Nashville, Tenn.: Broadman, 1974).
2. Robert A. Baker, *A Baptist Source Book* (Nashville, Tenn.: Broadman, 1966), 114.

3. The convention's earliest structures mirrored the older societies, with separate organizations for Home (and Indian) Missions, Foreign Missions, and literature.

4. Until the 1880s, men of God were also joined by a few women. From the 1880s until the 1920s, women were not allowed as messengers.

5. The Landmark movement, associated most frequently with J. R. Graves in Tennessee, has come to symbolize the Baptist insistence on local church autonomy. Landmarkers went so far as to insist that baptism and communion came down through ecclesiastical succession and only made sense when done for local church members in their church. They further insisted on an uninterrupted succession of baptism by immersion. They criticized any form of authority beyond the local congregation, though they were willing to admit the possibility of voluntary associations. The Landmarkers had mostly withdrawn from the "centralizing" convention by 1906, a development that William Barnes notes as a key point in the journey toward consolidation. See Barnes, *The Southern Baptist Convention, 1845-1953* (Nashville, Tenn.: Broadman, 1954), 167.

6. Baker, *Southern Baptist Convention,* 404 ff. See also Barnes, *Southern Baptist Convention.*

7. Paul M. Harrison, *Authority and Power in the Free Church Tradition* (Princeton, N.J.: Princeton Univ. Press, 1959), 227.

8. The current system is this: The president nominates a Committee on Committees that in turn nominates a Committee on Nominations. The Committee on Nominations nominates the various trustee slates. Each step of this process takes a full year (each new committee's work is voted on at the next convention) and each is subject to rejection by the convention as a whole. The terms are clearly marked, participation is usually designated on a per-state basis, and members regularly rotate on and off the various boards and committees.

9. Baker, *Southern Baptist Convention,* 314.

10. Samuel S. Hill, *Religion and the Solid South.* (Nashville, Tenn.: Abingdon, 1972).

11. Norris called the esteemed George Truett of Dallas "the Infallible Baptist Pope" and "The Great All-I-Am," doubtless among other things.

12. The best arguments for fundamentalism as a distinctly modern, reactionary movement are made by Frank Lechner in his "Modernity and Its Discontents," in *Neofunctionalism,* ed. J. Alexander (Beverly Hills, Calif.: Sage, 1985) and "Fundamentalism Revisited," *Society* 26 (Jan.-Feb. 1989): 51-59.
    Similarly, Nancy Ammerman's *Baptist Battles: Social Change and Religious Conflict in the Southern Baptist Convention* (New Brunswick, N.J.: Rutgers Univ. Press, 1990), 147 ff distinguishes between "big-F" and "little-f" fundamentalists. The latter are biblical literalists in a culture that supports such a position. That is, their beliefs do not deviate from the norm. "Big F" Fundamentalists are literalists who self-consciously pit themselves against their dominant culture. They are inerrantists who recognize their stance as not normal (though still quite correct). My claim here, like Ammerman's, is that although activists in the South may have sympathized with the "big-F" Fundamentalists in the North, they were turned back because they were speaking to a culture still dominated by "little-f" fundamentalism.

13. Although I do not wish to underestimate race as a factor in the anti-cosmopolitan attitudes of many southern whites, neither is it my place here to describe the extent or impact of either changes in racial percentages or the civil rights movement. Chapters in this volume by Hill, Knight, and Rosenberg adequately address that topic. For now it will suffice to say that urban centers were changing toward a new pluralism against which a segment of white southern culture reacted.

14. See Ammerman, *Baptist Battles,* 150 ff. Interestingly, she also has found the same tendency among those raised in the city who chose to move to suburban or rural settings, rejecting their cosmopolitan, heterogeneous, and racially mixed environment.

15. See Ammerman, *Baptist Battles,* esp. chap. 3.

16. I do not mean to imply here that either the South as a region or the SBC as a religious group approached anything we might consider "progressive" by world standards. I simply mean to say that the convention was gradually "opening up" at a pace with its surrounding culture.

17. The same has been said of most American denominations, perhaps most notably the United Methodist Church.

18. Although it is true that W. A. Criswell served as president of the SBC in 1969-70, he was elected in recognition of his status as pastor of the denomination's largest church and as one of its great orators. There was no concerted effort to elect fundamentalists afoot at the time. Several fundamentalist pastors have recounted to the Center for Religious Research that although they did not have any personal ambitions, they found it frustrating that they were never invited to serve in the denomination's hierarchy (a claim now repeated by moderate pastors).

19. These include Luther Rice Seminary in Jacksonville, Florida; Mid-America Seminary in Memphis, Tennessee; and the Criswell Biblical Studies Center (now Criswell Bible College) in Dallas, Texas.

20. The other coalition members were primarily "superchurch" pastors, including Bailey Smith (Del City, Oklahoma), James Draper (Euless, Texas), Adrian Rogers (Memphis), Charles Stanley (Atlanta), Jerry Vines (Jacksonville, Florida), Fred Wolfe (Mobile, Alabama) and W. A. Criswell, in a capacity akin to "pastor emeritus." Though details of organizational meetings are sketchy, those present at such meetings have confirmed their existence in various anonymous ways. Conservative journalist James Hefley has been present at some of these and has given some account of them as well.

21. See Ammerman, *Baptist Battles,* esp. chap. 6. The fundamentalists realized how easily the messenger system could be exploited. Fundamentalist churches within a day's drive of the convention site now sent their full complement of messengers—usually ten—to the presidential vote. Churches that had usually sent only a pastor and his wife, if anyone, now sent eight lay people as well, often on chartered buses.

22. Ammerman's data (*Baptist Battles,* chap. 4) support the contention that biblical conservatives, if not fundamentalists, were indeed the vast majority of the denomination.

23. More than one fundamentalist leader has said, in either conversation or formal interview, that it is misleading to think that the situation was not "winner take all" before, or that they were being more exclusive than the old establishment that had excluded them.

24. This is not to say that a vast majority of the convention is sympathetic to the new leadership. Ammerman (*Baptist Battles*) has established that

there is a very large middle, something near 50 percent of the denomination, which is inerrantist but not committed to any sort of political activism either within or without the convention.

25. Its executive, Stan Hastey, talked very freely about being prepared to offer the SBA's infrastructure as the basis for a new denomination or a merger, should the need ever arise.

26. The most telling book on this score has been O. S. Hawkins's *Unmasked: Recognizing and Dealing with Impostors in the Church* (Chicago: Moody, 1989). Hawkins, a sort of second-tier fundamentalist leader, outlines the way in which apostates gradually and insidiously hinder the work of the true church.

27. Most prominent of these is Richard Jackson, whose church gives the most to the Cooperative Program while still espousing inerrancy (and often leading the convention in baptisms, the key evangelical statistic).

28. These comments came from Eldon Miller at the meeting of the Executive Committee in Nashville, Tennessee, in February of 1989. I was present at that session.

29. Harrison, *Authority and Power,* 223.

30. Ibid.

31. I have heard Dunn deny this charge, but I have also heard Judge Paul Pressler insist that he knows it to be true.

32. Convention president Jerry Vines requested the withdrawal—technically a deferral at the time—so that tension within the convention would not hinder missionary efforts in the meeting's host city, Las Vegas. Although Vines's record on evangelism makes it difficult to call his request insincere, it was at least fortuitous that his request coincided with almost-certain defeat for the fundamentalist initiative.

33. Wolfgang Schluchter has suggested in his essay "The Future of Religion" (in *Religion and America,* ed. M. Douglas and S. M. Tipton [Boston: Beacon, 1982]) that our differentiated institutions, or spheres, appeal to political values located in political institutions to resolve differences that cannot be settled by appeal to "common" values. This struck me as so empirically accurate that I decided to push a step further to see if intra-institutional differences, based on differentiation and diversification, also might appeal to such political sources for conflict

resolution. For more on this, see Talcott Parsons's discussion of differentiation, value-generalization, and reintegration in, for example, *The Social System* (Glencoe, Ill.: Free Press, 1951).

34. With the moderate leaders gone, many messengers remarked that the 1991 meeting in Atlanta seemed like a return to the good old days. Although it is certainly true that 1991 was characterized by harmony and relative unanimity, memories of the turmoil lingered. Most interesting, from my perspective, is that Lee Porter, the recording secretary affiliated with the old establishment, retained his position despite the challenge of a candidate obviously chosen by the fundamentalist coalition. Although this event alone proves nothing, it may suggest an easing of hard feelings between fundamentalist sympathizers and other conservatives who have chosen to stay. In any event it surely points up that denominational politics are a cat that cannot be put back in the bag.

CHAPTER 5

RATIONALIZATION AND REACTION AMONG SOUTHERN BAPTISTS

David Ray Norsworthy

> The only thing on which two [Southern] Baptists will
> agree is how much the third ought to give to the
> Cooperative Program.
>
> —Anonymous

Bureaucracy enlisted in soul winning is still bureaucracy. This chapter will examine bureaucracy in the Southern Baptist Convention, with particular emphasis on its consequences for a conservative reaction. *Bureaucracy* will be understood as one of Max Weber's ideal types of legitimate authority or domination.[1] Correspondingly, *rationalization* here refers only to the process by which an organization takes on the formal properties of a bureaucracy.

The Southernness of Southern Baptists

To understand today's Southern Baptists, it helps to remember the nineteenth-century southern ambiance of the denomination.[2] The denomination was founded in 1845 amidst the sectional conflict over slavery. For more than one hundred years, Southern Baptists were shaped as the South was shaped. The influences, South and Baptist, were mutually reinforcing. Regional localism, familialism—and yes, white supremacy—were as much a part of being Southern Baptist as was zeal for evangelism and missions. Baptists were "at ease in

Zion."[3] As the denomination prospered, expanding in numbers and rising in social standing, the members in large part held onto their distinctive form of Baptist piety and biblicism. They lived in a society of rural communities and small towns, set off from, but uneasily part of, the more urban-industrial nation.

This nineteenth-century religion of southern whites is not properly called *fundamentalist*.[4] Fundamentalism was a reaction to modernism in religion and culture; the movement got its name from a Northern Baptist journalist. At the time the southern region and Southern Baptists were still close to their rural folk religion. Few southerners had encountered the relativizing and pluralizing effects that modernist beliefs had brought to the North. It was the very strength of their traditional religion, in fact, that enabled Southern Baptists throughout the first half of the twentieth century to retain confidence in the absolute truth of the "old time religion." Despite accelerating economic and social changes spawned by the dislocations of world wars and depression, southern rural and small-town religion had little of the militant reactionism associated with fundamentalism.

However, neither the region nor its civil religion were immune from all change. Even as doctrines took on the appearance of permanence, the organizational structures of the denomination were changing and modernizing. These structural changes may be summarized by saying that the Southern Baptist polity and the southern political economy experienced rationalization. In Max Weber's terms, this means that a change occurred in the manner by which claims to legitimacy were made by the religious and civil systems. Weber maintains three grounds for legitimate domination (authority): (1) *rational,* resting on legal rules and the right of officials to give commands; (2) *traditional,* resting on time-honored traditions and the right of leaders to exercise authority according to these customs; and (3) *charismatic,* resting on the heroic quality of a person and of the "truth" revealed or conveyed by that person.[5]

Rationalization in the SBC

From its inception in 1845, the Southern Baptist Convention was organized in a manner more conducive to centralized functions than was the parent body.[6] Actual formalization of the convention structure, however, was not the original intent; in fact, this move seems to have run roughshod over the Baptist principle of the autonomy of the local church. Ironically it has been the extraordinary success of Southern Baptists, measured by growth, that has forced the realization, time after time, that older, relatively simple and informal structures would no longer do. As Samuel Hill and Arthur Farnsley argue in this volume, the formation of the Cooperative Program and the Executive Committee were crucial centralizing, bureaucratizing moves.[7] These were followed, in 1931, by constitutional reforms, one of which created a regular method for electing and rotating boards of trustees to govern the various entities (agencies, boards, and educational institutions) of the denomination.

As new agencies and state conventions were added, the complexity of the denomination's governing task increased. In 1947, for instance, the Christian Life Commission (CLC) became a full-time bureau, with an expanded mandate to examine social and ethical issues, such as race relations and family problems, not traditionally on the agenda of organized Southern Baptist life.[8] The CLC is but one of thirteen such commissions. Finally, in 1956, the Inter-Agency Council, an extra layer of coordination, was created. Representatives from the staffs of all the boards and agencies serve on this council charged with coordinating programs and settling territorial disputes among staffs.

The denomination's structure not only began to look like a bureaucracy but its leaders began to act and think like bureaucrats. In the mid-1950s, the SBC undertook a management study with the guidance of the management firm of Booz, Allen, and Hamilton. Consultation with a secular management firm symbolized, as hardly anything else could, that the Southern Baptist leadership had adopted, for whatever reason, the rational-bureaucratic model of the modern organization. As of 1960, all agencies were required to have organizational manuals detailing their program assignments, lines of authority, internal procedures, and relationship with state and local bodies.

The Changing South after Midcentury

By 1950 extensive and cumulative changes in the social structure of the South started more rapidly to bring an end to rural and small-town isolation from national business, communications, and educational institutions. The immunity of southern culture and religion from modernist influences were sorely tested. By quantitative measures—statistics on migration and urbanization, income and education, and the division of labor—regional change was substantial, if not revolutionary, by 1960.[9] There was further diminution in the indexes of economic and social differences between the South and the rest of the country in the 1960s and 1970s.[10] With respect to the traditional system of white supremacy, too, change accelerated in the 1950s and in succeeding decades. No more appropriate symbol of the pressure for change can be imagined than the U.S. Supreme Court *Brown v. Board of Education* decision in 1954, striking down legally separated schools for whites and blacks.[11]

If the southern region and the Southern Baptist polity have undergone accelerated structural change, particularly after 1950, what have been the consequences of rationalization for the beliefs and actions of the members of this denomination? In the nineteenth century, it could be said that the culture of modernity and the fundamentalist reaction did not penetrate the South, because the enabling technological-economic structures had not become powerful enough. But even then the culture of the South, built as it was in reaction to the North before and after the Civil War, acted as an insulator against modernist culture. This insulation lasted for decades after all of the technological and economic prerequisites for a modern culture had been in place.[12]

Although the South and the SBC rationalized their structures, the world view of Southern Baptists—answers to core questions, rites, and religious priorities for individuals and groups—did not for a time change. Behind the protective wall of southernness, a vibrant and defensive culture-religion grew and prospered, though built to suit a society that was about to pass away. The strength and coherence of the Southern Baptist religion delayed the secularization that Weber called the "disenchantment of the world"[13] and Daniel Bell called the "profanation" of the traditional religious world view.[14] Powerful plausibility structures within the region and denomination, together with a continuing experience of conflict with an "alien" North, actually strengthened the claim to truth for the culture-religion. Statistics on material changes and structural trends, if interpreted deterministically, could lead one to miss the role that the culture-religion has played in shaping the effects of rationalization and the ensuing encounter between religious and secular-scientific world views. The argument is not that regional culture holds off modernism forever;

rather, it is that the ethnic religion was itself dynamic, making use of powerful resources with which to preserve and augment its distinctive character against intrusive cultural alternatives.

The 1950s changed the institutional environment more drastically than had any previous decade. The Supreme Court decision on schools, heightened conflict over implementation of the court's decision, and the larger civil rights movement were all powerful agents of cultural-religious change. This was a major moral issue framed and placed in the public sphere by blacks and *modernists,* not, for the most part, by southern white religious figures. The modernists, largely from outside Southern Baptist life, gave a nontraditional answer to a core question: How are people of different races going to relate to one another in this world?

Southern Baptist religious orthodoxy lost the moral authority to define race relations. The many related changes in relations between the South and the rest of the country helped to break down the wall that had denied modernism a hearing in the traditional order. By the end of the 1950s, and with increasing intensity in the 1960s, Southern Baptists themselves put the new questions to their religious community. During this period coinciding with strenuous moral and social activism within the country generally, the comfortable and well-worn grooves in which Southern Baptist beliefs had run were forcibly and irreparably damaged.

More and more Southern Baptists were now educated or living in cities or both. One consequence of this mobility was sharpened contradictions between their religious upbringing and the cultural messages to which they were exposed. Value confrontations occurred over school, family life, child rearing, and other issues. Unprecedented complexity had to be faced by ordinary people as they tried to make decisions about how to live their lives. The influence of modernist assumptions grew in tandem with the spread of pluralistic communities. There had to be some sort of response by people whose moral guide had been an absolutist, consensual religion.

Some Southern Baptists found the modern sensibility liberating and made for themselves an accommodation between their ethnic religion and the modern world. This response was especially likely in those with the most formal education, those in seminaries, and in top leaders of the denomination's agencies. These elites tried to take seriously the intellectual and ethical challenges that a scientific and humanistic ethos legitimately posed to the provincial South and to orthodox Southern Baptists.

Other Southern Baptists reacted with alarm to modernist intrusions. Some of these, too, were in positions of leadership in the denomination. They understood, perhaps better than their accommodative brethren, what the modernist challenge really meant for a Southern Baptist religion rooted in the nineteenth century. Heard in earlier generations, their voices had influenced, but not determined, the evolution of the denomination into the 1960s. [15] But at the end of the 1970s, and throughout the 1980s, the voice of fundamentalist reaction rose to a level that forced the denomination to take an unanticipated direction.

Leaders of this movement at first called themselves inerrantists or fundamentalists; later they eschewed the term fundamentalist, preferring to be known as conservative. By whatever name, however, they hold beliefs and attitudes closely resembling those of fundamentalist leaders in the North decades ago. But the shape of their protest was determined by both the enemy they now faced and the culture-religion they sought to defend. The ethnic or civil religion of the South had featured a powerful Protestant orthodoxy that erected a bulwark against modernism. Ironically it may be because of this defensive and insular orthodoxy that when cracks in the conservative structure occurred, one consequence was a harsh, uncompromising, and even more defensive movement to hold off change. Perhaps the very ease with which Southern Baptists were able for so long to put down or finesse dissenting voices among the "family" rendered the denomination ill equipped to deal with a massive structural cleavage at the point of crisis.

The response these southerners chose, then, built on the civil religion that had been so integral to their culture. The great mainstream of Southern Baptist religion has been characterized by powerful biblicism and oratory. Even as the denomination took on a hierarchy and a differentiation of functions, at the base local congregations continued to take their cues from Bible verses and stirring sermons. The rationalization process moderated these elements to different degrees in different segments of the church, but there persisted a duality of tendencies: moderation and civility on the one hand, and a fierce intolerance and condemnation of ways of life considered un-Christian (meaning deviant from orthodox Southern Baptist practices) on the other hand.

A rhetoric demanding public and unswerving fealty to an inerrant Bible attracted the attention of mainstream Southern Baptists who had cut their teeth on a biblicism just as certain but less insistent. Anyone who could be portrayed as an enemy of the Bible was automatically an enemy of the culture-religion.

The "Underside" of Rationalization

With the spread of bureaucracy in the SBC, there came to be a larger and larger gap between officials and ordinary Baptists in the local churches, and between professors and ordinary pastors. This situation allowed for the insulation of elites from the great majority of church members. Some Baptists who themselves had been insiders have spoken critically of the political behavior of denominational leaders before 1979, implying that fundamentalists had indeed been kept out of the top positions in the denomination.[16] Their reasoning, however, is especially revealing. One seminary professor, for instance, denied that *conservatives* were shut out, citing the clear conservatism of the presidents of the SBC from 1959 to 1979. If anyone was shut out, he said, "it was because of . . . incompetence or an uncooperative spirit."[17] Let us further examine this issue.

With expansion of the scale and complexity of denominational undertakings—from missions to education to pastors' pensions—the task of eliciting, distributing, and spending millions of dollars in yearly contributions could be managed only by an organization that came to look more and more like a business corporation or government. Yet as bureaucratic as the structure had to be, the grant of legitimacy to this rational-legal dominance was not enthusiastically given by grass-roots Baptists.[18]

The denomination-creating process has worked against cherished Baptist traditions: autonomy of the local church, the servanthood of leaders, and pioneer individualism. Growth and the professionalization of agency staffs brought tendencies toward rule by the expert—in short, competence. But competence in the agencies had the consequence of alienating many ordinary members of the denomination from the style and content of initiatives taken by these officials. By virtue of their education and career experience, bureaucratic officials were often able to mitigate direct control by elected boards—an informal power that became especially apparent in the controversies over various publications of the Sunday School Board and Broadman Press.

Within this informal but very real power system, one could predict that it might be people at middle and upper-middle levels of the larger structure who would, to the greatest degree, experience estrangement. Opposition to bureaucracy would be most likely among those who had positions as religious professionals (clergy) or lay leaders in their church, but had concluded that they or their point of view were insufficiently recognized by remote and insensitive wielders of power in seminaries and agencies.

Bureaucracy stresses formal procedure and rules over capricious or ideological grounds for action. As formal rationalization proceeds, therefore, the criteria for the selection of leaders change from traditional or charismatic gifts to other, more bureaucratic talents. This is the nature of the organization's requirements, once the road to bureaucracy is taken. People who do not go by the rules are quickly seen as having "uncooperative spirits."

All of this has nothing directly to do with belief in the Bible. But competence is usually defined by academic criteria, academic excellence is usually defined in ways that comport with modern thinking, and modern thinking is usually associated with new ways of approaching the Bible. Taken together, then, there may indeed be a tendency to pass over as uncooperative and incompetent those whose academic backgrounds are more limited to the conservative or fundamentalist schools, which have had poor reputations among both religious and secular elites. When the standards for evaluating institutions by Southern Baptists converge with those of secular leaders, "uncooperative spirits" see a modernist sellout.[19]

Discrimination against fundamentalists surely did exist in the educational institutions and denominational agencies of the Southern Baptist Convention during the generation before the take-over movement began. The issue, in a time when the bases of authority are changing, is what counts as appropriate discrimination: by what criteria is a candidate ruled unacceptable or less fit than another? Educational institutions discriminate against ignorance without being charged with unfairness. Bureaucratic appointments and decisions will match the requirements of the organization and the broad ideological consensus of its constituents. Bureaucracies, by their nature, do not serve any one small group taking a particular doctrinal position on a narrow range of matters over which there might be debate within the constituency.

The movement begun in 1979 by Paul Pressler and Paige Patterson has been described in various ways in other contributions to this book. Here the focus will be upon the antibureaucratic nature of the movement. My claim is that whatever else separated the inerrantist movement leaders from their opponents, the inerrantists clearly objected to the state of bureaucratic domination reached by the late 1970s in the operating structures of the denomination. This is supported by a study of the leading journal of the inerrantists, the *Southern Baptist Advocate*. In almost every issue from 1983 to 1989, under two different editors, attacks were made on the bureaucracy and bureaucrats. The following are summaries of a sampling of *Advocate* articles, with emphasis added to highlight the antibureaucratic nature of the complaints:

April 1984. It is reported that the aim of the inerrancy movement, as told by its leaders, is to wrest political control of the twenty national agencies from the enormous *bureaucracy* running them.[20]

November 1984. In an editorial a derisive reference is made to the Baylor University President and to the other *denominationalists*.[21]

January 1985. An attack is made on the Baylor president, accusing him of an attitude common to the "burgeoning bureaucracy, insensitive to grassroots concerns."[22]

March 1985. An article appears, titled "Centralization, Exclusivism, and Liberal Trends Generate Concerns by Baptist Pastor."[23]

June 1985. An editorial reports that a pastor who has voted against the conservatives for 6 years will be supporting Charles Stanley's reelection. One reason "had to do with the unprecedented efforts of denominational bureaucrats who are working to defeat Charles Stanley. . . . This pastor said . . . that controversy has become one of bureaucrats versus a ground-swell, grass-roots movement." The editorial goes on to identify the problem of "a burgeoning, insensitive bureaucracy which stands united against its constituents." The editor closes with the plea that "a message needs to be sent to the bureaucracy, whose salaries we pay, [a message that] we the people . . . will determine the course and direction our Convention will take."[24]

July 1986. There is a quotation from an article by Glenn Hinson that appeared in *Christian Century* on 7-14 June 1978. The *Advocate* quotes Hinson as follows: "In the corporate model, power is wielded by the heads of various companies and departments (in this case boards, commissions and agencies) and only nominally by the stockholders. When some 20,000 'messengers' of the churches gather for the annual convention, they make a lot of noise, but they, representing the stockholders, can do little besides rubber-stamp what their skilled force of executives, managers and other experts has decided after prolonged consideration. Even persons privy to the major policy meetings probably could not tell who really decided what. If forced to pinpoint a single body with the greatest overall clout, I would point to the Executive Board of the SBC and the committee which does its staff work. They decide who gets how much money from the Cooperative Program, and in this affluent corporation the power of the purse is a mighty one."[25]

July 1986. A guest editorial describes two groups, separated by differences in the philosophy that holds them together: those with a particular view of the Bible (moderate conservatives) and those with a philosophy of cooperation stressing liberty of interpretation (middle-of-the-road Bible believers). When controversy occurs, moderate conservatives run to methodology, procedure, and polity. Their philosophy of implementing theology is different from that of fundamentalist conservatives. Moderate conservatives have the tools, but tools do not win; philosophy does.[26]

July 1986. A letter to the editor is critical of a statement by Roy Honeycutt, president of Southern Baptist Theological Seminary, that the moderate minority will have to constitute "pockets of civility, intelligence and morality" and not be overcome by the hordes. The letter writer calls this "intellectual snobbery."[27]

December 1986. Protest is made against the elitism of denominational bureaucrats and executive directors, charging arrogance, insensitivity, and unfairness. It is believed that executives think they are better than the masses.[28]

June 1987. An editorial applauds a recent decision by the Foreign Mission Board to appoint missionaries regardless of whether they attended a Southern Baptist seminary. Objection is made to previous rules: "What a person believes should receive more consideration than where one goes to school."[29]

June 1988. An article asserts that in San Antonio "it will be determined whether the conservative resurgence continues or whether we will go back to the kind of *uncaring, unsympathetic and iron-clad* moderate/liberal control we knew before 1979.[30]

July 1988. An article begins, "All that we have experienced in the SBC is directly traceable to a calloused and insensitive bureaucracy."[31]

January 1989. An editorial attacks "closet conservatives" who, now that the inerrantists are in control, are willing to be identified as inerrantists and to be leaders. Some of them have been put on boards, and they show themselves as willing to "curry favor with the Bureaucrats."[32]

The above excerpts, and many others that could be adduced, show inerrancy-movement spokesmen as not only resentful of denominational leaders but hopeful that their appeal to the grass roots with antibureaucratic language would resonate broadly and well. Theirs is the language of populism, claiming that their party represents the views of the people against an elite who have forfeited the right to dominate by their imperious behavior and a philosophy that puts method, rules, and procedure ahead of right belief.

The inerrantists set out to delegitimate the Southern Baptist bureaucracy. The question arises as to where authority would be located if not in the structures evolved during more than a century of Southern Baptist expansion. The immediate answer, familiar to any Southern Baptist, is that the local church is autonomous and, therefore, there can be no higher authority. Another answer, reaching beyond polity to doctrine, is that only the Bible is authoritative. But in practice there will be, within so large and complex a body, a tendency for some individuals and small groups to exercise a disproportionate influence upon the actions of the thousands of local congregations and the millions of individual Baptists. To the extent that this influence causes people to do what they would not otherwise do, and to accept such direction as being "right," there will be a system of authority—beyond the Bible and beyond local churches—lodged in the denomination.[33]

Appealing to the democratic tradition in Baptist life, the inerrantists asserted that the messengers to annual conventions, as a presumed cross section of the grass roots, are authoritative. By their votes presidents of the denomination are elected and boards of trustees are put in control. These trustees, and not the agency executives, seminary professors, and bureaucrats, are supposed to make policy. In turn messengers at annual conventions give trustees guidance for their policies. Messengers are assumed to reflect the will of the millions of Baptists in local churches and are accorded the right to tell all of the functionaries within the denominational structure what is authoritatively Southern Baptist and what is not.

This democratic rhetoric was accompanied by a rhetoric of fealty to an inerrant Bible. By centering their insurgency upon the necessity of fidelity to the Bible, fundamentalists seemed to offer a choice between an elitist, doctrinally questionable, bureaucratic basis for authority and a democratically voiced allegiance to God's word. To ordinary Southern Baptists, this would be no contest.

Again the *Southern Baptist Advocate,* voice of the inerrantist movement, reveals much about their objectives. Reading issues of this journal published from 1983 to 1989, one finds repeated appeals to the grass roots and criticism of elites on behalf of the grass roots. But it is not as clear that the interests represented are of the grass roots or that the only authority being touted was the Bible. Rather than a grass-roots democratic movement, a counter-elite was being fostered, one of an ideological rather than bureaucratic sort. Editorials and articles supported pastors against denominational officials, and trustees against scholars and administrators. Favor was thus shown toward patrimonial or charismatic decrees spoken directly from on high to an undifferentiated mass, as against rationalized procedures and plans worked up and down a multi-layered structure of pragmatic functionaries and their constituents.

The journal repeatedly featured the most successful evangelists and pastors of giant and fast-growing churches, categories that included past and potential presidents of the SBC. Some examples follow:

January 1985. An article announced the first annual Bible conference by a new organization called Real Evangelism. Prominent pastors mentioned as participants in this three-day conference were Bailey Smith, Charles Stanley, Jimmy Draper, and Jerry Falwell. All except Falwell had been or were then president of the SBC, and Falwell was a superchurch independent Baptist pastor with a national television ministry. The director of the conference said, "We hope to make this an annual affair. It is Real Evangelism's way of saying thanks to the many pastors and people who have supported our ministry." [34]

March 1985. An article reports a dispute over a statement by Paige Patterson that his goal as president of the Center for Biblical Studies was "to create clones of Dr. [W. A.] Criswell," pastor of the First Baptist Church of Dallas. Patterson said that criticism of his statement reflects fear "of the powerful pulpiteer with an authoritative message from God." [35]

March 1986. An article by the editor makes the usual attack upon "a bureaucracy out of control," but adds that it is pastors and trustees who have been victims of imperious executives and seminary administrators. The editor complains about the social actionism of agencies, and presidents of colleges who want a board of trustees to be only fund raisers. [36]

July 1986. The editor compliments the new trustees as "good, solid, conservative men who come from the mainstream and grassroots of Southern Baptist life." He quotes Bylaw 16 of the SBC's constitution: "Boards, Commissions and Trustees . . . should represent the constituency of the Convention, rather than the Staff of the Agency." He instructs the trustees to "serve Southern Baptists," for they are "plainly responsible only to the SBC." In the past trustees have been rubber-stamp bodies for agency administrators. Sad to say, he adds, there have been times since the conservative resurgence began that conservatives have worked hard to get conservatives elected as trustees only to see them intimidated and voting with the liberals. This should stop. [37]

December 1986. An unsigned editorial takes the side of strong trustees against denominational executives and presidents of seminaries, emphasizing that trustees, given a mandate by the Convention, are in charge. Executives are hired hands; they should have no political role. By contrast the president of the Convention is free to be political, because he is elected by a majority at the Convention. There is no mention of the role for the minority point of view. [38]

December 1986. An unsigned article on the Baptist Joint Committee on Public Affairs identifies a problem in the structure of the Public

Affairs Committee (PAC), which has been the Southern Baptist advisory committee to the BJCPA. The problem seen is that of fifteen members on the PAC, nine are either executive officers or staff representatives of various denominational boards or agencies. Only five are elected at large through the Convention's normal process. There should be a change, so that although the president of the Convention would remain, all other members of the PAC would be elected and no one would be appointed by reason of being an executive or staff member. Although the article does not say, this change would sharply reduce bureaucratic, and increase presidential, authority.[39]

September 1987. An unsigned article reports a revision in the structure of the Public Affairs Committee in the direction of the proposal reported in the summary immediately preceding. The membership was increased from fifteen to eighteen, and the number of agency executives on the committee was reduced from nine to five. The net result was to increase the number of at-large members, elected directly by the Convention, from five to twelve.[40]

September 1987. An unsigned article is critical of alumni of Southeastern Baptist Theological Seminary for their affirmation of support for its administration and faculty and for making an effort to direct the trustees: "Trustees are not responsible to any Alumni Association but to the SBC." The position is that the alumni's role is to support the trustees, not to be critical.[41]

January 1988. An unsigned article reports that Dr. Larry Lewis, recently installed as Home Mission Board president by the now-dominant inerrantists, said to his employees and board of trustees, "We must give careful attention to the doctrinal integrity of our agency. This has been very clear to us that our Southern Baptist constituency want our agencies to be doctrinally sound. They don't want us to have a questionable or marginal theological stance. They are anxious about it; they are going to insist on it. Trustees who will not be responsive will be replaced. We have a mandate from our good bride, the SBC, to be very careful about the doctrinal integrity of our institution." An editor's note prefacing these remarks reads, "You will note that he never suggests that he would take the initiative in terminating Trustees or

present employees who do not concur with his particular interpretation . . ." Although apparently softening the impact of Lewis's words,
the editor is urging upon his readers the notion that a new structure of
authority is now in place—that bureaucratic rationality in trustee selection will not be allowed to circumvent the new "mandate from . . . the
SBC."[42]

January 1989. An editorial criticizes plans by moderate/liberal
churches to designate funds as a response to control of the denomination by conservatives. It suggests that because conservative churches
are just as autonomous as moderate/liberal churches, they might send
their entire check to Nashville. They could either designate a portion
to be returned to the state or let all their Cooperative Program contribution go to national causes.[43] The conclusion to be drawn from this
editorial is that the inerrantists, now in the ascendancy, will urge
among their constituents, ironically, a preference for more centralized
denominational activities than they did when their adversaries had
control.

I have shown why and how a bureaucratic mode of rationalization was
adopted by Southern Baptists, and have presented evidence that in reaction
to this adaptation to modernity a movement arose that opposed bureaucracy
and favored dominance by pastors and trustees. In little more than a decade,
as its leaders promised in 1979, the inerrantists have taken over the "commanding heights" of the denomination and have dramatically altered the personnel and functions of its major structures. In Weberian terms the grounds
of legitimate domination have shifted—away from rational rules and decisions by officials toward fidelity to tradition and the right of patrimonial or
heroic leaders to rule. Larry Lewis's statement on doctrinal integrity illustrates
the shift from bureaucratic manager to populist spokesman, away from ratio-
nally derived rules and procedures toward the primacy of tradition and inerrancy.

Such a system is open to being overwhelmed by the personal force of
even a single individual. Paul Pressler, for example, is officially vice-chairman
of the Executive Committee, but it was his personal clout as visible leader of
the successful inerrancy movement that enabled him to engineer the highly
irregular (from a bureaucratic perspective) 1990 firing of Al Shackleford and

Dan Martin from their Baptist Press posts.[44] Although these and other incidents do not warrant the conclusion that bureaucratic authority is being thoroughly dismantled, competing grounds for domination have gained strength on two sides—mobilized masses at the conventions and in the pews, and traditional or charismatic leaders speaking for God and the masses at the expense of officialdom.

Radical in its aim and ideology, the inerrantist movement nevertheless seldom had to use the language of radical politics. Instead it employed the language of its own culture. At times the fundamentalists in the 1980s seemed only to be attacking a few professors who do not believe the Bible and some bureaucrats who are arrogant. But the revolt went deeper, to the very heart of the modern system of rational and technical procedures that had entered the business of Southern Baptists. Never mind that in practice the conservatives used the latest media technology to communicate their condemnation of a technological order; they were really raising the issue of authority. Is the Bible absolutely authoritative? Shall any other authority supplant it?

Emerging Modes of Authority

Actually, as the evidence has suggested, the inerrantists offered more than the Book as authoritative. The movement was built upon the idea that certain pastors have a special calling or gift to be the voice of God. Extraordinary influence has been vested in those preachers who demonstrate the greatest skill in plying the themes and rhythms of Southern Baptist piety in a diagnosis and cure for ills of the southern soul and American civilization.

Probing deeper we might consider how the role of pastor has changed along with dramatic social change in the South and Southwest. In newly urban sections of the country, the pastoral role can be enhanced, the pastor becoming both an enforcer of individual morals and an overseer of the routine work of the church—attendance, service, and giving. The pastor fills a vacuum left by the decline of the social networks people had in more stable communities. In changing communities members of the congregation may depend more exclusively upon their church, under the guidance of their pastor, to provide the glue that holds their social lives together. The person who cultivates this bond also creates and maintains control over behavior. For certain personalities in communities of churning populations, the pastoral role can be transformed into that of an heroic figure. Upon the unusual power and visibility of these figures the inerrantists have built.

It is perhaps going too far to claim that these pastors come close to possessing Max Weber's ideal type of charismatic authority. Weber applied the term *charisma* to supernatural, or at least highly exceptional, powers.[45] Even when their congregations and followers treat them as larger than life, fundamentalist pastors do not depend upon charisma alone for authority. What Weber termed *patrimonial* domination refers to a system of authority involving a dependency relationship, broader than patriarchy but still based on loyalty and fidelity to a master.[46] This traditional system, in which custom requires that the subject support the master in all possible ways, is possibly being renewed today. Some chief pastors of large churches, especially if their influence extends by way of television beyond their congregation, develop something like patrimonial domination over their staff and membership, encompassing a wide circle of loyal supporters of a cause presented as the Lord's.

Although such a system of patrimony may work within a local church—even a superchurch—the question remains whether fundamentalist control of agencies and seminaries necessarily will result in the extirpation of instrumental and pragmatic modes of decision making. The bureaucracy, like a civil service that stays in place through political administration changes, has needed expertise and functional capabilities that inerrantist zealots cannot completely ignore. But just as a conservative administration can go over the heads of the bureaucracy to the voters, the new leadership of the Baptists can appeal annually to the convention messengers for passage of resolutions that are then used to police agency executives and seminary professors. The fact that Baptist tradition affirms the "autonomy of the local congregation" will not hinder this use of the convention, for usually it is not local congregations but the hierarchy of officials that is being disciplined.

Conflicting perceptions of pastoral authority found their way into the convention's public debate in 1988. The doctrine of the priesthood of all believers became the symbolic center of conflict over the pastor's legitimate power. This doctrine has been of great importance to Baptists, who cite Scripture as their authority and Martin Luther's writings as a precedent. Controversy started to build in 1986, when the Sunday School Board cited the priesthood of all believers as the scriptural foundation for their program of "Shared Ministry" to promote a "healthy relationship between pastors, church staff, deacons and church members."[47] What the Sunday School Board saw as "healthy," however, the fundamentalists saw as a bureaucratic attempt to undermine pastoral authority. At a public meeting, W. A. Criswell boldly asserted, "The pastor is the ruler of the church." Perhaps that is why a worried church historian wrote that "churches in the denomination increasingly are assigning more power to their ordained leaders."[48]

In 1988 Southern Baptists also observed the Year of the Laity, a "program emphasis" designed by agency leaders in Nashville. To go along with the emphasis, the topic of the annual Baptist Doctrine study was the priesthood of all believers, using a book published early that year by Walter Shurden.[49] Fundamentalists criticized both the study topic and the book. For them, it was all mounting evidence of the anti-pastor bias of bureaucrats.

In response to all of this, at the 1988 annual convention in San Antonio came the notorious Resolution 5: On the Priesthood of the Believer. This resolution stated that the doctrine is subject to misunderstanding and abuse, that it has been used to justify wrongly the attitude that a Christian may believe whatever he chooses, and that it can be used to justify the undermining of pastoral authority in the local church. It affirms that the doctrine of the priesthood of the believer "in no way contradicts the biblical understanding of the role, responsibility and authority of the pastor," and that "pastors are called of God to lead the local church."[50] The resolution passed by a sizable majority after a twenty-five-minute debate.

When the inerrantists were on the attack, their weapon was an unassailable Bible, used to hammer away at an overweening and poorly legitimated bureaucratic target. After years of strife, there were layers and layers of crosscutting polarizations. In such a presumably democratic polity, pastors and lay people had always been to some degree in an uncertain power relationship. The conflict in the 1980s heightened sensitivities to that uncertainty. Pastors were critical to the success of the inerrancy movement, if for no other reason than that they made up (and/or mobilized) the vast majority of the messengers at any given convention. It is no surprise, then, that so overtly political a group as the inerrancy leaders would exploit clergy-lay conflicts on behalf of the clergy. Whatever else it was, the 1988 resolution limiting the priesthood of the believer appealed to pastors besieged by unruly anti-authoritarian congregations.

Passage of Resolution Five set off a fire storm of protest, however, registered not only by oppositional forces at the 1988 convention but also in editorials and letters to editors of state papers.[51] The intensity of feelings aroused by this resolution suggests that it may have violated a core value of many grass-roots Southern Baptists. The inerrantists, sponsors of this resolution, had been shrewd readers in the 1980s of the doctrinal fears and social resentments of the broad mass of the Southern Baptist constituency. With the resolution on the priesthood of the believer, they may have won the convention vote but alienated an increasing segment of ordinary Baptists.

This resolution on the priesthood of the believer presented an issue that convention moderates attempted to use to rally the conservative middle. The resolution cast doubt on the virtue of individual freedom and raised the specter of pastoral authoritarianism. These were rich symbols for an oppositional movement advocating a return to a Baptist heritage of soul competency and the servanthood of leaders. It has been said that the Reformation meaning of the doctrine is often misunderstood today.[52] But it is in its most characteristically contemporary meaning—the idea of a right to private judgment—that the priesthood of the believer is most appealing even to many doctrinal conservatives.

Meanwhile, with moderates attempting to rally those to their right in a fight against patrimonial authority, those to their left were exploring other directions. More than a year before the priesthood resolution was presented, another opposition movement of moderates, the Southern Baptist Alliance, had emerged. The SBA described itself as "an alliance of individuals and churches dedicated to preservation of historic Baptist principles and freedoms and traditions, and to continuance of our ministries and mission within the Southern Baptist Convention."[53] Its commitments are to freedom of the individual and the local church, ecumenism, the servant role of leadership, theological education, evangelism, and a free church in a free state. In part the agenda was determined by prior moves of the "Pressler-Patterson-Rogers coalition." Formed to "provide a time and a place for like-minded Southern Baptists to meet together in fellowship and mutual support and to find a refuge from bitterness and divisiveness," the SBA as of March 1991 had over seventy thousand members and approximately 125 congregations.

Although respecting "historic Baptist principles," during its first two years the SBA applied these principles in new ways to new problems. By giving prominence to social justice for women and minorities, as well as to ecumenical outreach, the SBA is unlike any movement of comparable scale in Southern Baptist history. The movement both expresses and transcends a defense of the rationalized denominational structures under attack by fundamentalists. It contains, in tension, the goals of a dissident movement and a nascent institutional structure with reordered Baptist priorities. At the third annual meeting in Greenville, South Carolina, in March 1989, the discourse did not emphasize mere organizational mechanisms characteristic of a formally rational denominational polity.[54] They groped for what Max Weber called *substantive rationality,* wherein action is not based on rational calculation of the best technical methods of achieving a goal, but rather on the application of criteria of ultimate ends.[55] Content with neither the old substance nor its eclipse under bureaucracy, some SBA members reached for a new substance. They asked questions about the ends for which organization exists—questions revealing an intent to emancipate themselves from a cloying culture-religion. Resisting the legitimacy of tradition, charisma, and bureaucracy alike, SBA members sought a value rationality based on open communication in a diverse and participatory democratic order. The goals inchoately expressed were of the sort Jurgen Habermas discusses in his normative theory of rational action based on the centrality of uncoerced communication.[56]

As consistent as the Southern Baptist Alliance's interpretation of the priesthood of the believer is with mainstream Baptist belief, it will never attract many conservatives. Its agenda, style, and social base are too "progressive," too far from most mainstream Southern Baptist thinking. The SBA is more likely to incubate a new denomination or to join the American Baptists than to be the party that takes back the SBC from the inerrantists.

Perhaps the most important external effect the SBA has had so far is that it has opened room slightly to the left of center for other opposition movements to grow, movements that seek to mobilize people too conservative for the progressive SBA but infuriated by the tactics and agenda of the fundamentalists. Two such movements were formed successively. The first was Baptists Committed to the SBC, created in late 1988.[57] Avoiding the term *moderate* and calling itself *centrist,* this organization announced an agenda of "reclaiming the SBC from ultra-conservative control and depoliticizing the SBC presidency." Its purpose was to "unify our Convention behind the great distinctives of Southern Baptists: divinely inspired scripture as our authority; *priesthood of the believer* [emphasis added]; separation of church and state; and local church autonomy and democracy."[58] Baptists Committed supported the candidacy of Daniel Vestal for the SBC presidency. He lost in 1989 against an incumbent, and lost again in 1990 by an even wider margin.

After the convention in New Orleans in 1990, Baptists Committed spawned a second "movement from the middle."[59] At a meeting in Atlanta that August, this movement, called the Fellowship, created an alternative way to channel contributions from local churches to SBC institutions and to new causes. Although both Alliance and Baptists Committed members participated in the early phases of this new movement, it clearly began in the ranks of Baptists Committed. It signaled their turn away from partisan politics and was colored by their more conservative experience.

Despite widespread dismay over the new forms of authority and direction taken by the SBC's new leaders, the possible growth of any of these movements is limited by the strong conservative pull of the denomination's bureaucratic center. The connection between local churches and the centralized Cooperative Program has been legitimated as both biblical and successful. Few of those churches will be willing to sever that tie. It would ill serve fundamentalists to overthrow entirely the Southern Baptist bureaucracy.

Conclusion

I have argued that bureaucratic rationalization of the SBC produced a fundamentalist reaction strong enough in the 1980s to take secure control of the denomination's central agencies. Will this control be long lasting, bolstered by traditional and charismatic legitimations overriding bureaucratic requirements? Or will bureaucratic domination return? Or, finally, will the denomination split, allowing two or three denominations to emerge, each with its own distinct mode of authority?

Although these questions obviously cannot be given a satisfactory answer here and now, one viewpoint can be offered: Fundamentalism may be inherently unstable. Its replacement will probably not be the result of dethronement by one or a coalition of competing movements organized at annual conventions. Rather, the end of fundamentalist control, if and when it comes, will more likely be through deterioration of the legitimacy of the leadership cadre as a consequence of the inexorable infighting that their rigidity cannot let them escape.

There is, however, an alternative outcome. Fundamentalists can avoid delegitimation by holding onto a modified version of the rationalized bureaucratic procedures that were the objects of their attacks as they came to power. By discovering the modern bureaucratic imperative, they will moderate their rigidities based on belief, becoming less fundamentalist, even as they retain power. The extent to which they have to compromise will depend in part on how diverse their own denomination remains and whether the nation as a whole remains conservative. If disaffected moderates/progressives leave, and if the nation stays conservative, very little real compromise will be required to maintain control.

If a bureaucratized fundamentalism retains control of the SBC, how many disaffected moderates/centrists will make their peace with it? Probably the great majority. Because they are theologically conservative and culturally traditional, they will see the denomination as not really very different from what it was before the fundamentalist turmoil.

But there will be one difference: the Southern Baptists will in the meantime certainly have lost the tip of their Left wing—an event the fundamentalists devoutly wished for anyway. The great majority of Southern Baptists will remain as they are, though chastened and sensitized by the contradictory demands imposed upon a religious people living with modernity.

Notes

1. Max Weber, *Economy and Society: An Outline of Interpretive Sociology,* ed. Guenther Roth and Claus Wittich, 2 vols. (Berkeley and Los Angeles: Univ. of California Press, 1978).

2. Samuel S. Hill, *The South and the North in American Religion* (Athens: Univ. of Georgia Press, 1980); Bill J. Leonard, "Southern Baptists: In Search of a Century," *Christian Century* (17-24 July 1985): 682-84.

3. Rufus B. Spain, *At Ease in Zion: Social History of Southern Baptists, 1865-1900* (Nashville, Tenn.: Vanderbilt Univ. Press, 1961).

4. See also Glenn E. Hinson, "Neo-Fundamentalism: An Interpretation and Critique," *Baptist History and Heritage* 16, no. 2: 33-49; Leonard, "The Origin and Character of Fundamentalism," *Review and Expositor* 79 (1982): 5-17; George M. Marsden, *Fundamentalism and American Culture: The Shaping of Twentieth-Century Evangelism: 1870-1925* (Oxford: Oxford Univ. Press, 1980); and Martin Marty, "Fundamentalism as a Social Phenomenon," *Review and Expositor* 79 (Winter): 19-30.

5. Weber, *Economy and Society.*

6. See Robert A. Baker, *The Southern Baptist Convention and Its People, 1607-1972* (Nashville, Tenn.: Broadman, 1974).

7. See also Baker, *Southern Baptist Convention;* James L. Sullivan, *Baptist Polity as I See It* (Nashville, Tenn.: Broadman, 1983); and Nancy Tatom Ammerman, *Baptist Battles: Social Change and Religious Conflict in the Southern Baptist Convention* (New Brunswick, N.J.: Rutgers Univ. Press, 1990), esp. chap. 2.

8. Also in 1947, the convention adopted a Charter of Principles on Race Relations.

9. See John C. McKinney and Edgar T. Thompson, eds., *The South in Continuity and Change* (Durham, N.C.: Duke Univ. Press, 1965), especially Richard L. Simpson and David Ray Norsworthy, "The Changing Occupational Structure of the South," 198-224.

10. See Charles Hirschman and Kim Blankenship, "The North-South Earnings Gap: Changes During the 1960s and 1970s," *American Journal of Sociology* 84 (1981): 388-403.

11. Monro S. Edmonson and David Ray Norsworthy, "Industry and Race in the Southern United States," in *Industrialization and Race Relations,* ed. Guy Hunter (London: Oxford Univ. Press, 1965).

12. Joseph Fichter and George L. Maddox, "Religion in the South, Old and New," in *The South in Continuity and Change,* ed. John C. McKinney and Edgar T. Thompson (Durham, N.C.: Duke Univ. Press, 1965), 360.

13. Weber, *The Sociology of Religion,* trans. E. Fischoff (Boston: Beacon, 1964).

14. Daniel Bell, "The Return of the Sacred?" *British Journal of Sociology* 28 (1977): 419-49.

15. See Walter B. Shurden, "The 1980-1981 Carver-Barnes Lectures," delivered at Southeastern Baptist Theological Seminary, Wake Forest, N.C., 4-5 Nov. 1980. Manuscript circulated by Office of Communications, Southeastern Baptist Theological Seminary.

16. C. R. Daley, former editor of the *Western Recorder,* in 1984 told a class at Southern Baptist Theological Seminary that there have been behind-the-scenes politics by the establishment for a long time. His lecture was taped by a friend of the inerrantist party; extensive excerpts appeared in the *Southern Baptist Advocate* 6, no. 2: 1 ff.
Richard Jackson, losing candidate for the presidency of the SBC in 1988, had said earlier in the year that there had developed before 1979 an institutional arrogance among leaders of the denomination. See Toby Druin, "'Ask God for Sensitive Spirit', Says Jackson," *Baptist Standard* 100 (25 May 1988): 13.

17. Alan Neely, "Before SBC, Alliance director asked, 'What are our goals?'" *SBC Today* 6, no. 4 (July 1988): 22.

18. Paul M. Harrison, *Authority and Power in the Free Church Tradition* (Princeton, N.J.: Princeton Univ. Press, 1959) documented the similar dilemma among the Northern Baptists.

19. Secular influence upon accreditation of Southern Baptist educational institutions was under attack in 1989. In January the editor of the *Southern Baptist Advocate,* voice of the inerrancy movement, proposed that because the Association of Theological Schools and the Southern Association of Colleges and Schools had recently made an accreditation report critical of Southeastern Baptist Seminary, the convention authorize the president to appoint a committee to study whether the SBC should continue to affiliate with any outside accrediting agency for Southern Baptist seminaries, and to examine the feasibility of Southern Baptists' establishing their own accrediting agency with its own standards of accreditation.

20. The article, "Southeastern Seminary Students Host Conservative Sympathizers," was a Baptist Press release by Dan Martin in *The Southern Baptist Advocate* 5, no. 3 (Apr. 1984): 6 ff.

21. "Ziglar Explains Comments," Editorial, *The Southern Baptist Advocate* 5, no. 8: 4. The editor at the time was Russell Kaemmerling.

22. Russell Kaemmerling, "In Conclusion," *The Southern Baptist Advocate* 6, no. 1: 23.

23. J. Gerald Harris, "Centralization, Exclusivism, and Liberal Trends Generate Concerns by Baptist Pastor," *The Southern Baptist Advocate* 6, no. 3: 6-7.

24. Kaemmerling, "In Conclusion," 39.

25. "Quotable," *Southern Baptist Advocate* 7, no. 3: 1. The *Advocate* is quoting Hinson's statements in the 7-14 June 1978 issue of *The Christian Century*. Hinson, a professor at the Southern Baptist Theological Seminary, is no friend of the inerrantists, but his words are here being used to support their cause.

26. David Simpson, Editorial, *Southern Baptist Advocate* 7, no. 3: 4.

27. R. Elton Johnson, Jr. (a pastor from South Carolina), letter to the editor, *Southern Baptist Advocate* 7, no. 3: 6.

28. Robert M. Tenery (the new editor), "The Greatest Hazard to Peace," *Southern Baptist Advocate* 7, no. 4: 10-12.

29. Tenery, Editorial, *Southern Baptist Advocate* 7, no. 6: 6.

30. "Tips for the San Antonio Convention," *Southern Baptist Advocate* 8, no. 5: 1.

31. Tenery, "Have We Learned Anything?," *Southern Baptist Advocate* 8, no. 7: 25-26.

32. Tenery, "Remembering the Little Red Hen," *Southern Baptist Advocate* 9, no. 1: 3.

33. See Weber, *Economy and Society,* vol. 1, chap. 3.

34. "Real Evangelism Sponsors First Annual Bible Conference," *Southern Baptist Advocate* 6, no. 1: 3.

35. "Dilday Misleads Georgia Baptists," *Southern Baptist Advocate* 6, no. 3: 1 ff.

36. Tenery, "Unrest Spawned Conservative Resurgences," *Southern Baptist Advocate* 7, no. 1: 10-12.

37. Tenery, "To Our New Trustees," *Southern Baptist Advocate* 7, no. 3: 9.

38. "The Greatest Hazard to Peace," *Southern Baptist Advocate* 7, no. 4: 10-12.

39. "Baptist Joint Committee on Public Affairs Hearing," *Southern Baptist Advocate* 7, no. 4: 3 ff.

40. "Bennett Defies Public Affairs Committee," *Southern Baptist Advocate* 7, no. 7: 2.

41. "Who Owns the Institution?" *Southern Baptist Advocate* 7, no. 7: 7 ff.

42. "Dr. Larry Lewis Discusses the Peace Committee Report," *Southern Baptist Advocate* 8, no. 1: 4.

43. "Conservatives Have Options, Too," *Southern Baptist Advocate* 9, no. 1: 4.

44. See *SBC Today* 8, nos. 5 and 6 (Aug.-Sept. 1990) for accounts of these events.

45. Weber, *Economy and Society,* 241.

46. Ibid., 1010 ff.

47. Ken Camp, "Criswell Sets Limits On Shared Ministry," *Baptist Press,* 21 Feb. 1986.

48. Pat Cole, "Professor Sees More Authority by Clergy," *Baptist Press,* 3 June 1988. This article reports extensively on remarks made by Bill J. Leonard, professor of church history at Southern Baptist Theological Seminary in Louisville, Kentucky.

49. Jack U. Harwell, interview with author, 5 May 1989.

50. Michael Tutterow, "Vines Win Widens Rift," *SBC Today* 6, no. 4 (July 1988): 1-3.

51. See issues of *SBC Today* published in the latter half of 1988, especially vol. 6, no. 4, p. 1 ff.

52. James L. Holley, writing in *Southern Baptist Advocate* 9 (Mar. 1989): 14-17, says that "the drive in Southern Baptist life is for all Christians to be free spirits, accountable only to themselves and to God. . . ." Timothy George wrote in "The Reformation Roots of the Baptist Tradition" (*Review and Expositor* 86 [1989]: 9-22) that "for Luther the priesthood of all believers did not mean that every Christian is his or her own priest, . . . (but that) every Christian is someone else's priest, and we are priests to each other." Interestingly, the draftees of the resolution, perhaps inadvertently, make a concession to the modern reinterpretation of the doctrine's meaning when they titled it, not "Priesthood of All Believers" but the "Priesthood of the Believer."

53. Neely, "Before SBC, Alliance Directors Asked, 'What Are Our Goals?'" *SBC Today* 6, no. 4 (July 1988): 22. Three years later the SBA would drop the reference to the SBC in its statement of purpose.

54. Personal observations by the writer.

55. Weber, *Economy and Society,* 85-86.

56. Jurgen Habermas, *The Theory of Communicative Action,* vol. 1, *Reason and the Rationalization of Society,* trans. Thomas McCarthy (Boston: Beacon, 1984) and *The Theory of Communicative Action,* vol. 2, *Lifeworld and System: A Critique of Functionalist Reason,* trans. Thomas McCarthy (Boston: Beacon, 1987).

57. Reported in Jack Harwell, "Moore Leads Centrists," *SBC Today* 7, no. 2 (May 1989): 1.

58. From an ad in *SBC Today* 7, no. 2: 27.

59. See Jack U. Harwell, "Moderate Atlanta Meeting to Frame Alternate Funding," *SBC Today* 8, no. 5: 1, and "Moderates Create New Funding Mechanism for SBC Fellowship; Set Spring Convocation," *SBC Today* 8, no. 6: 1.

CHAPTER 6
MYTHS: STORIES OF THIS WORLD AND THE WORLD TO COME
Helen Lee Turner

After fundamentalist Adrian Rogers won the presidential election at the 1987 Southern Baptist Convention in St. Louis with nearly 60 percent of the vote, Robert Tenery, editor of the *Southern Baptist Advocate,* described the victory in decidedly daring and triumphal terms. He said that this "was the most significant day in American Christianity, because for the first time in history a major denomination was turned back to its conservative roots." He went on to say that these events were even "more significant than the Protestant Reformation." This victory, he said, "is a second Reformation that no one ever believed could happen, but it has happened."[1] For many these are incredibly bold statements, but to this man and many other conservative Southern Baptists, what has occurred in the convention has a powerful supernatural quality. It is, in effect, a proleptic experience of the kingdom of God, a present, albeit partial, fulfillment of a millennialist vision.

There is, indeed, no question that the coalition that has over the past decade risen to power in the Southern Baptist Convention has been driven by visions of grandeur and by a tremendous sense of urgency. This coalition has dramatically changed not only the denominational power structures but also the very nature of the SBC, especially through the promulgation of new attitudes toward pastoral authority. For most fundamentalists, the sense of urgency, expectation, and, now, victory have apparently overridden the pain of intense conflict. Surprisingly, despite serious divisions within the denomination wrought by this process, many nonfundamentalist Southern Baptists seem absolutely unconscious of the depth of the changes in their denomination, seeing them, if at all, as a return to their roots.

In this chapter I will argue that all this was accomplished through the use and reinterpretation of traditional Christian mythologies, especially eschatological myths. Indeed, this is probably the only way that such sweeping change could have been so readily achieved and then accepted as if it were Southern Baptist tradition. We will look first at what I consider to be the origin of the fundamentalist movement's sense of urgency—the millennialist mythology that gained new prominence in Southern Baptist life during the stressful decades of the fifties, sixties, and seventies. We will then consider how this millennial fervor helped give birth to new, exclusivistic forms of community that in turn sought self-identity through renewed emphasis on myths of origin, or *cosmogonies*. Through the new identity found there, fundamentalists were able to convince themselves and others that their efforts at reform were a return to earlier days—even though in significant ways that was not the case. Such reformulations of perceptions, in every way characteristic of movements theorists call *millennialist*, [2] inspired the remaking of the SBC and, undoubtedly, have had impact on the value structure of the larger society as well. Ironic as it may seem, out of apocalyptic expectation, new ways of understanding the world have been born.

Part 1
Social Stress and Apocalyptic Fervor

Anthropologists and sociologists have contended for some time that an anticipation of the destruction of the present world (millennial expectation) and movements focusing on this expectation often arise in cultures experiencing the severe disruption in traditional social, cultural, and value structures called *mazeway breakdown*. Threats to the moral structure are particularly constitutive here.[3] Psychologists also have observed that severe challenges to an individual's self-esteem, a kind of personal mazeway breakdown, frequently result in a preoccupation with death and a sense that the world is meaningless, or even in an incapacity to function in everyday life.[4] Thus social scientists have demonstrated what common sense might tell us. Visions of doom may well be a sign of the dysfunctional state of a society or individual.

There can be little argument that the period between World War I and the 1970s was a time of stress-producing change in the South and, consequently, in the Southern Baptist Convention. Compounded by the nationwide turmoil of the 1960s, social stress in Dixie became so intense by the 1970s that traditional mazeways collapsed. Certainly, from the present vantage point, not all of these changes were negative; many were quite positive. But even so, for white evangelicals they marked not only the death of many long-held southern values centered on rural family life but also the breakdown of a tenaciously held regional and racial identity. These changes wrought the kind of moral crisis on which millennialist movements thrive.

Corresponding changes in the SBC brought a similar sense of loss to many. The expansion of the denomination into "frontier territories," the centralizing of the bureaucracy and fund raising, liberal and ecumenical interests on the part of educators, and the decline of rural congregations dramatically changed the character of the convention. The latter development, a particularly painful process for many, seemed to be highlighted by the denominational emphasis on diversified programs for large urban churches. Moreover, the apparent endorsement by denominational leaders of "liberal" attitudes toward blacks, women, prayer in school, abortion, and so forth compounded the feeling on the part of many that the SBC had deserted them. No wonder people were convinced by the fundamentalist claim, made early in their campaign for denominational power, that the SBC was not what it used to be. The denomination had changed in very significant ways.[5]

Despite certain affinities with fundamentalism, however, most southern evangelicals, including Southern Baptists, were not fundamentalists during the first half of this century. As historian Samuel Hill asserts, popular southern religion in general has been traditionally "more world-affirming, inclusive, and oriented toward a heartfelt Christianity than the rational system of fundamentalism."[6] Prior to the seventies and eighties, for example, there is little question that most Southern Baptists were a staunchly noncreedal people who placed an emphasis on the priesthood of the believer. Congregational bonds were based primarily on shared moral values, spiritual experiences, and kinship ties, not doctrine.[7] Likewise, although pastors were generally respected, few would have been thought of as congregational "rulers." Language such as that would not emerge until the 1980s.[8] Mazeway collapse in the post-World War II South would instigate striking change indeed.

The Formation of Millennialist Mythology
Millennialist movements resulting from mazeway breakdown draw their life

from visionary mythology that often takes the apocalyptic form. The social situation does not in and of itself give birth to this mythology, however. Rather, it is derived from a reformulation of, or a renewed emphasis on, old myths. In a Christian context, these myths revolve around the expectation of the Second Coming of Christ, a hope that was central to the faith of the primitive church and, consequently, found expression in the earliest Christian creeds. In the midst of the mounting post-World War II social crisis, Southern Baptists began to give new emphasis to these ancient formulas. But they also drew heavily upon a newer, more elaborate interpretation of old beliefs that had come to America from England in the nineteenth century. This attractive, novel mythology, termed *dispensational premillennialism,* is based on the notion that in the creation God foreordained several distinct ages of time, during each of which he would relate differently to the world. Although in some sense these dispensations can be regarded as steps in a developmental scheme, God alone is believed to be in absolute control of the process. Because dispensationalism adamantly contends that the predestined return of Christ will come during a time of moral breakdown, this mythology is particularly well suited as the focus of a millennialist movement.

J. Frank Norris, a renowned fundamentalist of the first half of this century, played a significant role in spreading this novel but powerful eschatological myth in the SBC, even though his church's ties with the denomination were severed in 1924. During the 1920s, in his publication the *Searchlight,* Norris declared his conviction that signs of the end indicated the imminent arrival of the "Beast of Prophecy," and by 1926 he was using premillennialism as a test of orthodoxy. In 1931 Norris's interest in eschatology led to the formation of the Southwest Premillennial Conference. Even from outside the denomination's institutional structure, this organization, with *Searchlight,* fueled rising eschatological interest in the SBC.[9]

Even more influential, however, was the version of the Bible Norris encouraged people to use, the Scofield Reference Bible. This Bible supplies its readers with a key to the heavenly mysteries through its notations, nearly all of which are controlled by dispensational premillennialism. Though the actual usage or influence of this version is difficult to document, by midcentury it seemed to many observers that nearly all Southern Baptist pastors had one. According to a survey of Southern Baptist associational ministers (the Baptist equivalent of a Methodist district superintendent) that I conducted in November of 1987, the Scofield Bible has been more influential in the development of the eschatological beliefs of Southern Baptist ministers than anything, including seminary education. The question on the survey asked, "What has had the widest influence on the eschatology of the ministers in your area, besides the biblical text itself?" Although the figures are a bit inflated, because some of the ministers checked more than one answer, 41 percent of the 461 associational ministers who responded to the survey said that the Scofield Reference Bible had the greatest influence, whereas only 33.3 percent of those surveyed cited seminary education as the greatest influence. Other answers were significantly less popular.[10] If pastors were reading the Scofield Bible in such numbers, it is likely that many lay people were as well. By midcentury it was very clear that the mysteries of God's plan for the universe, as revealed in the Scofield Bible, held a profound attraction for many.

Another way in which this mythological system made its way into the SBC during the 1950s and 1960s was in the preaching of Billy Graham, who among Southern Baptists is without question the most respected of the popular evangelists.[11] During the fifties, when Graham was establishing himself as a model preacher, he regularly spoke of the Second Coming. In sermon after sermon, apocalyptic rhetoric was among the things that caught the ears of listeners.[12] For that reason alone, Southern Baptist pastors surely copied this as they did other elements of his preaching. Thus premillennial preaching, which had for some time been a mainstay of many Southern Baptist evangelists, began to enter the denominational mainstream.

As Graham was becoming famous, a network of premillennialist fellowships, built on the model of the group started by Norris, developed among Southern Baptists. According to Southern Baptist historian Robert A. Baker, by 1953 such organizations existed in every state in the SBC.[13] Baker's claim, though probably accurate, is difficult to document, because such groups are outside the denominational establishment and do not send reports to "headquarters." In my survey of associational ministers, however, information about the existence of premillennialist fellowships was requested. Nearly 10 percent of the ministers said they had known of such groups in the past. Although this percentage may seem rather low, when the limited information from those who had known of such groups was compiled, almost all of the states in the traditional SBC territory were mentioned. Because associational ministers clearly fall within the established SBC institutional structures, the fact that even a small percentage of their number had known of such nonestablishment organizations is rather compelling. Even from the fringes of the SBC, these fellowships undoubtedly served to further promulgate and legitimize dispensationalism among Southern Baptists.

It also appears that these premillennialist fellowships served as vehicles for the expression of feelings that would become more and more prevalent in the SBC as traditional southern value structures crumbled. Although very few records of such groups have been preserved, several copies of 1949 and 1950 issues of the occasional newspaper published by the Eastern Oklahoma Premillennialist Fellowship, the *Baptist Beacon,* are extant.[14] In those issues one can see expressions of the membership's discontent, sense of stress, and feelings of exclusion as society and the denominational structure changed around them. It was clear that many of the pastors associated with this publication believed that they had "failed to receive proper recognition" within the new SBC, and particularly evident was the tension between rural and urban congregations. As a consequence members apparently regarded themselves as being at odds with their state's denominational establishment, which they contended was housed in a "whitened sepulcher" built with money that should have been spent on rural missions.[15] The later fundamentalists in the SBC movement would play on and instigate similar feelings.

The hope of the Eastern Oklahoma Premillennialist Fellowship was centered quite clearly on the Second Coming, and the *Beacon* proclaimed on its masthead that it was "an Independent Pre-millennial Publication." In 1950 the editor of the *Beacon* doubted that the world has "ever known stark fear as it knows today." "Yes," he said, "fright is all about us," and the only answer is Jesus. Because of this "crisis," the editor urged churches to enter into simultaneous evangelistic crusades, because "it may be our last revival."[16] Although the writers of this publication were clearly biblical literalists and vigorously declared the evils of modernism, proclamation of their faith in the Second Coming was their primary reason for existence. The proclamation of the apocalypse provided not only an expression of their feelings about the state of the world but also hope that ultimately God is in control of the world and present in believers' lives. One writer for the *Beacon* declared that the fellowship's programs, "built around the glorious doctrine of the triumphant return of our Lord," were "spiritual banquets." Describing his own experience at fellowship meetings, he went on to say that the speakers "took us to the mountain peak and . . . lifted us clear off the mountain and walked around with us in the stratosphere. Yes, we were mighty close to heaven." [17] Although hearers of this message were also ready adherents to the message of biblical literalism, these millennialist visions of release from the problems of everyday life were more crucial.

Most of the premillennialist fellowships disappeared by the 1960s. For a number of reasons, the time was not right for a large-scale millennialist movement to develop within the SBC. Among other things, many churches were faced with immediate problems in their own neighborhoods. Although integration eventually contributed to the breakdown of traditional southern mazeways, for a time at least, resistance to integration offered the chance to make specific attempts to attack a definable problem. Such efforts are what millennialist theorist Michael Barkun terms *damage control mechanisms*.[18] These mechanisms did not stave off mazeway breakdown for very long— things were changing too rapidly in the South—but for a time energy was diverted from millennial expectation.

Another, and perhaps more significant reason, that premillennialist expectation did not give birth to a widespread movement during the fifties or sixties was the lack of a prophet to unite the Southern Baptists who had these concerns. As millennialist scholar Kenelm Burridge says, even when the social stage is set, "the curtain may go up to reveal a mêlée of actors looking for the proper parts. For the actions to become coherent a prophet is necessary."[19] By the early sixties, such a prophet was emerging. Dr. W. A. Criswell, dynamic pastor of the prestigious First Baptist Church of Dallas, would be the person to give life to a movement formed out of the eschatological interests provoked by societal stress.

Prophetic Voices Summon a New Community

Burridge says that a prophet in a millennialist context "focuses attention on the meaning of the millennium and brings order to inchoate activities."[20] W. A. Criswell fits this description well. Indeed, Criswell contends that his most important contribution to theology has been the exposition and advocacy of premillennialist doctrine.[21] And without question his messages on the subject

were viewed by many as groundbreaking and inspired—perhaps even prophetic in content. Criswell occasionally fed this notion by emphasizing the
neglect of such subjects by others, asserting that "in the many years that I
attended school . . . I never studied the Revelation. I never had a teacher
who took time to mention it." This he understands to have been a tragic
oversight of the learned establishment, because "to meditate upon that appearance and to look and watch and wait for the glorious triumph, the second coming of our Lord, is blessed above all things in the earth."[22] Increasingly in the 1960s, Criswell got attention with his talk about the end of time.

Beginning in 1961, during regular Sunday services at First Baptist of Dallas, Criswell spent three years preaching through the book of Revelation. (It
had taken him only fourteen years to cover the first sixty-five books of the
Bible.) With the publication of these sermons and others on Daniel,[23] Criswell
established himself as a revealer of God's promises, a prophet, to a people
who were experiencing the stress of social change, even as they enjoyed the
blessings of prosperity. Though today we might think of him first as a biblical
literalist, Criswell provided early formative charismatic leadership to the contemporary fundamentalist movement by presenting troubled people with a
vision that not only expressed their loss in the face of destroyed value systems but also gave them hope that God was in control of the future. Though
a number of things worked together to spur Criswell's rise to prominence in
the SBC, his notoriety as one of the leading denominational expositors of
biblical apocalyptic writings certainly was an important, indeed crucial, factor. Criswell's expertise on eschatology was still of great interest a decade
after his sermons on Revelation were first published. Taped copies of his
sermon, "Why I Am a Premillennialist" were widely distributed in the early
seventies by fundamentalists anxious to change the direction of their denomination.[24]

In the mid-1960s Criswell began to contend that conditions in the SBC
were contributing to the declining state of the world. In 1966 he declared that
"our church and denomination is [*sic*] beginning to die." Soon others, including 1967 convention preacher Landrum Leavell, echoed the warning.[25] As predictions of apocalyptic doom were projected in specific ways onto the SBC,
an important transformation of the eschatological vision began. Eventually
there would be the realization that the convention might be rescued even if

the larger society could not be. Criswell and a growing coalition of other "prophets" began to proclaim new interpretations of the crisis to a denomination ready to hear words of hope.

It was in this kind of atmosphere in 1968 that Criswell was elected president of the SBC, on the first ballot, over a well-known moderate (although that term was not yet in use). To his followers it seemed that his victory was part of God's great plan, and Criswell himself contended that his election was not entirely attributable to a political trend in the convention, because until six days before the Houston meeting he had requested that his name not be presented for nomination.[26] Apparently even Criswell believed that God had intervened in history, just as he was expected to do at the *parousia* (Second Coming). A decade later leaders of the emerging fundamentalist movement would claim similar divine leading,[27] thus associating themselves with the unfolding plan of God that was at the heart of dispensational eschatology.

Hal Lindsey's best-selling *Late Great Planet Earth* was published in 1970, both undergirding and reflecting the interest in the dispensationalist thinking that was already growing in the SBC. As indicated in my 1986-87 survey of a random sample of Southern Baptist clergy, only about 15 percent of Southern Baptist ministers were unfamiliar with Lindsey's work. More important, a considerable number said that their impressions of the book were largely favorable (28 percent) or very favorable (13.5 percent). Only 25 percent claimed to dislike the book. And, as one might guess, those who most liked the book were almost always supportive of the fundamentalist agenda in the SBC.

By the seventies talk of the Second Coming was obviously in the air and was no longer limited to the fringes of SBC life. Given this situation one might have expected premillennialist fellowships to find new life in the SBC. But this was not the case, probably because enthusiastic interest in the Second Coming was now quite widespread. One fellowship that did spring up in Oklahoma during the period gives us an indication of what was happening. Beginning in 1970 the Oklahoma Baptist Premillennial Fellowship, like its predecessors, sponsored conferences on the Second Coming. Among the speakers was Dr. Robert G. Lee of Bellevue Church in Memphis, who was soon to become a prominent elder statesman for the political movement gaining power in the SBC. The Oklahoma Baptist Premillennialist Fellowship enjoyed enthusiastic regional support for a while, but in the late seventies, the group disbanded. The death of one of the group's leaders was certainly a factor, but as Anson Justice, an officer of the organization, said, "The erupting of the inerrancy controversy . . . caught the attention of this constituency."[28] A new channel for expressing societal stress was developing.

In January of 1969, similarly disgruntled conservatives from North Carolina and Virginia had begun publication of a newsletter they entitled the *Sword and the Trowel,* the name used by British premillennialist Charles Spurgeon for his earlier publication. Contributor Clark H. Pinnock boldly declared that the SBC was "facing the greatest crisis in all her history."[29] Almost as if responding to the desire for change expressed in Pinnock's statement, that same year the eloquent R. G. Lee ended the Pastors' Conference (the SBC's annual preconvention festival of preaching) with a sermon entitled "The Second Coming of Christ." That message, on a topic for which he was already well known, so stirred the crowd that Reverend Lee became a popular fixture at the yearly meeting of that body over the next decade, until his death. Most of his sermons had strong apocalyptic undertones, if they were not overtly concerned with the issue, and no one seemed to tire of them. Indeed, the crowds grew. The very next year Lee's Pastors' Conference sermon was entitled "Hope—Evidence of the Unseen."[30]

During the next decade, a new generation of preachers emerged, and many gained attention for their vivid portrayals of doom and destruction contrasted with visions of final divine triumph. Their apocalyptic rhetoric not only gave voice to the painful loss of traditional mazeways but also provided a rallying point for new hope. People became convinced that even without the arrival of the Apocalypse, the SBC could change radically. New bonds, or *communitas,*[31] that stood outside of traditional denominational alliances were thus formed. A common vision of apocalyptic destruction that would be transformed into victory brought people together who might otherwise have had little basis for relationship. Under the sway of the millennial vision, traditional social distinctions faded into meaninglessness, thus allowing for new definitions of insiders and outsiders and also for new leadership. "Prophetic preachers" they were called, and many listeners believed they truly had the blessing of God.

Dr. Lee's proclamations of God's supernatural plan for the future gave him and the others an aura of authority. As fundamentalists gained the platform at the Pastors' Conference, they used their position to urge other preachers to claim this prophetic authority as well. In 1970 one segment of the program was entitled "The Minister: Christ's Man for the 70's." The next year the theme of the entire conference was "God's Preacher as Prophet." That year Criswell, still clearly the primary leader of the new movement, drew the lines between the true faithful and the "infidels" in prophetic terms. On one side were the "modern intellectuals" who say "the Bible is like Aesop's fables—full of fairy tales"; on the other side were the prophetic preachers with "a special mandate to preach the Word of God," which is eternal truth.[32] In that same year, Criswell also initiated a yearly Dallas pastors' workshop known as the School of the Prophets.

At the SBC Pastors' Conference in 1972, which was billed as a "Banquet of Preaching," speakers concentrated on "the centrality of the Bible, the approach of the Second Coming, the reliance on the Holy Spirit, and the need to stay on the main road that has made Southern Baptists the nation's largest Protestant denomination." In 1973 Jaroy Weber, who was elected president of the conference, summed up the sentiments of most of the speakers when he said, "We as pastors must . . . preach with awesome urgency because of the sinfulness of man and because of the second coming of Jesus Christ. Preach it and preach it with urgency."[33] Words like those prepared the way for the organization that year of the Baptist Faith and Message Fellowship.

The dominance of millennially inspired theological conservatives continued in 1974. Perhaps seeking to evoke something of the drama of the Second Coming, the main program was billed as a "Sunday night spectacular." Apocalyptic rhetoric prevailed and much of Criswell's keynote sermon dealt with the "blessed hope," which included an emphasis on the "marvelous rapture." The conference closed with a moving message by Cliff Barrows, entitled "The King is Coming." Again in 1975 Criswell preached, and again much of his message dealt with the prophetic hope. Fulfilled prophecies, he said, were for believers "signs of the presence of the True God." The next year's meeting was held in the midst of the national bicentennial. Press releases described the mood at the Pastors' Conference as "grim" as speaker after speaker, including W. A. Criswell, predicted a dire future for America unless it became a more Christian nation.[34] It was as though something were about to happen—the Apocalypse or some other divine intervention.

The now-regular recitations of the apocalyptic vision had become a kind of ritual encounter with the end of time. In much the same manner as an individual encounters the prospects of his or her own death, such ritual confrontations with the death of life as we know it encourage a people to examine their values and, as a consequence, to draw strict definitions of right and wrong (*binary contraries*).[35] More important, such encounters with the end time involve entering into the "strong or sacred time" of myth and are thus empowering.[36] The dispensationalist mythology presents one with fantastic promises, and those possibilities create new, urgent priorities as well as new loyalties. In this way the apocalyptic myth became the basis for both a new political agenda in the SBC and for a coalition to support it.

In 1977 a book by rising fundamentalist leader Jerry Vines, *"I Shall Return"—Jesus,* provoked apocalyptic conversation. But more important that year was the absence of R. G. Lee. He had had a heart attack, and Adrian Rogers, now the pastor of Lee's church in Memphis, took his place on the Pastors' Conference program. Rogers's sermon was on the evils of humanism, but his story about his visit with Lee captured the symbolic importance of the moment. Lee had gripped his hand and said, "Pastor, we can do it; . . . we can shake the world if we let God get hold of us one more time."[37] Captured in that statement from the well-known preacher was the transformation of the apocalyptic hope into a new millennialist vision for the SBC. Perhaps disaster, both ultimate disaster and the decline seen in other mainline denominations, could be averted if Southern Baptists followed the leading of God's prophets.

Part 2
Transformation of the Millennialist Vision

Historian of Religion Mircea Eliade says that the idea of the destruction of the world is not really pessimistic, for "even in eschatologies, the essential thing is not the fact of the End, but the certainty of a new beginning."[38] Even so, some scholars have suggested that millennialist movements always fail because they do not achieve the millennium. In one sense that is certainly true, but in a social sense that is not always the case, for the eschaton is not the real goal. Adherents may hope for the heavenly vision, but because such movements thrive in the context of social stress, one can argue that what millennialist movements really pursue is social reform. The central desire is the restoration of cultural values, so that once again the moral order might be trusted. Consequently millennialist visions often change over time, taking on a more worldly cast. Anthropologist Peter Worsley argues that all such movements experience an inevitable stage of "goal displacement."[39]

At first the *parousia* had been the focus of hope for those who were attracted by the messages of Criswell, Lee, and others. At that time the vision of the earth's destruction expressed their feelings about the moral state of society, and the new *communitas* composed of faithful believers in the apocalyptic vision was itself the primary solace from the world's fallen mazeways. But in time the faithful, quite unconsciously, experienced a transformation of their vision. Empowered by their ritual entrance into the "strong time" of millennialist mythology, Southern Baptist fundamentalists began to turn away from the prophecy's proclamations of doom and focused more on the prophecy's promise of God's glorious triumph. A kind of excitement about new possibilities was growing.

The Vision and Partisan Politics

By 1978 it was clear that the prophetic preachers had a new goal—control of the SBC. The urgent need to proclaim the coming of the end was transferred to this new cause, and thus the millennialist movement became political. Despite their growing power, however, fundamentalists did not choose to make an attempt for the SBC presidency in 1978, apparently because of the convention tradition of reelecting the incumbent. While they waited, the sense of apocalyptic urgency remained high as John Bisagno, pastor of the First Baptist Church of Houston, warned the crowd of twenty thousand at the Pastors' Conference that the time for evangelistic efforts was short because "everything points toward the next few years as the end of time."[40] The Apocalypse would not come as soon as Bisagno expected, but the end of the old SBC was clearly at hand.

Interestingly, as the political power of the new movement increased, it became clear that the denominational establishment had taken note of the widespread fascination with apocalyptic rhetoric. The attempts of the old guard to defuse the mythology speak further of the power of these images.

In 1972, for example, Broadman Press not only added to its commentary series a volume on Revelation by seminary professor Morris Ashcraft but also published *Highlights of the Book of Revelation* by George R. Beasley-Murray. Both volumes took a decidedly more academic approach than the works of Criswell or Lindsey. In 1975 the *Review and Expositor,* a journal published by the faculty of Southern Baptist Theological Seminary, devoted an entire issue to "The Revival of Apocalyptic." In that journal writers implored Baptists to pay attention to the theological concerns (not just the predictions) of apocalyptic biblical writings, going so far as to identify specific problems with Hal Lindsey's book.[41] In 1979 the SBC television program "At Home With the Bible" addressed a wider audience, featuring guest speakers who contended that "realistic thought" about the end of time should replace "sensational speculation."[42] It was as though denominational leaders sensed the institutional threat always associated with apocalyptic movements.[43]

Moderates outside the bureaucracy undertook their own efforts at damage control, attempting to redirect the energy generated by the apocalyptic rhetoric. In his presidential address in 1978, Jimmy Allen employed the fundamentalists' own slogans in a sermon entitled "Where There Is a Vision, the People Flourish." The vision for Allen and other moderates became embodied in the campaign known as Bold Mission Thrust, an ambitious plan to share the Christian message with the world by the year 2000. At the momentous 1979 convention in Houston, moderates attempted to make their own use of the now recurrent apocalyptic message of the fundamentalists; the convention theme was "Bold Mission While It Is Yet Day."

But it was too late. The moderate day had been swept away in the fundamentalist vision. Over five opponents, Adrian Rogers was elected president of the SBC on the first ballot. Everything about his election was seen by fundamentalists as part of a divine drama. As late as 6:00 P.M. on Monday before the Tuesday presidential election, he had refused to run for the office. But as Rogers later told reporters, during the night "God came down in tears of joy as I was praying."[44]

Millennialism and Denominational Politics among Clergy
What we have seen thus far demonstrates the history and use of millennialist rhetoric among the leadership of the fundamentalist movement in the SBC.

But is there evidence that all this was of real importance in the casting of votes? My 1986-87 survey of Southern Baptist clergy, undergirded with data from James Guth's 1988 survey, provides a hint of the broad-based importance of eschatology in Southern Baptist politics. First, both studies demonstrate that those who are fundamentalists are more likely than other ministers to be dissatisfied with the social changes brought about by the advent of modernity. For instance, respondents were asked to indicate (on a five-point, Likert-type scale) their agreement or disagreement with the following statement: "Things were better when there was public prayer in schools." Nearly 20 percent of the ministers indicated strong agreement with the statement, and an additional 36 percent agreed. The correlations between those in agreement with this statement and those who adhered to ideas associated with dispensational premillennialism were strong (see table 6.1).

To further test the relationship between dissatisfaction with the present world and belief in the doctrines of premillennialism, a cluster analysis was used. Three cluster groups were formed using the aforementioned question, with six other questions intended to test attitudes toward changing social values in the South. Three of the additional questions concerned attitudes toward blue laws, alcoholic beverages, and eating in restaurants on Sundays. Other questions used in the cluster analysis asked respondents to indicate whether they believed the world is getting worse, whether it is harder to be a Christian today than in times past, and whether unbelievers are trying to destroy the faith of Christians. There were 220 ministers in the "most dissatisfied" cluster, 246 ministers in the middle cluster, and 228 ministers whose responses reflected the least dissatisfaction with this world. As indicated in the right-hand column of table 6.1, correlations between the level of dissatisfaction and acceptance of the doctrines of premillennial dispensationalism were quite high.

As might be expected, my survey demonstrates that the more emphasis a minister puts on the doctrines of dispensationalism or premillennialism, the more likely he is to adhere to the doctrines most often associated with fundamentalism and with the fundamentalist agenda as it is expressed in the SBC. In particular, nearly 90 percent of the dispensationalists supported fundamentalist Adrian Rogers in the 1986 SBC election. Moreover, those who voted for Rogers generally placed a strong emphasis on the prophecies of Revelation,

Table 6.1
Correlations* between Beliefs about Prophecy and Beliefs about Modernity

Beliefs about Prophecy	Beliefs about Modernity	
	Things were better when there was public prayer in school	Dissatisfaction with Modernity (Cluster Analysis)
Book of Revelation emphasizes prophecy	.59	.47
Importance of the Rapture Doctrine	.60	.54
Dispensationalist Self-identification	.56	.51
Importance of Second Coming Doctrine to faith	.47	.42
Frequency of sermon references to eschaton	.45	.42
Israel's statehood a fulfillment of prophecy	.54	.47
Pre-Tribulation rapture	.51	.48

*All coefficients shown are gammas.

believed in the Rapture, considered the doctrine of the Second Coming to be important, believed the church will escape the Tribulation, and thought that the statehood of Israel is a fulfillment of prophecy. Most who voted for Rogers also said they make regular references to the second coming in preaching and were more likely than their colleagues to find the doctrine of the second Coming more important in their lives now than in the past.

By 1986 there were strong correlations among millennial views, theological self-identification (especially with *fundamentalist* versus *moderate*), and SBC politics. Millennialists and fundamentalists supported Adrian Rogers's candidacy, whereas nonmillennialists and moderates did not. Whether this political choice was the result of millennial views or of theological party preference is impossible to tell when the two ideologies are as closely tied as they were at the polar extremes of the convention. The relative importance of dispensational views can be seen most easily among those in the middle who resisted theological party labels by calling themselves *conservative* (about 69 percent of all SBC clergy). Among this group there are wide differences in adherence to dispensationalism, with roughly equal numbers on each side of that theological question. As table 6.2 suggests, among these nonpolitical conservatives, dispensational views had a marked impact on presidential choices. From 1985 to 1988, conservative ministers who indicated agreement with the doctrine of dispensationalism nearly always preferred the fundamentalist candidate, whereas the nondispensationalist conservative was far more likely to have supported the losing candidate.

Thus it would seem that dispensationalism is constitutive in the formation of denominational political perspectives. Even among those who had not claimed a party label, views on dispensationalism were closely linked to support for fundamentalist presidential candidates. Although one might argue about which is the primary doctrine—biblical inerrancy or dispensationalism—the tendency of millennialists to divide religion into absolute binary contraries of truth and untruth makes such an absolute doctrine about Scripture (and about those whose interpretations of Scripture differ) very likely. Millennialists are also likely to turn such ideas into a revolutionary political agenda.

Giving Specific Content to the SBC's Vision

Millennialist movements are not mere reactions to social stress; they are a social process through which new mazeways replace dysfunctional ones. Consequently the political success of 1979 could not have been maintained without the creation of a clear vision of what a reformed SBC would be like. Ultimately, as is the case with all millennialist movements, the fundamentalists' vision of the new convention would be created from the combination of two powerful forces: first, the retelling of origin stories, and second, the values of the new culture. We will look briefly at each of these forces and the way in which they influenced the fundamentalist dream for the SBC.

Eliade points to the importance of retelling origin stories. He says that the eschatological "rebeginning" is "the counterpart to the absolute beginning, the cosmogony." Eschatologies and cosmogonies are always tied together, and millennialist movements often envision a return to a "mythical

Table 6.2

Percent Conservative Support for Fundamentalist Candidates by
Attitude toward Dispensationalism

| | Support for Dispensationalism | | | | |
Candidate	Strongly Agree %	Agree %	Neutral %	Disagree %	Strongly Disagree %
1985, Charles Stanley gamma = .61	96	89	76	63	39
1986, Adrian Rogers gamma = .63	98	89	79	57	45
1987, Adrian Rogers gamma = .60	98	85	72	56	40
1988, Jerry Vines gamma = .59	92	80	64	47	27
Number of cases	48	114	76	110	51

Source: 1989 survey of SBC clergy by James L. Guth. There were 646 total respondents; 69% identified themselves as conservative and are included in this table (if they also responded to questions about presidential preferences).

golden age." Stories of origin are at the heart of a culture's self-understanding, and to societies in distress, creation myths "reveal that the world, man, and life have supernatural origin and history, and that this history is significant, precious, and exemplary."[45] Such stories ultimately free us from the present and thus bring healing. Hence there is no wonder that they are key to the development of new mazeways, and Southern Baptist fundamentalists followed the typical pattern by placing emphasis on origin stories.

The Scopes trial has permanently associated turn-of-the-century fundamentalism with creationism, and again in the SBC movement, belief that Adam and Eve were real people became a litmus test. In actuality most, if not all, of the issues on the Southern Baptist fundamentalist agenda are tied to cosmogonics. Even the all-important issue of the authority of the Bible is best understood as rooted in a story of origin. God breathed life into Adam; the Bible is

"God-breathed." The traditional role of women and an anti-abortion stance are likewise tied to the cosmogonic myth and God's created order. Fundamentalist attitudes toward America and American society issue from a belief that God had a plan for the United States even before it came into being. Both the *Advocate* and the *Journal* have been consumed with telling stories of sacred origins, and with calling people back to those roots. On virtually every page, in exhortations on virtually any topic, there are reminders that we must return "to the faith of our theological fathers." We must "restore our denomination." We must return to our "grassroots values." We must "get back to the Bible." We must look again to our origins to find out who we are. [46]

Though some would argue that fundamentalists are telling the same versions of these cosmogonies that Baptists have always told, I do not believe that is the case. In the millennial context, the eschatological myth in some sense controls the cosmogonic myth. Here our beliefs about the future actually influence our beliefs about the past. Among contemporary Southern Baptists, the dispensationalist belief that the end time will be brought about by the supernatural, predestined intervention of God has influenced the form of the related cosmogonic mythology and, thus, the reshaping of the Southern Baptist identity. Dispensationalism espouses the notion that God is in absolute control of all. As a result dispensationalism has made belief in a God-breathed Bible and certain related doctrines an absolute necessity. Among other things it has made the role of women a test of faith presumably not influenced by local custom. It has made preachers God's prophets, divinely appointed rulers of a congregation. It has blurred the traditional Baptist distinctions between church and state. And, ironically, because such ideas are derived from cosmogonic myths, many ordinary members have been convinced that this is what Southern Baptists have always believed.

The second crucial force in the fundamentalist vision of the reformed SBC grows out of the values of the contemporary culture. But to find acceptance, these values had to be reclothed in the language of the millennialist hope. As early as the 1950s, the standards of modernity had begun to be applied to local Southern Baptist churches. A good church was a growing church, and an even better church was a large church. Because many Southern Baptist congregations had fewer than three hundred members, a defeated outlook was quite common among small-church pastors. Although the fundamentalist reinterpretation of the millennial vision might have taken a variety of directions, the prevalence of the quantitative standard for success and the example set by the mega-church pastored by their primary prophet W. A. Criswell led to the creation of a vision drawn in these terms. Beginning early in their campaign, but especially after their first major successes, fundamentalists contended that God would dramatically intervene in the lives and churches of the true faithful. As Adrian Rogers said before his first election to the SBC presidency in 1979, every Baptist church with an excellent track record in annual baptisms is "a conservative, Bible-believing church."[47] In a short time fundamentalist mega-churches came to symbolize the heavenly vision, and candidates for state and national offices were chosen from among pastors of these large congregations. Fundamentalist nominees were regularly introduced with "This man is pastor of one of the fastest growing churches in the SBC."

The fundamentalist *Southern Baptist Journal* featured mega-churches and churches with increasing attendance on a "Record Attendance Scoreboard." They also told success stories. An article entitled "Fire in the Pasture," for example, told of the phenomenal growth of the Elliott Baptist Church in rural south Alabama. According to the report, the church, which was surrounded by dirt roads, had only about two hundred members until a new Bible-believing pastor enlisted the services of buses and "prayer warriors," who prayed for as many as eighteen hundred people by name each day. Within a short time, God intervened and Sunday morning worship attendance rose to somewhere between five hundred and 650 people.[48] Faith and the power of God brought victory out of the jaws of death and defeat—a story not unlike the story of the promised Rapture.

Adherence to the fundamentalist agenda thus became the formula for success. And with the establishment of this view as the criterion for acceptance into the new regime, it became in many ways a self-fulfilling prophecy.

Realizing the Millennial Vision

Visions of eschatological triumph have begun to take a very earthly form— not only in successful churches but also in rituals that allow the faithful to step for a moment into the future they envision. The fundamentalist movement in the SBC has not run out of steam, in part because it has continually found ways to allow adherents to taste the promise. At the 1988 convention in San Antonio, for instance, there was a grand victory pageant. Fundamentalists had declared the year before in St. Louis that the battle with liberalism had been won, and in 1988, they celebrated. Before Adrian Rogers came to deliver his presidential address, triumphal music accompanied a grand procession of banners and three gigantic crosses. As one observer put it, it was almost as though the Second Coming had already arrived. This was a ritual enacting the defeat of worldly enemies. And in it, no doubt, supporters of the now-institutionalized fundamentalist movement experienced something of the thrill they might associate with the Rapture. Such events and reports of them have kept the dreams and enthusiastic support of the movement alive.

In this and every way possible, fundamentalists have attempted to allow the average Southern Baptist to participate in their victory. But even with all of the news coverage of conventions, these events in themselves have not been enough. There are, however, other ways of proleptically seeing the heavenly kingdom. Fundamentalist mega-churches, even for people who realistically know that their congregation could never be a mega-church, provide inspiration and direction. Their earth-shaking choirs and charismatic preachers make them "exciting," an adjective often used by such congregations to describe themselves. They are a symbolic combination of the "mythical golden past" and the "meta-historical future." They are havens, preserving in an updated key the traditional values and life-styles that have been threatened by the onslaughts of modern society. Particularly attractive to families with young children, such churches make it possible for the whole family to fill much of their time and find most of their social contacts among people who believe and live much like they do, thus duplicating in a successful, modernized form something of the caring rural community they or their parents might have known in days gone by. These churches provide a community through which one can live in the kingdom (as envisioned by fundamentalists) now; they provide the loci for a realized eschatology.

However, the possibilities do not stop there. A taste of the Rapture also can be had in a "Bible Study Cruise." Led by pastors of the SBC's mega-churches, the apocalyptic conquest is symbolically enacted at sea. Worldly evils are literally pushed aside as "bars, casinos, and slot machines are closed, . . . the ship's entertainers are replaced by Christian entertainers, . . . the . . . ballroom is turned into a worship center. The stage is turned into a pulpit."[49]

But perhaps most meaningful is the music of victory. It is music, after all, that has most often touched Southern Baptists, and the fundamentalist movement in the SBC has successfully used choruses and hymns to bring heaven down to earth. Whether it is Mrs. Joyce Rogers's rendition of a song of apocalyptic expectation sung before her husband's message at the pivotal convention in San Antonio, or the stirring chorus "Victory in Jesus" sung by fundamentalist leaders during the 1990 convention in the New Orleans restaurant where plans for the take-over were born, music is for many the entryway to the kingdom. In triumphal singing there is the assurance of the heavenly vision and the confidence that once again all is right with the world.

Prophecies of doom, which once gave voice to widespread cultural stress in the South and fueled the early stages of the fundamentalist movement in the SBC, have been transformed into songs of victory. The millennialist impulse to define rigid values through a reexamination of cosmogonies has created a new self-understanding for Southern Baptists and, thus, a new SBC.

Notes

1. Robert Tenery in an interview in "God and Politics: Battle For the Bible," with Bill Moyers, produced by Gail Pellett, Public Affairs Television, 1987.

2. The more common term for such movements is *millennarian*. Other terms often used are *chiliastic, messianic, revitalization,* and *crisis cult*. Michael Barkun, in *Disaster and the Millennium* (New Haven, Conn.: Yale Univ. Press, 1974) contends that movements of this sort are looking for a "this-worldly salvation," which begins with the destruction of the existing social order. In a later study, *Crucible of the Millennium: The Burned-Over District of New York in the 1840s* (Syracuse, New York: Syracuse Univ. Press, 1986), Barkun further argues that millennarian movements need not center on the end of the physical world; rather, they may envision a radically new social order without being apocalyptic. The movement in the SBC ultimately evolved into this latter form. For this reason I have chosen to use the term *millennialist* here. It has more positive connotations, and it emphasizes the notion of change rather than ending.

3. Barkun, *Disaster and the Millennium,* 55, and elsewhere, emphasizes the importance of moral breakdown. His work is, of course, dependent upon early scholarship in the field, such as that of Kenelm Burridge, *New Heaven, New Earth: A Study of Millennarian Activities* (New York: Schocken Books, 1969) and A. F. C. Wallace, "Revitalization Movements," *American Anthropologist* 58 (1956): 264-81.

4. See, for example, Sheldon Solomon, Jeff Greenberg, Tom Pyszczynski, "A Terror Management Theory of Social Behavior: The Psychological Functions of Self-Esteem and Cultural Worldviews," *Advances in Experimental Social Psychology* 24 (1991): 93-159.

5. For further discussion of the social and denominational stress that led to this crisis, see Helen Lee Turner, "Societal Change and Millennialist Visions: Provocateurs of Denominational Strife," *Journal of the South Carolina Baptist Historical Society* 16 (Nov. 1990): 19-30.

6. Samuel S. Hill, "Fundamentalism and the South," *Perspectives in Religious Studies* 13 (Winter 1986): 62-63.

7. For a discussion of the bonds uniting traditional southern evangelicalism, see Donald Matthews, *Religion in the Old South* (Chicago: Univ. of Chicago Press, 1977).

8. One stunning example of this is Rev. T. A. Hall's "The Pastor A Ruler," *Southern Baptist Advocate* 9 (May 1989): 21-22.

9. For further discussion of Norris's premillennialism, see James J. Thompson, Jr., *Tried As by Fire: Southern Baptists and the Religious Controversies of the 1920s* (Macon, Ga.: Mercer Univ. Press, 1982), 146-56.

10. In my survey of associational ministers (1987), 17.8 percent of respondents said SBC literature has had the greatest influence (other than the Bible), 8.4 percent cited Hal Lindsey, 7.2 percent cited television preachers in general, and 12.2 percent cited other influences.

11. According to my 1985-86 survey of a random sample of fifteen hundred Southern Baptist ministers (48 percent response rate), Graham is without question the most favored of the television preachers, commanding respect from persons of moderate persuasion as well as from the conservative pastors. Of the ministers who responded to the survey, about 75 percent said they agreed with Dr. Graham. Virtually no one (1 percent) disagreed with him.

12. For examples of Graham's sermons see, William Franklin Graham, *The Challenge: Sermons from Madison Square Garden* (Garden City, N.Y.: Doubleday, 1969).

13. Robert A. Baker, "Pre-millennial Baptist Groups," in *Encyclopedia of Southern Baptists* (Nashville, Tenn.: Broadman, 1958).

14. We do not know how many issues of this newspaper there were. Those I consulted were acquired through the Oklahoma Baptist Historical Society and Reverend Anson Justice, a retired minister from the state who had collected them. Because Justice was not a member of the fellowship, we are uncertain whether he received all the issues or even preserved all he received.

15. "No. 3 Ed. Note," *Baptist Beacon* (June 1949): 2; J. Harvey Scott, "Lost A Head," *Baptist Beacon* (Sept. 1950): 1.

16. "Simultaneous Revivals," *Baptist Beacon* (Apr. 1950): 1.

17. "A Great Conference," *Baptist Beacon* (Apr. 1950): 4.

18. Barkun, *Crucible of the Millennium,* 143-44.

19. Burridge, *New Heaven,* 172.

20. Ibid., 172.

21. Dick J. Reavis, "The Politics of Armageddon," *Texas Monthly* (Oct. 1984): 237.

22. W. A. Criswell, "Pastor's Pen," 2 Dec. 1960, 1, 4, as quoted in Harold T. Bryson, "The Expository Preaching of W. A. Criswell In His Sermons on the Revelation" (Master's thesis, New Orleans Baptist Theological Seminary, 1967), 21. Criswell, *Expository Sermons on Revelation: Five Volumes Complete and Unabridged* (Grand Rapids, Mich.: Zondervan, 1969), 41.

23. Criswell's first volume on Revelation came out from Zondervan in 1962. He published regularly on the subject through the sixties and well into the seventies. Among his work is *Expository Sermons on the Book of Daniel: Four Volumes in One* (Grand Rapids, Mich.: Zondervan, 1972).

24. I received a taped copy of Criswell's "Why I Am a Pre-millennialist" directly from Dr. Criswell. He indicated that the sermon was originally prepared for his yearly pastors' conference, which is known as the School of the Prophets. That program was begun in 1971, but no date was attached to this particular sermon. However, the letter seemed to imply that the sermon was delivered at the first school.

25. As quoted in "Criswell says Christianity May Be Doomed by 2000," *Alabama Baptist* 131 (10 Nov. 1966): 9; SBC Convention Minutes, 1967.

26. "President Views Convention Needs," *Baptist Courier,* 13 June 1968, 3.

27. Perhaps most noteworthy in this regard is Adrian Rogers, who claimed a last minute call from God in 1979.

28. Anson Justice, "The Premillennial Baptist Fellowship Movement in Oklahoma," *Oklahoma Baptist Chronicle* 30 (Spring 1987): 7-21.

29. Editorial, *Sword and the Trowel* 1 (Jan. 1969): 10. It should also be noted that although Pinnock was originally identified with the fundamentalist movement, he later became severely critical of their tactics.

30. *Southern Baptist Convention Minutes,* 1969, 1970.

31. Victor Turner in *Ritual Process* (Chicago: Univ. of Chicago Press, 1969), 128, argues that the attainment of *communitas* is actually considered sacred because it "breaks through the interstices of structure" and "transgresses or dissolves the norms that govern institutionalized relationships."

32. *Southern Baptist Convention Minutes,* 1970, 1971.

33. Ibid., 1972, 1973.

34. Ibid., 1974, 1975, 1976.

35. Abram Rosenblatt, Jeff Greenberg, Sheldon Solomon, Tom Pyszczynski, and Deborah Lyon in "Evidence for Terror Management Theory: I. The Effects of Mortality Salience on Reactions to Those Who Violate or Uphold Cultural Values," *Journal of Personality and Social Psychology* 57, no. 4: 689 demonstrate that confronting one's death hardens one's value system. Burridge, *New Heaven,* 147 discusses the way in which millennialist expectation encourages the reordering of moral categories into sharply contrasting contraries.

36. Mircea Eliade, *Myth and Reality* (New York: Harper & Row: 1963), 19.

37. *Southern Baptist Convention Minutes,* 1977.

38. Eliade, *Myth and Reality,* 75, 76.

39. Peter Worsley, *A Trumpet Shall Sound: A Study of "Cargo" Cults in Melanesia* (New York: Schocken Books, 1968), xix.

40. *Southern Baptist Convention Minutes,* 1978.

41. Morris Ashcraft, *The Broadman Bible Commentary: Revelation* (Nashville, Tenn.: Broadman, 1972); George R. Beasley-Murray, *Highlights of the Book of Revelation* (Nashville, Tenn.: Broadman, 1972); Ashcraft,

"Preaching the Apocalyptic Message Today," *Review and Expositor* 72 (Summer 1975): 345-57; and Dale Moody, "The Eschatology of Hal Lindsey," *Review and Expositor* 72 (Summer 1975): 271-78.

42. "Heaven, Hell, the End of Time," *Baptist Courier,* 19 Apr. 1979, 12.

43. See Dennis R. MacDonald, *The Legend and the Apostle: The Battle for Paul in Story and Canon* (Philadelphia: Westminister, 1983) for a discussion of the effect of apocalypticism on the early institutional church.

44. James C. Hefley, *The Truth in Crisis: The Controversy in the Southern Baptist Convention,* vol. 1 (Hannibal, Mo.: Hannibal Books, 1986), 66, 67.

45. Eliade, *Myth and Reality,* 76, 19; Yonina Talmon, "Pursuit of the Millennium: The Relation Between Religious and Social Change," in *Reader in Comparative Religion, an Anthropological Approach,* ed. W. A. Lessa and E. Z. Vogt (New York: Harper & Row, 1965), 526.

46. For an in depth discussion of the use cosmogonies by fundamentalist Southern Baptists, see Helen Lee Turner, "Fundamentalism in the Southern Baptist Convention: The Crystallization of a Millennialist Movement" (Ph.D. diss., Univ. of Virginia, 1990), chap. 5.

47. *Southern Baptist Convention Minutes,* 1979.

48. "Fire in the Pasture," *Southern Baptist Journal* 3 (Oct.-Nov. 1975). Similar accounts appear in "A Country Church Comes Alive," *Southern Baptist Journal* 3 (May-June 1975), and "Tower Grove on the Grow Again," *Southern Baptist Journal* 6 (July 1978).

49. "Bible Cruises: New Phenomenon for Evangelical Christians," *Southern Baptist Advocate* 7 (Apr. 1987): 9, 10.

CHAPTER 7
WHAT'S ALL THE FIGHTING ABOUT? SOUTHERN BAPTISTS AND THE BIBLE
Joe E. Barnhart

The battle that threatens to turn Southern Baptists into at least two rival denominations, de facto if not de jure, has been waged at several levels. At one level,
the level to be addressed here, a fierce conflict over the Bible has been developing for at least four decades. But despite the rhetoric of the denomination's
fundamentalists, it would be erroneous to conclude that whereas one side ac-
cepts the Bible, the other rejects it. Because each side professes to regard the
Bible as an authoritative guide in matters of faith and practice, the dispute concerns *how* to accept the Bible.

It is also a popular notion that the controversy over the Bible can be
understood as a conflict between the literalists and the nonliteralists. This
explanation will not work either. There are more fruitful avenues for understanding how disputing Southern Baptists differ in the way they accept the
Bible.

General Revelation and Special Revelation
Today Southern Baptists are experiencing the tension between two putative
sources of divine revelation: general and special. General revelation, embodied in common or universal grace, is believed to be available to all members
of the human race. The Creator is said to be revealed everywhere in nature,
history, and human experience. Science, reason, the arts, literature, common
sense, and conscience are viewed as human interpretations of general revelation. Protestantism, like Catholicism, has insisted that none of these human

conceptualizations or interpretations is infallible, yet general revelation is acknowledged to be a genuine reality that human beings must interpret as best they can in order to survive and live meaningfully.

Special revelation is viewed not as initially universal or global but rather as embodied in the special salvation history of Israel and early Christianity, the ministry of Christ, and the inspired Scripture of the two Testaments. In the seventeenth, eighteenth, and early nineteenth centuries, Protestant scholars generally regarded science (as a window on general revelation) to be in harmony with the Scriptures of special revelation; the truths of divine revelation could not contradict one another, they thought. In the second half of the nineteenth century, however, Darwin appeared on the scene to disturb profoundly the measured bond of tranquillity between scientists and Protestant theologians. As both science and modes of critical inquiry have made assertions that seemingly lead away from accepted beliefs classified under special revelation, tensions have risen, occasionally resulting in battles such as the one in which Southern Baptists have been engaged.

Among those Southern Baptists who call themselves moderates are the students of the Bible who look upon historical and literary criticism as legitimate tools of biblical research. As disciplines alongside science and other forms of rational inquiry, historical and literary criticism are thought to be available to everyone who will spend the time and energy in learning them. Moderate leaders in the denomination, prone to regard science and critical disciplines as tools of general revelation that can assist scholars in interpreting special revelation, look upon "biblical criticism" as in some sense a divine gift for rightly discerning Scripture, a gift open to anyone, albeit only through years of training and rigorous discipline. The implications of this way of thinking are far reaching. One such implication is that Scripture *requires* light from the disciplines of general revelation if it is to be profoundly understood. Scripture is therefore neither a self-contained epistemological whole nor fully self-illuminating. Scholars within the moderate camp hold further that the two sources of revelation throw light upon each other, so that neither is truly complete or deeply understood apart from the other.

By contrast Southern Baptist inerrantists, leaders of the denomination's fundamentalist camp, are prone to regard historical and literary criticism as intrusions on the sacred ground of special revelation. They contend that the

Bible as revealed in its original autographs was inerrant. That is it neither taught nor implied any error in any subject or field of knowledge about which it made assertions or claims. The inerrantists appear on the surface at least to stress the epistemological self-containedness of Scripture. They are unlikely to view biblical revelation as somehow emerging out of a background of Mesopotamian hymns, Egyptian cosmology, Canaanite cultic practices, Zoroastrian myths, or Hellenistic magic and rhetoric. Apparent similarities between Old Testament Scripture and other Near Eastern texts and symbols are discounted. Inerrancy apologists stress the discontinuity between the Hebrew-Christian Scripture and the religions of either the Near East or the Hellenistic world. Inerrantists think in terms of the "one true religion" on one side and "false religions" on the other side. As does the Princeton scholar B. B. Warfield (1851-1921), they treat all "heathen religions" as "degrading to man and insulting to God." Far from embracing an evolutionary view of religion, they perceive "the origin of the heathen religions in the progressive *degradation* of man's thought of God, as man's repeated withdrawal of God . . . to [the point of] the steady destruction of all religious insight and moral perception alike . . ." (emphasis added).[1]

Those who follow the Warfield school hold further that the Hebrew faith of the Old Covenant and the Christian faith throw light on each other primarily because each is a part of special revelation. They hasten to add, however, that whereas the faith of the two Testaments may cast light on the heathen religions, the latter can cast little or no light on Scripture except to demonstrate how thoroughly removed heathen beliefs and practices are from the faith of Israel and the early Christian believers. Moreover, the religion of Israel is viewed as itself incomplete (and now rebellious) until it gains fulfillment in Christianity alone. Religious truth is to be found only in the special revelation of Christianity, never in the general revelation of other religions.

If leaders of the inerrantists have rejected the general revelation of the world's religions, their relationship to modern science is less clear. They may appear to be quite hostile to a number of theories of science as presented in most universities and science journals, but they appear to be open enthusiastically to certain areas of modern technology. There is a reason for this. Science presents hypotheses that seem at least prima facie to challenge directly many of the tenets of what fundamentalists call biblical Christianity. By contrast advanced technology in communications and travel does not appear, on the surface at least, to challenge those tenets, serving rather as instruments for spreading them around the world. It is misleading, therefore, to state categorically that fundamentalist leaders stand opposed to all modernity. What they intend to oppose is every element of modernity that threatens to change the content of what they regard as the settled, miraculous, and final revelation of God to humanity.

Inerrancy leaders among Southern Baptists are also ambivalent about the whole question of general revelation in the area of morality. For them virtually every worthwhile thing that human beings need to know about religion and morality exists in the self-contained Scriptures.[2] Most of church history until the sixteenth century is viewed as the story of the corruption of first-century Christianity. Southern Baptist fundamentalists are restorationists who think the mission of twentieth-century believers is to duplicate the purity of doctrine, polity, and practice exemplified by first-century Christians. Indeed, many of these leaders believe that most Southern Baptist churches have been and still are New Testament churches, that is, close approximations of first-century churches. They see the current Southern Baptist battle as a crucial and momentous contest between the defilers of doctrinal purity and those who have resolved to hold firmly to the pure faith once delivered to the prophets, apostles, and other ordained agents of the miraculous special revelation.[3] The result is that the fundamentalists' suspicion of biblical criticism and much of what the moderates regard as science is so strong that they are prone to perceive these disciplines as vile, heathenish corruptions or false religions to be purged from the camp of the faithful.

The Literalists

Although the two SBC camps can be distinguished by their differing views of general revelation, they cannot so easily be distinguished by their use of literal interpretations of Scripture. Both inerrantists and noninerrantists sometimes insist on drawing a sharp line between the literal meaning and the actual meaning of a text. Drawing the line in the right place can be a delicate art, and it is that interpretive task that often separates them.

It is misleading to identify inerrantists as literalists in reading and interpreting the Bible: many noninerrantist scholars take certain biblical passages more literally than do the defenders of inerrancy. Indeed, it might very well be that the noninerrantists find the inerrancy doctrine implausible *because* they take certain passages quite literally.

The story of Adam and Eve hearing the sound of God walking in the cool of the day (Gen. 3:8) is a case in point. Some noninerrantist scholars hold that the original author of this story believed that the deity literally walked in a literal garden while the day was literally cool. This is not to say that these same scholars today accept as true what the original author (or perhaps redactor) accepted as true. Rather, the point is that they do not rob the author/redactor of his or her belief in the literalness of some of the details of the story. Although excluding from their own personal twentieth-century framework the literalness of many (or perhaps all) of the details of the Genesis story, these scholars contend nevertheless that the original composer reflects his or her own historical setting and primitive cosmogony and anthropology.

Some inerrantists, by contrast, prove to be less literalistic, not only denying that the Creator of the universe literally took a walk in a literal garden but denying that the author of the story regarded the walk as literal. In short, even though they regard both the garden and the coolness of the day as literal, they deny that the Creator had feet and toes that enabled him to walk.[4]

Bible commentaries that embrace the inerrancy theory are uncomfortable with talk about anthropomorphic language and images in the Bible. Such talk suggests a slippery slope. If some God-talk in the Bible is anthropomorphic, perhaps all of it is. Along with an infallible Bible must there also be an infallible rule or theology that marks off the anthropomorphic from the nonanthropomorphic? If some aspects of the garden in Genesis 3 "must not be regarded as entirely anthropomorphic,"[5] are there other aspects that should be so regarded? In the attempt to back away from the concessions to anthropomorphism, one noted conservative Bible commentary insists that both the walk in the garden and the conversation God had with Adam and Eve "is not a mere figure of speech, but a reality."[6] It claims that God took a visible shape in order to converse with the first couple. But making such a claim about a literal occurrence creates problems. Does this necessitate that God became a literal man? Or was his appearance, as in the opinion of the commentator, an appearance (Docetic?) of a man? If it was a theophany, what does this mean literally? Does a theophanic being suffer hunger? Can it see through trees the way Clark Kent without his glasses looked through metal? These questions, and many more like them, are altogether proper, for according to Genesis 3:9, "the Lord God called to the man and said, 'Where are you?'" The prima facie reading of this story suggests that the Lord God asked the question in all sincerity, because he could not see Adam, who presumably was hiding in the garden because he feared being seen naked. In addition the Genesis author/redactor does not disclose if the Lord God was naked when he conversed with Adam and Eve, or if his body was concealed behind theophanic clothes or light. The point here is that if the problem of literalness is not itself tricky, interpreters have perhaps of necessity been clever and sometimes ingenious in the ways they permit their presuppositions and models to designate some passages as literal and others as not. In some cases difficult passages are avoided altogether.[7] Inerrancy, then, proves not to be a very good predictor of literalism.

Inerrantists among Southern Baptists also play down the sensual literalism of the Song of Songs (Song of Solomon) in order to frame its passionate passages as an allegorical or typological message. They are prone to view the passages almost mystically as a message of love between Christ and His church. In contrast the scholars of the moderate camp are willing to view the songs, or canticles, more literally as sensual and tender expressions between human lovers. Some of these scholars feel no need to treat the original canticles as anything beyond the erotic literature that they appear on the surface to be. If later a biblical writer used them for a theological purpose, that would not contradict the fact that the source material appropriated was originally erotic in intent and function.

One passage from the Pentateuch provides us with an opportunity to understand the vast differences between the inerrantists and the noninerrantists among Southern Baptist scholars. In Exodus is a passage that suggests that persistent Moses gained permission to see God's back but nothing more: ". . . I will cover you with my hand until I have passed by; but then I will take away my hand, and you shall see my back; but my face shall not be seen" (Ex. 33:22-23, RSV). Because the inerrantists take the Bible as a self-contained epistemological whole, they are strongly disposed to turn only to other biblical passages in the attempt to interpret this passage. They feel no need to refer to extrabiblical texts or religious cultures and concepts of deity outside the Bible to understand this admittedly difficult biblical passage. Inerrantists know that according to a New Testament text, John 1:18, "No man hath seen God at any time" (AV). This settles the question for them. Moses could not see God literally, although he saw something. He was not hallucinating. What he therefore saw literally was not God's essence, which cannot be seen, but God's theophany or physical manifestation or representation.

The noninerrantist Southern Baptists who know something about Near Eastern and Greek religions of antiquity are more likely to turn to extrabiblical sources to help them understand passages such as Exodus 33:22-23. Because they believe in general revelation, even in the area of religion, they believe they see a measure of continuity between the early Hebrews and their neighbors regarding concepts of God. Without wishing to deny the uniqueness of the Hebrew tradition, the noninerrantists believe that the Hebrew faith in especially its early stages struggled with the rather common assumption that God(s) literally possessed bodily features as well as certain human traits and characteristics. Indeed, according to Exodus 33:11, "the Lord used to speak to Moses face to face, as a man speaks to his friend" (RSV).

It is possible, according to some noninerrantists, that Exodus 24:10 and 33:11 represent one strain of the early Hebrew tradition, a strain that assumed that the deity could be seen and talked with literally face to face, whereas Exodus 33:20-23 represents a different strain, one that insisted that God's face could not be seen. The redactor of Exodus, therefore, incorporated the two strains or sources and gave them his own theological interpretation. Inerrantists oppose this analysis. W. A. Criswell, self-described literalist and grandfather of the fundamentalist movement in the SBC, writes in his commentary that the phrase "face to face" must be understood "figuratively."[8]

Similar strains between literal and figurative interpretations can be seen in treatments of the creation story. Ironically there are inerrantists and noninerrantists who agree that the "day" in the creation passages of Genesis 1 is to be taken as a literal twenty-four-hour period. The inerrantists who believe this conclude that creation was completed within one week. According to some noninerrantists, however, general revelation leads them to think that creation has been going on for eons despite the fact that the Genesis author mistakenly thought it took less than a full week. There are other inerrantists and noninerrantists who hold that the "day" of Genesis 1 is not a twenty-four-hour period but a vast stretch of time. Clearly, therefore, although interpreters can agree to take a given text literally, they often disagree as to what its literal meaning is.

The Explosive Issue of Extrabiblical Sources

It is perhaps over the question of extrabiblical sources that the scholars and leaders of the fundamentalists stand in sharpest disagreement with many moderate leaders and scholars. The inerrantists are exceedingly reluctant to acknowledge that the biblical writers drew ideas, images, and conclusions from a variety of human sources, whether written or oral. For them special revelation is a miraculous supernatural intervention into human history, not an example of religious and moral evolution. Far from depending on human culture, it rejects the heathen cultures surrounding the Hebrews and Christians. The noninerrantists' quest for extrabiblical sources and parallels of Scripture is regarded as the Enemy's drive to dilute the specialness of special revelation and to rob it of its supernatural authority and content.

The inerrantists do not categorically deny the existence of general revelation. They believe that the hand of the Creator could be seen clearly in visible creation *if* the eyes of unredeemed humanity were not blinded by wickedness and degeneracy. Following the thesis of the first chapter of Paul's Epistle to the Romans, they insist that heathen religions demonstrate how perverse minds have "changed the glory of the incorruptible God into an image made like to corruptible man, and to birds, and fourfooted beasts, and creeping things" (Rom. 1:23, AV). If very little truth and goodness is to be found in heathen religions, it would be erroneous to conclude that God's special revelation in Scripture could have drawn even a portion of its content from heathen sources. Fundamentalist leaders believe, therefore, that Baptist seminary and college instructors are degenerate at worst and misguided at best to search for profound moral and religious insight within heathen systems of belief. They contend that the purpose of a Christian seminary in particular is to train young men[9] to carry to the heathen the miraculously revealed truth of the Gospel. The purpose is not to learn morality and religion *from* the pagans.

It is not uncommon to hear a fundamentalist preacher proclaim that the Bible possesses the answers to all of this world's problems. This claim, in turn, creates pressure to perceive all problems as religious and moral problems whose solutions cannot in any way be solved by consulting the books and traditions of the heathen. "Professing themselves to be wise, they [i.e., the heathen] become fools" (Rom. 1:22, AV).

From the Authority of Scripture to the Authoritative Clergy

The fundamentalists' epistemological premise, which features the Bible as the sole authority in matters of religion and morality, has far-reaching consequences. Every area of general revelation—including medical research and every branch of science and learning—is reduced to the role of handmaiden to Scripture. In practice this means that when one group or party among the churches becomes the established interpreter of Scripture, it becomes in effect the authority in religion and morality. It furthermore builds a momentum to become the authority in vetoing cognitive claims and moral recommendations that conflict with the publicized conclusions of the established interpretations. I will elaborate this point later.

That the pastor is to be the authorized interpreter was made evident by the action of the 1988 Southern Baptist Convention in San Antonio. There the messengers voted (by slight majority) to circumscribe the principle of the priesthood of every believer in order to enhance the role of the pastor as the authoritative leader of the church. Emphasis was placed on the Hebrews 13:17 injunction: "Obey your leaders and submit to them; for they keep watch over your souls" (RSV). The most conspicuous intent of this resolution was to enhance the pastor in his capacity as guardian of sound doctrine and enforcer of the correct interpretation of Scripture. In effect this means that the senior pastors of the jumbo-sized Southern Baptist churches may become an elite class, setting the standards and guidelines of scriptural interpretation for other

Baptists. It also seems to be a device for curtailing not only the influence of college and seminary professors of religion but the boldness of Baptist lay people (who are increasingly college educated) in their tendency to interpret Scripture and determine for themselves what is or is not sound doctrine.

Perhaps the more significant corollary, if not the fully conscious purpose, of the 1988 pastoral leadership resolution is the erecting of a sea wall of resistance against the swelling waters of female influence in Southern Baptist churches. With women graduating from colleges and universities, and with an unprecedented rise in the number of women graduating from some of the Southern Baptist seminaries, the female threat seems real, especially to those pastors who align themselves with the fundamentalists. It is not mere coincidence that these same pastors had four years earlier, at the annual convention in Kansas City, succeeded in getting a resolution passed that claimed that the ordination of women was unsound doctrine as well as unscriptural and dangerous polity.

The claims of the leading fundamentalist pastors to positions as authoritative interpreters are seen also in the abortion controversy. They label abortion as murder and boldly profess to be able to prove from Scripture that the unborn are persons from the moment of their conception. What these pastors offer in support of their claim is a list of proof texts whose contexts had little or no direct bearing on the abortion question. But their interpretations of those texts are taken as the biblical basis for a single-minded denominational emphasis on stopping abortion. Sociologists and philosophers who study the dynamics of movements and organizations will find it exceedingly fruitful to continue studying the ability of fundamentalist pastors to mobilize swiftly in order to communicate quickly and effectively their own interpretations of selected proof texts as the authoritative judgment on the abortion question. As Nancy Ammerman notes, moderate scholars and leaders who do not accept the fundamentalist interpretations of these proof texts have been unable to mobilize and effectively communicate their own interpretations regarding the abortion question.[10]

The "battle for the Bible" among Southern Baptists is, according to Richard Land of the Christian Life Commission and Judge Paul Pressler (the fundamentalists' supreme strategist), about the nature of the Bible rather than about the interpretation of biblical texts. This claim does not, however, square with what is actually going on within the Southern Baptist Convention.[11] According to the apologists of the doctrine of inerrancy, the doctrine is itself rooted in certain texts of the Bible that are taken to be "Scripture's witness to itself." The point is that these texts, including 2 Timothy 3:16 and 17, have to be *interpreted*. The hypothesis of the inerrancy of the Bible is indeed a hypothesis or theory as to what is the proper interpretation of certain passages in the Bible.

As the controversy over inerrancy continues, it is becoming clearer that the affirmation of the inerrancy of any body of literature generates pressure to generate a *second* source of inerrancy, namely, the interpreter of the first source. The 1988 SBC resolution in San Antonio was in effect a significant step in the direction of affirming for all practical purposes an infallible or inerrant clergy class invested with the power (authority) to establish inerrant interpretations. The earlier step in this direction was, of course, the original demand for an inerrant source in Scripture.

The Presumption of Manifest Truth

Both the moderates and the fundamentalists represent contemporary Herculean efforts to come to terms with the naïve, optimistic view that truth is manifest for those who genuinely cleanse themselves of prejudice and open themselves to the pristine light. The Baptist tradition has a foot in the Enlightenment-democratic tradition that insists that truth is readily available to every mind and heart that is purged of the evil powers and impure influences that both corrupt the heart and poison the mind against truth. According to the optimistic classical liberal view, truth shines at the door of the mind, and its illuminating rays stand ready to enter as soon as the mind is cleansed of its love of falsehood.

This optimistic outlook branched off in diverse directions. One branch, the Jeffersonian, taught that the corrupting force that loves falsehood and abhors the manifest light of truth is external. This force takes the form of repressive governments and/or a repressive class composed of the clergy. If this evil influence can be broken, then the light of reason and truth will flood the mind and heart quite naturally.

Many Baptists of the eighteenth century shared much of this democratic way of thinking. Even though having their own members of the clergy to serve and lead them, the frontier Baptists in particular did not think of their clergy as a class but perceived them as fellow believers who could be dismissed from the pulpit on short notice. The Baptists tended to identify the oppressive clergy as those of the Church of England, the Church of Rome, Presbyterianism, and other denominations that Baptists resented for their use of the state to gain special favors. The New World Baptists tended to support Jefferson and Madison, because they shared the Baptist quasi-libertarian views on preventing the oppressive state from interfering with their religious life or giving special treatment to their rivals. The Baptists emphasized soul competency and the priesthood of every believer, and in doing so they contributed to the spread of the democratic ideal in the New World.[12]

A second branch or version of the optimistic epistemology that grew among the early Baptists of the seventeenth and eighteenth centuries may be described as follows: Truth is manifest and ready to enter the mind and heart of everyone. A great internal barrier, however, blocks the light. The heart itself is perverse and in love with falsehood and evil. The heart and mind must therefore be purged so that truth may flood it.

Baptists belong in part to the tradition of the Enlightenment, free-enterprise capitalism, and the strain of Protestantism that insists that an individual has to enter a covenant voluntarily without the mediation of a bureaucracy, whether secular or priestly. In religious terms Baptists belong to the born-again believers' tradition that teaches that it is possible to receive a new start in life, to move out into the world, relatively free of the chains of the past. The internal chain of original sin, the Adamic nature, can be sufficiently broken to permit the competent soul—that pure residue of the divine image—to receive light, grace, and truth.

Historically Baptists have never tired of proclaiming that the individual can interpret the Bible for himself or herself. The priestly bureaucracy is not needed. Once the internal and external barriers to truth and grace have been torn down, the individual, by enjoying inalienable soul competency, can open the Holy Bible and receive directly the word of God as light into his or her heart. Within this epistemological model resides the vague but pervasive assumption that because God is truthful and will never deceive us, falsehood and ignorance of God's grace are the product of corruption and sin, both internal and external. The optimistic classical liberal assumption is that once purification comes about, truth will readily flood the heart and mind.

Epistemological Pessimism

In the words of philosopher Karl Popper, "Epistemological pessimism is linked, historically, with a doctrine of human depravity, and it tends to lead to the demand for the establishment of powerful traditions and the entrenchment of a powerful authority which would save man from his folly and his wickedness."[13] At the close of the twentieth century, Southern Baptists, as well as most other denominations in America, are faced with somehow coming to terms with the inadequacy of both the optimistic epistemology of manifest truth and the pessimistic epistemology of incurable human corruption that requires an entrenched authority to establish truth and morality.

Feeling that today the relatively innocent people in the Baptist pews, as well as the young people in Baptist colleges and seminaries, are being exposed to false teachings such as women's liberation and higher criticism of the Bible, fundamentalist leaders have been forced to doubt their assumption of the doctrine of manifest truth. This doubt only increases as the charismatic movement makes inroads into some Southern Baptist churches. Hence even inerrantists are forced to doubt that born-again lay people will readily detect heresy and interpret the Bible properly if they have only the Holy Spirit to guide them.

What or who, then, must guide the believers in gaining the truth and avoiding falsehood? One answer emerging on the Southern Baptist horizon is that God has called a special group of believers to whom all others must yield, especially in matters of sound doctrine and morality. Baptist believers must obey and submit not only to Scripture and the Holy Spirit, but to their pastors. These three complete the sacred *troika* of epistemological and moral authority. To oppose this divinely instituted troika is to rebel against God.

To the degree that seminary professors and Baptist college teachers of religion see themselves as divinely ordained authoritative interpreters, they become merely a part of the troika. To the degree that they do not see themselves in this light, they are more likely to be a part of the Enlightenment-democratic-Protestant tradition that is resolute in its drive to open all believers to what they believe is a deeper understanding of Scripture. But in order to maintain this latter self-image, they can no longer embrace either the optimistic epistemology of manifest truth or the pessimistic epistemology that requires an entrenched elite class possessing the authority to enforce the proper interpretations of Scripture. A completely new model of epistemology is required among Southern Baptists in order to do justice to the Enlightenment-democratic-Protestant tradition and to transcend the doctrine of manifest truth. But what is this new emerging model among Southern Baptists?

Beyond Epistemological Primitivism

Perhaps no Southern Baptist has punctured the myth of manifest truth with more succinctness than Charles H. Talbert, one of the leaders of the National Association of Baptist Professors of Religion. He writes:

> After the New Testament period and up until Augustine of Hippo (A.D. 354-430), there was a widespread tendency in Christianity to *identify sin and evil with the ignorance of the finite mind*. But that way of thinking comes from Hellenistic culture, not from biblical faith.
>
> Our finitude moreover is not something evil, but something good, because it is created by God (Gen. 1:31). It is, however, sin to reject one's finitude and to grasp for divine knowledge (Gen. 3:5,6).
>
> For Jesus to have been a man of his own time in his knowledge of matters of fact would not have subverted either his divinity or his full humanity, including . . . the finitude of limited knowledge in matters of fact. Only if he were truly human (including finitude), as well as divine and sinless, could he be our Savior (emphasis added).[14]

Talbert's perspective stands in sharp opposition to that of one of the noted protagonists of inerrancy, Edwin J. Young, who makes the staggering claim that "fallibility is the consequence of sin."[15] Taken to its logical conclusion, Young would have to hold that Adam and Eve (whom Young takes to have been a literal couple in a literal garden) possessed omniscience prior to the Fall and that Lucifer (whom Young takes also to have been a literal angel before his fall) was already equal to God in one respect, namely, omniscience.

The theological issues of Christ's nature—whether one nature, as Monophysites contended, or two natures, as B. B. Warfield contended—are outside this chapter's scope of discussion. The epistemological issues alone are sufficiently complicated to require full attention. It is probably safe to conclude that as the twentieth century approaches its close, epistemological primitivism has been severely wounded if not put to rest. It is perhaps no longer possible for Southern Baptist leaders to believe that any literate born-again believer can simply pick up the Bible and intelligently say to himself or herself, "Well, now, I shall ignore all the commentaries and all the many human interpretations that have been set forth. All I want to do is read what the Bible itself says." There are no born-again epistemological noble savages possessing an innocent tabula rasa mind who can read the Bible in pristine child-like faith. No putative pure heart can glean the pure meaning of Scripture without aid and guidance. And it is certainly the case that no putative innocent born-again minds reading the Bible in simple faith can be counted on to arrive at a common theological body of doctrinal truth.

Herein lies the contemporary Southern Baptist epistemological dilemma: either try to breathe life into the dead horse of epistemological primitivism (with its doctrine of manifest truth) or deal with the harsh fact that born-again believers require help and guidance in interpreting the Bible. The new epistemological battle likely will become a political battle over how the authoritative interpretations of Scripture are to emerge.

Versions of the Inerrancy Hypothesis

There is a certain irony in the recent demand of some that Southern Baptist leaders in particular be put to the test to determine their adherence or lack of adherence to the doctrine of inerrancy. It is ironic because those Baptists who resent being tested will more likely support subjecting the doctrine of inerrancy itself to the test. The more central and crucial the doctrine becomes in the politico-economic decisions of the SBC, the more likely it is to be subjected to rigorous analysis and scrutiny. The price to be paid in debating and probing the epistemological depths of the inerrancy theory is so heavy, however, that both sides of the battle may eventually allow the terms of the controversy to be significantly revised or even shifted to an altogether different issue or theory. Every human theory that passes beyond the infancy stage of verbal ritual tends to develop revisions that either improve or undermine it. In the debate over the inerrancy theory both inside and outside the Southern Baptist Convention, at least three versions of inerrancy and infallibility have already evolved:

1. *Extended inerrancy.* Francis Schaeffer and the Southern Baptist fundamentalist Harold Lindsell insist that when the Scriptures affirm something as true, it is true exactly and precisely as stated. When the Bible makes what purport to be true claims in chronology, geography, astronomy, measurement, physics, theology, philosophy, psychology, or any other field of knowledge, it is free of all error in every way. In trying to harmonize the Gospels in their accounts of Peter's denial and the cock crowing, Lindsell cannot bring himself to believe that there is even a slight discrepancy in the accounts. Adding up all the accounts and trying to harmonize them so that there are no inconsistencies, he thus feels compelled to conclude that the cock crowed six times.

2. *Limited infallibility.* According to evangelical author Dewey Beegle, there exist minor irreconcilable conflict passages in the biblical reports of Christ's Resurrection, but this fact does not imply that the Resurrection event did not happen. Even though there are other errors in the Scriptures that the authors did not recognize as errors, God used a partially flawed means (i.e., the Scriptures) to communicate his perfect Gospel. To demand that the Scriptures be in every way more error free than in fact they are, Beegle argues, is to impose a human expectation on divine special revelation.

3. *Appropriate inerrancy.* Daniel Fuller of Fuller Theological Seminary and Southern Baptist scholar Clark Pinnock contend that the Scriptures do not teach error and are inerrant in accord with the range of their overall purpose. Each passage serves flawlessly and appropriately its purpose. Both Pinnock and Fuller note, however, that the Scriptures reflect a much greater variety and richness of genres than many of their fellow evangelicals have admitted. There are pseudonymous writings, scientific inaccuracies, inferior moral passages, cultural accommodations, and other imperfections included in the texts. But these are not taught or even implied as belonging to the essential truths of the Gospel.

With Fuller and Pinnock, many Southern Baptist scholars believe that proponents of extended inerrancy such Harold Lindsell have themselves erred grievously in demanding of the Bible a degree of precision that is precision either for its own sake or for the sake of an abstract and arbitrary human standards. Lindsell's standard is said to be irrelevant to the whole purpose of the Scriptures, which is to communicate the Gospel and serve as the guide to redemption and righteousness. Some of these Southern Baptists use the terms *inerrancy* and *infallibility* to refer to the Bible in its capacity to lead the earnest reader unfailingly to saving grace. Others think the terms should be bypassed, because they miscommunicate as much as they communicate.

The Inerrancy Battle into the Next Century

Controversies, like fevers, rise and fall in intensity. The inerrancy controversy among Southern Baptists likely will continue into the next century, but in the process numerous refinements and qualifications could cause a major shift in the way the whole issue is perceived and defined. Some theories either die the death of a thousand qualifications or survive by becoming a mutation that grows to resemble its parent only remotely. The process of mutating has already begun with the inerrancy theory and will probably continue with unpredictable results.

Fundamentalist leaders sometimes grow impatient with moderates who are accused of weaseling or twisting the words *infallible* and *inerrant* to mean whatever they want them to mean. These accused moderates reply that they are merely taking the definitions given by some of the most notable inerrantists—J. I. Packer, for example—and applying them more consistently than the self-appointed extended inerrantists. "'Infallible' denotes the quality of never deceiving or misleading," Packer writes, and "'inerrant' means 'wholly true.'"[16] The Bible does not mislead, the accused moderates say. It is people such as Harold Lindsell who mislead themselves by ignoring the great diversity of literary genres used in the Bible.[17]

The moderate scholars who claim that the first eleven chapters of Genesis are not a historical narrative seem to divide roughly into two groups. The first group agrees somewhat with the extended inerrantists in asserting that the author thought he or she was writing an actual historical narrative. The moderates of this group then add that the author/redactor was clearly wrong in thinking he was writing a historical account. These scholars do not, therefore, describe the Bible as inerrant. The second group of moderates argues that the author/redactor of Genesis 1-11 used a highly poetic and dramatic genre, not a historical narrative, to express his or her theistic and providential view of the universe. The author was not in error in doing this, they contend. Those who insist on reading the chapters as a historical narrative have simply mistaken one genre for another.

The Bible within the Bible

Some moderates will use the terms *infallible* and *inerrant* to mean that God unfailingly reveals only what he intended to reveal through the Scriptures. That and nothing more. The controversy about the Bible, then, for many Southern Baptists turns on the question of what it is that God intended to reveal in each passage of Scripture. Unfortunately neither the moderates nor the proponents of extended inerrancy have direct access to the Creator's putative intentions. In every case talk of specific divine intentions is rooted in their human conjectures, many of which are based on years of serious scholarly research.

Ironically, many moderates insist that the Scriptures do not advance a doctrine of inerrancy in the first place; that is, the theory of inerrancy is itself unscriptural. Most inerrantist scholars acknowledge that inerrancy is taught neither explicitly nor systematically in the Bible. It is nevertheless surely implied and presupposed, they contend. But that, too, is a matter of conjecture and interpretation. And that is why the pressure is building within the convention to establish for the people in the pews authoritative interpretations that do not appear to be interpretations at all, and certainly not interpretations that must always prove themselves against challenges. Because the Bible is a very large and complex book with no single theological thread on which to string all the stones and pearls contained within it, the controversy over inerrancy seems to be moving toward developing a Bible or story within the Bible as a meaningful "story" around which individuals can build their religious lives. One camp is currently weaving one story; a second camp (and perhaps even a third) is weaving another story. Whether the rival parties can find common cause (or a common enemy) that will allow them to remain together in peace has yet to be determined. In the meantime there remains the continuing Southern Baptist saga: Can this unhappy marriage be saved?

Notes

1. B. B. Warfield, *Biblical and Theological Studies,* ed. Samuel G. Craig (Philadelphia: Presbyterian and Reformed, 1952), 565-66.

2. See, for example, James T. Draper, *Authority: The Critical Issue for Southern Baptists* (Old Tappan, N.J.: Fleming H. Revell, 1984), 38-43; and Cornelius Van Til, *Coming Grace* (Philadelphia: Presbyterian and Reformed, 1954), 3-5.

3. Ironically, there is among secular humanists a small group that looks upon every religion (whether of professed special revelation or of professed general revelation) as both moral corruption and defilement of human reason. They are able to find nothing in any religion from which they can learn anything except examples of moral decay and intellectual rot. It is as if these particular secular humanists have taken the fundamentalists' position and extended it one additional step, thereby goring the inerrancy ox with its own horns.

4. The plot thickens, however, for the literal translation is "the voice of Yahweh" rather than "the sound of Yahweh" walking in the cool of the day. The King James Version uses the literal translation—"voice of." But is the literal meaning the actual meaning the author/redactor wished to communicate? Is it possible that even though a more primitive oral version of the story portrayed Yahweh as talking to the animals or to beings other than Adam and Eve, the redactor later intended to communicate that the first couple heard only the sound of Yahweh moving about in the garden?
   The King James Version speaks of the Lord walking "in the cool of the day," even though a more literal translation would speak of "the wind of the day." In order to grasp the actual meaning, rather than the strictly literal meaning, readers of the text would need to presuppose that toward sunset the wind began to blow and cool things down. Perhaps a more primitive version of the story portrayed the wind as the breath (voice) of a god stirring noisily among the trees of a garden (see 2 Sam. 5:24 and 1 Kings 14:6).

5. F. Davidson, ed., *The New Bible Commentary,* 2d ed. (Grand Rapids, Mich.: Eerdmans, 1960), 80.

6. C. F. Keil and F. Delitzsch, *Biblical Commentary on the Old Testament,* vol. 1, *The Pentateuch,* trans. James Martin (Grand Rapids, Mich.: Eerdmans, 1951), 97.

7. Dr. W. A. Criswell, former SBC president and grandfather of the fundamentalists, published a book titled *Why I Preach That the Bible Is Literally True* (Nashville, Tenn.: Broadman, 1969). Unfortunately *The Criswell Study Bible,* a commentary on the Bible, avoids commenting about the thorny problem of literalness in Genesis 3:8-13.

8. Criswell, *Criswell Study Bible* (Nashville, Tenn.: Thomas Nelson, 1979), 119.

9. Seminaries may also train young women, in this view, but only as "helpmeets" for the men who will be ordained to carry the gospel.

10. Nancy Tatom Ammerman, "Organizational Conflict in the Southern Baptist Convention," in *Secularization and Fundamentalism Reconsidered,* ed. J. Hadden and A. Shupe (New York: Paragon, 1989).

11. See Joe E. Barnhart, *The Southern Baptist Holy War* (Austin, Tex.: Texas Monthly, 1986), 8-16.

12. For an argument about the continued influence of these ideas in Baptist life, see Arthur Farnsley's chapter in this volume.

13. Karl Popper, *Conjectures and Refutations: The Growth of Scientific Knowledge* (New York: Harper & Row, 1965), 6.

14. Charles H. Talbert, "The Bible's Truth is Relational," in *The Unfettered Word,* ed. Robinson B. James (Waco, Tex.: Word, 1987), 46.

15. Edward J. Young, *Thy Word is Truth* (Grand Rapids, Mich.: Eerdmans, 1957), 77-78.

16. J. I. Packer, *"Fundamentalism" and the Word of God: Some Evangelical Principles* (Grand Rapids, Mich.: Eerdmans, 1958), 95.

17. For an expansion of this argument, see Barnhart, *Religion and the Challenge of Philosophy* (Totowa, N.J.: Littlefield, Adams & Co., 1975), chap. 2; and Bob E. Patterson, *C. F. H. Henry* (Waco, Tex.: Word, 1983), 112-26.

CHAPTER 8
THE SOUTHERN BAPTIST RESPONSE TO THE NEWEST SOUTH
Ellen M. Rosenberg

The New Right, with which many of Southern Baptists' fundamentalist leaders are obviously allied, is one in a long line of reactionary responses with religious coloration that have been organized throughout American history. It may be seen as a successor to the anti-evolution movement of the 1920s, when the threats of modern science, the end of Anglo-American world domination, and the labor union movement galvanized sections of evangelical religion into unprecedented political involvement.[1] That movement gained its greatest legislative success in the South, and the New Right is rooted in that region as well, although the magic of national television has made it seem broader. The special and most pointed reason for reaction in the South today is the erosion of the historic supremacy of whites, especially males.

In historical perspective the trauma of the Southern Baptist Convention was inevitable, although it did not, of course, have to take this particular form. Three powerful institutions had evolved to maintain white solidarity—the edifice of customary and legal segregation, or Jim Crow; the Democratic party in solid form; and white evangelical religion, in which the Southern Baptist Convention was the largest institution. When segregation fell, inevitably the other two great institutions would be profoundly affected.

Southern Baptist pastors had historically voiced the ideology of the culture, and prominent Southern Baptist laymen, as political leaders, implemented it in their shaping of the regional social structure. Southern Baptist involvement in state and local government needs to be fully documented, but it was certainly deep and broad in the Deep South. *New York Times* reporter Roy Reed noted, for example, the proximity of the First Baptist Church to the state capitol in Jackson. "From its pews, 20 years ago, a handful of families ruled Mississippi".[2] Theirs is no passive reflection of a regional culture designed by others. Southern Baptists had, and still have, tremendous power to shape, create, and construe the culture of the South and should rightly be held substantially responsible for the results. No group including the Talmadges, Theodore Bilbo, Lester Maddox, Jesse Helms, and Strom Thurmond, let alone Harry Truman and Jimmy Carter, can claim to have been mere spectators at the parade.

With the erosion of segregation, the southern political landscape was altered significantly as millions of African Americans registered to vote, mostly as Democrats, and millions of whites consequently switched to the Republican party. As political scientists Black and Black put it, "The breadth of the Democratic collapse is staggering. It would be difficult to find comparable instances in American political history of such a rapid and comprehensive desertion of an established majority party by an entire region."[3]

And the Southern Baptist Convention's reaction has taken the form of a successful take-over by a well-organized, New Right-aligned faction. The movements led by Jerry Falwell and Pat Robertson were weak in the Deep South, plausibly because the Southern Baptist Convention was so strong. Success of the New Right therefore required that the SBC be co-opted, something that was easy to do given the somewhat casual structure of the Convention's bylaws.

The pretense of theological disagreement should be exposed by now; the inerrancy shibboleth, with its highly selective biblical literalism, is but a cover for a kind of controlled political mobilization. Playing on a powerful combination of theological, political, and emotional insecurities, using sex in classic fashion to attract attention, New Right leaders have skillfully manipulated the male-oriented tribal authoritarianism of the Old Testament to support their own political agenda.

When placed in this context, the storms of the last few years lose their bewildering quality and become comprehensible. First, trustworthy people (mostly men, but also a few of their agreeable wives) were placed in all possible important posts, as trustees of the seminaries and agencies. In every case a person's stated theological position was less important than his or her fidelity to the fundamentalist cause. Nonaligned conservatives and inerrantists were replaced with fundamentalist supporters, even if this meant, as the bottom of the barrel was approached, the candidacy of some with very weak backgrounds.

The Shape of the Take-over

Where have these new leaders led? Southeastern Seminary was thought to be a center of liberal opposition; the opportunity came along for a particularly brutal assault on administration and faculty. A coup was effected to widespread attention outside the denomination, American Association of University Professors (AAUP) censure, doubt about accreditation, and a disastrous decline in enrollment. There was continuing pressure on churches with women deacons, would-be women pastors, and the divorced. In addition there was tighter scrutiny of prospective missionaries and their possible deviations. Discipline was tightened up and down, including bold assertions of pastoral authority, particularly in the infamous "priesthood of believers" resolution, aiding pastors who wished to lead their congregations into political action.

If Southern Baptists were to become an effective element in the New Right movement, fundamentalists also would have to control the Southern Baptist voice in Washington, the agency that lobbies Congress and the White House and makes public pronouncements about what policies Southern Baptists favor. For fifty years that voice was the Baptist Joint Committee on Public Affairs, a consortium representing nine Baptist denominations, including several black groups, and inevitably led by Southern Baptists due to their size and resources. The director and counsel of the BJCPA, both Southern Baptists, would not lobby for New Right causes—the Bork nomination and a vetoed Civil Rights Restoration Act conspicuously—and on most issues defended the historic Baptist commitment to church-state separation. As Arthur Farnsley's chapter in this volume suggests, the fundamentalist leadership tried a variety of tactics to weaken, restrict the freedom of, pack, supplant, then defund completely the BJCPA. Finally the relationship was severed and fundamentalists got their own new and powerful voice, backed with denominational money.

At the other agencies and seminaries there was increased secrecy and nervousness about academic, press, and professional freedom. As pressure for doctrinal conformity grew, the fundamentalist leadership even flirted with the idea of its own accrediting agency, like a corporation having its own auditors. Respected journalists at the Baptist Press were removed, and the head of the Sunday School Board was pushed into premature retirement. Board-staff boundaries eroded as trustees involved themselves in personnel decisions at all levels. Those incumbents who could not because of their prominence be forced out easily were harassed, needled, and kept on the defensive in the hope that they would retire early or become neutralized or paralyzed. Meanwhile across the denomination, baptisms and receipts were just about flat, and several big Baptist universities loosened denominational ties to prevent take-over.

Southern Baptists and Southern Culture

The background to the SBC's current controversy reaches deeply into the past. Historically, vast numbers of Southern Baptists have been economic marginals, those who had most to lose from the competition of black labor both before and after slavery. Before the Civil War, however, there were also some with a stake in the slave system, as either owners or potential owners of slaves. And there were always some who were urban and educated, who either adopted the southern point of view during the polemic over slavery or left the denomination. The Southern Baptist Convention as a denomination was born in the midst of this polemic, and, indeed, because of it. Resenting northern pressure to disqualify slave owners as missionaries, it forced a test case and then separated from the denomination in 1845. (Two other big evangelical churches divided about the same time over the same cause; both have been reconciled nationally: Methodists before World War II and Presbyterians during the 1980s.)

The 1840s were also a peak time of white evangelical activity among blacks. Many thousands of slaves were persuaded into white churches, where they worshipped in segregated sections or in the balconies. After the war they were pushed out, sometimes with help in founding their own churches. At the Southern Baptist annual meeting in 1869, it took a day and a half to dispose of the issue—and of the blacks, now in a position (they thought) to contemplate social equality. In describing this event, historian Kenneth Bailey points out that the importance of this debate to Southern Baptist—and southern—history has been neglected or denied by Southern Baptist social historians, even by "race relations" specialists and ethicists, as they have interpreted this and other related aspects of their past in their own way.

The Southern Baptist role in Reconstruction and the imposition of Jim Crow raise interesting questions about subjects and objects. The overwhelming mass of Southern Baptists were the tenant farmers and, later, mill workers who, according to populist thinking, were themselves the victims of the Great

Race Settlement as their claims to economic justice were bought off with the chimera of white supremacy. Social equality with blacks and the possibility of intermarriage were prevented by segregation of public accommodations, job reservation obviated direct economic competition, and literacy requirements deterred black voting from altering the system. Separate and vastly unequal schools were crucial to all of these processes.

There were also, however, Southern Baptists in the power structure, engineers of the new southern class system. During the populist upheaval in Alabama, the class cleavage among Baptists was exposed. Some Southern Baptists expressed their discontent by withholding donations to missions, donations that were received and administered by Southern Baptist "elites."[4] As part of their response, Southern Baptists largely rejected the Social Gospel reform movement, spreading in from the North, in favor of an emphasis on personal sins and vices and a new enthusiasm for otherworldly theology.

Any more than a minimal concern for the living, schooling, or working conditions of blacks or for their legal and political rights was masked largely by the necessity of maintaining white solidarity. The national Southern Baptist meetings passed resolutions deploring lynching even as Southern Baptist pastors officiated at Ku Klux Klan funerals. Southern Baptist women, however, pioneered work with black women on a more human level.

The few prophetic Southern Baptist voices, noting the common misery of blacks and their own poor whites, preached of legal rights, but not of social equality. Pressure came from the margins, from groups like the global Baptist World Alliance; but their efforts were rejected as meddling by Southern Baptists in the United States.

Then, in the midst of a second decade of agricultural depression, the New Deal brought a modest ration of economic help to the most desperately needy, and the second segregated World War brought boom to some southern areas. Postwar, President Truman, a Southern Baptist, integrated the armed services and proposed doing the same for federal employment. There were a few Southern Baptist responses to the currents in the air, with the seminaries officially desegregated in the early fifties, along with some of the state-convention-sponsored colleges. And some patient, low-key concern by social ethicists was present, as well.

The Brown decision in 1954 and its aftermath were, of course, traumatic for Southern Baptists. Although the denomination's annual meeting passed resolutions of endorsement, unofficial responses were quite the opposite. The denomination spanned the center-to-right part of the southern spectrum; many of the few pastors on the left lost their churches, and many pastors and laity left the denomination completely. Southern specialist Marshall Frady complained, "Whatever became of the moderates? . . . Where was the spirit of Christian brotherhood? . . . Where was the Southern Baptist Convention?"[5] Taylor Branch described the uproar when Martin Luther King, Jr., spoke at the Southern Baptist Theological Seminary:

> So sensitive was King's name . . . that the white Southern Baptist Convention forced its seminary to apologize for allowing King to discuss religion on the Louisville campus. Within the church, this simple invitation was a racial and theological heresy, such that churches across the South rescinded their regular donations to the seminary. "Steps have been taken to help prevent the recurrence of this kind of error," announced one of the trustees, pastor of the First Baptist Church of Montgomery, Alabama.[6]

By the late 1960s, the topic that was convulsing the entire region was the subject of so much compromise at the national meetings that the resolutions sounded nearly incoherent and incomprehensible. The white South, and Southern Baptists, reacted to the whole trauma by flight from city neighborhoods that were "in transition," establishing "Christian schools," defecting to the Republican party, and becoming deeply involved in a politico-religious amalgam called the New Right.

Southern Baptists, the New Right, and the Politics of Race

As a typical reactionary movement, an identity-group whose presumed cultural control is threatened attempted to redefine the conditions of membership. For Southern Baptists it was no longer enough to be evangelical, conservative in theology, and grounded in biblical authority—inerrancy became the shibboleth. It was, of course, an inerrancy that focused on excluding women from the pulpit and other positions of authority, defined everything from homosexual "perversions" to sex education as threatening to "traditional family values," and found new devices for segregating blacks within the denomination.

For many Southern Baptists, the essential appeal of the New Right agenda, and the Reagan-Bush programs that have been in reciprocal relationship with it, is the construction of a vanished imaginary South, an authoritarian world in which women, children, and blacks kept their places. Southern Baptists moved upward in the class structure after World War II, enabled by that glorious one-time era of economic growth and upward mobility from which they especially benefited (for reasons embedded in regional economic history). They confidently expected to inherit the leadership and representation of the whole South, to take their places as modern Bourbons. But they were cheated out of that legacy by the Supreme Court, and, in their frustration, have struck back in hurt, confusion, and anger.

The ways in which discontents old and new have been blended in this movement can be seen in the issues at its core. At a Southern Baptist Christian Life Commission conference in Atlanta, in March 1982, Jerry Falwell was a guest speaker. During the question period after his talk, he was asked, "Why the New Right now?" He replied with reference to three great Supreme Court decisions, each roughly a decade apart: school desegregation in 1954, prohibition of Bible reading and prayer in the schools in the early 1960s, and the abortion decision of 1973. Each decision provoked fresh outrage, but was also linked to the others in complex ways.

When the New Right came to national prominence in the late 1970s and Reagan became its spokesman in 1980, the color-related issues were clearly part of the agenda. Richard Viguerie listed the agenda as "busing, abortion, pornography, education, traditional biblical moral values, and quotas."[7] Lincoln Caplan summarized the Reagan social agenda as "eliminating abortion, affirmative action, school busing, and some established rights of criminal suspects; permitting school prayer; and so on."[8] Greenhaw's version: the "social issues of right-to-life, anti-busing, capital punishment, and family protection."[9] Allen Hunter pointed out that "the silent majority . . . excludes blacks, not Catholics . . . [T]he rhetoric of Christianity is a way of saying white without mentioning race."[10]

Modern southern Republicans have adapted the old messages. As political scientists Black and Black stated, "There are carefully calibrated and relatively subtle racial appeals."[11] Roger Wilkins, then at the Institute of Policy Studies, was more direct: "Ronald Reagan's dirty little secret is that he has found a way to make racism palatable and politically potent again." [12] Historian David Bennett felt that "they [today's reactionaries] sometimes traffic in the code words . . . attacking 'welfare chiselers' and 'urban rioters'—they have no need for the divisive rhetoric of the old days of southern white supremacy. . . . But they do provide an explanation for the defeats, disappointments, and social disorders of the recent past." [13]

But after the first few years of the Reagan administration, references to desegregation and related issues—busing and affirmative action, for instance—went underground. Thus Reagan's letter to the Southern Baptist Convention annual meeting in Atlanta in 1986 mentioned only abortion and school prayer. The key year for the change seems to have been 1982. An IRS ruling had denied tax exemptions to institutions practicing racial discrimination. Congress, on several occasions, could have changed this but clearly chose not to. Bob Jones University and Goldsboro Christian School challenged the ruling in the late 1970s, and the attorney general's office, at the time, defended the IRS. Then, under Reagan-appointed personnel, and the special urging of Senators Trent Lott and Strom Thurmond (both Southern Baptists), the Justice Department reversed its position and defended discrimination. The furor over this about-face, and later over the Senate's unsuccessful attempt to prohibit busing, led to a politically astute effort to disguise that portion of the Reagan agenda. Symbolic issues began to be used instead—the Martin Luther King, Jr., holiday, South African sanctions, the "welfare trap," statehood for the District of Columbia.

In addition the vaunted "family" issues have been used in such a way as to use blacks once again as a negative reference group. Pat Robertson argued in a *Sojourners* interview that "the home . . . is the basic unit of the church. . . . You have to have some unit, and the home/family has been it, so far. But when this goes, you have the corollary problems. . . . You have the flotsam and jetsam of the ghetto where young people don't know who their parents are. . . ." [14] Bruce Fein, a lawyer and New Right ideologue, explained, "If you look at the cultural ethos of blacks, the numbers of those who are illegitimate, the numbers of those raised in single-parent families, the drug trafficking, the numbers in jail, obviously you are going to have a difficult time in maintaining minority enrollment in professional schools." [15] The most egregious example was Bill Moyers's 1985 CBS documentary entitled "The Vanishing Family," in which unmarried black parents in Newark were essentially ridiculed. Despite former Southern Baptist Moyers's supposed liberalism, he was not able to empathize with the hopelessness of these individuals' economic circumstances enough to understand that marriage is something people have to be able to afford. Many blacks, especially feminists, were heartsick.[16] The emphasis on family issues, then, has the advantage of reinforcing the importance of the institution that is the last bastion of white male authority.

The Reagan administration, with ideological contributions and political support from the religious New Right, used every available means in its assault on civil rights—the presidential decree, the administrative regulation, and the power of the Justice Department (which, for example, in the fall of 1988 offered Georgia school districts federal aid for legal preparation costs toward a return to neighborhood—thus, segregated—school assignments). The most powerful weapon has been the federal budget process and its impact on various health and welfare programs, programs that most directly affect the life and death status of the poor (who are, of course, disproportionately black). Bensman and Vidich call this "budgetary racism,"[17] and a crucial ideological mechanism in this effort was termed the New Federalism. At bottom it was a return to the states of the most important programs affecting black life chances, a plan of wide appeal in the South for historic reasons, and a vital part of the Republican "Southern strategy."

The whole symbolism of states' rights and the role of state power in black-white relationships in the past need not be belabored. William Riker's statement is classic: "The main beneficiary [of federalism] throughout American history has been the Southern whites, who have been given the freedom to oppress Negroes, first as slaves and later as a depressed caste. . . . The significance of federal benefits to economic interests pales beside the significance of benefits to the Southern segregationist whites."[18] More fine-grained analyses show how southern congressmen manipulated New Deal welfare legislation so that federal regulations would not interfere with local control of the black (and sometimes white) labor supply. The pattern is striking: the administration of programs that applied to agricultural workers (as Social Security does not) was left largely to the states.[19] Workplace safety regulations are still, in fact, under state control.

Reagan introduced his ideas of the New Federalism in a speech in 1976 and enlarged on the theme during the 1980 campaign. Close analysis indicates that much of the rhetoric about bringing government closer to the people was exactly that, rhetoric. One summary: "The President's actions indicate that the preferred level of government is simply the level perceived as most able and amenable to bring about a specific result or to further some social value of the President's choosing."[20] Municipalities had been emphasized by both Nixon and Ford in their decentralization efforts; but they were largely bypassed during the Reagan years. "The level is most often the state level, . . . no matter the fact that local government is closer to the people. This is not because Reagan loves state government more, he simply loves both the federal government and giving authority to the teeming masses of the cities less."[21] Most of the largest cities, of course, now have black governments and problems and demands. Although federalism and curtailment of federal power were important Reagan goals, his administration did not hesitate to override them when it suited other policy objectives, such as operation of nuclear power plants.

The principal mechanism for Reagan's New Federalism was the Omnibus Budget and Reconciliation Act of 1981 (OBRA), called by some the most important piece of domestic legislation since the Social Security Act of 1935. It took fifty-seven health and welfare programs, folded them into nine giant block grants, handed them to the states, and cut federal fiscal support by 25 percent. As economist Robert Lekachman wrote, "The politics of block grants are cynical and divisive, setting group against group, cities against states, and race against race."[22] Directing implementation of the Reagan plan were Senators Strom Thurmond, Bennett Johnston, and Jesse Helms (three Southern Baptists), Senator Orrin Hatch (a Mormon), and the Methodist technocrat David Stockman. Later budgets proposed further cuts, but Congress blocked most of them as the impact of OBRA was felt in their home constituencies.

Some of the Reagan administration policies have resulted in a very large increase in working-age rural poverty, with blacks and southerners among the most persistent rural poor. Lloyd Bentsen charged in his 1988 campaign speeches that federal spending for rural development was cut by 58 percent during the Reagan years, and the Office of Rural Development was abolished.[23] Summary figures also show that federal funds for low-income programs were cut 54 percent between 1981 and 1988.[24] Although total spending for so-called social programs increased during the Reagan years, the additional

funds went overwhelmingly to entitlement, or non-means-tested, programs—
Social Security, Medicare, and veterans' and civil service retirement benefits.

In contrast to the Reagan rhetoric of "the safety net" and re-targeting to
"the truly needy," the facts show that over the years, "those programs most
clearly intended to be redistributive fared the worst," as Nathan and Doolittle
put it.[25] Marian Palley concludes that "cutbacks disproportionately affected
both single women with young children—who have a greater risk of being in
poverty than any other population sub-class—and older women."[26] The Center for Budget and Policy Priorities concurs: "The group hit most severely by
the decline in the anti-poverty effectiveness of government programs has been
female-headed families with children."[27] As Lyndon Johnson "'reconceived'
poverty in a manner that allowed him to construct a domestic program whose
primary beneficiaries were urban blacks,"[28] so Reagan reconceived federalism
in a way that allowed program constrictions whose primary victims were
blacks, both urban and rural. Conservative southern whites were handed
back, in effect, power that the war on poverty had taken away.   .

Although Reagan's primary impact on black Americans was economic,
he also took on the Civil Rights Commission (CRC) itself, firing pro-minority
holdovers (unprecedented in itself, because the CRC was supposed to be
nonpolitical) and replacing them with weak or purposefully inactive people.
Congress became so annoyed at the CRC's mismanagement and ineffective-
ness that it cut the agency budget severely. It remains impotent and useless.

Even more important, Reagan sought a fundamental reorientation in the
Supreme Court. The decisions of his three appointees and their conservative
allies during the 1988-89 term "dispelled much of any remaining doubt about
whether former President Ronald Reagan accomplished his goal of moving
the Court in a more conservative direction on civil rights."[29] In March 1988
Reagan vetoed the important Civil Rights Restoration Act, although it became
law through congressional override.

"In recent times," according to Black and Black, "no politician has exploited the mismatch in party symbols more skillfully than Ronald Reagan, who
is much more conventionally 'southern' in his style and practice of politics than
either Lyndon Johnson or Jimmy Carter. Shrewdly blending themes from the
entrepreneurial individualistic culture and the traditionalist heritage, Reagan's
positions on most issues . . . appear eminently reasonable to most middle-class

southern whites."[30] These programs, then, are important factors in explaining why so many Southern Baptists, eminently reasonable middle-class southern whites, became Republicans, voted for Reagan and Bush with such enthusiasm, and ushered fundamentalist leaders into their denomination's hierarchy.

George Bush inherited the Reagan legacy, and his record suggested a continuation of its policies with only a change in the style and tone of the covering rhetoric. Six months after he took office, when the Supreme Court handed down five decisions seriously weakening established civil rights laws, Bush let it be known that he felt no need for legislative correction and subsequently vetoed such action, only reversing himself as a former Ku Klux Klan leader ran for office wearing a Republican label. He nominated candidates for the crucial Justice Department civil rights post who had almost no experience in this complex field of litigation. He left the Civil Rights Commission without direction. And he allowed the whole focus of "civil rights" to be moved away from blacks, ethnics, and females to include the elderly, disabled, and AIDS patients—thereby diffusing and weakening the framework for future action. His budget proposals reinforced the power of the states to bypass urban (minority) problems. However, he also ignored the Republican commitment to federalism when it came to the funding of abortion for poor women, or to support for legislation enabling Bible study in public schools (even at the risk of overriding local school boards). The anti-black impact remains implicit. It does not, obviously, explain everything, but a revealing amount of energy and ingenuity has gone into concealing and denying it.

For some Southern Baptists, there is still a lurking belief in the inherent inferiority of blacks, and, thus, a justification for denying them equality and the opportunity to operate freely in American culture. For others there is a lingering horror of miscegenation. Like hundreds of millions in other parts of the world, they feel that marriage is much too important to be left to the individuals involved. Endogamy (marriage within a specific group) is enforced by propinquity and private exclusiveness, if no longer by law. So as schools and public accommodations, particularly recreational facilities, became desegregated in the South, churches were the last protected places. Consequently the growth of the Christian school movement, and the enormous investment of southern churches in basketball courts, saunas, jogging tracks, restaurants, and movie theaters (the recent $35 million addition to the Second Baptist Church of Houston has all of these, as well as a nine-hundred-pupil K-12 school). These expanded church-sponsored facilities are open only to a few carefully chosen blacks.

Building on these fears, but anxious not to express them overtly, the New Right and the Reagan and Bush administrations have, with considerable skill, disguised the anti-black strategy that is part of their appeal. Enough Southern Baptists have responded positively to these messages to ensure the capitulation of the convention to New Right forces and the mobilization of the SBC for grass-roots lobbying through local churches. They have been willing to politicize their religion in order to make claims on the larger polity as an ethnic group. The fundamentalist-dominated Southern Baptist Public Affairs Committee's support for the nomination of Robert Bork to the Supreme Court, and for Reagan's veto of the Civil Rights Restoration Act, are most telling evidence of this assertion. In both cases, intriguingly, the issues of race and abortion were carefully fused so that opposition would not be perceived as racist.

As Marjorie Williams described it in the *Washington Post,* the Southern Baptist Convention has a similar problem: "To scoop up [the] disaffected . . . who are revolting against the pace of change in the South—without appearing to appeal to bigotry."[31] As the late Republican party chairman Lee Atwater stated, "Making black voters welcome in the Republican Party is my pre-eminent goal; . . . our outreach to minority voters is not a short-term tactic. It is a longterm political necessity and, more than that, a moral imperative."[32] Atwater was "reaching out," *Boston Globe* columnist Thomas Oliphant commented, "with only the barest minimum of a mea culpa for his party's embrace of racial politics over the last twenty-five years and in the 1988 campaign."[33]

Race Relations and the New Southern Baptists

But the Southern Baptist Convention's problem is considerably greater in duration, and the nostra culpa would have to be of more massive dimensions. If the convention wants to continue to grow, it can no longer depend on large families and country churches. The ominous figures for decreasing family size and the stark demography of southern urbanism indicate that Southern Baptists must reach out to blacks for new members. They must also reach out to the deaf, to Native Americans, to Koreans and Vietnamese, and to millions of

Hispanics in their heartland—but all of these present only the problem of language. Just as bilingual education should be transitional to full competence in English and eventual mainstreaming, so there is a reason for language missions as a bridge to eventual undifferentiated participation. But with blacks there is no language barrier, and still Southern Baptists insist on segregating them in separate bureaucracies: the Black Church Extension Fellowship or a Black Unit in the Foreign Mission Board, and putting on conferences on Resources of Black Baptist Churches or for Black Pastors' Wives.

The comparative historian George Frederickson, expert on slave systems, points out that "race" is losing its saliency, and "culture" is supplanting it—as more acceptable and less redolent of the past and of discredited biological determinism. Emmanuel McCall, former head of Black Church Relations for the Southern Baptist Home Mission Board, illustrates this trend: "The gospel was presented contextually (in the language, culture and traditions of the hearers). . . . Many Anglo churches have seriously attempted to reach black people in their communities; . . . others have failed because people in black communities often prefer a cultural lifestyle different than in Anglo churches where they feel uncomfortable. . . ."[34] This approach places the responsibility for separatism on blacks, as Southern Baptists did after the end of slavery. But the record suggests otherwise.

There is something very moving about this huge organization in its struggle with its past. It is not simple to contemplate relinquishing one of the main sources of group identity, especially when the future seems uncertain and insecure. Signs of the struggle are everywhere: efforts to define racism as a spiritual problem; the recipe for Race Relations Sunday to "focus . . . think about . . . consider . . . and find ways to be God's servants to bring about racial harmony"[35]—not, note, justice or equity, let alone equality; and the defensive enumeration of the efforts to include blacks in other than menial capacities. If the identity of one group has been based on the exclusion of another, if people are encouraged to develop a sense of pride because of what they are not, the effort for whatever reason to include the not-group will be perceived as threatening—a zero-sum game if there ever was one. In a stratified society, the group immediately above the one whose status is rising will be the most aggrieved. So the historic class position of most Southern Baptists explains their special pain.

The new Southern Baptist fundamentalist leadership, like the Republican party, has made elaborate efforts to indicate a new openness on black-white relations, principally with a conference, hastily organized as its conveners acknowledged, over the Martin Luther King, Jr., holiday in January 1989. The official audio tapes and photographs of the event presented a curious record.

From the black speakers, there were some moving anecdotes of personal pain, of condescension and exclusion and hurt, and some affirmation of gradual change, but a long future agenda. Emmanuel McCall seemed to accept a completely segregated status for black churches within the denomination; some of the other black officials did not. McCall cited, with pride, the fact that a former assistant, black, was now on the planning committee at the Home Mission Board. Only because of his presence have the ethnic and black departments been included in the Board's projections of its major evangelical efforts for the next decade. McCall took pains to contrast, as monolithic wholes, the worship styles of "the white community" and "the black community" as reasons for separate approaches to them. But then he took further pains to describe the identical ranges of variation within each of the two. He raised some hard issues: "If we are planting churches in the black communities only because we do not want them in ours . . . if the racial mentality of the federal government of the last eight years is influencing the agenda of the Southern Baptist Convention. . . ."[36]

There was also a mixture of opinion from white speakers. Some, such as Carolyn Weatherford (now Crumpler), former head of the Woman's Missionary Union (WMU), and Foy Valentine, former head of the Christian Life Commission, spoke of past experiences that had made them different from southern norms, and of prophetic roles they had played throughout their lives as Southern Baptists. Weatherford's account confirmed the advance role played by the women's organization, whose financial independence from the SBC allowed it to be light years ahead on this issue. From other speakers there was more than a whiff of defensiveness—elaborate enumerations of the number and function of black employees, for example, and little stories about "fine black families" or about the speakers' cleaning women—none of which brought any laughter. The condescension is hard to abandon: even the well-meaning Dr. Richard Land (then newly installed fundamentalist head of the Christian Life Commission) described how, in planning this very conference on "race relations," he called Emmanuel McCall, the most senior and best known of all the black executives in the Southern Baptist Convention, to ask him for his ideas. Said Land, "That gives you a measure of the stature McCall has in this Convention on this issue." Lloyd Elder, head of the Sunday School Board, responded to a question about publishing more black writers with a plea for "some really disciplined prose."

The really hard questions were asked mostly by Sid Smith, head of the Black Church Development unit in the Sunday School Board. Baptist Press featured two of them in its syndicated coverage: "How long before a black is president of the Southern Baptist Convention?" and "How long before there is a rainbow of God's people on Southern Baptist Convention boards and agencies?" Baptist Press did not, however, publicize Smith's "difficult question" about intermarriage: "We need a Christian response to it," Smith said. He also reminded his audience of other sensitive issues—"investing with a conscience," "utilizing minority vendors . . . especially banks," and "multi-racial social justice causes" such as the Martin Luther King, Jr., holiday (against which Southern Baptist Senator Jesse Helms of North Carolina has been extremely outspoken).

The Southern Baptist Convention lost many of its progressive people during the 1960s, because it resisted change. Like the Republican party, they risk losing more now if they change too fast or go too far. As one member of the audience asked, "Is what we are learning about churches in transition [i.e., white flight] going to become a Convention in transition? . . . When and if we have a black President, will Anglo Saxons leave?" (McCall ducked the implications of this with a plea to blacks to get involved at all levels.)

These conference tapes indicated that all the agencies, except possibly WMU, have blacks working only on black issues. The real question (as it is with women) is whether Southern Baptists can accept blacks in authority over whites. No integrated church congregations were mentioned except in northern urban ministries. The "language" missions are really irrelevant as examples; Southern Baptists do not have a solid 150-year history of fear, hostility, and discrimination toward Koreans or Vietnamese. Later events indicate a resegregation of agency personnel and a restriction of national SBC work with blacks to liaison with black churches. A policy of subsidies to train black pastors and build black churches may engender black Southern Baptist growth, but only at the expense of established black denominations, which will clearly cause resentment.

The other major historic southern denominations have aggressively integrated at the highest levels. The Presbyterian Church (USA) elected a black woman as moderator in 1989, and the Episcopalians a black woman bishop. The United Methodists have forty-nine active bishops; ten of them are black, some serving in the Southeast. Maybe someday Southern Baptists will start living in a truly integrated denomination, with not only a black president, but many black trustees on the boards of the seminaries and agencies; many black professionals working with all aspects of Southern Baptist life, not just black issues; many black senior pastors in integrated churches; and many black professors at all of the seminaries, teaching theology and church history and ethics, as well as black sociology (whatever that may be). And people will have stopped paying attention. But that day is a long way off, and unlikely to be hastened as long as the denomination is yoked to the New Right.

The New Right leaders have aligned the Southern Baptist Convention solidly with the pro-life movement, pushing the abortion issue into as many agency activities and aspects of public policy as their imaginations can conceive. Although much thought has gone into discouraging people from interpreting their stand as antifeminist, the fact remains that those religious denominations in the anti-abortion forefront are also those most adamantly opposed to the admission of women to their principal religious statuses (Roman Catholics, Orthodox Jews, Missouri Synod Lutherans, and Mormons, as well as the dominant fundamentalists of the Southern Baptist Convention). These efforts and the intensity of the anti-abortion movement are clearly in reaction to organized strivings of women for more autonomy and authority in public roles.

Prayer in schools (and before high school sports events) and the related issues of religious displays on public property and the treatment of evolution in public school textbooks raise questions about the cultural diversity of American life and the control of its expression. As the United States and the South become more heterogeneous, the placid hegemony that used to be taken for granted is challenged, and the potential losers fight back.

Meanwhile the moderates have slowly but increasingly surely moved in another direction. Very reluctant to confirm a schism, they have at least set up a separate coordinating structure with some female leadership; organized alternative mechanisms for press relations, ethics analysis, and missions activity; and established a consortial seminary framework that includes plans for blacks to teach, among other things, theology. All of these structures are open to women, blacks (and other minorities), and divorced persons, although specific welcome of homosexuals, an issue of great concern to most other American Protestant groups, has not yet been demonstrated. Cooperative links have also been forged with the Progressive National Baptists, a black group formed by M. L. King and others during the civil rights revolution of the sixties. Some of the tentative quality of these moves is due, of course, to uncertainty about finances. But the contrast in outlook and emphasis with the fundamentalists is clear.

Moderate voices were absent or suppressed at the 1991 annual meeting. Featured speakers included George Bush, Oliver North, and Tim LaHaye; and Jerry Falwell was there. The resolutions were right out of the New Right agenda; the resolution claiming that the Bible authorizes sex only within marriage seems as out of touch with American life as does the Roman Catholic prohibition of artificial contraception. The battle for control of the norms for family structure is almost obsessive in its intensity. Beverly LaHaye, president of Concerned Women of America and featured token female at the 1992 SBC Ethics Conference (entitled "Citizen Christians: Their Rights and Responsibilities"), said, "Everything we are doing right now is turning out to be a homosexual issue. . . . We are now being consumed by it."[37]

Conservatism on sexual issues makes the fundamentalists strange bedfellows with the Roman Catholics. As Catholic social activist George Wesolek put it, "Although some hate to admit it, Roman Catholic social activists may have more in common with Evangelicals than with mainstream Protestants. . . . Who, as it turns out, are our natural allies on sexual and family issues? The Evangelicals."[38] And, not surprisingly, priest-sociologist Andrew Greeley finds that analysis of one large-scale opinion survey makes "a persuasive though not absolutely certain case that Catholic 'conservatism' is motivated largely by negative attitudes toward changing roles for women; . . . the Catholics the church has been able to hold in orthodox sexual attitudes tend to be both racist and sexist."[39]

These issues are dividing religions all over the world. As the force of the market is felt, Islam, Judaism, and the various Far Eastern traditions all face the same issues and are being fractured. The connection between institutional religion and the state, the use of religious affiliation as a ground for social and political identity, and the transformation of family systems with changes in economic organization are splintering all these ancient movements and leading to the same dramatic struggles for control.

Some of these groups, however, including American Roman Catholics, also have "justice-and-peace" activists, who work effectively on issues such as human rights, nuclear proliferation, and global distribution of economic resources. Southern Baptist groups have not made these a priority, nor did they (as far as is retrievable from national press accounts) take a position against the Persian Gulf War, as did some Catholics and many mainstream Protestant groups in the United States.

Once more many southern whites, especially males, feel beleaguered, victimized, betrayed by cultural change. Not long ago Strom Thurmond could get away with saying, "The white people of the South are the greatest minority in the nation."[40] The present Southern Baptist Convention leadership will pass, but the turmoil that allowed them to come to power will enmesh the Southern Baptist Convention in reaction until real economic and political change has penetrated their society. The moderates have moved on.

There was once not only a Counter-Reformation but a Catholic Reformation, and then, not only a Vatican I but, after a generation, a *Rerum Novarum*. The Southern Baptists, with their great resources and the confidence that comes from their sense of divine approval, have the capacity for the same achievement. Although appearing to stand firmly with their gaze to the rear, their heels dug in, they may find the strength to move ahead, to take their place in meeting the challenges of the newest South. Or they will stop being Baptists.

Notes

1. See Ferenc M. Szasz, *The Divided Mind of Protestant America* (University: Univ. of Alabama Press), 182, on movements in the 1920s.
2. Roy Reed, "Mississippi: 20 Years of Wide Racial Change," *New York Times,* 18 Aug. 1983, B14.
3. Earl Black and Merle Black, *Politics and Society in the South* (Cambridge: Harvard Univ. Press, 1987), 267-68.
4. J. Wayne Flynt, *Dixie's Forgotten People: The South's Poor Whites* (Bloomington: Indiana Univ. Press, 1979).
5. Marshall Frady, "God and Man in the South," *Atlantic Monthly,* Jan. 1967, 37.

6. Taylor Branch, *Parting the Waters: America in the King Years, 1954-1963* (New York: Simon & Schuster, 1988), 488.

7. Cited in James A. Reichley, *Religion in American Public Life* (Washington, D.C.: Brookings Institution, 1985), 319.

8. Lincoln Caplan, "The Tenth Justice." *New Yorker,* 10 Aug. 1987, 31.

9. Wayne Greenhaw, *Elephants in the Cottonfields* (New York: Macmillan, 1982), 113.

10. Allen Hunter, "In the Wings: New Right Ideology and Organization," *Radical America* 15, nos. 1 and 2 (Spring 1981): 126.

11. Black and Black, *Politics and Society,* 271.

12. Roger Wilkins, "Smiling Racism," *The Nation,* 3 Nov. 1984, 437.

13. David Bennett, *The Party of Fear: From Nativist Movements to the New Right in American History* (Chapel Hill: Univ. of North Carolina Press, 1988), 390.

14. Pat Robertson, "Politics, Power, and the Christian Citizen," *Sojourners,* Sept. 1979, 3.

15. Quoted in Pamela Reynolds, "After Bakke, Minority Students Still Flagging," *Danbury News-Times,* 5 July 1988, 8.

16. See "Scapegoating the Black Family," *Nation,* July 1989, 24, 31.

17. Joseph Bensman and Arthur J. Vidich, *American Society, Revised: The Welfare State and Beyond* (South Hadley, Mass.: Bergin & Garvey, 1987), viii.

18. William H. Riker, *Federalism: Origin, Operation, Significance* (Boston: Little, Brown, 1964), 115.

19. Lee J. Alston and Joseph P. Ferrie. "Labor Costs, Paternalism and Loyalty in Southern Agriculture: A Constraint on the Growth of the Welfare State." *Journal of Economic History* 45 (1985): 95-117.

20. Lester M. Salamon and Michael S. Lund, eds., *The Reagan Presidency and the Governing of America* (Washington, D.C.: Urban Institute Press, 1984), 443.

21. Salamon and Lund, *The Reagan Presidency,* 444.

22. Robert Lekachman, *Greed Is Not Enough* (New York: Pantheon, 1982), 99.

23. Warren Weaver, Jr., "Bentsen Accuses Republicans of Farm 'Mismanagement'." *New York Times,* 10 Sept. 1988, 9.

24. Center for Budget and Policy Priorities, press release, 2 Sept. 1988, "Impact of Government Benefits Declines, Adds to Number of Poor Families," 2 (Washington, D.C.).

25. Richard P. Nathan and Fred C. Doolittle. "Federal Grants: Giving and Taking Away," *Political Science Quarterly* 100, no. 1: 69.

26. Marian Palley, "Shifts in the Distribution of Aid," in Salamon and Lund, *The Reagan Presidency,* 452.

27. Center for Budget and Policy Priorities, press release, 5.

28. Robert Huckfeldt and Carol Weitzel Kohfeld, *Race and the Decline of Class in American Politics* (Urbana: Univ. of Illinois Press, 1989), 9.

29. Linda Greenhouse, "The Court's Shift to the Right," *New York Times,* 7 July 1989, 1.

30. Black and Black, *Politics and Society,* 315.

31. Marjorie Williams, "The Bad Boy of American Politics," *Washington Post National Weekly,* 27 Nov.-3 Dec. 1989, 8.

32. "Toward a G.O.P. Rainbow." *New York Times,* 26 Feb. 1989, E23.

33. Thomas Oliphant, "Atwater Woos Blacks," *Danbury News-Times,* 27 Aug. 1989, B2.

34. "Black Church Extension Continues." *Missions USA* (Mar.-Apr. 1989) 21.

35. Robert Parham, "Room for all at God's Table," *Biblical Recorder,* 3 Feb. 1989, 3.

36. Quotations from the conference in this and following paragraphs are from the audio tapes of the proceedings and the official press release from the Baptist Press.

37. Cited in "Religious Right Rallies for Gay-Rights Battles," *Christianity Today,* 22 July 1991, 38.

38. George A. Wesolek, "A New Reality—A New Alliance," *America,* 9 Nov. 1991, 340, 341.

39. Andrew M. Greeley, "Who Are the Catholic Conservatives?" *America,* 22 Sept. 1991, 160.

40. Cited in Greenhaw, *Elephants in the Cottonfields,* 227.

CHAPTER 9

RACE RELATIONS: CHANGING PATTERNS AND PRACTICES

Walker L. Knight

The question was never, Was the Southern Baptist Convention racist?, for the denomination was born in 1845 when slaveholding missionaries were denied appointment by the Triennial Convention. Rather the questions were: How racist was the SBC a century and a half later? What forces were working for change? How does a major denomination change something so basic to its identity? Can a "people's" denomination ever rise above its culture? And, most important for the 1990s, Did the changes significantly fuel the fundamentalist renascence of the 1980s?

The SBC had been able to resist all efforts to change the denomination's segregationist positions previous to 1954, primarily because society had not changed. Baptists and Methodists, the two largest denominations in the South, were aligned with the established leadership in the region. With the Supreme Court ruling in 1954 on public schools, however, forces were set in motion that would eventually change the South, the nation, and the SBC.

Since its origin in 1845, the SBC had sought to evangelize blacks, and had appointed white missionaries for the task. In fact before the SBC was organized, there were one hundred thousand black Baptists among the 350,000 Baptists of the South, but they were second class—balcony—members of the churches. After emancipation blacks organized their own churches, and in 1897 they formed the National Baptist Convention. At the time of a 1960 report, the National Baptist Convention had an estimated fifty thousand churches and nearly eight million members.

In 1845 the SBC instructed its Board of Domestic Missions to "take all prudent measures for the religious instruction of our colored population." The board, later named the Home Mission Board (HMB), worked extensively at this task, but always from a separated position. After the National Baptist Convention was formed, the board's work program was named Department of Work with National Baptists, even avoiding the use of the word *Negro.* The work aided black churches, trained black pastors, and helped evangelize blacks through revivals, vacation Bible schools, and other activities.

I discovered firsthand the reluctance of Southern Baptist leaders to deal directly with the prejudice of the denomination while I was director of the editorial department of the HMB. My primary responsibility was to edit *Home Missions Magazine.* I set the tone of my editorship during the first full year of my work—1960—when I published the first comprehensive look at the involvement of Southern Baptists with blacks. The report came from a study by the Advisory Council on Southern Baptist Work with Negroes. The council was formed in 1954, the year of the Supreme Court decision on school desegregation, and included a representative from each agency or institution in the SBC working with Negroes.

The study revealed extensive involvement of the denomination with blacks, but that involvement reflected the culture of the nation and, especially, of the South—separation of the races and a paternalistic approach to ministry. The report indicated more than five thousand Southern Baptist churches engaged in some type of activity with Negroes. One surprising figure in the report was that a third of the 654 associations reporting said they had black churches as members. State Baptist conventions affiliated with the SBC reported employing 125 workers, many of them black, who worked with the black churches.

All six of the denomination's seminaries reported that they were open to Negroes, but the operative word was *open,* for not all had black students. Blacks instead were encouraged to attend the American Baptist Seminary in Nashville, a school for blacks supported for the most part by Southern Baptists. It was operated by National Baptists but primarily financed by Southern Baptist money. Only seven of the 63 SBC colleges, junior colleges, academies and Bible schools were even open. The colleges and the SBC seminaries combined included only 150 black students, and a large number of these were from Africa or other mission fields. The report said that the Woman's Missionary Union, Brotherhood Commission, Christian Life Commission, Sunday School Board, Foreign Mission Board, and Home Mission Board had devoted "space in their periodicals to Christian attitudes and actions toward other races." The report was entirely positive, and it reflected the extent of SBC involvement, but it did not touch the extent of the prejudice that affected the membership and kept the races separate in local black and white churches.

Local Church Struggles

In a "people's" denomination, with locally autonomous churches, the front-line battles were local ones. But churches rarely integrated without incident, and pastors were not able to take public stands on racial matters without extreme pressure from their congregations. In the wake of the Supreme Court's 1954 ruling, for example, segregationists in Louisiana threatened in 1960 to close the public school system in favor of private schools. Although the tension was greatest in New Orleans, other communities were profoundly affected. In Baton Rouge fifty-three ministers, including thirteen Southern Baptists, signed a strongly worded "Affirmation of Basic Religious Principles." The statement and the ministers' signatures, published 7 May 1961 in the Baton Rouge *Morning Advocate,* affirmed God's creation of all persons in God's image, with superiority given to no group, as well as God's condemnation of all injustice. "It is impossible to love God without loving one's fellow man," it read. The statement also affirmed freedom of speech for all; urged moral responsibility to neighbors, the public, and the family; and asked for the improvement of relations among the races. In closing the statement asked that the public school system of the state be maintained, stated that every citizen possesses equal rights under law, and declared that discrimination on account of race or religion is a violation of divine law.

Charles McCullin, one of the Southern Baptist pastors who signed the statement, said publication of the affirmation brought a fire storm of reaction against each of the ministers. McCullin, and the others, were investigated by the FBI on more than one occasion. A significant number of members left the church where he was pastor. Obscene and insulting phone calls came at all hours. Opposition plagued him and his family for the years he remained at the church. For months a motion was made at each monthly church business meeting calling for his dismissal as pastor, until finally a motion passed that a dismissal motion would be in order only once a year. He could propose no new direction for the church without opposition, and although many remained faithful, the church never recovered from the loss of members and the attitudes of prejudice and distrust.

McCullin said all of the Southern Baptist pastors reported similar harassment, and eventually each one left the city because of it. He stayed for seven years, hoping to wear the opposition down or see a change in racist attitudes; but when change did not come, he accepted a position as director of Baptist Centers in New Orleans, employed by the Baptist HMB in Atlanta.

Churches attempting to open their membership to blacks met with mixed results. So rare was the action in the South that they often received national publicity in the process. In 1966, for example, Tattnall Square Baptist Church of Macon, Georgia, whose buildings were located adjacent to the campus of Mercer University, dismissed its pastor, minister of education, and minister of music because they had openly advocated the acceptance of blacks in worship and membership. Thomas J. Holmes, formerly on both the faculty and the administrative staff of Mercer University, had accepted the pastorate of Tattnall Square Church in December of 1964. He had been led to believe that the church would be open to blacks, but later found that the deacons, when faced in 1963 with the possibility that a student from Ghana—Sam Oni—might join, sent word that he would not be welcome. The pastor informed Oni of this, and Oni joined Vineville Baptist Church instead.

However, Holmes wrote in *Ashes for Breakfast: A Diary of Racism in an American Church,* "Oni felt himself bound on a historic mission. He was a convert of Baptist missionaries to his country. He had come to Mercer, the Georgia Baptist university, because a missionary and Mercer graduate had guided him there. He was preparing himself for a public service career in his native Ghana."[1] Oni in 1963 had broken the racial barrier at Mercer University, becoming the first black student at the school. He felt compelled, according to Holmes, to go to Tattnall Square Church. Holmes and the other ministers of the church supported his action. They worked with the church during 1965 and 1966 to create an inclusive, ministering congregation in tune with the needs of both Mercer students and the inner-city area where the church buildings were located. But they were not able to overcome the cultural resistance in such a short time.

When Oni appeared on the steps of the auditorium on 25 September, deacons blocked his way. They had been instructed by the deacon body to turn all Negroes away. He was forcibly dragged down the steps. The police were called, and they kept Oni in their car until he agreed to leave. Meanwhile the congregation inside the building was voting 250 to 189 to oust their three ministers. In the preface to his book, Holmes wrote, "The tragedy of this church is the nearly universal disgrace of the churches—they might have led the way to community, but, alas, they would not!"[2]

Not all reports from churches were entirely negative. In the late 1960s, in Decatur, Georgia, a small town of twenty thousand neighboring Atlanta, the movement of blacks from the inner city seeking better housing or from newly mechanized Georgia farms forced many all-white churches to face the racial issue in concrete terms in their own communities. Churches generally took one of four options: fleeing to the new all-white suburbs, remaining as a white island, staying in the community and changing, or disbanding.

Beginning in 1965, under the leadership of newly called pastor John Nichol, Oakhurst Baptist Church in Decatur chose to wrestle with staying and changing, one of the few Southern Baptist churches in the Atlanta area to do so at the time. The denomination provided no guidelines for a congregation facing such change. In fact during the decade to follow, the Atlanta Baptist Association was to lose more than forty churches to racial change: many disbanded, others moved. Many who stayed have been unable to reach newcomers to their communities, white or black, and remain today with aging memberships, slowing dying.

Oakhurst started its consideration of the issues from the position of strength, with an average of more than 650 attending Sunday school each week, and before the community near the buildings changed to 95 percent black. Nichol began to challenge the dominant white culture by preaching for years on the inclusive nature and mission of the church. This was coupled with a strong weekday ministry to the community, especially directed toward the increasing number of children: tutoring, skating parties, movies, vacation Bible school activities, an aggressive library ministry, well-baby clinics, boys' clubs, and other similar ministries.

The effort was costly and the struggle ugly at times, with threats of violence, obscene calls to the pastor, and months of tension. Through it all Nichol avoided any direct vote on racial matters, as the church gradually accepted blacks in all phases of its life, including membership. Nichol often told the congregation, "Whether or not to accept a person as a member because of color is

not up for votes, for we would be voting on whether or not to be church."
Members did vote in another way, however—hundreds left. The once-large con-
gregation fell from a membership of nearly twelve hundred to five hundred.
Staff was reduced, ministries were dropped, and building plans were abandoned.

The struggle, nevertheless, eventually contributed to the creation of
a refined, dedicated congregation taking seriously the nature and mission of
the church, creating its own covenant emphasizing God's leadership in the
making of an open and inclusive fellowship.[3] The church under Nichol and
the pastors who followed him, because of a willingness to run counter to
culture, eventually began to attract scores of socially aware young couples.
Nurseries were once again opened, and there was new energy to start creative ministries: a national hunger publication, *Seeds;* a shelter for the home-
less using the church buildings; an AIDS ministry; a group home for the men-
tally retarded; a mission to Cuban detainees at the Atlanta Federal Penitentiary;
and a refugee resettlement ministry. Office space was granted to many other
ministries, including three national missions, the publication *SBC Today* (now
Baptists Today), regional offices for Clergy and Laity Concerned, and the Baptist Peace Fellowship of North America (now in Memphis).

The Southern Baptist congregations in Birmingham were also touched
by the racial controversy in that city, and one of the results was the creation
of a new congregation. At the First Baptist Church in 1970, the congregation
voted on whether to accept Mrs. Winfred Bryant and her daughter Twila,
who had been a part of the church's tutoring ministry, as their first black
members. A majority voted to accept them, but church procedure called for a
two-thirds favorable vote, and the count fell far short. They were not accepted,
and the controversy split the church. Two hundred members followed Pastor
J. Herbert Gilmore, Jr., when he left to start another congregation.

Struggles in the Denomination

Within and without the denomination, Southern Baptists exhibited both resis-
tance and courageous leadership. Clarence Jordan (founder in 1942, with
American Baptist P. D. East, of Koinonia Farms at Americus, Georgia) and
Will D. Campbell (author and civil rights activist with the National Council of

Churches) were two of the most notable Southern Baptists to influence the denomination, especially its youth. Their influence was exerted through their writing; records; and speeches at churches, college campuses, and denominational meetings.[4] Not the least of their influence came in national reporting on the witness of their lives.

Before 1954 few within the SBC challenged the segregationist practices of the denomination's agencies and churches. Among the clearest voices to speak out were seminary professors, especially those teaching ethics. In 1949 T. B. Maston of Southwestern Baptist Theological Seminary in Fort Worth, Texas, wrote a small study book, *Of One,* for use by Woman's Missionary Union, then incorporated much of that volume into *The Bible and Race,* published in 1959 by Broadman Press. In the later book, Maston challenged segregationists on biblical grounds, destroying their use of favorite defenses such as the curse of Canaan or Ham (Gen. 9:25) and the setting of "the bounds of habitation" for humankind (Acts 17:26).

From Maston's classroom came more than one denominational leader who would challenge the racist attitudes of Southern Baptists. Most widely known are Foy Valentine, longtime director of the Christian Life Commission (CLC); Jimmy Allen, director of the Texas CLC for many years, then pastor in San Antonio when he was elected president of the SBC and, later, director of the Radio and Television Commission; and James Dunn, also director of the Texas CLC before heading the Baptist Joint Committee on Public Affairs.

The Home Mission Board reflected both the tendency to resist change and the courageous leadership to make change. Although the administration was slow to act before Arthur B. Rutledge headed the agency in 1965, those leading the work with Negroes, such as Noble Y. Beall, Guy Bellamy, and Victor Glass pushed and pulled Southern Baptists to the limits of their tolerance. In 1958, for example, the agency published *The Long Bridge,* a mission study book on the denomination's work with Negroes, but before the book could be studied—even though already in the bookstores—it was recalled in response to widespread criticism. At the last minute, a book on another phase of home mission work was substituted.

After 1960 I began extensive reporting of Baptist work with blacks, only to encounter consternation: "We have never done it this way before." Supervisors suggested that I let up on the reporting. Then in 1962 the CLC, the one agency that consistently called on the denomination to adopt strong positions on race, led the SBC calendar committee to include a Race Relations Sunday. Because of the advance planning necessary, it would not appear on the calendar until 1965.

In 1963 I suggested that the churches did not need to wait. They could immediately do the following: gather information about the races; study the history of the denomination's work with blacks; and inform Southern Baptists about the progressive steps already taken by their schools, hospitals, and other agencies. I also suggested that pastors' conferences could take positive positions and churches as they can should announce they are open to all people.

Had I avoided the final suggestion, I might have escaped a reprimand. Instead I was called to the office of Courts Redford, executive director of the HMB, who informed me that "if you want to continue the kind of editorial freedom you have been practicing you need to go somewhere else." The agency had for the first time hired a black secretary, and, he said, "We've got all of the integration we can take here." There was always the fear that the Cooperative Program gifts for missions and the annual Annie Armstrong Offering for Home Missions would be threatened by any controversy.

I was excused from Redford's office without his asking if I would comply or not. I determined that I would continue exercising my editorial freedom, being careful that I did not supply him with any other reasons for dismissal, gambling that it would be too embarrassing for the agency to fire me over the racial issue. Redford retired the next year; and Arthur Rutledge, an advocate of racial equality, succeeded him. Under Rutledge all programs of the agency began to stress racial equality. The magazine took the lead, but we paid a price with a falling circulation.

Nineteen-sixty-eight became a watershed year for those in the denomination wanting change. Churches were finally receiving encouragement from the denomination, but it took the assassinations of Robert Kennedy and, more important for Baptists, of civil rights leader Martin Luther King, Jr., to shake the reluctant SBC into action. At the convention, meeting in Houston, a "Statement Concerning the Crisis in Our Nation" was adopted on 5 June by a vote of 5,687 to 2,119. The statement had been generated by state, SBC, and agency leaders, representing a consensus never before present. It was not the usual resolution, but an action instructing the agencies to take steps to address the situation, and the HMB was directed to lead in its implementation. The statement confessed past failures by Southern Baptists, called for respect of individuals, equality for all persons, a defense against injustice, a refusal to be part of racism or violence, and acceptance of Christians as brothers. It urged Southern Baptists to work at reconciliation and to bridge divisive barriers.

A week after the convention, Arthur Rutledge of the HMB called agency heads and program leaders to Atlanta to assess where Southern Baptists were and to develop plans for the future. Thirty-five leaders responded, and an assessment was made of what was and was not being done. The major change was that agencies were freed to examine procedures and to take actions. No dramatic steps were immediately taken, but a series of minor ones began to change the huge denomination.

The Home Mission Board employed Emmanuel McCall in 1968 as its first black staff member with an office in its headquarters. In fact, he helped draft the crisis statement, and until 1991 headed what is now called the Black Church Extension Division, which went through a series of name changes reflecting the move away from paternalism. With an annual budget of $4 million, the division's efforts today are directed primarily at starting churches in black communities. It is now estimated that there are more than one thousand predominantly black churches affiliated with Southern Baptists, the most being in California, Michigan, Texas, and the Northeast—but every state has its share. In fact, so aggressive has the SBC become in starting churches in black communities that it has created a backlash among many black leaders who are saying that the denomination is contributing to divisiveness in the black community.[5]

In 1969 the Christian Life Commission held its annual seminar in Chicago under the theme "The Church's Mission in the National Crisis." One of the speakers was a young divinity student at the University of Chicago, Jesse Jackson. He opened his speech by saying, "I'm glad to see you Southern Baptist ministers here in Chicago. When I was growing up in South Carolina I wish I could have joined some of your churches, but I couldn't and that's part of the problem."[6]

The Sunday School Board began in the 1970s to adapt its literature to teach brotherhood, and to include photographs of blacks and whites together. Seminaries sought black faculty members but had little success in competing with other institutions for their first and even second choices of strong candidates. Baptist associations and state conventions began to take some actions, but the real struggle was left to the churches.

A number of factors strengthened the hands of those working for racial reconciliation in the 1970s. First and foremost was the force of federal law, coupled with the moral imperatives of the civil rights movement. Second, the evangelistic and expansionistic drive of the SBC, the natural outgrowth of its theology and sense of a divine mandate, was creating a national denomination, breaking out of the regionalism that had contained it before World War II. As the SBC grew nationally, it incorporated areas without the South and its segregation. Southern Baptists in California, Michigan, New York, Texas, and other non-South or border states grew to include hundreds of black churches and thousands of integrated churches.

The third factor was the Southern Baptists' reverence of missions. They had created their denomination for mission purposes. When the Home Mission Board under Arthur Rutledge, with reinforcement from the Woman's Missionary Union, the CLC, and the Foreign Mission Board, began to insist that Southern Baptists change, the denomination began to respond.

That response may have been slow, but it was certain. Following the adoption of the "Crisis in Our Nation" statement, Southern Baptists began a systematic effort to reach blacks and to include blacks.

The Current Status of Integration

The first black churches to affiliate with Southern Baptists through an association were in California in 1951. By 1956 there were perhaps five such churches, then by 1973 there were 191. The number was to nearly double in the next five years, and double again each five years after that. Today there are more than one thousand churches with more than 350,000 members. The last state to report a black church affiliate was Mississippi, in 1984. The states with the largest representation are Texas, California, and Michigan. The most—20 percent—are in New York.

With burgeoning numbers of black churches and the influx of black members into integrated Southern Baptist congregations, there has come a greater push to include blacks in denominational literature. The Sunday School Board (SSB) added its Ethnic Ministries Department in 1979, after being inundated with indignant reaction to the withdrawal in 1971 of an issue of the periodical *Becoming,* which included a photograph of two white women witnessing to a black youth. Grady Cothen, SSB president at the time, was asked by a newspaper reporter what would be done to correct such prejudice. Cothen revealed new guidelines for materials and suggested the reporter come back in a year; Cothen promised the reporter a copy of every publication that included blacks. When the reporter returned, it is said he was presented with a pickup truck load of materials.

As late as 1989, however, the SSB was still working at making progress in the use of art and photographs depicting ethnic people. A Baptist Press report on 15 February 1989 indicated that a review of 2,274 pictures in 158 SSB periodicals revealed that 216 included ethnics—that is, at least one person who obviously was Hispanic, black, or Asian—a percentage of 9.6. That was nearly double the percentage in the report of three years previous. A spokesperson for the agency said the quality is improving as well, that is, the persons are not depicted as poor or down-and-out and receiving services rather than participating in a church activity. "In five years, we should be right where we ought to be," the spokesperson said.

Until 1991, despite earlier efforts, none of the SBC seminaries had a full-time black faculty member. Black leaders have been added at most of the agencies (in 1989 there were seventeen), but generally they relate only to other blacks. In assignments transcending race—evangelism, for example—they have yet to be given the chance to lead. Only one, Emmanuel McCall of the Home Mission Board, headed a division (Black Church Extension) and had a significant role in decision making and budgeting, and he has since left.

In December 1989 David D. Benham, a Native American on the HMB staff in the Church Extension Division, resigned, accusing the agency of "resurgent racism." Benham wrote:

> The HMB in the 1960s and 1970s took a stand which did not reflect the majority of Southern Baptists, but which proved to place the agency in a pathfinder role for equality and Christ-like posture, and many of our

churches have come to an attitude of acceptance of all races. . . . I am
saddened that after 15 years of experience as a staff member of the HMB,
I can see little progress; . . . the HMB now demonstrates an attitude and
message of segregation and a regression to an old but resurging racism;
there will now be no ethnic person serving in any of the SBC programs
assigned to the HMB, except in those so designated as the segregated
units: language church extension and black church extension.[7]

Other staff took issue with Benham's charge, defending president Larry Lewis
as having worked for racial reconciliation in St. Louis, and saying that the
organization had been successful in reaching ethnics; but none refuted Benham's
charge as to staff in areas other than the areas he noted.

On the other hand, state conventions and associations have elected
blacks to responsible positions. Seven have served as presidents of state conventions. The Alaska convention had a black president in the early 1970s.
Don Sharp of Chicago served as president of the Illinois state association in
1983 and 1984; others have served as presidents and vice-presidents in other
states, such as the District of Columbia and New York. But at the national
SBC level, only eight blacks in 1991 served among the more than nine hundred trustees, directors, and standing committees; and the number of ethnics,
as well as women, has been decreasing in recent years.

Fundamentalism and Race Relations

When the fundamentalists began their concerted attempt to take over the
Southern Baptist Convention in 1979, progress toward better race relations
within the denomination began to slow and almost ground to a halt. This
happened for a variety of reasons. First, as Ellen Rosenberg contends in this
volume, the conservative movement in the United States—and in the Southern Baptist Convention—has been identified with a segregationist position.
As early as 1955, for example, W. J. Simmons, executive secretary of the Mississippi Citizens' Council, had this to say: "[The White Citizens' Council] is
much more than a white supremacist group, and I think it is much more than
a protectionist group. I think it is fundamentally the first real stirrings of a
conservative revolt in this country."[8]

In Alabama as well, race and "conservatism" were mixed. The charges against Herbert Gilmore at First Baptist Church of Birmingham clearly showed a fundamentalist mind-set against the moderate pastor, linking civil rights with "liberal" religion. The event, reported extensively by the national press, set in motion a process in which members sought to fire Gilmore and part of his staff. Public charges brought against him by the segregationists in the church avoided the race issue, centering on his "liberalism." Their substance is an eerie forewarning of the fundamentalist storm to hit the denomination nearly ten years later. Gilmore was charged with not believing the Bible is infallible, with being a member of the liberal E. Y. Mullins Fellowship, with not accepting the Baptist Faith and Message statement, and with the fostering of "social" ministries. The controversy eventually split the congregation. All of the staff and more than two hundred members, most of whom were in leadership positions, left to form a new church—the Company of the Committed, today known as the Baptist Church of the Covenant. The church in 1970 was one of the first in the state with an open membership. Today First Baptist Church also has black members.[9]

In speeches in South Carolina in 1956, W. A. Criswell, the "godfather" of SBC fundamentalists, called integrationists "a bunch of infidels, dying from the neck up," and he charged that they were "good-for-nothing fellows who are trying to upset all the things we love as good Southern Baptists." Criswell and many other conservative Southern Baptists were to change, but not to the extent that they would work to change the denomination.

Since 1979, the year fundamentalists gained control of the Southern Baptist Convention and thus control of the process by which resolutions are created and adopted, only two resolutions have dealt with civil rights, and neither of these asked Southern Baptists for any action to improve race relations. Instead each was concerned over the intrusion of the federal government in church affairs, wanting exemption of religious organizations in the adoption of civil rights legislation. One resolution, in 1986, did encourage "agencies and committees to increase the involvement of blacks and other minorities in employment, missions, and programs." But aside from the establishment of churches in black communities, just the opposite has been taking place.

When fundamentalist Richard Land was elected to head the CLC, to his credit he immediately called for action in the area of race. He and other fundamentalists were embarrassed, however, by the outspoken remarks of commission member Curtis W. Caine, Sr., a medical doctor from Jackson, Mississippi. Speaking of race relations, Caine said: "We have to be very careful that we do not get caught in the trap that is closing in around us about apartheid in South Africa, which doesn't exist anymore and was beneficial when it did, because it meant separate development. We have to be very careful that we don't get caught up in the endorsement of—quote, the reverend, unquote—Martin Luther King" (whom Caine then called a "fraud"). [10]

Today fundamentalist leaders are trying to distance themselves from that heritage, but the results are mixed. Four months after Caine's statements, Land held a race relations conference in Nashville on Martin Luther King's birthday. But only 190 people attended, most of them agency people or Southern Baptist moderates. Land and five other denominational leaders issued a call for a revival of race relations as a primary concern with Southern Baptists. However, the HMB was absent from this group, as also were the better known fundamentalist leaders.

Emmanuel McCall, the most prominent black staff member of the HMB, has gone on record saying that although the "conservative group in power [in the SBC] now identifies with the extreme political right, their attitude to race is not where their political ideas are." [11] And Jerry Vines, president of the SBC in 1989 told a reporter that "Southern Baptists have grown in our understanding that the Gospel is for all people everywhere. To integrate is consistent with the Gospel I have always preached." All the mega-churches that have spawned the fundamentalist leaders of the denomination, including Criswell's First Baptist Church of Dallas, now have black members, but none of these fundamentalists have shown leadership nationally in race relations.

Nancy Ammerman's research challenges McCall's assessment of the fundamentalists in the SBC, however, showing the strong correlations between their political conservatism, their religious conservatism, and their feelings about civil rights. Ammerman surveyed a randomly selected sample of Southern Baptist pastors and lay leaders, asking them, in 1986, whether they agreed or disagreed with the statement, "The civil rights movement helped to move this country in the right direction." "Fifty-three percent of self-identified fundamentalists agreed with the statement as opposed to 90 percent of the self-identified moderates. The civil rights movement is a very important part of how moderates define themselves. Fundamentalists don't so much disapprove as they are equivocal," she said. [12]

Southern Baptist Moderates and Civil Rights

Ammerman's finding relates to the second reason Southern Baptists lost their impetus for greater change in regards to race: moderates in the denomination, including most of the agency leaders and outstanding pastors who had worked for change, began to shift their energies into opposing the fundamentalists. And as the fundamentalists took over, the moderates had less and less power with which to instigate change.

Finally, ironically, the civil rights of women, although not in opposition to the civil rights of blacks, attracted the loyalty of many who had been working in race relations. This was especially true of moderate Southern Baptists. The moderate Southern Baptist Alliance, for instance, has opened leadership to women, published a book entitled *The New Has Come, Emerging Roles Among Southern Baptist Women,* and has given financial aid to the Women in Ministry organization. But the SBA and the newly formed Cooperative Baptist Fellowship have few blacks in their organizations. Many moderates apparently feel the battle for women's rights is more critical at this time than race, especially within the denomination. Moderates of all stripes have turned their energies, then, to opposing fundamentalists and becoming advocates for women. And because moderates have lost their positions of power, they are less effective in challenging any denominational policy or attitude.

At their 1990 annual meeting in St. Louis, however, the Southern Baptist Alliance adopted "A Call to Repentance." This resolution acknowledged that slavery was a factor in the organization of the SBC, calling these sins "a spiritual blight upon the relationships between African-Americans and whites in the South which has lasted unto this generation." The lengthy resolution called for repentance, saying "we publicly repent and apologize to all African-Americans." Although the resolution was presented to the larger SBC through its resolutions committee in June of 1990, the committee did not even present it to the convention for consideration. Nevertheless SBA president Richard Groves, in an appearance before the Progressive National Baptist Convention in August of 1991, read the resolution and proposed a dialogue between representatives of the two groups. The proposal was promptly accepted and representatives from both organizations have been named and have been meeting.

It is not surprising that such initiatives came from moderate Southern Baptists, for the willingness to take stands, to work for racial equality, and to open churches and other institutions to all persons has characterized moderates. As the sides formed in the denominational controversy, nearly all of the leaders who had effectively worked for change in race relations aligned themselves with moderates. On the other hand, those opposing such efforts, those linking civil rights with liberalism, aligned themselves with fundamentalists.

The Future for Southern Baptists

On racial equality the SBC always has lagged behind the culture, never leading the way, even though its churches counted a large number of civic leaders as members. After the Supreme Court eliminated the law's support of a segregated school system, the culture slowly changed. Southern Baptists, being a denomination reflecting its culture, slowly changed also, but few Southern Baptists were among the leaders of the civil rights movement, and the few who were—such as Clarence Jordan or Will Campbell—labored as virtual outcasts of the SBC.

In the 1980s, in part as a reaction to the great gains of the civil rights movement, the nation slowed its drive to give equality to blacks. The Supreme Court, changed by the addition of more conservative members, no longer supported radical change. The executive branch of government, which once had supported civil rights efforts, now appeared to impede them. During the 1980s the SBC, led by fundamentalists, regressed in making racial changes. Fewer blacks served as trustees of boards and agencies. Fewer blacks were in leadership roles. Fewer resolutions, speeches, or articles appeared to challenge the move back to segregation. The areas in which blacks and other ethnic groups are engaged by Southern Baptists are evangelism and church founding. If they are successful here, however, the SBC may eventually include a contingent large enough to challenge its practices.

In the 1990s, as the nation witnesses racism in the code words of a David Duke running for political office or in a presidency holding the racial line with vetoes over "quotas," so the SBC appears to move backwards. There is once again an atmosphere that allows overt racism to be voiced. In his evaluation of a recent national conference that had less than ten blacks present, one SBC leader wrote, "Too many niggers."

The SBC reflects the culture, showing an inability or an unwillingness to change the culture, being, instead, the one changed. With moderates out of power and distracted by controversy and other issues, can Southern Baptists under fundamentalists offer any hope of saving the nation or themselves from a serious relapse into racial bigotry? The answer is no. In fact, the SBC may lead in the other direction.

Notes

1. Thomas J. Holmes, *Ashes for Breakfast: A Diary of Racism in an American Church* (Valley Forge, Pa.: Judson, 1969), 13.
2. Ibid., iv.
3. For an account of this church's history, see Walker Knight, *Struggle for Integrity* (Waco, Tex.: Word, 1969).
4. Dallas Lee's *The Cotton Patch Evidence* (New York: Harper & Row, 1971) recounts Jordan's story. Will Campbell tells his own story in *Forty Acres and a Goat* (Atlanta, Ga.: Peachtree, 1986).
5. Cited in the Atlanta *Constitution,* 5 Mar. 1990.
6. Jesse Jackson, "Chastising the Rich Young Ruler," *Home Missions* 40, no. 7 (July 1969): 23.
7. *SBC Today* 7, no. 10 (Jan. 1990): 1.
8. Will D. Campbell, *Race and the Renewal of the Church* (Philadelphia: Westminster Press, 1962), 18.
9. See J. Herbert Gilmore, Jr., *They Chose to Live: The Racial Agony of an American Church* (Grand Rapids, Mich.: Eerdmans, 1972).
10. Cited in *Baptist Press,* 16 Sept. 1988.
11. "HMB veteran responds to charges of racism," *SBC Today* 7, no. 10 (Jan. 1990): 2.
12. Nancy Tatom Ammerman, *Baptist Battles: Social Change and Religious Conflict in the Southern Baptist Convention* (New Brunswick, N.J.: Rutgers Univ. Press, 1990), 102-4.

CHAPTER 10

THEOLOGY AND POLITICS IN SOUTHERN BAPTIST INSTITUTIONS

James L. Guth

The movement that has swept the Southern Baptist Convention since 1979 has had unmistakable ties to the secular political movement known as the Christian Right. Leaders such as Paul Pressler, Paige Patterson, Charles Stanley, and Adrian Rogers not only fostered rank-and-file discontent with denominational agencies but joined the conservative political movement outside the convention. During the 1980s these men were often quite visible in Christian Right causes and by 1990 had succeeded in establishing a new Baptist lobby in Washington, an extension of the Christian Life Commission that would bypass the "liberal" Baptist Joint Committee.

Most analyses of the larger Christian Right movement have focused on what might be called *macro,* or cultural- and societal-level explanations of its rise: its emergence from the electronic church, its dependence upon preexisting fundamentalist networks, and the modern state's assault on traditionalist values.[1] Most studies have concluded that the early estimates of the Christian Right's potential were badly exaggerated: the television audiences were smaller, the organizational networks less effective, and the shared values less powerful in evoking political action than most observers first thought. The failure of Pat Robertson's drive for the GOP nomination in 1988 and the disbanding of the Moral Majority in 1989 seem to confirm this assessment.

And yet there are contrary indications that the Christian Right may have more breadth and depth than this interpretation suggests. Survey after survey demonstrates that a great many religious people differ from the nonreligious in their views on social and moral issues, such as abortion, prayer in school, gay rights, and sex education, to name just a few. And political activists are also characterized by consistent religious differences, with religious traditionalists disproportionately giving their allegiance and dollars to the Republican party and affiliated conservative groups.[2] Such conservative activists are found in virtually every American denomination, including the so-called liberal mainline churches. These findings hint that the Christian Right is much more deeply embedded in many denominations than we have hitherto suspected. The broader Christian Right, as opposed to its recent organizational manifestations, is the offshoot of historic controversies within American Protestantism (and, perhaps, within Catholicism as well). As Martin Marty suggests, these battles created two "parties" among and within American denominations: a "public," or liberal, party and a "private," or conservative, party—which has now gone "public" in its own way.[3] In most denominations, the old public party has dominated the organizational bureaucracy and clergy, whereas the previously private party has been stronger among laity. In the last few years, especially, this old division has reemerged, albeit in new form, as almost every large denomination has witnessed conflict between liberal establishment and conservative insurgents—and nowhere has that conflict been as noisy as in the SBC.

How to interpret these developments has been the subject of some contention. Many observers see the entire SBC Controversy as a theological protest, an effort to bring the denomination back to strict orthodoxy, or perhaps to an even more demanding dispensationalist stance. The movement's leaders may be political conservatives, these people say, but that is incidental to their doctrinal purposes within the SBC.[4] Others believe the movement to be essentially political (in the national, not the Baptist, sense), fomented and aided throughout by New Right activists hoping to add the SBC's weight to conservative social and political causes, using theological arguments as cover.[5] Still other observers see a "politics of resentment": Baptists outside the hierarchy and long excluded from participation in SBC affairs have provided the shock troops for the take-over, led by power-hungry malcontents seeking to unseat established elites.[6] A fourth interpretation, which is often combined with the third, sees the Controversy as a social one. Pastors from small churches, in rural areas, with modest schooling, have been most responsive to appeals to turn the convention back to God and to, incidentally, eject the urban (and urbane) modernized leadership of the denomination.[7]

The Surveys

Whatever the cause, it is apparent that enough Baptists became discontented enough with their denominational institutions to create a revolt. This chapter is an assessment of various approaches to explaining that revolt. The data are drawn from two surveys of Baptist ministers in 1980 and 1984. The 1980 survey was a 110-item questionnaire sent to a random sample of 756 ministers, drawn from approximately forty thousand pastors listed in the SBC's *1980 Convention Annual*. The final response rate was 62 percent, yielding 460 respondents.[8] The 1984 form, a somewhat longer instrument, was sent to 1,710 ministers and elicited 902 responses, for a 53 percent response rate.[9] Comparison of both sets of respondents with Southern Baptist ministers generally (based on information from the SBC's *Quarterly Review*), shows that respondents are slightly better educated, from larger churches, and thus of somewhat higher status than the average SBC pastor. This slight response bias should not be a major problem, as our interest is less in estimating the distribution of particular attitudes than in explaining what influences those attitudes.

Here we use ministers' evaluation of denominational agencies as an indicator of institutional discontent. We shall consider the four hypotheses suggested above: (1) the fundamentalist movement is rooted in theological disputes; (2) broader social and political agitation is responsible; (3) the struggle is, at base, one between different factions, between "ins" and "outs"; and (4) social group differences are primarily responsible. We do not, of course, exclude the "blind men and the elephant" possibility: all four approaches have merit.

To determine the degree of ministerial discontent with SBC institutions, we gave pastors a checklist in the 1980 and 1984 surveys, allowing them to rate agency performance as "excellent," "good," "fair," or "poor." The 1984 survey added one institution to the 1980 list, the Baptist Joint Committee on Public Affairs (BJCPA). As the 1984 survey had a much wider range of potential explanatory variables, in this chapter we use those data. Our inspection of variables highly correlated with institutional assessment in both years suggested essential continuity in the factors influencing ratings.

As table 10.1 indicates, there is considerable variation in ministerial evaluations. The Foreign Mission Board gets the best ratings in both years, followed by the Home Mission Board, Sunday School Board, the seminaries, and, finally, the Christian Life Commission and Baptist Joint Committee. Note also that between 1980 and 1984 the ratings were fairly stable, with a slight deterioration over the period. More recent data derived from a 1988-89 study show very similar results.

This pattern invites several kinds of explanation. First, those agencies most directly involved in mission activities, long the highest organizational priority among Southern Baptists, get the best ratings. On the other hand, agencies dealing with inherently controversial issues (the CLC and the BJCPA)

Table 10.1
Ministerial Ratings of Southern Baptist Institutions
(percent)

Institution	Excellent	Good	Fair	Poor
Foreign Mission Board				
1980	44	42	8	1
1984	41	44	12	1
Home Mission Board				
1980	35	44	14	3
1984	32	49	15	2
Sunday School Board				
1980	30	41	19	6
1984	25	46	22	6
Seminaries				
1980	29	37	22	8
1984	23	39	23	11
Christian Life Commission				
1980	20	38	19	13
1984	13	33	25	19
Baptist Joint Committee				
1980	—	—	—	—
1984	11	26	24	23

are themselves more controversial, with much greater variation in responses. In addition, the seminaries have historically been distrusted by fundamentalist elements in the SBC, as centers of unorthodox theological innovations,[10] and both the Christian Life Commission and Baptist Joint Committee have often taken liberal political stances at odds with most fundamentalist and some mainstream Southern Baptists. The poorer ratings of the seminaries, the CLC, and the BJCPA may reflect not only this history, but the incessant attacks in recent years by fundamentalist dissidents (now the SBC establishment), perhaps channeling generalized discontent toward these agencies.

Our first step was to determine whether there was a single "institutional evaluation" factor at work here or whether evaluations of each agency were being made independently. A correlation matrix revealed a fairly strong set of relationships, but with some interesting variations. The relationships among agency evaluations were quite robust—people who liked one were also likely to favor the others. Evaluations of the seminaries correlated at about .50 with the other institutions, meaning that how a pastor felt about the seminaries was a good, but not perfect, predictor of how he felt about the other agencies. The correlations among mission board ratings were also quite strong, but those between the political and mission agencies were smaller. How one evaluated mission boards was a less reliable predictor of political agency evaluations. This pattern was confirmed by a principal-components analysis, a statistical procedure designed to find patterns of common variation. All six agencies exhibited loadings of over .74 on the first principal component, accounting for well over half the variance, but a second smaller factor also appeared, on which the CLC (.52) and BJCPA (.56) loaded. A varimax rotation (a procedure to clarify the meaning of the factors) showed the mission boards loading heavily on one factor, the CLC and BJCPA on the other, and the seminaries modestly on both. Although evaluations are clearly related, there are also distinctly separable dimensions.

On this basis we decided to use four separate measures: a factor score for "general evaluation" of denominational agencies (based on the first unrotated principal component) that would be a measure of overall satisfaction; the seminary rating; and factor scores for the mission boards and for the political agencies.[11] This strategy will permit us to both see the larger patterns of influence and preserve some important nuances.

Theological Variables and Institutional Discontent

If the battles in the SBC are at base theological, as most observers contend, institutional discontent should be associated primarily with fundamentalist theology. To evaluate this possibility, we analyzed the relationship between theological beliefs and discontent.

Although Southern Baptist pastors are overwhelmingly orthodox, there are important theological differences among them.[12] To simplify the task of relating a formidable variety of intercorrelated theological measures to agency evaluations, we first sought to reduce twelve belief items to one or two combined factors.[13] Virtually all twelve items demonstrate a strong interrelationship, with most loading at .5 or better on the first unrotated principal component, which we call *general conservatism*. After further testing this larger pattern was separated into two distinct subfactors. The first we call *orthodoxy*, because it contains items such as the physical resurrection and the Virgin birth of Jesus; the second constitutes a clear *fundamentalism* measure: the highest loadings appear on women's ordination, biblical inerrancy, the historicity of Adam and Eve, fundamentalist self-identification, biblical literalism, a literal hell, and original sin. (Using the same procedure in our 1988-89 study and incorporating dispensationalist self-identification confirms this interpretation: dispensationalism loads heavily on this factor, as well.) For further analysis, then, we assigned each respondent three factor scores: one each for general conservatism, orthodoxy, and fundamentalism.

Whether the SBC holy war is really "about" theology, ministers' beliefs are clearly associated with institutional ratings (see table 10.2). General theological conservatism is strongly linked to negative assessments of the seminaries and political agencies, but is not significantly related to mission-board ratings. When theological conservatism is separated into orthodoxy and fundamentalism factors, the results are interesting. Although orthodoxy modestly depresses political agency evaluations, it actually has a very mild positive effect on mission-board ratings, and no effect whatever on evaluations of the seminaries.

Not surprisingly, it is high scores on fundamentalism that are strongly—and negatively—related to institutional ratings, especially those of the seminaries and political agencies. Overall, as the general evaluation factor correlation indicates, fundamentalist orientation—not simply orthodoxy—is the key influence in institutional negativism.

Table 10.2

Theological Attitudes and Institutional Evaluations

Institution	Theological Attitude		
	General Conservatism	Orthodoxy	Fundamentalism
Seminary	-.33**	-.05	-.44**
Mission	-.07	.09*	-.20**
Political	-.35**	-.14**	-.37**
General	-.26**	-.02	-.37**

Note: All coefficients are Pearson's R correlation coefficients.
   * Significant in one-tailed test at .01.
   ** Significant at .001.

Political Orientation and Institutional Discontent

Many analysts (especially secular journalists and political scientists) are inclined to see the SBC's Controversy in political, more than religious, terms.[14] According to this interpretation, the battle is really between social and political traditionalists and more modern ministers. The former simply do not like the way the world is going and want SBC institutions to fight America's drift away from conservative values, whether in family matters, national economic life, or international affairs.[15] According to this view, theological controversies merely provide one vocabulary for the conflict. Other analysts argue that once theological and background differences are taken into account, there are few direct connections between the theological and political movements.[16]

To assess these contentions, we used three political-factor scores, based on twenty political variables. Once again we initially produced a first principal component, on which all the political variables loaded. This unrotated factor we call *general conservatism.*[17] The highest loadings represent social issues—abortion, the equal rights amendment, school prayer, and belief that liberals cannot be Christian—rather than economic or public-welfare questions. But everything from voting for Reagan in 1984 to favoring more defense spending is contained in this factor.

Table 10.3

Political Attitudes and Institutional Evaluations

Institution	Political Attitude			
	General Conservatism	New Right	New Deal Liberal	New Liberal
Seminary	-.46**	-.43**	.15**	.19**
Mission	-.25**	-.20**	.09*	.16**
Political	-.55**	-.42**	.30**	.23**
General	-.47**	-.38**	.20**	.23**

Note: All coefficients are Pearson's R correlation coefficients.
   * Significant in one-tailed test at .01.
   ** Significant at .001.

Further analysis produces a major *New Right* subfactor, on which the school prayer, abortion, and conservative ideology items loaded most strongly, along with the belief that free enterprise is Christian and liberalism is not; support for more defense spending, tuition tax credits, and the Moral Majority; opposition to gay rights; and the perception of oneself as more conservative than one's church.

There were also two smaller liberal factors, with negative loadings on the conservatism items. We call them the *New Deal Liberal* and *New Liberal* factors. The New Deal factor is comprised of party identification (Democratic), support for a greater federal role in social problems, concern with fighting unemployment, voting for Mondale in 1984, and support for the ERA. The New Liberal factor includes environmental issues, gun control, affirmative action, and strategic arms reduction.

How do political orientations relate to institutional evaluations? As table 10.3 suggests, general political conservatism is strongly—and negatively—correlated with institutional ratings. As expected the strongest relationships are with the political agencies, but the correlations with the general evaluation and the seminary ratings are also quite robust. Quite clearly discontent is based on the New Right social-issue conservatism, whereas the smaller New Deal and New Liberal factors are modestly conducive to positive agency ratings. A quick comparison with the correlations in table 10.2 shows that general political conservatism is even more strongly related to institutional evaluations than is theological conservatism. The relatively high correlations in both cases may suggest, of course, that theological and political indicators are intercorrelated and, perhaps, reinforce each other in producing institutional alienation. We shall attempt to untangle this relationship later.

Denominational Politics and Institutional Discontent

Some observers have seen the rebellion and successful coup d'état in the SBC as stemming from internal discontent with participatory opportunities for all factions in the denomination. The decade-long insurgency often has been portrayed as one of organized outsiders attempting to move in. Indeed this portrayal is a common one, albeit with different overtones, among both moderate and fundamentalist activists and among some academic observers as well. To assess the influence of internal organizational politics, we used seventeen internal variables. These included measures of status (the size and social class of the church), measures of access and participation in the system (attendance at recent national meetings and office holding in local, state, and national Baptist associations), and factional alignment in the Controversy, that is, preferences for specific SBC presidential candidates during this period. Again we used principal-components analysis to produce a single measure for "insurgent" preferences for fundamentalist presidential candidates in 1981, 1982, and 1984 (loading at .89, .89, and .83, respectively). We also produced one factor for attendance at SBC conventions over the previous decade (with loadings from .60 to .81), and three factors for office holding: one which tapped office holding at national and state levels prior to 1984, one representing local office holding in 1984 and the past, and one representing current state and national office holding.

As table 10.4 illustrates, factional preferences are strongly correlated with evaluations of both seminaries and political agencies. In other words supporters of the fundamentalist candidates for SBC president tend to be especially critical of the seminaries and political agencies, but also less supportive of mission institutions. This overall displeasure is summarized in the strong

Table 10.4

Denominational Politics and Institutional Evaluations

Institution	Denominational Politics						
	Fundamentalist Faction	Frequent Attender	Class of Church	Size of Church	Office Holding		
					Past	Local	Current
Seminary	-.48**	.18**	.12**	.14**	.15**	.10**	.08**
Mission	-.24**	.11**	.02	.07	.05	.12**	.11**
Political	-.53**	.04	.06	-.03	.06	.07	.01
General	-.46**	.12**	.06	.05	.07	.11*	.08*

Note: All coefficients are Pearson's R correlation coefficients.
* Significant in one-tailed test at .01.
** Significant at .001.

negative correlation between factional preference and general evaluation scores. It is clear that institutional dissatisfaction is part of the platform on which these SBC presidential candidates have successfully mobilized a following.

The other measures of participation and access are less clearly related to pastors' evaluations of their institutions. Frequent attendance at conventions, and pastoring a middle-class congregation—or a large church—are mildly correlated with positive evaluations for the seminaries, as are all three office-holding measures. Frequent attendance, local office holding, and current national office also correlate weakly with positive ratings for the mission boards. But *none* of the denominational status and participation measures predict support for the political agencies. Evaluations of these agencies are influenced only by a pastor's factional alignment, not by his history as an insider or the status of his church.

Some of these indicators may really be proxies for others. The fact that ministers from smaller and poorer churches are more unhappy with the seminaries may really be measuring the effects of their own limited ministerial education rather than their current institutional locus as such (see the next section). Nevertheless, institutional discontent is characteristic of supporters of the fundamentalist candidates, who both rode on and encouraged this sentiment. And that discontent was somewhat more prevalent among those marginal to the older leadership structures of the denomination, at least as defined by office holding and attendance at national meetings.

Ministers' Backgrounds and Institutional Discontent

The revolution in the SBC also has social roots, although scholars dispute what they are. The uprising is often pictured as a classic rural fundamentalist versus urban moderate fight, with the former contesting the onset of modernity. To explore the social bases of ministerial conflict over denominational institutions, we used twenty-three indicators of social status, educational achievement, and other demographic variables. As table 10.5 demonstrates, however, only a few of these exhibit significant correlations with the institutional ratings.

Almost all of the significant background factors were related to education, and the most powerful predictor is which seminary the pastor attended. We used a four-point rating scale for seminaries, with Southern and Southeastern seminaries at the liberal end and (independent) fundamentalist institutions, such as Mid-America Seminary and Criswell Bible College, at the other. Generally the more liberal the seminary, the more positive the evaluations of all denominational institutions, and especially of the seminaries. The length of seminary education also contributes to institutional support: pastors with no seminary training are most critical and those with graduate degrees rate all institutions more highly. The extent of college education also has an

Table 10.5

Ministers' Backgrounds and Institutional Evaluations

Institution	Ministers' Background					
	College Degree	Elite College	Liberal Arts Major	Years of Seminary	Liberal Seminary	Rural
Seminary	.23**	.15**	.11*	.25**	.31**	.08*
Mission	.09*	.07	.05	.13**	.18**	.01
Political	.03	.01	.06	.12*	.24**	-.01
General	.11**	.07	.07	.17**	.26**	.01

Note: All coefficients are Pearson's R correlation coefficients.
   * Significant in one-tailed test at .01.
   ** Significant at .001.

effect, but mostly on seminary ratings. Similarly, attendance at one of the elite Southern Baptist colleges and having a college major in the social sciences or humanities also correlate slightly with seminary ratings, but not with evaluations of the missions or political institutions. The picture here is of an educational establishment valued by its graduates, but devalued by those with different educational experiences.

Rural origins had only one small effect—on seminary evaluations—and that effect was in a positive direction. Age, father's social class, and an upbringing in the Southeast have no significant relationship with evaluations—indicating that, among ministers at least, these social background factors are not a primary direct determinant of factional alignment.

In summary, Southern Baptist ministers in 1984 had different evaluations of their central denominational agencies. The mission boards generally received positive ratings, albeit with minor variations. The seminaries, as expected, were more controversial, eliciting many negative ratings. The most negative assessments went to the SBC's social and political arms, especially the BJCPA, which had been the center of several prolonged controversies. Both theological and political beliefs are strongly correlated with the seminary and political agency ratings, the political measures being a little stronger. Factors inside the SBC social system also are highly correlated with ratings: those supporting fundamentalist-faction candidates for SBC president tend to be critical of denominational agencies, as—to a lesser extent—are pastors who infrequently attend SBC annual meetings; they tend to be from smaller, working-class churches; or have not held national, state, or local office in the denomination. Of the demographic variables, only education really matters much: less-educated ministers and those educated outside the SBC's colleges and seminaries are most critical.

Which Factors Are Most Important?

To develop a more complex model of institutional discontent, we experimented with the four types of predictors for the general institutional evaluations. Of all the demographic, theological, political, and internal SBC factors, which were related to which? We eventually produced a "path model" that used the fewest possible variables to explain pastors' evaluations of their institutions, at the same time relating various measures to one another in theoretically meaningful ways. The model presumes that institutional evaluations are the complex product of theological and political orientations, as well as of the factional alignments these generate. Table 10.6 and figure 10.1 provide the regression coefficients for the hypothesized path model.

Starting on the left in figure 10.1, note that only a few factors influence the critical educational variables. Father's social class and attendance at an elite Baptist college produce slightly longer seminary training, whereas attending such a college and having been reared in the Southeast (the locale of Southern and Southeastern seminaries) influence the likelihood of attendance at a liberal divinity school. Notice in table 10.6 that the amount of variance actually explained is small: demographics have modest influence over the nature of Baptist ministers' education. Past generations of Baptist leaders have been determined to make theological education readily and economically available for aspiring ministers, and that has apparently minimized the class barrier to seminary training.[18]

The role of educational factors in producing some degree of theological moderation is suggested by the third column in table 10.6. Attendance at a liberal seminary and advanced seminary education produce decreasing conservatism, as, to a lesser extent, do southeastern regional origins and attendance at an elite Baptist college. Seminary training is thus largely responsible for the critical theological divide among Southern Baptist ministers.

In turn theological conservatism has a powerful impact on political conservatism, with attendance at a liberal seminary having some direct politically liberalizing effects, as well. Theological conservatism, in close conjunction with political conservatism, produces the SBC's factional alignments. Note that these two factors alone explain almost three-fifths of the variance in factional choices. Knowing where pastors stand on theological and political issues tells us a great deal about which presidential candidates they will support. Although the beta for political conservatism (.47) exceeds that for theological conservatism (.36), the total effects for theological conservatism are considerably greater, because of the additional effects of theology on political beliefs. In other words theology produces factional alignments in two ways: directly, and indirectly via its influence over political attitudes. Still, political views are important in their own right: no matter how the regression is run, political attitudes make a large independent contribution.[19] As much as theology tells

Table 10.6

Regression Coefficients for a Path Model of Institutional Evaluations

Independent Variable	Dependent Variable					
	Years of Seminary	Liberal Seminary	Theological Conservatism	Political Conservatism	Fundamentalist Faction	General Evaluations
Father's class	.18					
Elite college	.10	.25	-.10			
Southeast		.25	-.12			
Years of seminary			-.25			
Liberal seminary			-.28	-.17		
Theological conservatism				.62	.36	.26
Political conservatism					-.47	-.39
Fundamentalist faction						-.36
R = .21		.36	.48	.70	.77	.53
Adjusted R squared = .04		.12	.23	.49	.59	.28

Figure 10.1

Path Diagram for General Evaluations of Southern Baptist Institutions

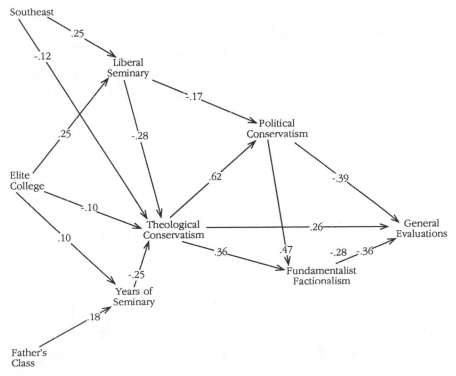

us about the preferences and discontents of these pastors, political beliefs give us additional insight into their SBC factional alignments.

Finally, the evidence indicates that factional preference, political conservatism, and theological conservatism all influence pastors' overall assessment of denominational institutions. Political conservatism has the largest direct impact on evaluations, followed closely by factional alignment: the more conservative the politics and the more identified with the fundamentalist faction, the more critical the assessment of denominational institutions. Note that factional alignment does seem to be the independent variable: reversing the causal arrow and using institutional evaluations to predict factional alignments produces little added predictive power. In other words ministers become more critical of SBC agencies as they align with the fundamentalist faction; it is not their discontent that leads them to the fundamentalist faction. Their factional alignment, of course, is primarily the result of their theological and political perspectives, which also contribute to their criticism of agency performance.

The influence of theology on evaluation is two-fold. First, theological conservatism produces both political conservatism (especially in its New Right aspect) and identification with the internal fundamentalist cause. But once these indirect effects are incorporated in the model, the direct link between theological conservatism and evaluation persists—*and is positive*. This no doubt represents the impact of traditional orthodoxy on cooperative missions work. As noted earlier it is primarily the fundamentalist aspect of theological conservatism that produces political conservatism, factional fundamentalism, and critical assessments of SBC institutions. Those who are merely conservative in traditionally orthodox ways—but do not identify with either the denomination's fundamentalist movement or New Right political causes—are still positively attached to their denomination's institutions. Overall the model explains 28 percent of the variance in the general evaluation score.

We also experimented statistically with the possibility that evaluations of the seminaries or political agencies were really the critical dependent variables, but these models yielded only marginally different results. As might be expected, the role of theological variables was slightly larger in predicting seminary ratings, whereas ministers' political attitudes were a little more predictive of the CLC/BJCPA factor. And the total amount of variance explained was somewhat higher for the political agencies (35 percent) than for the seminaries (27 percent). On the other hand, this set of factors in the backgrounds of pastors told us little about their ratings of mission boards, accounting for only 11 percent of the rather modest variance in that rating. There simply is not enough difference of opinion among SBC pastors over their mission boards for those differences to correlate with other differences among them.

Thus each of the four hypotheses has at least some merit. Perhaps least useful is the demographic argument: social background does influence the education ministers receive, but it is the location and nature of the college and, especially, of the seminary education that shapes ministers' world view and commitments. In this sense the fundamentalists' fear of liberalism in the seminaries is on target.[20] Higher education, especially at elite SBC colleges and seminaries, attenuates orthodoxy, especially in its fundamentalist aspect, and also produces greater political liberalism.

The relative importance of theological, as opposed to political, factors is less clear. Those espousing both theological and political conservatism identify strongly with the 1979-89 insurgency against denominational agencies. Theological and political conservatism are intimately linked in this insurgency; it makes little sense to argue about their respective importance. As several analysts have suggested, the conflict is really one between two competing world views, incorporating clashing perspectives on theology, society, and politics. The struggle is at once a "battle for the Bible," a "holy war for the family," and a "struggle for the soul of America." The multiple meanings give the Controversy a kind of ultimate significance for all the combatants.

Our findings here leave a good many questions unanswered. The first concerns the role of social background factors in the genesis of the Controversy. Although social position does not seem a powerful explanation for ministers' attachment to fundamentalist insurgencies, such influences may be more important for Baptist laity, as a host of studies of the general public suggest. For ministers the nature of professional socialization clearly is the critical element, but for laity factors directly related to social and economic modernization may be crucial.[21] Nor is it obvious that political beliefs influence laity in their factional choices: the connection between theology and political orientation has always been stronger among clergy. In any case these issues deserve careful study.

Finally, there is evidence that the fundamentalist faction's success in dominating many agency boards is widely perceived among pastors and is already having an impact on institutional evaluations. In our 1988-89 study, for example, identification with the fundamentalist faction results in continuing negative evaluation of the seminaries and the BJCPA, which are still fighting fundamentalist control; but fundamentalist factional alignment is now *positively* related to attitudes toward the Home Mission Board and Christian Life Commission, now under fundamentalist rule. Thus we may well be watching the transformation of support for SBC institutions: former denominational loyalists are becoming the opposition, whereas the former dissidents are becoming the establishment. Whether the opposition will be a "loyal" opposition is yet unclear.

Notes

1. On the electronic church, see Jeffrey Hadden and Charles Swann, *Prime Time Preachers* (Reading, Mass.: Addison-Wesley, 1981); on fundamentalist networks, see Robert Liebman's "Mobilizing the Moral Majority," in *The New Christian Right,* ed. Liebman and Robert Wuthnow (New York: Aldine, 1983); and John Green and James L. Guth's "The Christian Right in the Republican Party: The Case of Pat Robertson's Supporters," *Journal of Politics* 50 (1988): 150-65. On the modern state, see Wuthnow's *The Restructuring of American Religion* (Princeton, N.J.: Princeton Univ. Press, 1988).

2. Green and Guth, "Faith and Politics: Religion and Ideology among Political Contributors," *American Politics Quarterly* 14 (1986): 186-99; and Guth and Green, "God and the GOP," in *Religion and American Political Behavior,* ed. Ted G. Jelen (New York: Praeger, 1989).

3. Martin Marty, "Fundamentalism as a Social Phenomenon," *Review and Expositor* 79 (Winter): 19-30.

4. James C. Hefley, *The Truth in Crisis: The Controversy in the Southern Baptist Convention* (Dallas, Tex.: Criterion, 1986).

5. Ellen M. Rosenberg, *The Southern Baptists: A Subculture in Transition* (Knoxville: Univ. of Tennessee Press, 1989).

6. Douglas Reed, "Politics within the Southern Baptist Convention: A Political Party Analysis" (Paper presented at the annual meeting of the Southern Political Science Association, Memphis, Tennessee, 1989), esp. 30-33.

7. See Nancy Tatom Ammerman, *Baptist Battles: Social Change and Religious Conflict in the Southern Baptist Convention* (New Brunswick, N.J.: Rutgers Univ. Press, 1990), chap. 5.

8. For more detail, see Guth, "The Southern Baptist Clergy: Vanguard of the Christian Right?" in *The New Christian Right;* also Guth, "The Politics of Preachers," in *New Christian Politics,* ed. David Bromley and Anson Shupe (Macon, Ga.: Mercer Univ. Press, 1984).

9. See Guth, "Political Converts: Partisan Realignment among Southern Baptist Ministers," *Election Politics* 3, no. 1: 2-6; and "Southern Baptists and the New Right," in *Religion in American Politics,* ed. Charles W. Dunn (Washington, D.C.: Congressional Quarterly, 1988).

10. Joe E. Barnhart, *The Southern Baptist Holy War* (Austin, Tex.: Texas Monthly, 1986).

11. On this methodology, see George H. Dunteman, *Principal Components Analysis* (Newbury Park, Calif.: Sage, 1989).

12. See Guth, "Political Converts," 5-6.

13. The twelve items—in the order of their loading on the general conservatism factor—concerned the historicity of Adam and Eve, the actual reality of the devil, the inerrancy of the Bible, Jesus as the only way to salvation, the physical Second Coming, the absence of a Bible basis for female clergy, the reality of hell, the Virgin birth, fundamentalist self-identification, Jesus' physical Resurrection, humans capable only of sin, and the absence of symbol and myth in the Bible. The first factor accounted for 44 percent of the variance. Only the question on the importance of symbol and myth in the Bible exhibited modest loadings on that factor. The second smaller factor accounted for about 11 percent of the variance. The orthodoxy factor contained the items on Jesus' physical resurrection, the physical Second Coming, the Virgin birth, Jesus as the only way to salvation, and the reality of the Devil. The fundamentalism factor contained the remaining seven items.

14. See, for example, Thomas Edsall, "New Right Finally Gains Control of Huge Southern Baptist Convention," *Washington Post,* 14 June 1986.

15. Rosenberg, *The Southern Baptists,* 180-214.

16. Ammerman, "Southern Baptists and the New Christian Right," *Review of Religious Research* 32, no. 3: 213-34.

17. The political items included (in descending order of loading on the first principal component) self-identified conservatism, belief that political liberals cannot be Christian, support for an abortion amendment, support for more defense spending, opposition to the Equal Rights Amendment, support for a school prayer amendment, support for the Moral Majority, support for privatization of government programs, identification as more conservative than one's church, identification as Republican, belief that only free enterprise can be Christian, opposition to equal rights for gays, opposition to federal action on social ills, vote for Reagan in 1984, opposition to gun control, belief that affirmative action is unnecessary, opposition to strategic arms control, support for tuition tax credits, support for fighting inflation rather than unemployment, and saying that the environment is not a priority.

18. Rosenberg, *The Southern Baptists,* 57.

19. These results are quite compatible with those reported in Ammerman, "Southern Baptists."

20. See also Ammerman, *Baptist Battles,* 134 ff.

21. Ibid., chap. 5.

CHAPTER 11

WOMEN AS LAY LEADERS AND CLERGY: A CRITICAL ISSUE

Sarah Frances Anders and Marilyn Metcalf-Whittaker

The roles of Baptist women would be expected to reflect broad cultural changes as well as the internal demographic and structural dynamics of their denomination. This chapter is a look at those interlocking changes.

Women played vital, visible roles in early Christendom, and the names of notable devout women surfaced occasionally in those early centuries. Many centuries later early Baptist laywomen made a persistent impact on the religious nurturing of children and the cause of missions. Is their role still confined to the care of children and missionaries, or is the influence of women any more significant or widespread in the contemporary church, particularly among evangelical Southern Baptists?

A generation has passed since the first feminist winds of change began to rustle the gender roles of American Christendom. Interestingly, feminist writings in American mainline religion appeared concurrently with the secular feminist writings of the 1960s. These were reinforced by the National Council of Churches' 1969 stand on the deplorable position of women in church hierarchies. That council, representing American mainline Christianity, confessed that the church had reflected rather than transcended the male-dominated culture of which it is a part.

Cultural Revolutions

Only three major revolutions have created significant sex-role shifts in the history of humankind. The first was the domestication revolution, which was precipitated ten to fifteen thousand years ago by the taming of small animals and the cultivation of the soil. It is likely that women were responsible for these advances, because mothers and elderly women remained at the local campsite while men hunted and foraged for food. Improving their living conditions no doubt enhanced women's status as well—for a time. This first revolution led to a more settled life-style and clearly differentiated sex roles in the emerging plow and herding cultures.

The second great "wave," according to Toffler,[1] euphemistically called the Industrial Revolution by most, was in reality several stages of economic development beginning at least two centuries ago and culminating in technology and services that would eventually sweep away the major rationalizations for fixed and discrete sex-role separation (or *sexegration*).

Some would claim that the third great revolution was the move to an information-based, electronic age; but feminists assert it was the gender revolution. The tip of this iceberg was seen in Abigail Adams's letter in 1777 to her husband John, the future president, as she asked that the members of the constitutional convention be generous to the women, lest they foment a rebellion.[2] Foretastes of the revolution also appeared in the women's education movement and in the abolition of slavery in the nineteenth century. In the twentieth century, suffragism and the vital employment of women during the major wars reveal the broadside of an emerging modern feminist movement in a high-tech culture.

Early Baptists and Women

Baptists and Protestants emerged in the plow culture of western and central Europe; and Southern Baptists now are scarcely three generations removed from that milieu. Their early English forebears could not suppress the creative and persistent contributions of some women who served as deacons, preachers, and hostesses for church-home meetings. Thus Baptists often became the objects of criticism for having "she-preachers" as much as for abounding in the lower-status trades groups. Women shared more than leadership roles, however; like their male counterparts, they were whipped, imprisoned, and otherwise persecuted for their beliefs and practices.

Two Baptist groups from England settled in America, the Regular Baptists (or Particular Baptists, as they often were called) and the General Baptists. In England women had had a much more active leadership role among the latter group. In America women voted in most Baptist churches, and some were deaconesses and elderesses. In the mid-1700s the role of women began to disturb some Baptists in the colonies, especially those under the influence of Particular Baptists in New England and the middle colonies, resulting in diminished female roles.

In the South Baptist women had a more active leadership role, largely due to the influence of Separate Baptists, who emerged during the widespread revival that followed the Great Awakening. The new Separate churches ordained women as deaconesses and elderesses, but some women also gained reputations as effective and eloquent preachers. These frontier Baptists flourished in rural areas of the Carolinas and Virginia and aroused opposition from the Regulars, who were settled more in the cities of those colonies. These urban Baptists were more Calvinistic in theology, more educated, and valued an orderly worship alien to the frontier.

When the two types of Baptists eventually merged, they maintained the warm, informal, evangelistic mode of the Separates and for the most part followed the doctrine of the Regulars, thus suppressing the visible and vocal roles of women. After the split into Northern and Southern Baptists in the pre-Civil War period, patterns of gender roles shifted again. Northern Baptists (later American Baptists) eventually became more open to women's leadership participation, and Southern Baptists became increasingly conservative. Southern Baptist women appeared to compensate by taking a major role in children's moral and religious education, vacation Bible schools, and missionary education and promotion.[3]

Early Twentieth-Century Patterns

In the late nineteenth and early twentieth centuries, the development of factories, urbanism, immigration, wars, and economic shifts produced unique movements and upheavals in personal and family roles. For many house-holds factory production removed the male from the household economy of the farm and locked in place the adage "A woman's place is in the home." Nevertheless, during this period women founded or endorsed a number of movements seeking goals in social reform such as suffrage, abolition of sla-very, compulsory education, child labor laws, and temperance—all of which did little to improve their own status and power in society or the church. Methodists, Congregationalists, and Quakers were among the few denomina-tions allowing women to preach. However, some new religious sects were being formed by pathfinders such as Mary Baker Eddy, Ann Lee, the Fox sisters, and Aimee Semple McPherson.

Every decade of the twentieth century has chipped away at familiar man-woman roles and relations. The erratic shifts between liberalism and conserva-tism in church and society have created a roller coaster journey for women—in and out of higher education, to and from the labor force, and up and down in the pulpit.

The Contemporary Scene

The various women's movements are now a generation old, but the advances are modest even in the secular areas of our culture. Religious backlashes against the secular movements have not been uncommon. Yet the proportion of women in law, medicine, management, and engineering is steadily climbing (though generally not exceeding 25 percent by the close of the 1980s). By no means, however, have similar gains been made in the evangelical ministry.

Southern Baptists were not among the first to publish declarative state-ments about the status of women in the church. Conferences and books on the issue of equity for women did not appear in this denomination until the mid-1970s. And never have Southern Baptist women and their supporters among the brethren been as strident, for instance, about language changes in hymns and services as those in some evangelical and mainline bodies.

Southern Baptist women began to hold state and national denominational offices by the mid-1970s. Although their election to the major boards, commis-sions, and standing committees of the conventions constituted only 1.9 percent of the total membership of 772, distributed among twenty-five such groups in 1962, the proportion of these women had grown to 6 percent by 1975 and reached its peak of 13 percent in 1978, just as the convention began to make a swing toward fundamentalism. During that period in the late 1970s, women also occasionally were being recognized for distinguished denominational service beyond their traditional roles with children, music, and missions. And in 1978, after most other major evangelical bodies had held such consciousness-raising conferences, three hundred invited participants attended the National Convocation on Women in the Southern Baptist Convention, held in Nashville.

As a result of the fundamentalist movement's growing success and the fundamentalist view on the role of women in the denomination, the percentage of women on decision-making boards dropped to a low of 6 percent in the mid-1980s. The gradual increase to 10.6 percent female representation on these boards late in the decade could not be interpreted as a major change of perspective on the equal status of women, however; many of the new appointments appeared to be fundamentalist pastors' wives and other women who shared the fundamentalist position. What this eventually would mean in the actual working of the convention remained to be seen.

As Southern Baptist women had, in the 1970s, slowly been making their way into positions of denominational leadership, women throughout Protestantism also were making their way into local church pulpits. By 1970 there were an estimated seven thousand clergywomen throughout the nation,[4] the largest number being Pentecostals, with only a handful being Southern Baptists. During the next decade, Jeanette Stokes reported that the number of clergywomen in the top ten Protestant bodies alone had grown to four thousand, with the United Methodists and American Baptists leading.[5] Her findings are supported by those of Carroll, Hargrove, and Lummis, who enumerated women clergy in the mainline Protestant denominations (see table 11.1). At that time they asserted that there were too few Southern Baptist clergywomen to be included in their study.[6]

In truth there were then more Southern Baptist than Lutheran clergywomen, but fewer Southern Baptist women pastors of local churches. A studied estimate would indicate that the number of evangelical clergywomen has probably more than doubled during the decade of the eighties, but the records maintained by Anders indicate that at least a four-fold increase occurred among Southern Baptist clergywomen during this period. By 1991 there were more than eight hundred ordained Southern Baptist women, but

Table 11.1

Women Clergy in Selected Denominations

Denomination	Number of Women Clergy		Women Clergy as % of Total	
	1977	1981	1977	1981
American Baptist	157	NA	1.8	NA
American Lutheran	18	93	0.3	1.3
Christian (Disciples)*	388	317	5.7	4.8
Episcopal	94	425	0.8	3.4
Lutheran in America	55	210	0.7	2.6
Presbyterian (USA)	75	180	1.4	3.3
United Church of Christ	400	757	4.1	7.8
United Methodist	319	1316	0.8	3.6
United Presbyterian (USA)	295	630	2.1	4.5

Sources: 1977 data from Jacquet, Constant H., Jr. *Women Ministers in 1977* (Office of Research, Evaluation and Planning, National Council of Churches, March 1978), 9–13; 1981 data from Carroll, Jackson W., Barbara Hargrove, and Adair T. Lummis. *Women of the Cloth: A New Opportunity for the Churches* (San Francisco: Harper & Row, 1983)

* includes ordained and licensed ministers; not all are in parish ministry.

only thirty-eight were serving as local church pastors, with fifty-six serving as associate pastors. Among these women the pastoral role remains the most visible, desired—and controversial—form of leadership.

Assessing Contemporary SBC Women and Their Denomination

The two authors of this chapter have been engaged in three relevant research projects attempting to measure and describe the present role of Southern Baptist women at various levels of their denominational participation. The first project is Anders's ongoing research on women's roles in all types of lay and ordained ministry. The second project is Anders's compilation of a detailed file on the clergywomen, containing descriptions of their calls, their education, their professional positions, and assessments of their status. The third report is Metcalf-Whittaker's case studies of women pastors and assistant/associate pastors, their supporters, their opponents, and the ordained women's personal responses to their uncommon or nontraditional roles.

Women as members of local congregations. Southern Baptist women are probably in a clear majority in the pews of most local churches, at least 53 to 57 percent of the total congregation, as in most major Protestant groups. Records in the SBC annuals indicate that women serve as messengers from those congregations to the annual conventions in much fewer numbers than do men, recently between 39 percent and 42 percent of total registrants. More revealing has been the fact that although the overwhelming majority of male messengers are local church staff professionals, only 8 to 10 percent of the women have been. Most women registrants are homemakers (spouses of male staff and denominational workers) or lay messengers.

On the staffs of local churches, women have been in a very small minority (around 10 percent) in the last two decades. This stands in ironic contrast to their numbers during the late 1940s and early 1950s. During that time women occupied as many as one-third to 40 percent of nonpastoral church-staff positions.

Women as denominational employees. Various convention records for this generation indicate that women have fairly consistently made up about one-fourth of the denominational employees. In 1991 women comprised only 20 percent of the denominational work force (see table 11.2). Investigation of their job titles in the SBC annuals places them almost exclusively in middle management or office-support systems. At the 1978 National Convocation on Women, an employment report attested to the fact that these women employees considered themselves overqualified and underpaid when they compared themselves to their male counterparts.

Women on decision-making boards. The total number of elected decision makers on the denomination's eighteen major boards and commissions has ranged between seven hundred and eight hundred sixty-four during the last two decades, with the number of women members ranging between twelve and ninety-two. The percentage has never exceeded 13 percent of the total. The boards are predominantly clergy, but no ordained clergywomen have thus far served. Even if there were equal distribution between male and female laity and between

Table 11.2

Women in the Southern Baptist Convention, 1991

SBC Churches	37,974		
SBC Membership	15,044,413		

Ministers	Total	Women	Percentage
Pastors	@ 33,194	38	0.11
Retired pastors	4,899	3	0.06
Evangelists	898	NA	
Associate pastors	3,154	56	1.80
Chaplains	@ 3,400	182	5.40
Denominational jobs	3,985	31	0.80
District missionaries	@ 1,000	0	0.00
Newly ordained	1,921	100	5.20
Other ordained	11,922	400	3.40
Professional Church Staff (Ordained and Nonordained)	27,167	@ 2,225	8.20
Full-time employees	@ 1,316	@ 264	20.1
Boards (18)	864	92	10.6
Committees	108	15	13.9
State campus-ministry directors	34	4	11.8
Seminaries (6)			
Faculty/administration	522	57	10.9
Trustees	286	13	5.5
State Conventions:			
Executvie directors	42	0	0.00
Asst. directors	19	0	0.00
Presidents	39	1	2.60
Editors	40	4	10.00
Assistant editors	19	5	26.30

Sources: Southern Baptist Handbook, 1991; interviews with SBC Research and Statistics Division, Nashville, Tenn. and Anders Master List of SBC Ordained Clergywomen, Jan. 1992.

clergy and laity, with the dearth of female clergy from which to draw, 25 percent would be the highest probable proportion of women serving in these crucial decision-making positions.

Women as denominational officials. Women are scarce in the upper echelons of state and national conventions. There have been no executive directors at either level, and the highest proportion of women assistant state directors has been 15 percent. There were none in 1990. There have been more women assistant editors than senior editors for the state papers, but the numbers in both positions can be counted on one's fingers.

The National Student Ministries Department also is heavily male. In the post-World War II years, women were common among local campus directors, but they have comprised less than 20 percent in the last twenty years. They are certainly less likely than the men to be ordained, in spite of the "minister" label they wear. Women in these campus positions could, if they were present, be strong role models for women students as they make vocational choices.

Women within the seminary environs. Southern Baptist seminaries have been consistently coeducational for the past fifty years, although the earliest female students were not granted diplomas from the seminaries themselves. The proportion of women seminarians fluctuated in every decade, but they remained concentrated in religious education and music programs. In the last fifteen years, however, the number of women theology students has steadily increased, according to SBC Education Commission annual reports.

Until the 1980s there were no women faculty members in the theology schools of the seminaries, and the proportion of these women professors had not reached even 10 percent by the end of the decade. After the 1984 SBC resolution against the ordination of women, two seminaries (Southeastern and Southern) reacted by appointing between them one female assistant professor of theology (now tenured), one female dean of a new program, and one female chaplain.[7] Were the seminaries expressing their displeasure with the convention's decision? As suggested by table 11.3, they are still far from balancing the numbers of women and men they employ.

Table 11.3

Women* Faculty and Administrators in Southern Baptist Seminaries, 1989

Seminary	Total Faculty	Women Faculty	Total Administrators	Women Administrators
Golden Gate	24	1	16	1
Midwestern	27	1	18	2
New Orleans	47	3	7	0
Southeastern	34	1	12	1
Southern School of:			62	21
Theology	49	3		
Church Music	15	1		
Christian Education	11	2		
Carver School of Social Work	7	3		
Southwestern School of:			40	12
Theology	49	0		
Religious Education	26	4		
Church Music	24	6		
Others with faculty status	9	1		

Source: Southern Baptist Convention Annual, 1990.
* Numbers of women could only be estimated based on apparent gender of names.

Consequently there have been few role models for women on these campuses to help as they search out their specific calls to ministry. The problem is increased as one notes that women have remained under 30 percent of the administrative staff (almost always supportive office personnel) and under 5 percent of the trustees. Actually, only the three more moderate seminaries have routinely had *any* women on their boards. Thus although one-third or more of Baptist seminary students are women preparing for a wide variety of professional ministries, they are taught by faculties with fewer than 8 percent women professors, directed by higher administrations that are almost exclusively male, and governed by trustee policy makers that are only 5 percent female.

Southern Baptist Clergywomen

Southern Baptists were slow to admit the contemporary relevance of the Old Testament prophet's words, "Your sons and your daughters shall prophesy" (Joel 2:28). When Virginia Baptist Addie Davis was ordained in 1964, she became the modern pioneer (now retired) who quietly led the way in the ordination of women in her denomination. Though ordained in a Southern Baptist church, she found her place of ministry as pastor of an American Baptist congregation.

Because Southern Baptists have no national hierarchy that governs ordination, each local church has had to make its own decisions. And where national records were kept, no one thought to ask about the gender of the ordained. Those women who have followed in Davis's train have not then been officially categorized as a denominational statistic. Keeping track of ordained women was not a task people at headquarters were eager to assume; those who cared to know have had to work from the ground up.

Since 1981 Anders has been seeking to identify all existing and newly ordained Southern Baptist clergywomen. Information on the circumstances of their ordination and their current position has been gathered from whatever sources possible (from the "grapevine" to various Baptist news sources). An inventory has been mailed to each woman identified to secure data on her educational and professional experience, including the nature of her present ministry. Out of more than six hundred confirmed clergywomen contacted, almost one-half have completed inventories, often including candid accounts of their experiences. The 308 who had completed inventories by the end of 1991 were representative of the larger master list in locale, education, and position.

Although a few Southern Baptists had written accounts of the status of the church woman, none had dealt exclusively with the ordination of women for the diaconate and the pastoral ministry. Certainly Alma Hunt's *History of Woman's Missionary Union* and its predecessor *In Royal Service: The Mission Work of Southern Baptist Women* by Fannie E. S. Heck dealt with a very important contribution of women to one phase of Southern Baptist life.[8]

The first general treatment of women in the denomination, Leon McBeth's *Women in Baptist Life,* was also the first treatment of women as deacons and clergy. At the time of its publication in 1979, the number of ordained

Southern Baptist clergywomen was evidently under one hundred. McBeth mentions Helen Turner's personal file of just under sixty names of clergywomen (including herself), fifteen years after the ordination of Davis in North Carolina.[9] In the span of a decade, then, that estimate had grown tenfold.

Estimates of women in the diaconate are understandably even less accurate, but they far exceed the number of women ministers. In the SBC publication the *Deacon,* a 1973 report indicated that there had been churches with women deacons as early as the 1920s, but their numbers had mushroomed during the early 1970s. By 1976, in Virginia alone, the state Christian Life Commission reported 520 women deacons. There were also women chairs of deacons during these years.[10] One can safely estimate that several hundred churches have ordained women on their boards of deacons, a number that is likely still growing.[11]

Greater than 80 percent of the Southern Baptist women who have been ordained to the ministry have achieved that status during the last decade—ironically also the decade of shift toward strong conservatism in the convention. Indeed the greatest number of ordinations were in 1984 and 1986, years when significant actions were taken asserting the subordinate roles of women in the convention and at the Home Mission Board. In 1984 the SBC adopted a resolution stating that in order to reduce confusion and preserve submission, and because woman sinned first, women should not assume roles of authority in the church. In 1986, citing this resolution as justification, the Home Mission Board refused thereafter to give financial aid to churches that called female pastors. Rather than subduing women, these actions seem to have spurred them to greater action.

In addition to historical forces, regional factors certainly operate in the present denominational climate. The same four states in the SBC—North Carolina, Texas, Virginia, and Kentucky—account for more than 46 percent of the ordinations of clergywomen and more than 47 percent of the churches and institutions employing them. That is, of course, no accident, because the two Southern Baptist seminaries that historically have accepted the movement of women into ministry are located in Louisville, Kentucky, and Wake Forest, North Carolina. Although the Atlantic seaboard states in general are the most open, ordained women serve in at least twenty-two states and four foreign countries. Some of the most successful of these women—successful in the sense of being in positions to which they felt called and for which they specifically trained—are those who received clinical pastoral education and now serve as chaplains in the military or in a variety of hospital and correctional institutions.

Almost all Southern Baptist clergywomen (90 percent) have a seminary degree. This is roughly double the rate for Southern Baptist clergymen. [12] In addition 21 percent of the clergywomen have university graduate degrees, and 13.5 percent either have doctorates or are completing their doctoral programs. Almost one-third of them reported they had clinical pastoral education certification (CPE). As is often the case for women entering a previously male-dominated profession, the educational qualifications of these women place them far ahead of their male colleagues.

Table 11.4 gives an account of the kinds of positions held by these women. As illustrated, in 1991 there were thirty-eight women serving congregations as pastors (three others were retired), fifty-six as associate pastors, and 182 as chaplains. Considerable diversity in their roles is evident. Second to the chaplains (in varied settings) were those occupying supporting—"associate"—ministerial roles (youth, education, music, children, and other profes-

Table 11.4

Employment of Southern Baptist Clergywomen, 1991

Position	Number	Percentage
Pastors	38	4.7
Retired pastors	3	.4
Associate pastors	56	6.9
Chaplains	182	22.5
Other professional staff	166	20.5
Missionaries	9	1.1
Social work/counseling	21	2.6
Professors (college or seminary)	15	1.8
Other ordained	320	39.5
Total	810	100.0%

sional staff positions). Noteworthy are those who have pursued counseling and social work professions.

That many Southern Baptists still strongly oppose the ordination of women is evident in the actions of some of the denomination's 1209 local associations. Churches in Oklahoma, Kentucky, California, and Tennessee, which have ordained women, have been dismissed from their respective associations. Some state conventions also have adopted resolutions voicing their disfavor of the practice; but, of course, local Baptist congregations remain autonomous. Associational and state actions create a good deal of publicity and may intimidate other churches, but they rarely have any real effect on the functioning of the censured churches.

Such actions do, however, create a climate in which the status of ordained women is an issue. The response of these women to that situation is reflected in their answers to questions posed on the inventory, some of which are shown in table 11.5. As we can see there, almost all of these clergywomen view the issue of women's status in the convention as important, the vast majority as *very* important. On this they are even more convinced than average Baptists—Nancy Ammerman reports that 52 percent of the local church leaders she surveyed saw the ordination of women as a "major issue."[13] We can also see that a considerable majority (59 percent) of Southern Baptist clergywomen report that they frequently have experienced prejudice because of their ordination, and 14 percent believe there exists a general attitude of hostility toward them within the denomination.

Ordained women are naturally controversial and symbolic, and they are aware of it. They sit at the heart of the fundamentalist-moderate controversy, representing each side's cause—either to be purged from the Southern Baptist Convention as the embodiment of liberalism or to be held up in triumph as the symbol of open-mindedness and independence.

Their symbolic importance is, in the eyes of ordained women and those who work closely with them, a problem at times. They do not want to be exhibited as emblems of anyone's theology. They want to work in church or denominational settings as ministers recognized for their abilities, not their gender. One woman who is a leading advocate of women's ordination declared, "I'm so tired of walking into a meeting and being an issue." Another woman, a minister, said, "We've become a flag that each side waves. The moderates say, 'Look at how liberal we are. We even support women being pastors.'" One conservative male pastor admitted that he listens to tapes of a female Bible teacher who he says actually preaches. His friends tease him about being a liberal for listening to "women preachers."

The symbolic importance of women does not relate only to the SBC conflict. Women who take on pastoral roles are threatening a traditional division of sexes that is desired not only by conservative men but by conservative women. As one female pastor described her encounters with other women:

> One of the issues that I've had a great deal of trouble with is that because I am ordained I've found that there are some women who are very threatened by that . . . as if that [ordination] puts me in an elite category. And I have had to deal with that in women's groups . . . also that I'm a pastor . . . I have gotten a lot of attention. But I've paid for my legitimacy, and there are a lot of women who are afraid to ask for ordination, and therefore find it frightening that other women are.

She went on to describe a meeting at which an unordained woman tried to express her support for women "in ministry," but assumed that only "radical feminists" would support women as pastors. The female pastor said of her own reaction, "I felt incredibly disappointed. And my own view is that I feel like I'm willing to accept women on a wide spectrum. I think we need the variety. Ordination for me is not an issue of something that's [of] value or importance as a minister."

Some of the strains faced by Southern Baptist clergywomen are common to other working women as well. There is evidence of concern, for instance, about family issues. After the 1985 convocation on women held at Southeastern Baptist Theological Seminary, one clergywoman reported that "several" of the women ministers who attended the convocation reported that family responsibilities, particularly being a mother, are a "hurdle," as they termed it, in their ministry. They have to balance ministry and family responsibilities and sometimes fear a "breakdown of family life".[14] This obviously has been a longtime dilemma for clergymen as well. And working women at all levels of secular life have had to perform balancing acts among their numerous contemporary roles, including their family ones.

Some of the research on women in the ministry has dealt with the dilemmas of role conflict. As Carroll, Hargrove, and Lummis hypothesize, "We suspect that, even for some women, a part of socialization into the status of ordained ministry involves having to come to terms with their own ambivalence about occupying two statuses that have traditionally been kept separate" [i.e., "minister" and "woman"].[15] They found that women were significantly less likely than men to decide to enter seminary before they had finished college. Women were more likely to have interrupted career paths toward the ministry, trying other occupations first.[16] The findings of Anders and Metcalf-Whittaker on Southern Baptist women differ. Most Southern Baptist clergywomen they questioned did not delay long after college before going to seminary, although they did not decide to become ordained at the same time as they decided to attend seminary.

Whether to become ordained, in fact, was not a theologically straightforward decision for these women. Most of these respondents (82 percent) believe that ordination is more ecclesiastical than biblical. "Baptists need more of a theology for ordination. . . . I don't need to be ordained but my church needs to ordain me," explained one associate minister. But many wrote in that if a denomination chooses to set apart and affirm a calling, there should be no gender barriers or discriminations.

A large proportion of these Baptist clergywomen (93 percent) believe that the seminaries could and should support them in a more active manner (something less likely to happen now that seminary boards are controlled by fundamentalists). But even if gender barriers came down in the seminaries, the local churches would prove a problem. Whether ordained women can find places to serve in local churches is an issue about which the women surveyed have doubts. A very large number of the respondents (88 percent) feel that there are still areas closed to women, the chiefs of which are the local church pastorate and denominational positions. (Only about 5 percent of them have held any state or national elected offices.)

Not surprisingly, then, they believe that only a minority of SBC churches are ready to consider a woman as a pastor. Ammerman reported that 45 percent of her 1986 respondents claimed they would support the hiring of a "qualified ordained woman to their staff." Most indicated, however, that they would support her in roles other than the pastorate. In the 1985 survey, 26 percent said they felt that women could be ordained as pastors, but these

Table 11.5
SBC Women in Ministry Inventory

Item (Number of Responses)	Response	Percentage
Do you feel that the role of women in the SBC is an important issue in the current controversy? (296)	Very important	81.7
	Somewhat important	17.6
	Not important	.7
Have you experienced prejudice or resentment about ordained women? (297)	Frequently	58.9
	Seldom	39.4
	Never	1.7
What is the general attitude of SBC men toward your status as an ordained woman? (373)	Favorable	23.3
	Tolerate	52.0
	Hostile	13.9
	Indifferent	10.7
Are there still areas of ministry that you feel are closed to you? (290)	Yes	87.9
	No	12.1
What do you think is the future for ordained SBC women? (304)	Bright	1.9
	Long-range hope	57.6
	Bleak	40.5
Do you think the seminaries should take a more active role in supporting ordained women? (300)	Yes	88.0
	No	12.0
Have you ever considered leaving for another, more open denomination (273) [17 of those responding have left.]	Often	44.3
	Rarely	39.6
	Never	16.1
How many SBC local churches do you think would consider a woman minister? (291)	Majority	.3
	Minority	99.7
Do you believe ordination is biblical or ecclesiastical? (260)	Biblical	17.7
	Ecclesiastical	82.3
Are you a member of the SBC Women in Ministry organization? (300)	Yes	53.0
	No	47.0
Have you attended one of these one or more times? (461)	SBC convention	61.7
	Pastors' Conference	22.0
	Women in Ministry	45.3
	Southern Baptist Alliance	24.7
Have you held a state or SBC office? (300)	Yes	5.0

opinions varied widely between the moderate and the fundamentalist camps. On the moderate side, a large majority of both laity and clergy would ordain and/or hire a woman; on the fundamentalist side, there was a considerable gap between laity and clergy: ministers were almost totally opposed to the practice, whereas the laity were somewhat less opposed.[17]

Given the recent direction of the convention, it is not surprising that most of the clergywomen sample (58 percent) profess only long-range hopefulness that their denominational climate will change, whereas 41 percent declare that the outlook is decidedly bleak. The somewhat cautious optimism of the majority is reflected in the comments of the 1989 president of Southern Baptist Women in Ministry: "Change doesn't come easily. It's worth waiting for. We need to be prophetic and call for the change while at the same time being realistic that it takes time. . . . And despite convention resolutions and slow change, we're not destroyed. We're building a bridge for the next generation."[18]

A few are not willing to wait for bridges to be built. Seventeen respondents indicated on the inventory that they have already left the denomination for other roles, and 84 percent admitted to having considered leaving their mother denomination for more tolerant and affirming bodies. The churches most mentioned as providing this openness were Presbyterian, American Baptist, United Church of Christ, and United Methodists. All of the ordained women interviewed by Metcalf-Whittaker indicated that they preferred to remain Southern Baptist but would rather change denominations than cease working as ministers.

One of the women who has left, Rev. Frances Browne, was reared and educated as a Southern Baptist but is now a Methodist pastor serving two rural churches. Another, who has stayed, told the *Atlanta Constitution,* "It angers me that seminary teaches that we are all called of God. They give us Masters of Divinity degrees and then say, 'there are no places for you.'"[19] Women who have pastoral jobs often receive lower salaries than men in similar positions.

Some of the clergywomen recognize the attempts that have been made to support them, even when that support is not quite what they had expected or hoped for. Said one woman interviewed by Metcalf-Whittaker:

Everybody's not at the same place on women. But there are people
trying to be open and some people are taking steps and it's hard, . . .
and there are some people who aren't where I want them to be. . . .
Sometimes I get angry 'cause I think, 'I'm just a token.' But at other
times I look at it and I say, 'These are people trying hard, who are
trying to behave with what they say they believe. They're just not totally there yet, but they're making an effort.'

Even with good intentions and efforts by some, it is clear that no dramatic
change can be expected toward the universal acceptance of clergywomen
among Southern Baptists. This is particularly the case as long as the overall
theological and political climate is dominated by fundamentalists.

During the period covered by this research, a continuing upward trend
has been charted among moderate states and churches. There is no reason to
believe they will diminish in their ordination and employment of these well-
educated, committed women. Both the Alliance of Baptists and the Cooperative Baptist Fellowship are clearly supportive of women ministers, with virtually all of those surveyed at the fellowship's May 1991 convocation saying
they approve of ordaining women. In fact, nearly one-fifth of the clergy
present at that meeting were female.[20]

Among the women themselves, some are fairly comfortably serving in
vocations for which they have trained and to which they feel called. For that
large group of women who are in positions to which they do not feel ultimately called and for which they are not specifically trained, the frustration
runs deep. And almost everyone experiences considerable hurt from the perceived intolerance in much of the convention.

The present conflict between fundamentalists and moderates in the
Southern Baptist Convention serves as a model of the much larger tension
between tradition and change. Within an organization whose purpose in part
is to preserve tradition, the very difficult struggle of women to take on the
highest leadership roles (i.e., pastor, deacon, and denomination leader) probably will continue for some time. With tradition-minded fundamentalists in
charge, that will be all the more true. Although inerrancy in biblical interpretation may be their avowed first concern, the ordination of women serves as
a visible test of the "inerrant" biblical interpretations they support.

Yet there are women who will continue to answer the personal call they feel. Ironically, it is a call about which they learned from the very denomination that now questions it. Southern Baptists believe that individuals should answer God's call, no matter who questions it, and that is what some women are doing and will continue to do.

Notes

1. Alvin Toffler, *The Third Wave* (New York: William Morrow, 1980).
2. Published in Charles Adams, *Familiar Letters of John and Abigail Adams* (Boston: Houghton, Mifflin, 1899).
3. For more detailed historical data on early American women in Baptist life, see William L. Lumpkin, "The Role of Women in Eighteenth Century Virginia Baptist life," *Baptist History and Heritage* 8, no. 3 (July 1973): 163; and Leon McBeth, *Women in Baptist Life* (Nashville, Tenn.: Broadman, 1979), 37.
4. *Newsweek,* 2 Nov. 1970, 81.
5. *South of the Garden,* 3 Dec. 1981, 4.
6. Jackson Carroll, Barbara Hargrove, and Adair T. Lummis, *Women of the Cloth: A New Opportunity for the Churches* (San Francisco: Harper & Row, 1983), 2.
7. Recounted, ironically, in David O. Beale. *S.B.C.: House on the Sand?* (Greenville, S.C.: Unusual Publications, 1985), 181.
8. Alma Hunt, *History of Woman's Missionary Union* (Birmingham, Ala.: Woman's Missionary Union, 1964); Fannie E. S. Heck, *In Royal Service: The Mission Work of Southern Baptist Women* (Nashville, Tenn.: Broadman, 1913).
9. McBeth, *Women in Baptist Life* (Nashville, Tenn.: Broadman, 1979), 154.
10. Ibid., 144.
11. Nancy Tatom Ammerman in *Baptist Battles: Social Change and Religious Conflict in the Southern Baptist Convention* (New Brunswick, N.J.: Rutgers Univ. Press, 1990), 97 reports 37 percent of local church leaders *individually* support ordaining women deacons; 17 percent say their

church supports it; but only 7 percent report that they have women currently serving. Still that may amount to nearly two thousand churches.

12. A 1983 survey by the Home Mission Board indicated that 43.2 percent had completed seminary or beyond. This compared closely with the 45 percent figure reported by churches on their 1982 Uniform Church Letter (their annual report to the denomination). See C. Price, "A Study of the Educational Attainment of Southern Baptist Pastors, 1983" (Atlanta: Home Mission Board, 1984).

13. Ammerman, *Baptist Battles,* 94.

14. Felicia Stewart Hoyle, "Partnership in the Gospel. Convocation on Women: A Report from the Workgroups" (unpublished, 1985), 8.

15. Carroll, Hargrove, and Lummis, *Women of the Cloth,* 11.

16. Ibid., 70.

17. Ammerman, *Baptist Battles,* 96-97.

18. Adelle M. Banks, "Female Ministers Fidget But Stick with Baptists" *Orlando Sentinel,* 17 June 1989, 9D.

19. Nancy Hastings Sehested, quoted in Lee Walburn, "Southern Baptist Leaders Rejecting Women Pastors," *Atlanta Constitution,* Apr. 21, 1987, 1C, 4C.

20. Ammerman, "Convocation Survey Reveals Much Experience, Many Shared Priorities," *Fellowship News,* Dec. 1991, 3-4.

CHAPTER 12

PERCEPTIONS OF ACADEMIC FREEDOM IN SOUTHERN BAPTIST COLLEGES

Larry C. Ingram, Robert Thornton, and Reneé L. Edwards

Conflict is certainly not new for Baptists. They were born in disagreements over slavery and have experienced periodic conflicts over beliefs and polity through-out their history. But the conflict of the 1980s was different. According to long-time observer Porter Routh, the novel aspect of the contemporary struggle has been the level of overt political activity.[1] The extent to which candidates for denominational office have openly campaigned, maneuvered for position, sought endorsements, and used paid advertisements has increased to the point where election competition can be characterized as qualitatively different. And the force driving this high level of political activity is the existence, for the first time, of an explicit platform, a reform agenda tying the presidency of the SBC to eliminating theological opponents and changing the denomination's institutions. By 1990 fundamentalists had accomplished their goal, and most, if not all, SBC agencies were controlled by reform-minded trustees.

Because of the division of labor among Southern Baptists, however, control over the denomination allows for control over the seminaries but not the colleges. The colleges are owned and operated by the state conventions, so that intrusion into college affairs requires dominance at the state level. Fundamentalists have not been as successful in the state conventions as they have at the national level.[2] Consequently they have not been in position to bring as much pressure on the colleges as they can on the seminaries.

This does not mean that the colleges have avoided controversy. Throughout Baptist history, educational institutions have been targets of criticism. But a growing number of incidents have been reported over the last three years. Probably the most widely publicized was the "open letter" sent by Lee Roberts to some six thousand Georgia Baptists. The letter accused the president of Mercer University of holding a heretical theological viewpoint, identified a variety of moral problems Roberts perceived at Mercer, took issue with the way in which Mercer selects its trustees, and put forth Roberts's solutions to these problems.

Baylor University has long been the target of Texas fundamentalists. It was the concerns of Baylor students, according to Paul Pressler, that galvanized his interest in SBC affairs. The university has been publicly criticized for hiring a Mormon in its foreign language department, but the school has resisted efforts to have the individual terminated. The question of whether to have dances on campus has often made the news. And the film society at Baylor was dissolved for showing morally offensive movies.

A student at Missouri Baptist College complained to her pastor about a textbook, producing a series of events that led to an administrative decision to emphasize creationism as opposed to evolution. Apparently the college's faculty were instructed in how to conduct their classes. Two faculty members were not rehired, and a third longtime teacher chose to resign. A trustee also resigned in protest against the school's infringement on academic freedom.

At the Alabama Baptist Convention in 1987, messengers passed a resolution calling on its agencies to "build their professional staffs and faculties from those who clearly reflect the dominant convictions and beliefs held by Southern Baptists at large" (language adopted from the SBC Peace Committee report, passed earlier that year). This followed a strong campaign by fundamentalists to prevent the hiring at Samford University of a provost they suspected of theological error.

These and other incidents represent intrusions into the educational process as it had been in place in Southern Baptist colleges. Their occurrence has to do not only with the cognitive position of fundamentalism—a way of thinking that is often alien to secular educators—but also with the peculiar role of the denominational college as a nonsecular educational institution. Denominational colleges exist under a set of contradictory expectations that often manifest themselves in goal or mission statements.[3] These statements express the goal of such colleges to support—or at least not to undermine—the world view of the churches while providing an exposure to knowledge and values upon which alternative world views have been based. Much of the criticism against Baptist colleges has been that they have not taught students to discount these alternatives.[4] The irony in this is that the colleges are accused of taking seriously the very knowledge that justifies their existence as institutions separate from the churches.

Thus Baptist colleges operate out of a dilemma. If the dilemma is not managed well, the school is vulnerable. On the one hand, to lean too far in the direction of religious socialization diminishes their standing as educational structures. They might as well be extensions of the churches themselves. On the other hand, to question the traditions and practices of the church threatens their relation with significant segments of the supporting constituency. To eschew all religious commitments would be to give up their unique status as *denominational* colleges.

Maintaining their relationship to the Baptist constituency is important to the colleges in a variety of ways. First, most colleges receive from their state conventions operating funds of about 5 to 10 percent of their total budget.[5] Second, a highly variable but usually large percentage of the student body comes from Baptist churches. Tuition and fees represent 40 to 60 percent of the budget. Third, many churches and individuals make gifts or donations to the colleges out of their interest in Baptist life. Together these facts mean that Baptist colleges, particularly the smaller and less prestigious ones, are economically dependent upon denominational support.

Beyond that it would be a serious omission to ignore the factor of denominational and theological loyalty in assessing the position of the colleges. In the survey reported here, almost two-thirds of the respondents (62.7 percent) claim to be members of Baptist churches, and the overwhelming majority (80 percent) of these state that they are active participants. Although these schools see themselves as Christian colleges first, there is no evidence here that they wish to pursue their task independently of the denomination.

Baptist colleges are therefore locked into a denomination that makes contradictory demands upon them. The denomination itself is in a state of disarray, the outcome of which may well determine the developmental direction of the colleges.[6]

Many in the SBC are convinced that their colleges are not faithful to the Baptist cause. Nancy Ammerman found that about two-thirds of her national sample of clergy and lay leaders agree that there are people teaching in Baptist schools who "do not believe what Baptists ought to believe." Furthermore, those who accept this view are much more willing to see the governing boards of SBC agencies stacked with fundamentalists. They also express considerably lower levels of confidence in the doctrinal soundness of other SBC agencies.[7]

Such a situation could hardly fail to have some impact upon the people who work in these institutions. It was with this understanding in mind that the survey reported below was undertaken.

Sample and Method

The population from which this sample was drawn consisted of full-time faculty members at the forty-six senior colleges and universities affiliated with the Southern Baptist Convention. The sample was selected in two stages. First, twelve colleges were chosen at random from the list of forty-six. Of these twelve, three could be described as larger and more prestigious than the other nine. Because of this it was decided to select a larger number of professors at these schools than at the others. In the second stage, then, twenty professors were randomly drawn from each of the three large colleges and ten professors from each smaller college.

In mid-February of 1988, the first mailing was sent to each of the 150 faculty members in the sample. Each packet contained a cover letter explaining the purpose of the survey, disclaiming any attachment to the parties in the dispute, and promising anonymity to all respondents. The letter was attached to a three-page questionnaire soliciting information on a number of background variables, including theological position, and containing several open-ended questions about academic freedom, obligations to their constituency, effects of the Controversy on their college, and support for colleagues who were criticized. Respondents also were asked to list any incidents that had occurred on their campus in the last five years. Finally, a stamped, self-addressed envelope was provided for returning the questionnaire.

In April a second mailing went to all nonrespondents, including those who had refused participation in the first instance. In this cover letter a promise of anonymity for both the respondent and the college was made. From the second mailing an additional thirty questionnaires were received. In all seventy-nine people (53 percent) replied in one way or another, and sixty-nine usable questionnaires (46 percent) were obtained.

Coding of the background items was a relatively straightforward procedure, with one exception. The theological viewpoint was determined by asking subjects to locate themselves on a ten-point scale, with one being fundamentalist and ten being liberal. Although three respondents resisted this continuum, the great majority of those who answered the questionnaire located themselves on the scale without comment. After inspecting the data, we opted to place the respondents into three categories: fundamentalist (1-3), moderate (4-6), and liberal (7-10). The reader is cautioned against attributing specific theological content to the positions, for the scale addressed no specific beliefs as properties of a position. In point of fact, our procedure probably inflates the liberal category by including those faculty who used higher numbers merely to distance themselves from fundamentalists. Regardless of the proper labels for these categories, those who placed themselves at different points on the continuum manifested consistently different response patterns to the questions.

Coding of the open-ended questions involved judgments by the two junior authors of the paper. Each, working independently, categorized the response as clearly positive, positive with qualifications, clearly negative, or negative with qualifications. In the event that ratings were in disagreement, the authors were instructed to reconcile their ratings through discussion. This proved to be almost unnecessary, as rater reliability exceeded 90 percent. Because the two "with qualifications" categories were usually very small, they have been collapsed into "yes" and "no" responses for this paper.

Although this research is descriptive in nature, the relationships among variables were subjected to statistical testing. Because the sample was small and because the differences among subgroups were not dramatic, most relationships were not statistically significant by usual sociological standards. Thus the reader is cautioned that the differences discussed do not have strong statistical support. At the same time, because certain of the relationships point consistently in terms of direction, we believe they may be empirically and substantively significant.

Results

Respondents were asked to give a definition of academic freedom, according to their personal view. Then they were asked, "Given your viewpoint, does academic freedom exist at your school?" Over three-quarters (78.9 percent) said without qualification that academic freedom does exist at their institution. An additional 14.1 percent agreed that it does exist, but placed some qualification on their statements. Only four respondents (7 percent) were classified as giving a negative response.

This strong perception of academic freedom as a property of Baptist colleges suggests that Baptist faculty are relatively comfortable with the conditions that exist on campus. In fact the comments indicate that most administrators work hard to deflect criticism and maintain an open environment. Professors would appear to perceive more support than threat from their campus administrators.

It should be borne in mind, of course, that the views of academic freedom held by persons who teach in Baptist colleges are likely to differ from those who teach elsewhere. Although the data here do not allow for a rigorous test of this supposition, a content analysis of the definitions of academic freedom shows some directions that such a test might take. Four themes appeared with considerable frequency in these definitions. The most frequent theme referred to "teaching the truth as one sees it." With some variation in wording, this idea was expressed in more than one-third (35.3 percent) of the responses. Yet almost one-fourth of the responses contained a second theme (third in frequency) that emphasized teaching "both" or "all" sides of an issue as a condition of academic freedom. One historian suggested that the highest of compliments is for students not to know the position of the teacher. Thus it seems that there is no consensus among these professors concerning whether the essence of academic freedom is to be found in exposing students to the instructor's considered judgment or in exposing students to a variety of viewpoints without necessarily taking sides.

In any case the second most prominent (30.8 percent) theme revolved around the notions of responsibility and limits (guidelines, boundaries). For these faculty members, academic freedom must take into account the potential impact of their statements on students or on the sponsoring organization. Four respondents clearly stated that those who cannot operate within the limits established by the school "should go elsewhere." Academic freedom for a sizable number of those faculty may not include the right to make others uncomfortable. This group is probably quite different from the fifteen respondents (22 percent) who said that the essence of academic freedom is the right to teach or publish "without fear of reprisal" (the fourth theme).

A second question asked, "If a person teaches at a Southern Baptist college, does this mean that he/she is obligated to support traditional or majority Baptist views on social or moral issues?" (See table 12.1.) Although the position implied in this question is a key plank in the fundamentalist platform, it was rejected by the majority of faculty polled here. Fifty-seven percent responded negatively, and almost one-half of those who gave a positive response offered some qualification to their positions.

Three of the background variables are associated with whether faculty think they must support dominant Baptist views on social or moral issues: theological leaning, tenure status, and length of service. But none of these differences are in the direction one might predict. Ironically, faculty who identify themselves as fundamentalist are *more* likely than either moderates or liberals to reject this position. Those who have tenure and those who have at least sixteen years of service at their school are more likely to endorse the necessity of conforming (see table 12.1). It appears that the more "established" one is, the more likely is the insistence on conformity.

Table 12.2 reports responses to the question "Would you defend a faculty member who took a controversial position on some issue relevant to his/her area of expertise?" A resounding 83.6 percent indicated a willingness to support a colleague, although this figure does include seventeen who placed some qualification on their involvement. As one forthrightly put it, "I would not place my job on the line." Nevertheless this figure indicates considerable faculty resistance to intrusive forces.

And here the differences along theological lines are more predictable. Fundamentalists (55.6 percent) are considerably less likely than liberals (100 percent) to say they are willing to defend a controversial colleague. In addition, active Southern Baptists are more likely than either inactive or non-SBC faculty to say they would defend others. And those who have long service at the school seem more willing to resist intrusion than more recent appointees.

A fourth question faculty were asked to consider was, "Do you think that the controversy in the Southern Baptist Convention has produced more pressure on faculty at your college to take conservative positions in their teaching and scholarship?" Almost 60 percent of those replying to this question answered in the negative (see table 12.3), reflecting their strong affirmation that academic freedom is still viable in Baptist schools. Still, more than four out of ten (40.3 percent) believe that there is more pressure to take conservative positions.

Again a marked difference exists in the responses of fundamentalists and

Table 12.1

Perceived Obligation to Teach Majority Views

"If a person teaches at a Southern Baptist College, does this mean that he/she is obligated to support traditional or majority Baptist views on social or moral issues?

Social Characteristic (Number of Cases)	% Replying Yes
Theological viewpoint	
Fundamentalist (10)	30.0
Moderate (26)	46.1
Liberal (24)	50.0
Highest earned degree	
Doctorate (42)	45.2
Master's (21)	38.1
Tenure Status	
Tenured (28)	57.2
Nontenured (35)	31.4
Church Affiliation	
SBC-active (34)	38.2
SBC-inactive (6)	83.3
Non-SBC (23)	39.1
Gender	
Male (43)	44.2
Female (17)	35.3
Length of Service	
15 years or fewer (44)	36.7
16 years or more (19)	57.9
Age	
40 or younger (19)	36.8
41–50 (17)	35.3
51–60 (17)	61.9
61 and older (6)	33.3

those less conservative theologically. The small group of fundamentalists was almost unanimous in rejecting the view that the Controversy has had a conservative impact on their campuses. If people have changed, the change is evidently not enough to be noticed by those who are the most conservative. Moderates and liberals, on the other hand, are almost evenly divided on whether or

Table 12.2

Willingness to Defend a Colleague

"Would you defend a faculty member who took a controversial position on some issue relevant to his/her area of expertise?"

Social Characteristic (Number of Cases)	% Replying Yes
Theological viewpoint*	
Fundamentalist (9)	55.6
Moderate (29)	75.1
Liberal (25)	100.0
Highest earned degree	
Doctorate (44)	86.3
Master's (23)	78.3
Tenure Status	
Tenured (28)	85.7
Nontenured (39)	82.1
Church Affiliation	
SBC-active (34)	88.2
SBC-inactive (8)	75.0
Non-SBC (26)	76.9
Gender	
Male (48)	85.4
Female (19)	78.9
Length of Service	
15 years or fewer (45)	80.0
16 years or more (21)	90.5
Age	
40 or younger (20)	90.0
41–50 (17)	82.4
51–60 (24)	79.2
61 and older (6)	83.3

*Differences are significant at .004 level.

not the Controversy has created conservative pressure. Table 12.3 also suggests that tenured more than nontenured, males more than females, and those with longer rather than shorter service agree that pressure in a conservative direction has been generated. Finally, those active in Southern Baptist churches are more likely than others to sense pressure.

Table 12.3

Perceived Conservative Pressure

"Do you think that the controversy in the Southern Baptist Convention has produced more pressure on faculty at your college to take conservative positions in their teaching and scholarship?"

Social Characteristic (Number of Cases)	% Replying Yes
Theological viewpoint*	
Fundamentalist (10)	10.0
Moderate (29)	27.6
Liberal (25)	36.0
Highest earned degree	
Doctorate (45)	31.1
Master's (23)	21.7
Tenure Status	
Tenured (29)	37.9
Nontenured (39)	20.5
Church Affiliation	
SBC-active (35)	25.7
SBC-inactive (7)	42.9
Non-SBC (26)	26.9
Gender	
Male (49)	26.5
Female (19)	31.6
Length of Service	
15 years or fewer (46)	28.3
16 years or more (22)	31.8
Age	
40 or younger (20)	30.0
41–50 (18)	38.9
51–60 (24)	25.0
61 and older (6)	0.0

Another question dealt directly with the effects of the Controversy: "Have you been affected in your role as professor by the controversy?" The responses are summarized in table 12.4. Slightly more than one out of four (27.9 percent) admit that they have altered their professorial role as a result of the Controversy. When asked how they have been affected, the replies indicated that generally

Table 12.4
Perceived Effects on Teaching

"If a person teaches at a Southern Baptist College, does this mean that he/she is obligated to support traditional or majority Baptist views on social or moral issues?"

Social Characteristic (Number of Cases)	% Replying Yes
Theological viewpoint*	
Fundamentalist (10)	30.0
Moderate (26)	46.1
Liberal (24)	50.0
Highest earned degree	
Doctorate (42)	45.2
Master's (21)	38.1
Tenure Status	
Tenured (28)	57.2
Nontenured (35)	31.4
Church Affiliation	
SBC-active (34)	38.2
SBC-inactive (6)	83.3
Non-SBC (23)	39.1
Gender	
Male (43)	44.2
Female (17)	35.3
Length of Service	
15 years or fewer (44)	36.7
16 years or more (19)	57.9
Age	
40 or younger (19)	36.8
41–50 (17)	35.3
51–60 (21)	61.9
61 and older (6)	33.3

these professors had "toned down" or "become more cautious" in the classroom. A different kind of response came from several professors who said that they had been "grieved" or "saddened" by the Controversy. As in other cases, there is a discrepancy in the replies of those who hold differing theological views. Liberals (36 percent) much more than fundamentalists (10 percent) claim to have been affected personally by the Controversy. Those with tenure believe they have accommodated more than the nontenured.

Conclusion

This chapter set out to explore the effects of Controversy on the faculties of colleges owned and operated by the state conventions of the Southern Baptist Convention. As often happens in such research, the results are somewhat mixed. A majority affirm that academic freedom exists in their schools. They deny that those who teach in Southern Baptist colleges are obligated to support dominant views, and they indicate their willingness to defend a colleague who takes a controversial position. A substantial minority, however, are convinced that pressure for conservative views has indeed increased, with many admitting to becoming more cautious in the classroom.

It would appear that the effects of the denominational struggle have been for the most part subtle rather than blatant. Although fundamentalists have not been able to position themselves to dominate Baptist colleges in the manner that they have positioned themselves to dominate the seminaries, it would seem that they have created an atmosphere threatening enough to influence the internal processes of Baptist colleges.

Comments on the questionnaires demonstrate a variety of subtle changes:

> I am more careful of what I say and of what examples I use.
>
> . . . [L]et me say that the controversy is affecting our ability to employ the top people. . . . every one of them has quizzed us very closely about the likely impact of a fundamentalist takeover on his own position. At least two strong candidates have withdrawn their names after a visit. This is virtually unprecedented.
>
> . . . if you felt that there were people out there who were looking over your shoulder, wouldn't you be somewhat inhibited?
>
> I cannot really trust many people to be open and honest with about academic issues.
>
> The throwing around of labels in order to protect the faithful from heretics has had the effect of pressuring many faculty to keep many opinions unspoken—effectively stunting intellectual growth.
>
> Caused administration to develop a severe case of paranoia.
>
> I know the presidents of this and every other SBC institution are being watched.

Despite such comments, only twenty respondents (29 percent) could, or would, supply even a single instance of a violation of academic freedom at their colleges over the last five years. Fully one-half of these twenty respondents came from two institutions. It thus appears that fundamentalists have intruded symbolically and indirectly rather than organizationally and directly.

If this is true, then administrators of Baptist schools face the prospect of many fundamentalist victories without having fought any battles. It may be that apprehension is fundamentalism's greatest weapon. Only when a given college has shown itself both willing and able to deflect intrusion can its professors concentrate on their disciplines and their students rather than on the denominational political struggle. Comments on the questionnaires suggest that the perception of administrative support is crucial:

> I feel we have good academic freedom here. Some of our faculty members have been challenged, but I felt our faculty and administration was supportive.
>
> I believe that academic freedom does exist at [this] College primarily because the faculty and administration have effectively resisted outside forces.
>
> I do not think that academic freedom exists at my institution, primarily because the university and its trustees and upper-level administrators are more attentive to forestalling a fundamentalist assault upon this school than they are to furthering the full and open exposition of ideas.
>
> [We have academic freedom] because of the force of tradition, at least since the 1920s and the commitment of most students, faculty and administrators.
>
> Academic freedom is very limited here because the administration is too sensitive to outside influence.

If one asks how, in the face of their answers to questions about the effects of the Controversy, these professors are able to maintain their belief that academic freedom is still manifest in their schools, we would suggest that the answer lies in a phenomenological view of society. The work of Peter Berger and Thomas Luckmann on the social construction of reality argues that humans act to produce institutions that then set limits and conditions for the behavior of those who produced them.[8] In the course of time, people adjust to these limits and conditions, come to think of them as normal and natural, and desire that their behavior and the behavior of others conform to the institutional patterns of expectation. They make peace with the society they create.

In the present case, these professors work in Baptist colleges. Over the course of time, they have come to accept the limitations, especially those imposed by concerned Baptist constituents, prescribed by their institutions as facts of existence. The situation does not seem to them restrictive because they identify with those limitations. Hofstadter and Metzger have expressed this idea cogently:

> A man is objectively free insofar as his society will allow him to express novel or critical ideas without the threat of formal or informal punishment of any serious kind. He is subjectively free insofar as he *feels* free to say what he wishes. Subjective freedom may exist without objective freedom wherever men are so completely confined by the common assumptions of their place, time, or class that they are incapable of engendering any novel or critical ideas that they care to express, and where in fact the expression of such ideas would be dangerous. Such men would be conscious of no restraints, but they would not be free.[9]

This "constructionist" point of view would seem to gain support from the fact that it is those who have been most absorbed into the colleges (those with tenure and those with longer service) who endorse most strongly the obligation to conform to Baptist ways of thinking. And it is these same types of people who are most sensitive to the effects of the SBC Controversy (see tables 12.3 and 12.4). Having made peace with their institutions, they feel more strongly the effects of change. To defend a colleague's right to take a controversial position is to defend an institutional practice.

This argument may be extended to the differences in responses between fundamentalists and their colleagues. The institutions to which these professors have become accustomed are indeed conservative—they are loyal to the denomination that supports them—but they have also been relatively open to an exchange of ideas and a variety of viewpoints. Confronted with the possibility that the range of expression may be shortened, those who cannot endorse the fundamentalist position are more inclined to defend their colleagues, as well as more willing to believe that both they and their institutions are being threatened by the direction in which the SBC Controversy is being resolved.

Notes

Funds for this research were provided by a faculty research grant from the University of Tennessee at Martin.

1. "An Interview with Dr. Porter Routh," *Theological Educator* (1985 special issue): 25-27.
2. James C. Hefley, *The Truth in Crisis: Conservative Resurgence or Political Takeover?* vol. 3 Hannibal, Mo.: Hannibal Books, 1988).
3. Larry C. Ingram, "Sectarian Colleges and Academic Freedom," *Review of Religious Research* 27 (1986): 300-314.
4. Paige Patterson, "Academic Freedom—Liberty or License?" *Southern Baptist Advocate* 8 (May 1988): 7.
5. *Southern Baptist Convention Annual,* 1987.
6. In fact it appears that several colleges have responded to the Controversy by adopting a strategy of disengagement from the denomination. Thus although claiming to remain loyal to Baptist causes and professing to desire a continuing relationship with the denomination, these schools have developed policies that give them control over appointments to their governing boards. In a case that may have to be settled in court, Baylor University trustees established a new board of regents outside the control of the Baptist General Convention of Texas. The trustees then passed their authority to govern the university over to the regents. In less controversial ways, Wake Forest University, Stetson University, Furman University, and others have (or soon will) become relatively autonomous. The model used approximates that of the Presbyterian colleges, which describe themselves as having a "covenant relationship" with the denomination.
7. Nancy Tatom Ammerman, *Baptist Battles: Social Change and Religious Conflict in the Southern Baptist Convention* (New Brunswick, N.J.: Rutgers Univ. Press, 1990), 159-61.
8. Peter L. Berger and Thomas Luckman, *The Social Construction of Reality* (Garden City, N.Y.: Doubleday, 1966).
9. Richard Hofstadter and Walter P. Metzger, *The Development of Academic Freedom in the United States* (New York: Columbia Univ. Press, 1955), 16.

CHAPTER 13

RURAL INTERPRETATIONS OF CONFLICT

M. Jean Heriot

The ongoing dispute between the moderate and the fundamentalist factions of the Southern Baptist Convention (SBC) has forced members of local churches to reassess the nature of conflict within the family of faith. Many members appear bewildered as they confront what seemed to them unthinkable; their Southern Baptist rhetoric, strategies of interaction, and, indeed, their very perception of the Christian faith are based on the assumption that conflict should not exist within their own ranks.[1] Nevertheless the denominational infighting that surfaced in 1979 increased year by year to reach its zenith during the period in which I did ethnographic fieldwork (1985-86) in the Southern Baptist hinterland. News of the discord reached members through media portrayals on television and in newspapers, through their pastors' attendance at the SBC annual convention meetings, and from their fellow members' discussions.[2]

During the 1985 and 1986 annual conventions of the SBC, I conducted participant observation research with members of a Southern Baptist church in South Carolina. Members of Cypress Pond Baptist Church, like many other small, rural congregations, struggled to understand the national strife.[3] This paper examines these members' attempts to comprehend the incomprehensible and how pastors used traditional Southern religious practices and rhetoric to persuade their congregations' political and theological positions. We will see that rural SBC churches, such as Cypress Pond, that have not yet confronted the full force of modernity retain an evangelical world view that shifts all conflict from the here and now to another, transcendent reality.

Although commitment to this evangelical world view establishes the boundaries within which these Southern Baptists interpret disputes, that self-same commitment creates what appear to be unresolvable problems in settling the SBC Controversy. In the past this world view was able to subsume variation and translate it into the group's primary metaphor, the salvation of the world through the grace of Jesus Christ. Now the SBC faces immense difficulties because variation has polarized into two factions, both claiming to be right. Taken to this extreme, variation threatens the world view at its foundations, for the existence of two points of view, two truths, cannot coexist with the claim that there is only one eternally right way to live.

At the congregational level, members of Cypress Pond experienced the national conflict when they were influenced by two pastors, one a moderate and the other a fundamentalist. These pastors created confusion among their congregation, because each supported his position using the ostensibly familiar call to spread the message of salvation.

Thus at the level of world view, this chapter sketches the framework in which disputes are addressed, and at the level of the local congregation, it illustrates the stress placed on that framework when variation in political and theological positions can no longer be avoided. It is necessary to comprehend both levels in order to understand how Southern Baptists traditionally approach political struggles and why they have so few tools for dealing with disputes.

An account of the social characteristics of Cypress Pond—agrarian, southern, kin-based, traditional, white, and small—sets the historical and demographic scene for the subsequent discussions of their perceptions of conflict. These characteristics are also those of approximately half the Southern Baptist Convention's churches.[4] Although noting the dangers of generalizations based on one case, I argue that the qualitative data gathered at Cypress Pond is representative of the larger, overarching concerns facing a significant and defining segment of SBC churches.

Green Pastures and Country Roads

To visualize Cypress Pond, fix your mind's eye on church buildings set in pastoral splendor. The countryside shimmers with a deep forest green of pine and hardwood trees, interspersed with rolling fields of grasses or crops. A panoramic view includes sloping pastureland directly in front of the buildings, a thinly forested region behind, a cemetery to the right, and a sawmill to the left. One can see only a few homes from the church grounds: most are distant and concealed by trees. No stores are visible and only one paved road fronts the church. All other roads near the church are dirt and disappear into the surrounding forest.

In such a location the church grounds and buildings seem incongruous, especially to a non-southern visitor. The two church buildings, the sanctuary and "educational building," are large and impressive, with brick veneers. Inside the educational building are classrooms, a large meeting room, and a kitchen. Amid the pastures facing the church is a softball field complete with lights for night games, spectator stands, and a concessions building.

These modern facilities do not stand on a main road. Their rural location means members must drive six miles to the nearest town of five thousand and forty-five miles to the nearest movie theater. Most of the membership consists of people who live within a four-mile radius of the church itself. Average attendance at Sunday worship services is 125, with almost all of the three hundred resident members kin in one way or another. Those who attend Cypress Pond do so, they say, in part because their families have come here for generations. Local kin networks remain complex and intertwined.

In terms of its community setting, Cypress Pond represents, in many ways, quintessential southern Protestant historical and demographic features. For at least 175 years, Salkehatchie County (a pseudonym), South Carolina, has been overwhelmingly Protestant, with the oldest and largest churches being Baptist.[5] In 1980 members of SBC churches constituted about 70 percent of the county's population. The only non-Protestant religious group located in the county is the Catholic church. With approximately two hundred adherents in 1980 and with no resident parish priest, the Catholics in the community are swamped numerically by their Protestant neighbors.[6]

Several demographic and economic trends have contributed to this homogeneity in religious beliefs and population. First, Salkehatchie County has continued to have a low population density and, until the 1950s was economically dependent on agriculture. Second, from the early 1800s until the 1950s this region of South Carolina was characterized by major emigration with relatively little immigration.[7] In effect this has meant that there have been only two ethnic groups since the Civil War, blacks and whites, whose separation is still manifested in segregated churches. (The twenty-two SBC churches in Salkehatchie County have no black members. Blacks, instead, predominantly attend independent Baptist churches.) The lack of immigration also has meant that those born in Salkehatchie County are born to families whose ties to the land go back to the early 1800s.

Beginning in the 1950s, as part of a general upswing in the state's economy, industries moved into Salkehatchie. Within driving distance now are the Federal Plant (a government-funded plant), a waste processing center, two textile mills, and an optical plant. With depressions in the farm economy, these employers have become increasingly important as sources of income; as a result, the sources of income for Cypress Pond church members also have changed. During the time of my fieldwork, the county's last full-time farmer was forced to take a job at one of the local manufacturing plants to make ends meet. He and several other farmers are working full-time industrial jobs while farming part time. Forty-four percent of the adults (male and female, excluding those who have retired) now work for one of the five local plants. Others work in local stores or in government service agencies, such as schools or state offices, and a privileged few operate their own small businesses.[8]

Despite this economic change, members continue to identify themselves as part of an agrarian community. Pastors preaching at Cypress Pond make frequent references to the lives of farmers and the farming life-style. Church members refer to themselves as country people. They grow vegetables for home canning and assess the weather with an eye to its effects on crops.

As a whole church members see themselves as either working class or middle class. If income is the measure of middle-class standing, most Cypress Pond members are indeed middle class. If, however, education is used as the standard, few would fit the typical description of middle class: only a handful of church members have attended any school of higher learning, and even fewer have attained degrees.

Salvation in Societal Context

To view Cypress Pond as a representative case for understanding the approaches of rural SBC churches to conflict resolution entails examining larger societal forces that have shaped their evangelical world view. As a community Cypress Pond exists in a milieu that has just begun to be touched by the forces of modernity. The existence of cultural homogeneity means that these Southern Baptists do not have to confront alternative belief systems on a daily basis. That fact alone sets Cypress Pond apart from many other cultural contexts in American society, contexts in which believers must face alternative belief systems not just on television but across the street and at work in their day-to-day lives.

According to Nancy Ammerman, the differences between fundamentalist and evangelical Protestants in America often stem from such differences in societal contexts and from believers' corresponding responses to modernity. In her typology both evangelicals and fundamentalists believe that the Bible is the word of God. They believe that one must be born again to be saved, and they believe God created the world. The distinguishing mark of the fundamentalist is the added insistence on a radical separation from the world. Fundamentalists are found where their traditional belief systems come in contact with competing belief systems in the modern, pluralistic world of city and suburb.[9] Because Cypress Pond members can adhere to traditional evangelical beliefs without insisting on a radical separation from the world, they are not yet fundamentalists by this criterion. They will remain simply evangelicals until shifting cultural contexts demand of them a reevaluation of their belief system. Indeed, I found that the term *fundamentalist* was not one invoked either to classify or explain the SBC controversies at Cypress Pond. Members spoke of conservatives (or ultra-conservatives) and moderates (or liberals and moderate conservatives) rather than fundamentalists and moderates, and pastors and members alike overtly affirmed an evangelical identity no matter what stand they took within the SBC.

Not only are they evangelicals by virtue of their beliefs and their isolation from many forces of modernity, they are also direct heirs of the Protestant Reformation in their outlook on life. Boldly stated, church members maintain the world view of early Protestantism with few modifications. As Robert Bellah characterized this religious system (drawing heavily on Weber), the beliefs espoused by members of Cypress Pond resonate strongly with those of their forebears. They, like their predecessors, postulate a dualistic world view. A sharp demarcation exists between this world and a transcendent other world where individuals will dwell in heaven or in hell upon death. To achieve these transcendent goals, Cypress Pond members also declare the process of salvation "potentially available to any man no matter what his station or calling might be" and attempt to manifest this salvation in the midst of this world. Their stress on inner faith leads to a view of religious action as "identical with the whole of life." [10]

This form of Protestantism emphasizes a view of salvation that minimizes disagreements, at least among the saved. Conflicts are both perceived and interpreted in the context of the great, ongoing, dualistic battle between God and Satan. For the purposes of this chapter, the issue of central importance is the members' conception of salvation; that is, because they attempt to live salvation in this world "for the sake of the world beyond," [11] all conflict is translated into this cosmological framework and then projected onto individuals who play out this otherworldly battle in daily life. A type of circular reasoning acts here to reinforce the belief system. Living as saved persons requires manifesting salvation, and manifesting salvation entails absolute certainty that one lives for the life to come. All conflicts, at whatever level they are encountered—interpersonal, communal, national, or international—must be interpreted in this context for the logic of salvation to hold true.

To view Cypress Pond Baptists as evangelical exemplars of early Protestantism is to set their belief system in the context of what has been a relatively stable cultural milieu. This is not to deny the influence of television, VCRs, modern transportation, or a host of other factors that have rapidly transformed American society. At Cypress Pond the tensions of the modern world, though by no means absent, remain remote. What seems to occur among the committed is an orientation toward living that places their identity as saved individuals paramount in their definitions of themselves. A positive evaluation of such definitions sees that commitment as strength of character in the face of daily temptation. A more negative evaluation sees that same commitment as a form of "blinder," effectively separating these Christians from the "reality" of the modern, pluralistic world. Whatever the evaluation, the effect of this world view in this cultural context promotes among members a view of social solidarity in which the tensions of this world have ramifications for the next.

To view conflict solely in terms of a cosmic struggle between salvation and damnation has, however, created confusion when that conflict takes on shades of gray. Members have trouble interpreting strife if it threatens, in any way, to shake their faith in their traditional world view. Then they look to their pastors, those they consider their spiritual leaders, for guidance. If they have pastors who differ, problems spring into being. Just such differences were evident at Cypress Pond during my fieldwork. In 1985 Cypress Pond's pastor was Reverend Squires (a pseudonym), a fundamentalist who voted for the fundamentalist candidate at the 1985 annual SBC convention. In 1986 Cypress Pond engaged an interim pastor, Reverend Manning (pseudonym), who was moderate in outlook and who voted moderate at the 1986 convention. Let us look at each pastor's presentation of the conflict to their congregation. We will see that both Squires and Manning broadly interpreted the SBC discord within the shared framework of salvation. But because their positions differed substantially, members who supported Squires in 1985 and Manning in 1986 must have felt a certain disjunction. Or did they? We will return to this question after the following case accounts.

Squires: Conservative Pastor during the 1985 Convention

Reverend Squires had been preaching at Cypress Pond for six years prior to my arrival in May 1985. "Called by God" to become a pastor in his twenties, he subsequently went to a southern Bible college for two years while he pastored his first church. Before attending this Bible college, he had never attended a postsecondary school. At the time I met him, he was in his early fifties, having pastored several churches. My initial impression of him as an expert tactician at the level of local church politics was slowly confirmed over the next few months. When questioned about conflict at any level in the Baptist church, he tended to minimize it as much as possible.

When discussing the SBC, Squires overtly framed his conservative political views in terms of salvation. During an interview he told me that the problems within the denomination could be boiled down to a few people in key positions who were "throwing daggers at each other." Although he considered the main area of contention to be theological, concerning the question of whether or not the Bible is without error (the inerrancy debate), he viewed this question in terms of ultimate salvation. Squires articulated his perspective well, devoting a sermon to the theme of "Teamwork" within the local church and at the level of the convention. He used Paul's analogy of the church as the Body of Christ (1 Cor. 12:12-31) and preached that the purpose of the church is to work together as a body. Addressing the question of unity in the church, Squires implied that those causing the problems in the convention are only attached to the church and are not actually members of the Body of Christ. That is, he questioned their very salvation.

In addition Squires criticized the nature of the infighting itself, proclaiming the evangelical goal of world salvation as the primary goal of Southern Baptists. His use of rhetorical strategy minimized the conflict for his congregation and sought to reaffirm the purpose of leadership as rooted in the God-given Great Commission. From the pulpit, he stated:

> The people who are in leadership positions in our Convention have been name calling. God has had His hand on this Convention for years. He's used Southern Baptists to reach around the world to save the lost. Including both Home and Foreign Missions, we've got over 5,000 missionaries serving on the field at the present time. I'm proud of that and I know you are, you've had a part of it. But we can so easily let little things sidetrack us from the main objective of what we believe that we're about. I think that God's got His hand on us to reach the world by [the year] 2000. But we need to pray for that convention, we need to pray for those persons who are in leadership, and I want you to be much in prayer.

Squires stressed that he did not approve of the "politics" within the convention and that the SBC needed to "get its priorities straight."

Thus anyone who causes discord that takes attention away from the goal of salvation is not saved. From this perspective it follows that there is only one true path to salvation. Squires assumed this when he told me that the way he voted at the 1985 national meeting of the SBC in Dallas would be the way that "100 percent of the church feels." In ranging himself with the fundamentalist side, Squires also assumed he had been given the authority, perhaps even the duty, to speak for his congregation, that they tacitly agreed to his assumption of authority, and that he could invoke this authority to prove his points. That absolute authority comes from, he believes, the Bible.

As Squires informed me in an interview, the whole Bible, not parts of it, is inspired. His view of salvation is based on the Bible and represents the truth for both himself and his congregation. Shortly after returning from the SBC national meetings, he preached another sermon stating this theological position and expressing the belief that his conservative viewpoints stood for all within the congregation. His sermon was entitled "The Infallible Word of God." In it he recapitulated the stand of the fundamentalists on inerrancy. He claimed that the Bible was without error and criticized those in the SBC who did not agree:

> Now sad to say, if you've been keeping up with the news or listening to the radio, or reading the newspapers. If you know anything about our life as a Southern Baptist Convention, in the past few weeks and months it's been brought to our attention that we have problems within the family of Southern Baptists. We have those who deny, literally deny, the historical and scientific proofs that are found in Genesis, Chapters 1-11. We have some in our Convention that say that the theory of evolution is as good as anything they have ever seen. And in making that statement, as far as I'm concerned, they are denying the creative ability of God. Men and women today are still attacking the Word of God. The devil, working through men and women, are still trying to change the meaning of the Word of God. . . . And I believe that you are the same kind of people I am. I think you believe the same way I do, I believe this is God's word. Now when we look at the Bible, some people say it contains God's word. *It is God's word.*

Squire made three main points: God inspired every word of the Bible, the purpose of Scripture is to bring a lost and dying world to know the Savior, and the Bible is the work of the Holy Spirit. He exhorted members to be certain of their own doctrinal beliefs in order to guard themselves against those who preach false doctrine, that is, those who deliberately attempt to draw believers away from the position of inerrancy. He concluded that "truth is based not on who believes it. Truth is based on who says it." By this he refers to the Bible as the word of God.

Aside from questioning the salvation of the opposing side, the only strategy Squires mentioned for dealing with the national strife is personal prayer. Because Squires has already given his congregation his interpretation of the right way, prayer then is a plea for others to see the "truth," to see the "light," and, in essence, to acknowledge that his side is right because God has so defined it. This approach once again derives from the view that there can only be one correct stance for the truly saved. Cosmological truths justify and enhance the personal, making the conflict intelligible in absolute terms: the good, the fundamentalists, the saved, versus the bad, the moderates, the unsaved.

From the strategies and content of both sermons cited above, it appears that Squires follows a time-honored Baptist tradition. In his priestly role, he spoke for and to his congregation. They, from my observations, endorsed his role and his position. Squires's second sermon ended the immediate concern over the actions of the national convention at this church, and no further overt discussion was initiated until the following year.

Manning: Moderate Pastor during the 1986 Convention

Reverend Manning began his interim appointment at Cypress Pond in November 1985, after Squires left to pastor another church. Then in his seventies, Manning had been a loyal Southern Baptist pastor for more than 70 years. After his retirement from full-time pastoral work, he frequently served as interim pastor when churches were in the process of locating a permanent pastor who felt called to serve them in a full-time capacity. Manning entered the ministry in his thirties, after completing a four-year college degree and three years of seminary in Baptist-affiliated schools. Although judged as sincere and "smart," there were those among his audience who said that his preaching was "above their heads" and that they did not understand him.

As a moderate Manning gave the SBC political conflict a different interpretation, although he too ultimately cast the conflict in terms of salvation. Many of Manning's strategies reflect his subtle attempts to lead a conservative congregation to a moderate stance. His interpretations highlight the uneasy tension between the "truth" of salvation and Baptist believers' responsibilities in coming to know that truth. Manning's views represent the moderate stance and the problems it encounters with a congregation adhering to the early Protestant world view.

Beginning in late April, about six weeks before the 1986 annual convention in Atlanta, Manning attempted to inform the general congregation of his views. He announced in Sunday morning worship service that he would devote the next Wednesday night prayer service to a discussion of the SBC. Attendance was not noticeably altered for that service (it was less than twenty), at which Manning did indeed offer a clear statement of his position. His presentation, rather than a sermon, forms the basis of my discussion, because Manning, in contrast to Squires, did not use the sermon as the vehicle for informing the congregation of his political views. Rather he chose the small-group format of the Wednesday night prayer service. Here he invoked the authority of the teacher more than that of the preacher. He noted that as pastor of the church, he might be said to have influence over the congregation, but that he wanted the congregation to think about what he said and to form their own opinions. He also pointed out that authority within the local Baptist church rests with the congregation.

Manning then moved to a discussion of the question of inerrancy. This was not the real question, however; the real question, he said, was over control of the seminaries. He characterized the two opposing groups within the SBC as the "ultraconservatives" and "moderate conservatives." Identifying himself as a moderate conservative, he claimed that ultraconservatives were pastors who want to be "rulers" of the local church and who tend to be located in the large city churches. Such churches resemble independent churches in which what the pastor says is the "law." They tend to support the SBC's Cooperative Program in a minimal manner. Ultraconservatives, he further informed the group, often have seminaries that are not affiliated with the SBC. There they teach a limited, literalist perspective on the Bible. They hold that theirs is the right and only interpretation possible, and they are attempting to force this interpretation on SBC seminaries. As such, these ultraconservatives are trying to limit the Baptist doctrine of the priesthood of the believer by defining the "truth" of the Bible. For instance, in their literal interpretation of the Bible, they can and do say that the role of women should be severely limited in the church. If you follow that interpretation, he argued, then women would not even be able to teach mixed classes in the church (a practice routinely occurring at Cypress Pond).

As an example of the tactics being used by the ultraconservatives, Manning displayed a recent copy of the *Baptist Courier* (the South Carolina state Baptist newsletter, dated 5 May 1986). In it Lee Roberts, an "ultraconservative" spokesman, had said that the SBC was teaching "slop" in its seminaries.

Manning strongly objected to this article, indicating that he believed that the seminaries should teach more than one interpretation of the Bible to their students. Then individuals could decide on a position, because there would be room for the believer to make his or her own interpretations. In his own experience at the seminary, he said, all of his teachers loved the Lord and were trying to strengthen the faith of their students, not weaken it.

In the next six weeks, Manning made references to his position in the main worship services, asked church members to pray for the convention in Atlanta, and organized the trip for members who planned to attend. He did not preach any sermons overtly denouncing the opposing side; instead, he explained that he himself was a member of the church voting as the spirit led him. He even left the pulpit, descending from its raised platform, to speak to the congregation "on their level." This symbolic movement served to highlight his dedication to a belief in the priesthood of the believer. Each member was urged to pray and to consider attending the conference as a messenger. As SBC messengers, they would vote according to their own convictions rather than representing predetermined congregational stands.

From that point on, he repeatedly asked for volunteers to attend the convention as messengers from the church and for moneys to fund their attendance in Atlanta. By dint of much effort and persuasion, he eventually mustered four messengers in addition to himself, and the church did pay for their attendance. This was the first time that the church had ever sent messengers other than the pastor and his wife.

After returning he followed the same format as Squires, presenting the results of the convention to the congregation on the following Sunday morning in the form of an announcement. Because the SBC had elected the "ultraconservative" Adrian Rogers as its president, Manning told the congregation that he now knew exactly who was in control of the SBC. But, using the convention's own theme from 1 Corinthians 13:8, "Love Never Fails," Manning stressed that the SBC was his church and that he was not going to leave it. He would continue to work within the SBC, despite his disagreement with it. He admitted his disappointment with the results and agreed with his wife's evaluation that the SBC appeared to have changed so much that they felt as though they were out of place. Still Manning expressed hope that the seminaries would survive as they are and that "womanhood" will be able to hold its own against the onslaught of the ultraconservatives. He urged that the convention go forward in evangelism efforts and cited with pleasure the preliminary reports from the SBC's coordinated "Good News America: God Loves You," simultaneous revivals in which a record number of baptisms occurred.

The strategies employed by Manning served to mask his differences with Squires. He changed the nomenclature from fundamentalist versus moderate to ultraconservative versus moderate conservative. He emphasized the role of the priesthood of the believer in biblical interpretation and illustrated these beliefs with a symbolic move from the pulpit to the congregational level. He made public a basic fear of the congregationally governed church: someone else will tell them what to do. Yet in the end, he interpreted the conflict in terms of the same goal Squires had, that of saving the world. His solution to the problem, despite his rhetoric to the contrary, was similar to that of Squires. Those who sought to limit basic Baptist beliefs were wrong, according to Manning. His criticism of their financial contributions and of their attacks on the seminaries questioned their commitment to being Baptist and to cooperative efforts to bring salvation to the world. The only possible solutions to conflict remained prayer and the unthinkable—nevertheless stated—threat of leaving the SBC.

Evaluating Congregational Responses

Even though I had been at Cypress Pond for more than a year, the depth of misunderstanding apparent among members of the congregation after the 1986 SBC elections still managed to surprise me. Those who actually had attended the convention seemed to have a fair grasp of the political issues involved, but most other members did not. During a Wednesday night discussion of the SBC, for example, one deacon finally expressed his perplexity by asking, "But did the person we wanted get elected?" Still others later told me in private that they were confused about the outcome of the elections. These members had talked with representatives of other local Southern Baptist churches who, unlike Manning, had voted fundamentalist. Suddenly a handful of members apparently realized that Manning and Squires (along with pastors in their neighboring churches) represented different factions within the SBC.

In attempting to make sense of their confusion, I had to rethink my own perceptions of the Controversy and of the pastoral actions of Squires and Manning. Before observing the reactions of the puzzled few, I had naïvely assumed that members either knew that these pastors differed or simply did not care enough about the conflict to determine which side their pastor took. Somehow in my understanding of the pastoral positions I overlooked the point that Squires had made. Church members do think of themselves as conservative politically and morally. Building his sermons around that conservative (fundamentalist) identity, Squires could assume that he spoke for the whole congregation. Manning, too, was savvy enough to portray his moderate stance so that he drew upon his congregation's conservative bent, though he pointed to different kinds of conservatism.

Now some members were forced to confront conflict not just at the national level but within their very congregation. Squires and Manning represented two diametrically opposed doctrinal stands, both claiming to be right and both denouncing their opponents' side. When members reached this understanding regarding Manning and Squires, they were surprised. Cypress Pond found itself touched by the national debates in a heretofore unknown manner. Pastoral rhetorical skills and leadership roles had succeeded in transforming the debate from something "out there" to something that affected their own church. After all, they sent congregational messengers to the 1986 convention who voted moderate, not fundamentalist. When the differences were realized by a few congregational members, the aftermath was initially confusion. Because I left the field shortly after the 1986 convention, I do not know the extended ramifications of this discovery.

Implications for Conflict Resolution

We have seen that Cypress Pond pastors and members interpret conflict in terms of the struggle between good and evil. Although Manning attempted to mitigate this dualistic world view by bringing in the priesthood of the believer, he could not escape the either/or thinking predicated by his own salvation rhetoric. Carol Greenhouse, in a study of Hopewell, a suburban SBC church, similarly argued that Hopewell Baptists must displace their congregational conflicts onto the next world. She concluded that the emphasis on personal salvation, combined with the theological doctrine of the priesthood of the believer, meant that disputes cannot be addressed directly in this religious system. By holding to the individual's rights to make decisions, this doctrine does not admit of any authority save that gotten directly from God. Nor can disputes be settled by compromise, because doing God's will can only admit one answer. Thus Greenhouse notes that the only avenues open to Baptists in situations of church conflict are prayer and/or witnessing.[12] According to Greenhouse, "The logic of their [SBC] faith denies them any means for engaging in disputes or other sorts of confrontations that would create winners and losers—or more generally—authorities and constituents. Instead, they define their community as being harmonious a priori by virtue of having accepted Jesus."[13]

Greenhouse builds her thesis using both ethnographic and historical data concerning local strife in the town of Hopewell, Georgia. Because the church she studied was urban, all her conclusions cannot be generalized to rural SBC churches. In addition, the cases of actual conflict she discusses are primarily historical rather than current local disputes or contentions over SBC politics. In the case of Cypress Pond, we have a local congregation in which pastors differed, spoke and acted on their differences, and consequently, engaged their congregation in SBC political disputes. De facto, Cypress Pond was in a state of conflict. What happens when strife exists where, by their own definitions of faith, it should not?

Cypress Pond pastors and members advocated prayer as one method for coping with the SBC political struggle. Both pastors modeled this solution when they prayed for the outcome of convention meetings during worship services and prayer meetings. Members, too, prayed that the situation would be resolved in a manner consistent with their belief system. For example, one deacon reacted to the media coverage in 1985 by praying that something good would come from the national convention, because "the whole world would be watching" and for some people "we [Baptists] would represent Christianity." Although some members have their doubts about the efficacy of prayer as it affects their lives, the situation within the SBC, though troubling, had not raised, prior to 1986, the same degree of concern. When they expressed the desire for the conflict to be completely resolved, the first response proffered was always the traditional one of prayer.

Charles Conrad's study gives us further clues to the actual processes that inform decision making in local SBC churches. He used data from six Southern Baptist churches, transcribing and analyzing audio tapes of church decision-making events.[14] Conrad argues that members communicate in meetings, among other things, their stands on tensions within the local church and between "the church's theology and the organizational structure."[15] Among the cycles of communication he identifies is one he terms *politicization of the process*. Given the doctrine of the priesthood of the believer, conflict can arise over competing theologies. When these were expressed by different members in local meetings, Conrad found two outcomes:

> Either the discussion ends (abruptly) and a vote is taken, or other parishioners begin to support one of the theologies and continue to do so until it is clear that both forms are supported by a significant segment of the group. At this point the time allocated for the meeting runs out and the discussion is tabled until the next meeting. Before the meeting ends the pastor or discussion leader urges the group to spend the intervening days in prayer and Bible study about the issue.[16]

If the issue is tabled, it may be brought up again later, and eventually a vote is taken—on the immediate issue, if not on the theological dispute. Thus we have conflict uneasily resolved through majority vote, with no real resolution of the competing theologies. If the losers accede to the majority and accept the majority vote as indicative of God's will at work in the world, harmony prevails. Cypress Pond business meetings generally followed this format whenever there was controversy. Although the problem of which side to support at the SBC annual conventions had not been formally debated during the time of my fieldwork, other meetings displayed this strategy of finding God's will in the will of the majority.

Manning, given his moderate stance, continued throughout his tenure to urge members to think and decide for themselves on all matters of church policy and church doctrine, to vote as they were led by God. He nevertheless expressed considerable skepticism that this method would continue to function as it had in the past. The problem with majority rule within the SBC, he stated on more than one occasion, was that it was predicated on the assumption that the majority acted and voted by the will of God. He voiced considerable doubt that all affiliated with the church were truly saved. And if the "world" (i.e., the lost or unsaved) invades the church and comes to form the majority of its membership, then the decisions made by the majority will be tainted.

Manning's concern identifies the heart of the problem facing the SBC. As Arthur Farnsley argues in this volume, majority rule as an expression of the will of God works well where consensus is relatively high; it begins to fall apart where members' theologies clash on issues that cannot be resolved through appeal to traditional authority. What happens if members align along two seemingly irreconcilable platforms? Then, according to this world view, one group must be wrong. They must not be following God's will; they must not be saved; they may even be led by the Devil. The argument once again reaches the cosmological level where, in some sense, it remains unsolvable.

Two avenues for conflict resolution are currently open to members of local congregations. One, identified by Greenhouse and repeatedly invoked at Cypress Pond, stresses working together toward achieving the goals of salvation, using prayer to achieve this goal. The other, discussed by Conrad, uses majority rule to resolve theological issues, again invoked within the context of doing God's will on earth. It too presumes that prayer leads one to vote for truth. Both strategies seem inadequate when the disputants each claim the prerogative of speaking for God.

Conclusion

In terms of the world view considered here, it is not that these Baptists are unfamiliar with strife, for they know conflict intimately. But their belief system leaves them with few choices when faced with conflict within their own ranks. Members, especially committed members, view conflict in the terms discussed throughout this chapter. They believe in salvation as their reason for existence and as their goal in life. Living salvation means living for the world to come, for heaven and its rewards. Anything threatening these beliefs, these goals, threatens their self-identity as well as their religious system. Thus basic internal strife attacks their primary metaphor for interpreting life—salvation. When complicated by the doctrine of the priesthood of the believer, members have limited tools for handling doctrinal conflict within their congregation. They instead transpose it to the transcendent level, a fight for the fate of the souls of humanity.

Within a cultural context in which pluralism has, until recently, been kept to a minimum, enduring doctrinal conflict is a new development. Without the tools for debate and compromise, these Southern Baptists will probably remain confused and relatively powerless. They watch the national controversy, endure its appearance in their own backyard, and still pray that their view of salvation will triumph.

Notes

1. Carol Greenhouse, *Praying for Justice: Faith, Order, and Community in an American Town* (Ithaca, N.Y.: Cornell Univ. Press, 1986).
2. Nancy Tatom Ammerman's data, for instance, indicate that virtually all the local church leaders she surveyed routinely got convention news and had heard about the Atlanta convention in 1986. Eighty-two percent had read about it in their state Baptist paper; 60 percent had seen local news accounts; and one-third had heard an official report at church (Ammerman, private communication from Center for Religious Research Survey, 1986); also Ammerman, *Baptist Battles: Social Change and Religious Conflict in the Southern Baptist Convention* (New Brunswick, N.J.: Rutgers Univ. Press, 1990), 181 ff.
3. The names of the county, the church, and the pastors and members of the church are pseudonyms.
4. Ammerman, *Baptist Battles,* 53.
5. M. Jean Heriot, *Blessed Assurance: Assessing Religious Beliefs through Actions in a Carolina Baptist Church* (Ph.D. diss., Department of Anthropology, University of California, Los Angeles, 1989).
6. Bernard Quinn et al., *Churches and Church Membership in the United States in 1980* (Atlanta, Ga.: Glenmary Research Center, 1982).
7. Charles F. Kovacik and John J. Winberry, *South Carolina: A Geography* (Boulder, Colo.: Westview, 1987).
8. Heriot, *Blessed Assurance,* 70-71.
9. Ammerman, *Bible Believers: Fundamentalists in the Modern World* (New Brunswick, N.J.: Rutgers Univ. Press, 1987), 8.

10. Robert N. Bellah, "Religious Evolution," in *Reader in Comparative Religion,* 3d ed., ed. William Lessa and Evon Vogt (New York: Harper & Row, 1972), 45-46.

11. Max Weber, *The Protestant Ethic and the Spirit of Capitalism,* trans. Talcott Parsons (New York: Charles Scribner's Sons, 1958), 154.

12. Greenhouse, *Praying for Justice,* 104.

13. Ibid., 105.

14. Charles Conrad, "Communicative Action in Church Decision-Making," *Journal for the Scientific Study of Religion* 27 (1988): 345-61.

15. Ibid., 345.

16. Ibid., 353.

CHAPTER 14

SWINGING PENDULUMS: REFORM, RESISTANCE, AND INSTITUTIONAL CHANGE

Larry L. McSwain

The Southern Baptist Convention is undergoing a wrenching transformation that affects every level of its institutional life. Most observers of SBC history consider the present tension the most painful of many controversies to plague a naturally conflicted body.[1] In some sense its survival with relative organizational unity for nearly 145 years is a miracle of American denominational experience.

The jury is still out on the long-term effects of a decade of bitter infighting. The short-term effects are obvious—slowed numerical growth, increasing losses of members into inactive status, budget cutbacks in personnel and programs at denominational agency levels, and the diffusion of energy to political activities to balance power rather than to work at a mission with consensus. At another level the primary result of the Controversy is a fundamental realignment of the control of the agencies and institutions owned by the denomination. It is only in the 1990s that the results of that realignment will be known fully.

Institutional Change

Whatever else has been the result of this internal warfare, change in the control of SBC agencies is now a reality. Whether the change has been worth the costs—loss of trust and disruption of the SBC—depends on which side one favored. The contest between moderates and a new kind of conservatism—an organized fundamentalist movement—has been won by the fundamentalists. The presidency, and thus the appointment of the Committee on Committees, has been consistently controlled by these new conservatives, allowing a clear ideological perspective to become dominant in the work of every denominational entity in SBC life.

Some of those agencies are more crucial to the fundamentalist agenda than others. For instance, little change in policy is apparent thus far at the Annuity Board, the Historical Commission, the Southern Baptist Foundation, the Education Commission, or the Stewardship Commission.[2] Clearly identified moderates are not appointed to these units—just as they are not appointed anywhere else—but middle-of-the-road types can be appointed to these rather innocuous positions, helping the conservatives to create some apparent balance in the appointment process.

Although change has been minimal within these structures, the future will likely bring attention to these groups in the same way the larger agencies have been affected. One example is a proposal for the Education Commission to develop an in-house SBC accreditation body. Such a plan would enable fundamentalist-controlled schools to avoid sanctions from secular accrediting agencies.

The central mission program and the educational functions of the denomination, on the other hand, have been affected in significant ways. The most obvious change is in the direction of executive leadership of denominational structures. Six units have chosen seven new executives since 1985, when conservative majorities began to emerge in the trustees of the agencies: the Home Mission Board, Christian Life Commission, Golden Gate Seminary, Southeastern Seminary, Annuity Board, and Sunday School Board. Five of the seven new executives have been clearly identified conservatives. One moderate, Larry Baker at the Christian Life Commission, was selected and then replaced as quickly as a fundamentalist majority of the commissioners took control. That commission has emerged as a strongly unified political force for New Right political and moral issues, most notably abortion. The president of the Annuity Board is in the least ideological agency, in which competency in administration and money management serve the interests of both sides; hence a moderate pastor was chosen in the summer of 1989 to serve as that agency's president.

The second legacy of the conflict is serious friction within denominational units. That friction has been most apparent in places with changing executive leadership. The transition at Southeastern Seminary has brought the resignations of nearly all the previous faculty and staff, with replacements in about three-fourths of the positions by persons the pre-transition seminary community could not support. The fundamentalist reform at Southeastern has resulted in a 50 percent loss of students, censure by the American Association of University Professors for loss of academic freedom, and accreditation reviews by the Southern Association of Colleges and Schools and the Association of Theological Schools.

Several staff terminations for doctrinal concerns, a budget crisis as a consequence of overspending, and fundamental shifts in priorities are visible at the Home Mission Board. All holdover staff members at the Christian Life Commission have been replaced, and budget woes plague Golden Gate Seminary.

In other agencies, where there are holdover moderate executives, the internal conflict focuses more sharply on differences between them and their new fundamentalist trustees. Policies in hiring, program emphases, and trustee reviews have changed in virtually every unit to some extent. The changes are most apparent at the Home Mission Board and Sunday School Board, the largest and most influential agencies affecting local church programs. Even where policies or personnel have not yet changed, conflict has created a difficult working environment. Other agency executives, notably seminary presidents, have faced criticism, opposition, and public efforts at embarrassment from their own trustees—those charged with the legal responsibility of guiding and supporting the institutions. The publication in 1990 of charges of heresy and cover-up against Southern Seminary's president, Roy Honeycutt, Jr., by trustee Jerry Johnson is one of many indications of the tenuous relationship within all denominational agencies.

The third effect of the Controversy has been the tightening of money at the denominational level. One of the myths perpetuated by many in the early years of the conflict was that fundamentalists would pour dollars into denominational programs and institutions, if they had a voice in the affairs of the convention. Although growth of the Cooperative Program, the primary program of denominational support, has continued, its rate of growth has been minimal and below even the lower rates of inflation in the 1980s. Twenty million dollars in approved capital funding projects have gone unfunded; the

Radio and Television Commission has assumed $10 million in debts; the Home Mission Board has overspent $20 million in reserves; and Golden Gate Seminary is seeking a purchaser for its unique San Francisco properties to balance its deficit budget. Meanwhile all agencies struggle to convince long-time moderate benefactors to support institutions whose future is uncertain.

The Controversy has also cost millions of dollars in new direct expenditures—expenditures for political activity. When one adds the total costs of the annual mailings of information promoting SBC presidential candidates, the costs of the news publications not covered by subscriptions, the travel expenses for the annual meeting by those who attend only to vote on the president, and the travel by those promoting the conflict, the impact is staggering. Added to this are the additional costs of massive annual meetings with a professional parliamentarian and increased legal costs associated with a lawsuit filed by Alabama layman Robert Crowder (protesting Charles Stanley's handling of the 1985 convention). In addition the new leaders have established new standards of growing opulence for their board meetings. The drain of resources for the denominational institutions created by this dissension has been substantial.

A fourth effect of the Controversy is the development of an even more cautious attitude toward innovation at every level of denominational life. Although the denomination has never been known for its innovation, as Samuel Hill's chapter in this book documents, the fundamentalist movement in the convention is a movement even less experimental in methodology than was the denomination in the 1960s and 1970s. It is rooted in a style more conducive to a southern rural and blue-collar cultural past than in the growing urban sophistication and pluralism faced by the churches of a national denomination. New leaders have been rather uniformly recruited from the margins of the denomination's life. Their educational levels are significantly lower than those of their counterparts of a decade ago. They often represent smaller, more isolated congregations. Fewer have established credentials of success in professions or business. The consequence is that conservatism has been translated into methodological traditionalism. If it is new, it is likely to be attacked by the new trustees, or at least not supported. Thus the energy to attempt new programs, experiment in the marketplace of ideas, or propose controversial approaches is drained by an attitude of anxiety. "If it will not appeal to the average church member, do not do it" is the new creed.

Another effect of this ten-year battle is its impact on the young. Evidence of a dramatic drop in the number of persons entering ministry at all levels is beginning to mount. Southern Baptist seminaries were at the height of an enrollment surge in the early 1980s, with as many of 25 percent of all U.S. seminary students studying in SBC institutions. That enrollment was fed by an equally high number of ministerial students in the more than fifty colleges and universities supported by Southern Baptist state conventions. Since 1985 there has been a 25 percent drop in the number of church vocation students in these same schools. This portends significant changes in seminary enrollment in the 1990s. Added to this is the drop in the numbers of college-aged youth in the general population as a result of birthrate changes in the 1970s. A rather dramatic decline in the pool of persons available for church vocations may be evident. Already every SBC seminary is experiencing enrollment decline. The applicants for missionary appointment with the Foreign Mission Board are half what they were in 1985. Southern Baptists may have to cease attributing their numerical successes in missions, education, and church growth to Providence.

Another institutional consequence of the Controversy is the emergence of new structures to counter the influences of the new conservatism. The formation of the Southern Baptist Alliance (now Alliance of Baptists) and the subsequent efforts to start new moderate seminaries portend of future splinters in the once-homogeneous fabric of the convention. Even more such divisions have followed the stunning defeat of moderate presidential candidate Daniel Vestal at the 1990 convention in New Orleans. The fundamentalists have not understood correctly the depth of concern they have stimulated in churches in vast regions of the convention.

Understanding Religious Reform

How then did this denomination end up in a topsy-turvy swirl of accusations, recriminations, polarized parties, and power struggles to control the agencies of its denominational life? Such a question calls for some theory of change that takes into account both the institutions within which people find their faith shaped and the culture of which they are a part. My thesis, drawn from contemporary studies of cultural change, suggests change as the result of the introduction of a new ideology of belief that upsets a traditional commonsense view of denominational life. As discussed in other chapters in this volume, traditional Southern Baptist identity was shaped by a culture that had coherence prior to World War II.[3] The changes in the South over the last forty years required a new ideology to make sense of this changing world. The SBC's fundamentalists provided such an ideology in the form of the nineteenth-century doctrine of biblical inerrancy. This ideology won in the SBC because it was merged with modern methods of political reform learned in the right wing of the Republican party under Ronald Reagan. This new method of functioning has had the unintended effect of establishing conflict, rather than belief, as the carrier of the new.[4]

Recent cultural studies provide something of the framework for this view. How and when does social change occur? Ann Swidler argues, rather persuasively in my judgment, that change is carried by ideologies that are a part of the "tool kit" of adaptation during unsettled periods of a culture. During settled periods "traditions" shape a stable definition of beliefs and practices that are taken for granted. They become so entrenched that they become a part of an unconscious "commonsense" view of reality by means of which the world is understood. "Ideologies," however, establish new ways of acting by organizing individuals to function in ways that may become traditions and eventually commonsense thinking. What ideology does is to offer a new way of handling the unsettled quality of social change.[5]

Such a view is a rather useful way of understanding the SBC conflict. The leadership for the grass-roots inerrancy movement in the SBC (the ideology) has come from places most affected by the changes in southern culture—the largest, most urban churches of the convention, where the transitions from the Old South have been most visible. What leaders of these churches discovered was that the old traditions of denominational programs did not prove effective in their environments. Rather, an authoritarian doctrine that created new enthusiasm was essential in the changing environments in which they worked. What they did was to challenge the traditions of denominational functioning operative since the 1940s by substituting a particular ideology for the old commonsense ways of being Southern Baptist. What is ironic in this argument is that a nineteenth-century ideology became the framework for addressing late twentieth-century modernity. Yet it was exactly the same unsettled quality that gave rise to fundamentalism in the nineteenth century.[6]

Such a view is also consistent with Robert Wuthnow's innovation theory applied to the religious sources of social change. Wuthnow's first application of change theory was to the new religious movements of the 1960s and 1970s. His argument was that the diversification of American religion was the result of the secularizing effects of science as a world view. By creating questions regarding the adequacy of theistic traditions, a new consciousness rooted in mysticism grew. He suggested, however, that the long-term consequence might be a reaction to new directions from more traditional modes of thinking and behaving.[7] For him religious change is a social process in which people have to be exposed to new understandings, innovations have to be given legitimacy, opportunities for experimentation must exist, and some motivation is necessary to adopt new conceptions.[8]

By the 1980s Wuthnow broadened his understanding of innovation to include the importance of ritual and ideology in social and cultural changes. Without the ordering character of meaning in culture, innovations do not endure. Therefore change must be meaning-full to be adopted. Ideology functions to provide the ordering component of change. In bringing forth a moral order, there are three phases of ideology at work: *production* of a new ideology as a result of disturbance in the existing order, *selection* of a particular ideology that succeeds by mobilizing the resources for survival, and *institutionalization* in which the new ideology takes root in the culture.[9]

Moving the Pendulum: Conservative Ideological Reform

Wuthnow's theory of ideology fits well the experience of Southern Baptists during the past decade, though moderates in the denomination have not understood it. The production of the new ideology of conformity to inerrancy was a twenty-five-year process in which the denomination struggled through a series of theological skirmishes, beginning with the Elliott controversy of 1963.[10] Between 1979 and 1985 the resources for winning the ideological battle were gathered, and since 1986 the process of institutionalization of the new ideology has been underway.

The rest of this chapter explores the resistance to that process. How was it this new conservatism succeeded with such apparent speed? Why has it been so difficult to resist? Some understanding of the commonsense wisdom governing the decision-making processes of the SBC prior to 1979 is necessary to answer these questions.[11] First, the center of denominational polity and life is the congregation. Southern Baptist congregations are, by and large, reflections of a conservative religious faith representing Christians who have constructed their faith to fit an ordinary rural, southern culture. It is the function and responsibility of all denominational agencies to serve this constituency in congregations by developing those programs that help them do their work.

Second, there is a diversity of congregations within Southern Baptist life and this diversity can be placed on a continuum of liberal to conservative. The most liberal of Southern Baptists would fall just to the left of center on the general continuum of American religion, but the Southern Baptist spectrum also would extend all the way to the most conservative side of that general continuum. Thus all Southern Baptist congregations are generally conservative, and much more so than the nation's churches as a whole. Within this continuum there have always been churches on either extreme that cannot be served by the denomination because they deviate too much from the norm or center of the denominational continuum. According to the old commonsense wisdom, it is the function of the denomination to serve the center of this conservative collection of folks.

Finally, there is a pendulum effect at work defining the center. As cultural shifts occur, the pendulum swings from the center to the left and then back to the center and to the right. There is a rhythm at work. If discontented people on one side or the other wait a few years, the pendulum will shift. This view was enunciated most clearly by long-term denominational executive James L. Sullivan:

> These two groups of about 10 percent each (liberal and fundamentalist) are the ones who debate every controversial issue that comes up on the floor of the Convention. The 80 percent in the middle, called the "silent middle," are listening intently, and by the ensuing discus-

sions are able to separate truth from error and present a motion that will be generally acceptable to Southern Baptists before the vote is taken. . . .

At times the Convention has been swept into extremism, most frequently by ultraconservatives. This has brought problems each time. Revisions usually were made the following year at one of the subsequent Conventions when messengers realized that they had moved away from the center of the constituency too drastically, and they moved back toward the center. . . .

Sometimes it is hard to determine where the "middle" is with Southern Baptists. There are certain identifiable characteristics which change as we move. For instance, if one starts at the Atlantic and moves westward, theology gets more conservative. As one moves from the Canadian border to the Gulf of Mexico, stands on social issues become more conservative. As one starts at the Pacific and moves eastward, music gets more conservative. So one can in honesty ask, "Where is the middle?"[12]

Quite obviously there is an intrinsic pendulum rooted in the democratic processes of the convention, according to this view. As a result the denominational leadership viewed the conflict in the SBC in 1979 as simply one more swing of the pendulum that would shift back to the center before any major dislocation of the denominational structure could occur.

The innovation introduced by the conservative movement was one of changing this homeostatic situation by means of organized political action to institutionalize the values of the 10 percent on the right into the structures of the denominational fabric. How? By generating a new constituency attending the annual meetings of the SBC while appealing to the old "middle" with the rhetoric of "problems in River City."

Historically the messengers to the annual meetings were largely pastors and staff members of medium- to large-sized congregations, their families, older active lay persons involved in the women's and men's auxiliary organizations, and denominational employees. Those with the budgets and time to attend were the attendees. Typical conventions were collections of eight to fifteen thousand persons, depending on the geography of the meeting. To jump to more than forty-five thousand messengers in 1985 indicated a major shift in the constituency of the annual meetings.

There were two sources of these new messengers: new conservatives and moderate resisters. Pastors of smaller churches and laity within one day's travel time of the meeting were aroused by the rhetoric of biblical inerrancy and a carefully orchestrated effort to recruit new voters. In reaction, moderate leaders organized laity and more pastors to counter the new movement.

The story of this innovative core of fundamentalist leaders has been the focus of numerous descriptions.[13] The emphasis of the following discussion is on the moderate resistance, to which less attention has been given.

Reactionary Tradition: Moderate Resistance to Change

As might be anticipated, the initial victories of the new SBC leadership in 1979 were greeted with a general sigh of "so what" by most of the denominational and local-church leadership. The election of Adrian Rogers as the first of a string of fundamentalists was viewed as a midcourse correction that would move the denomination back to its centrist roots without serious dislocations. After all, many of the changes in the denomination toward more tolerance in racial matters, the embracing of human rights agendas, the adoption of historical-critical studies of Scripture in the seminaries, the ordination of women, and participation in the national political forum (symbolized by the election of Jimmy Carter in 1976) were viewed as a loss of the conservative ethos of the Old South Convention base. Increasing numbers of blacks, women, and ethnics were to be found in leadership roles of the convention, especially during the presidency of Jimmy Allen, a former social ethics activist who served as SBC president in from 1977 to 1979.

Only a few voiced public concern about the growing fundamentalist movement, most notably Duke K. McCall, soon to retire as president of the Southern Baptist Theological Seminary. The concern was so lacking that no serious effort was made to challenge the presidential bid of Bailey Smith in 1980. Accordingly, the youngest president in SBC history was elected easily that year in St. Louis, from a church, the First Southern Baptist of Del City, Oklahoma, that had never before provided such national leadership.

Before the next convention, however, a group of moderates met in Gatlinburg, Tennessee, to begin organizing moderate resistance. What was most surprising about that effort was the rather immediate negative reaction to it from the denominational structures. The very fact that they were dubbed the "Gatlinburg Gang" by the denominational press indicated the attitude toward these resisters. For their efforts at counterorganizing, the moderates were pictured in the popular press as the "spoilers" and instigators of conflict. The early abuse suffered by these outspoken moderate leaders caused many in the middle camp to remain silent and uninvolved. Eventually most of the denominational leadership would join the resisters, but only after it was too late.

The moderates were able to marshal 41 percent of the 1981 Los Angeles presidential vote for retiring Baylor University president Abner McCall against the incumbent Bailey Smith, surprising even themselves. McCall was a rather unlikely candidate—university president against popular evangelist, retiree against youthful preacher, educator versus popularizer. But moderates were encouraged that they not only mobilized a sizable group to cross the continent for a vote but won several votes on the second day of the convention, replacing several fundamentalist trustee nominees.

Moderates were unable to build on this beginning, however. For all of their effort—ten years of meetings, strategy work, and enormous volunteer effort—they have yet to win the presidency. The moderates' presidential candidate in 1990, Daniel Vestal, won only two percentage points more than had Abner McCall in 1981. Yet Vestal was a youthful, attractive, biblically conservative candidate who campaigned hard for more than a year, was not opposing an incumbent, and was the beneficiary of years of accumulated concern over fundamentalist actions on the boards and agencies of the convention.

Why have moderates not succeeded in moving the pendulum back to the middle perspective they have supported? After all, moderates have been supported by most of the older mainline churches of the body, by most of the editors of state news publications, and by the majority of denominational agency leaders. Why have they consistently been defeated? The reasons, in my view, are several.

To begin with, moderates have never been willing to counter biblical inerrancy with an ideology of their own. They define the "problem" as political, not ideological—theology is just a strategy for control, they say. Moderates have never conceded that the inerrancy ideology is a deeply seated world view that is held by vast numbers of Southern Baptists who genuinely want that world view to control the decisions of convention life. The moderate view has been that the issue is *solely* political. For SBC moderates, operating as if these were "settled" times, ideology is irrelevant. What matters are larger loyalties of institutional cooperation and cultural consensus. In their view it is a *program* holding Southern Baptists together, not a doctrine. For fundamentalist leaders, however, a program that does not embody a true theology is not worthy of support. Purity of ideology is paramount. Therefore loss of institutional vitality in the conflict and transition is of little concern, if such loss purifies the doctrinal base of the organization.

Ironically this moderate lack of concern for ideology is part of the reason Southern Baptists have not divided more deeply than they have. The moderate perspective is genuinely "moderate," in that it will compromise ideology. Most moderates are willing to accept the leadership of the fundamentalists, allowing them representation and the freedom to hold their ideology—as long as it is not imposed on others. Such a compromise the fundamentalist leaders will not allow. Had moderates openly espoused a decisive counterideology, as those most liberal in their group have advocated, another denomination would already be in the making. Moderates therefore minimize the differences between the competing groups. "We are all conservative in theology," goes the common moderate wisdom. This very *moderation* has kept the convention together, but has made it impossible for moderates to win politically. The fundamentalists have won because of their driving passion for ideologically based change. This passion motivates people to give their money, attend rallies to hear their leaders and candidates, and organize messengers to attend the conventions at considerable expense. A commonsense tradition is difficult to mobilize, especially when it does not exist anymore!

Thus the first problem of moderates is identity. It extends even to the nomenclature of the conflict. The faction on the right resents the terms *fundamentalist* or *take-over group*; those on the left resent *liberal* or *moderate*. Both have claimed *conservative* as the label that best fits their followers. Baptist Press finally developed guidelines, calling one group *moderate conservative* and the other group *fundamentalist conservative*. The term that has been most used by moderates as a self-identifying label is *loyalist*. They have eschewed an ideological identity in favor of an organizational one. That reveals the difficulty of strategy. How do defenders of institutions prevail against an ideological force claiming the bankruptcy of those very institutions? By choosing to make theology the primary issue of their campaign, namely, insistence on adherence to the doctrine of inerrancy for all denominational employees, fundamentalists have tapped the passion necessary for political success.

The argument against inerrancy often was twisted in the popular mindset as a disregard for the authority of Scripture, a hallmark of orthodoxy for virtually all of the middle of the convention. Cecil Sherman was one of the few to accept the ideological challenge when he debated inerrantist Paige Patterson on the topic of biblical inerrancy prior to the Los Angeles convention in 1981. Copies of the debate tape unfortunately were distributed widely by fundamentalists, using Sherman as an example of liberal deviation. Virtually every leader who has attempted rational discussion on the theological issue has found himself (the male pronoun is chosen deliberately, for this has been a male dominated fight) publicly ridiculed for liberalism. Moderates could challenge the necessity of inerrancy as a basis for biblical authority, but they have had no competing ideology *for* which they could argue.

A second problem the moderates have is their difficulty in nominating candidates capable of winning against the fundamentalist candidates. Historically, the president of the SBC has been the pastor of a large, growing congregation. Not surprisingly, these pastors are also popular preachers. They are highly visible as speakers on the circuit of state convention meetings and as hosts of para-denominational conferences. Such individuals tend to be ambitious and are highly conscious of their future reputation. Because being moderate was seen as being a troublemaker, any ambitious pastor who aspired to win the presidency was cautious about identifying publicly with the moderate cause. Consequently, in nearly every year of the Controversy, moderate network leaders were turned down by pastors who were asked to allow themselves to become candidates. Had they agreed, moderates might have won and avoided the depth of the dispute. Too few pastors of influential churches believed in the ability of moderates to get them elected.

In addition, moderate leaders faced internal conflicts over their own candidate-selection strategy. They divided over whether to support conservative pastors capable of attracting fundamentalist voters or to nominate clear supporters of the resistance movement. Resistance leaders, however, were often aging and identified with the denominational establishment. At nearly every moderate strategy session the preferred candidate was a leading denomina-tional agency head, such as the president of the Foreign Mission Board, or a retiring denominational executive. The first three moderate candidates were retiring denominational leaders opposing young and dynamic pastors. By 1985 moderates had convinced the first pastor to allow himself to be nominated. An ultraconservative in theology, Winfred Moore was also of retirement age. Each pastor who ran after Moore could have been a candidate of the funda-mentalists in terms of theology but opposed the conflict generated in the de-nomination. Hence they were loyalists.

Not until 1990 were moderates able to run a pastor with the kind of qualifications that might have won the election earlier in the conflict. Daniel Vestal was youthful, theologically conservative, an effective speaker, smart in his political strategy, and highly visible. Even so he was not able to win the endorsement of other highly visible conservative pastors or garner adequate political support from the moderate organization.

A third problem moderates have is their inability to organize a unified movement with clear lines of responsibility and authority. The commitment of moderates to a democratic approach to shared leadership created difficulty in organizing a consensus. Not that the attempt has not been made. Moderate organizers have met every year but one since 1981 to select a candidate—only to return home to responses such as "Why did you choose him?" or "Pastor X would have been a far better candidate" or "We will never win until you ask me how to win!" In an effort to broaden leadership, nearly anyone willing to become involved was allowed to offer strategy decisions. Little dis-cipline was exercised as followers attending strategy meetings for the first time became spokespersons for the moderate movement. The constituency of the moderates is largely well educated, from larger congregations, and ac-customed to participation in denominational decisions. Thus everyone wanted to be consulted. Yet few wanted to do the hard work of organizing people to attend the convention and vote for a moderate candidate.

The result was a loose-knit moderate confederacy of volunteers operat-ing against the resources of well-funded and highly organized conservative structures. Moderates met infrequently and usually at the national conven-tions, when it was too late to make meaningful decisions. In the early years, vice-presidential candidates were chosen on Monday night of the convention and word was passed in the hallways the next day. Even in 1989 moderates had not agreed upon candidates for vice-president; consequently, three were nominated against one conservative candidate. When moderates did meet, participants were busy pastors with the resources to pay their own expenses. They had time for meetings and decisions, but then seldom had the time to lead in the day-to-day work of arranging rooms and transportation and telephoning to get out the vote.

Not until 1986 was there anything like a public staff arrangement funded by moderates, but that was focused rather exclusively in Texas, through the work of the Baptist Laity. Modest organizational efforts were made prior to 1986, as individuals raised small amounts of money to employ a retired person to function as a network coordinator. Some funds were made available to denominational employees who worked incognito in addition to their full-time employment. The initial funds to begin *SBC Today* in 1984 were raised by the same network of people attempting to elect new leaders. When the paper turned out to be not clearly identified with their concerns, they funded the *Call,* a more direct voice, for one year. Otherwise almost all of the work of moderates was a volunteer effort with little coordination and much local initiative.

Some of these organizational weaknesses were confronted in 1990. That year Baptists Committed to the SBC provided the most overt organizational effort of the decade, with paid staff, publications, and extensive telephone networks. Again it was too little and too late.

Contrast this to the resources of the fundamentalists. The two most visible leaders of the movement traveled nearly full time for much of this decade of change. Paul Pressler had a judgeship that required his attendance in the office one-half day per week. With a staff to do much of the routine work and his own prodigious capacity to work on legal briefs in airplanes and motel rooms, Pressler met with as many as five hundred groups annually as the primary carrier of information about the Controversy. Pressler's foundation, established in the early 1960s to support conservative theological education, was the likely source of the funds for this effort. Accompanying him was Paige Patterson, president of the independent Criswell Bible College. His role gave him visibility and, possibly, the Criswell budget for travel. On the other hand, denominational leaders were criticized severely whenever they traveled to speak on behalf of the moderate effort, even though they refused to use denominational funds to do so.

Beyond these efforts, fundamentalists funded two newspapers during the period, with full-time editors who engaged in organizing transportation, hotel accommodations, and strategy sessions at the SBC. Several of the larger churches assigned staffs to assist in the effort, with the associate pastor of one SBC president serving as the de facto staff for monthly meetings of leaders and for the annual election effort.

Conflict Dissemination: The Future Agenda

Where is the denomination headed? Prognostication is hardly a sociological science, yet if the thesis of this chapter is accurate, one can anticipate something of the future of Southern Baptist churches, associations, and conventions. Can the consensus that has held the disparate elements of the denomination together—namely, programs of missions and congregational ministry—be maintained amid the new emphases on ideology and conformity? Will a split in the denomination occur? Will the pendulum swing back to a kind of pre-1979 era of moderate leadership with renewed vigor in missions and evangelism?

Organizational innovations follow established networks. Although change is brought about as a consequence of numerous forces, it is only revolutionary change that alters the mechanisms in a structure whereby those changes are disseminated. My contention has been that conflict, whether intentional or unintentional, is the primary innovation that has been introduced into the fabric of SBC life. What conservatives thought they were introducing when they unstuck the pendulum of the 1970s was an ideological commitment to a particular theology, namely, the inerrancy of the Bible. What was introduced into the denomination was not just a new ideology but the use of ideology as a strategy of institutional change.

Another part of the common wisdom of Southern Baptist leaders is that it takes seven years for a new idea to filter from the leadership to the grassroots members of the local congregation. That filtering process begins with national agencies. The leadership organizes around a slogan or program formulated for adoption by the national convention. Money is committed to its dissemination. Gradually the state convention leadership buys into the new concept. State papers publicize the new emphasis. Conferences are held throughout church associations stressing the new emphasis. Eventually, having lived with repeated rhetoric emphasizing the new idea, local pastors adopt the innovation. Soon the new language of the concept has infiltrated sermons, Sunday school lessons, local associational meetings, and, finally, the committees and conversations of local church members.[14]

I argue that a process that once worked for the dissemination of a new *program* (such as Bold Mission Thrust) will now work for the dissemination of a new *method*—conflict as the means of change. The strategy of conflict for the redirection of the convention at a national level has worked. A new control is now the order of the day in national agencies and commissions. The moderate holdover leaders have been forced into accommodations with their more conservative trustees, and power is being consolidated quickly in those agencies with fundamentalist leaders. Moderate dissenters either leave or become quiet in the face of new majorities. Accordingly, at the national level, conflict is quickly being replaced by quiet resignation on one side and exuberant embracing of the new agenda of fundamentalist ideology on the other.

The pendulum is not going to swing back to the middle way of the old common sense approach to SBC life. The "new conservatives" now guide the direction of the SBC. Moderates have been whipped, and there is no likelihood of any resurgence of strength to move the denomination to a more centrist position during the coming decade. The most important question of the future is no longer "Will the fundamentalists win?" but "What happens now to the moderates?"

The most likely scenario, in my judgment, is simply a shift of the arena of the conflict. Resistance will continue, but at the level of state conventions and local associational and congregational structures. As Arthur Farnsley notes, partisan-style politics are now a fact of SBC life. The same conflicts that were played out at the SBC level during the 1980s will be played out at the local level in the 1990s. A 1989 special convention, called in Florida to address the abortion issue, is simply one evidence of the direction of the decade to come.

For moderates the alternative to internal conflict as a way of life is to build programs and institutions to compete with the old SBC institutions they built, which are now controlled by others. The emergence of the Southern Baptist Alliance and the Cooperative Baptist Fellowship provide strong bases from which moderate churches can move in alternative directions—something that was much more likely in 1990 than, even, in 1989. New seminaries, parallel curricula for local churches, and alternative mission programs may be the outcome.

Moderates also may form a new denominational structure. Given the strong resistance to leaving the SBC in toto, a societal approach to the future is more likely than a new denomination. Societies provide a structure for organizing efforts around a specific cause rather than centralizing all the causes supported by a group. Societies could provide the means for individuals and churches to direct local church funds, which once were given through the Cooperative Program, in a number of new directions. Such churches would continue to participate in state and local structures, but not participate in the national convention.

Finally, some churches will simply leave the SBC. Although a mass exodus is unlikely, those most alienated will probably seek alignments with American Baptist regional bodies or become independent congregations.

Why have I suggested that spreading conflict and continued moderate losses is the most likely outcome? Simply this: If moderates had the organizational savvy and the energy required for a major new effort, with the passion needed for new structures to become effective, they would never have lost the SBC in the first place. The same energy and commitment it takes to elect an SBC president is required to build a new denominational organization. Moderates have not had enough of either the past decade. Neither do they appear to have the energy and commitment to set a new course for the future of their churches in the 1990s.

Notes

Parts of this chapter originally appeared in substantially different form as "Anatomy of the SBC Institutional Crisis" in *Review and Expositor* 88, no.1 (Winter 1991): 25-35.

1. Walter B. Shurden, *Not a Silent People: Controversies that Have Shaped Southern Baptists* (Nashville, Tenn.: Broadman, 1972).

2. There also has been little change at the single "auxiliary" to the convention over which official SBC authorities have no control, the Woman's Missionary Union.

3. See Arthur Farnsley's chapter, for instance, for a description of the traditional "consensus" of common sense decision making.

4. Not all inerrantists are carriers of conflict. In fact one must separate the scholarly definitions of inerrancy, which are highly nuanced, from the popular use of the term to mobilize political followers. The fact that most inerrantist scholars who participated in the Ridgecrest conference sponsored by the six seminaries in April 1987 disavowed adherence to the political agendas of the new conservative leadership indicates the distance between popular uses and more technical uses of the term. Many Southern Baptist moderates would accept a modified definition of inerrancy, such as that proposed by David S. Dockery: "Inerrancy means when all the facts are known, the Bible (in its autographs) properly interpreted in light of which culture and communication means had developed by the time of its composition will be shown to be completely true (and therefore not false) in all that it affirms, to the degree of precision intended by the author, in all matters relating to God and his creation." David S. Dockery, "Biblical Inerrancy: Pro or Con?" *Theological Educator* 37 (Spring 1988): 25.

5. Ann Swidler, "Culture in Action: Symbols and Strategies," *American Sociological Review* 51 (Apr. 1986): 273-86.

6. There are numerous histories exploring the context of the rise of nineteenth-century evangelicalism. Linda K. Pritchard, "Religious Change in Nineteenth-Century America," in *The New Religious Consciousness,* ed. Charles Y. Glock and Robert N. Bellah (Berkeley and Los Angeles: Univ. of California Press, 1976), 297-329, is a creative summary of how evangelical theology emerged as dominant in a context of considerable social and religious change.

7. Robert Wuthnow, *The Consciousness Reformation* (Berkeley and Los Angeles: Univ. of California Press, 1976). In his conclusion he wrote, "Modernity does not replace tradition; it simply builds on top of it. The shape of the new is powerfully influenced by the old. But in the process, the old is often revitalized by the new. Misplaced emphases and ideals

gone sour often become corrected from the vantage of new perspectives" (212).

8. Wuthnow, *Experimentation in American Religion: The New Mysticisms and Their Implications for the Churches* (Berkeley and Los Angeles: Univ. of California Press, 1978), 18.

9. Wuthnow, *Meaning and Moral Order: Explorations in Cultural Analysis* (Berkeley and Los Angeles: Univ. of California Press, 1987), 151.

10. See Samuel Hill's chapter in this volume for an account of this controversy. I have given a brief history of this development in Larry L. McSwain, "Anatomy of the SBC Crisis," *SBC Today* (June 1986): 10-11, 18.

11. See Farnsley's chapter in this volume for a fuller description of the way polity and decision-making processes have shaped organizational understandings of the denomination.

12. James L. Sullivan, *Baptist Polity as I See It* (Nashville, Tenn.: Broadman, 1983), 200-202.

13. See, for instance, Joe E. Barnhart, *The Southern Baptist Holy War* (Austin, Tex.: Texas Monthly, 1986); Robison B. James, ed., *The Takeover in the Southern Baptist Convention* (Decatur, Ga.: SBC Today Publications, 1989); and Nancy Tatom Ammerman's *Baptist Battles: Social Change and Religious Conflict in the Southern Baptist Convention* (New Brunswick, N.J.: Rutgers Univ. Press, 1990). See also the three volumes by James C. Hefley, *The Truth in Crisis*.

14. The best example of this delayed acceptance is the time it took to convince the convention to defund the Baptist Joint Committee on Public Affairs, an effort that succeeded in 1990 only after years of defeat on the convention floor.

CHAPTER 15

TOWARD AN EVANGELICAL FUTURE

Timothy George

> If I did not believe in God, I would predict the demise
> of the SBC during the 80s.
>
> —Duke K. McCall, May 1980

The Controversy in the Southern Baptist Convention is over. This does not mean that all the fighting has stopped, much less that the belligerents on either side have suddenly been seized with the spirit of genuine reconciliation. Far from it. Ecclesiastical wars, like wars fought with real bullets and bombs, leave lingering scars that only time and a new generation of noncombatants can begin to heal. For this shalom we must wait.

Still, as everyone on all sides now admits, the battle for control of America's largest Protestant denomination has resulted in a decisive shift in direction for the SBC—called a "take-over" by moderates, and a "turnaround" by conservatives.[1] This process is not likely to be reversed in the foreseeable future, despite continuing skirmishes between incumbents and insurgents, and numerous guerrilla maneuvers played out at all levels of local Baptist politics.

The thesis of this chapter can be stated quite simply: The recent conflict in the SBC is part of the wider struggle of American evangelicals to come to grips with the crisis of modernity and can only properly be understood in that larger context. Of course there are many other aspects of the Controversy that can be and have been studied with much profit: its southern dimension, its economic implications, its demographic makeup, its populist appeal, its political configurations, and so forth. However, when viewed against the background of recent religious history, one fact stands out above all others. For only the second time in this century the veering of a major American denomination away from its historic, evangelical roots toward a more liberal, mainline Protestant posture has been arrested and reversed.[2] Moreover, this change has been as sweeping and dramatic as it was unexpected. It is little wonder, then, that sociologists of religion would seize on a phenomenon that even a close reading of American denominational history would not have prepared one to predict. Several chapters in this volume track the process by which this remarkable reorientation has occurred.

Although I shall also touch upon this aspect of the story, I am more interested in the theological forces that gave rise to the Controversy in the first place, and in the profound crisis of identity that its aftermath has posed for Southern Baptists. Moderates, as defenders of the latest Lost Cause, must now decide to either find a place to stand in the new order or seek alternative alignments. For most of them, secession is not an option; but how to function within a fractured family is not at all clear at present. Conservatives have an even greater worry: Can they survive their own success? Can they forge a new consensus that will include most, if not all, Southern Baptists without replicating the very system their movement was launched to correct? The mere replacement of one set of bureaucrats with another doth not a reformation make.

Throughout its long and fractious history, the Church of Jesus Christ has ever been pulled between the poles of identity and adaptability. Where identity has triumphed exclusively, the church has become insular, cloistered, turned in on itself. Where adaptability has reigned as the orthodoxy of the day, the church has become diffuse, assimilated, bereft of transcendence. As Southern Baptists move from an era of conflict toward one of reintegration, this tension will set the bounds in the quest for a new consensus and the recovery of a vision worthy to reclaim. Following a brief overview of the developing rift in the convention, I shall focus on three areas of concern that press for clarification and restatement as we move toward an evangelical future for the SBC: biblical authority, Baptist heritage, and theological renewal.[3]

From Synthesis to Schism

In 1900 the Southern Baptist Sunday School Board, then only nine years old, published a remarkable collection of essays entitled *Baptist Why and Why Not*. In the opening paragraph, James M. Frost declared, "Baptists are one in contending for the faith; one in their history and the heritage of their fathers; one in their purpose to preach the gospel of the grace of God among all nations."[4] The chapter titles of the book have a polemical ring: "Why Baptist and Not Campbellite," "Why Immersion and Not Sprinkling," "Why Missionary and Not 'Omissionary.'" This was to be a "campaign book," a tool for the promotion of denominational interests such as Baptist schools, missionary endeavors, and benevolent concerns.[5] A "Declaration of Faith" was appended to the volume, incorporating many of the articles later adopted in the Baptist Faith and Message of 1925. In that same year, the convention also approved the Cooperative Program, thus providing both a confessional and an organizational basis for its consolidation and expansion.

Recognizing diversity among themselves on many ancillary matters, the twenty-five contributors to this volume, including college presidents, seminary professors, leading pastors, and missions strategists, nevertheless stood together on a common doctrinal foundation: "We accept the Scriptures as an all-sufficient and infallible rule of faith and practice, and insist upon the absolute inerrancy and sole authority of the Word of God. We recognize at this point no room for division, either of practice or belief, or even sentiment."[6]

Although there has never been absolute uniformity among Southern Baptist congregations, the denomination entered the twentieth century remarkably united in its basic mission and purpose. Three developments during the early decades of the century further solidified the Southern Baptist synthesis: the refusal to join the emerging ecumenical movement, the containment of the fundamentalist-modernist controversy, and the construction of an impressive denominational bureaucracy supported by a systematic plan of finance. These were not isolated strands but interconnected facets of the developing Southern Baptist consciousness. Each reinforced the other, and each provided a common enemy to oppose—the "bastard" union movement, as one denominational executive described early ecumenical efforts; theological liberalism, safely sequestered in the northern denominations; and ecclesiastical separatism, the "noncooperation" epitomized by J. Frank Norris (whose guerrilla tactics against the denominational machine were more of a nuisance than a genuine threat).[7] All three factors entered into the report of a special committee, unanimously adopted by the SBC in 1951. Although affirming the missions efforts of Southern Baptists outside the traditional "Southland," the report focused on the doctrinal deviation of many ecumenical leaders who deny "such scriptural truths as the Virgin birth, the deity of Christ, and the inerrancy of the Holy Scriptures."[8]

In the 1950s two trends portended ill for the conflicts of the next three decades: the introduction of historical-critical studies in Baptist seminaries and colleges and the dominance of a program-centered approach to ministry. The success of the latter imbued convention leaders with a heady sense of invincibility as they steered the denomination in an increasingly progressivist direction during the 1960s and 1970s. As early as 1963, historian Samuel Hill predicted that the denominational applecart could be upset by a populist, grass-roots reaction: "The convention's polity being as it is, wresting of control by the ultra-conservatives from the moderates is not impossible."[9]

To some extent the term *inerrancy* became the rallying cry for conservatives, because other targets were too mobile to hit squarely. As Nancy Ammerman explains, the "actual moderate agenda" was camouflaged by an amorphous appeal to "freedom," because moderate leaders were convinced that "they could not rally majority support" for their progressivist ideas.[10] In both cases the underlying theological basis of the conflict was seldom explored—moderates largely denying that there was a theological rationale for the Controversy, conservatives fixated so narrowly on inerrancy that doctrinal concerns in other areas were ignored or pushed to the sidelines.

By the early sixties, Southern Baptists had developed a style of denominational life characterized not so much by theological perversity as by theological vacuity. This was the result of a long process of slippage going back at least fifty years. For example, George McDaniels, a leading pastor and later president of the SBC, issued the following jeremiad in 1919:

> In other decades Baptists were better indoctrinated than they are today. The environment in which they lived, sometimes inimicable to them, was conducive to the mastery of their principles. Of later years, a tendency to depreciate doctrinal discussion is easily discernible, and

young converts particularly are not rooted and grounded in the faith. Modern nonchalance acts as if it made little difference what one believes.[11]

By the 1960s the very word *indoctrinated*, which McDaniels used in a positive sense, had taken on a sinister connotation for many Baptists. Whatever it was, they did not want it done to them!

Earlier generations had been nurtured on the Baptist catechisms of Spurgeon, Broadus, and Boyce and, later, the solid instruction of BYPU, the Baptist Young People's Union. Gradually, however, these models of explicit Christian education yielded to the philosophy of John Dewey, and the discourse of conviction gave way to the religion of civility. Within the polite circles of the Baptist establishment, to ask about one's theology was taken as a gauche intrusion into the realm of privacy, almost like inquiring into the method of birth control one used: it was something everyone assumed, but as a deeply personal matter, it was hardly relevant to the public practice of religion. Even conservatives who were still sure that they "believed the Bible" were often woefully ignorant of its contents and even less aware of the rich doctrinal heritage to which they were heirs. Thus Billy Bob Baptist, as a recent SBC president dubbed the typical preacher boy (preacher girls in those days were beyond the imagination), was totally unprepared for the vigorous assault on the traditional understanding of Scripture that he encountered at—of all places!—his home-state Baptist college and his pastor's recommended seminary. This saga, repeated and no doubt exaggerated over twenty years, reinforced the sense of mistrust, alienation, and betrayal that would eventually issue in revolution. When later, in the midst of crisis, denominational leaders tried to reassure an aroused constituency that "all was well in River City," vast numbers of them thought they had reason to know better.

It would be a gross mistake, of course, to assume that SBC seminaries were suddenly filled with death-of-God liberals, and even more preposterous to imagine that mainstream Southern Baptists were seduced by the theology of the secular city. Most Southern Baptists, then as now, remained strongly committed to a conservative, evangelistic expression of faith. What did occur, however, was a discernible loosening of these commitments and an increasing preoccupation with a mainline Protestant agenda on the part of many of the educational and bureaucratic elites who set the policies and guided the boards and agencies of the convention. Their focus subtly shifted from SBC evangelical distinctiveness toward mainstream cultural accommodation. This trend was subtle and usually held in check by a pragmatic concern not to overturn the applecart. But it manifested itself in various ways: a one-way ecumenism to the left, a flirtation with the faddish theologies of the day, the uncritical dissemination of historical critical presuppositions concerning the Bible, an intellectualist disdain for the kind of piety held dear by the grass-roots constituency, an affinity for left-of-center politics, and a covert pro-choice advocacy on abortion. Most Southern Baptists, for example, would have been outraged to know that the head of their Christian Life Commission during this period was supportive of the Religious Coalition for Abortion Rights.

The most convincing sociological explanation of this phenomenon is Peter Berger's New Class hypothesis. According to this analysis, the American middle class underwent a wrenching bifurcation in the sixties and early seventies, a split between the traditional bourgeoisie with its conservative political and religious leanings, and the "new middle class," based in the educational system and communication media of the nation, a culture-shaping elite with outright disdain for the traditional mores and virtues of the old middle class. Not surprisingly, the cultural fault lines present in society at large also characterized the mainline Protestant churches. "The gathering storm in the churches," as one analyst depicted the increasing ferment of the late sixties, was simply a reaction to the "ability of a bureaucracy to maintain itself even against the will of a majority of constituents and their elected representatives." Berger argues that "in denomination after denomination, people who represented the new culture took over the bureaucratic machinery and thus the public face of the community."[12]

David Norsworthy's chapter in this volume shows how the structural rationalization of the SBC led to the "insulation of elites" from the great majority of church members. More and more ordinary Baptists in local churches sensed a growing gap between themselves and their church leaders in Nashville and Atlanta. To be sure, many of the Baptist bureaucrats of this era were sincere and devout, if somewhat colorless, persons; only a few were true convictional liberals in the theological sense. Many others, however, were not a little embarrassed by the fundamentalist roots of their own religious past. They had left the sawdust trail long ago. Now they were eager to nudge their buoyant if backwards denomination along the same path of liberation they had found so personally emancipating. Alert to all the evils of Baptist fundamentalism, of which they were true cultured despisers, they were themselves theologically naïve and ill prepared to believe any warnings of a leftward drift within the denomination.

In most mainline denominations, evangelicals voted against the new culture with their pocketbooks and their feet—they quit giving and going. Some Southern Baptists also became frustrated and gave up on their denomination. A few of these were bright progressives on the radical left fringe, the "missing generation" referred to by Nancy Ammerman. But another "missing generation," far larger and very different, were the thousands of Southern Baptists who became Independent Baptists and non-Baptist evangelicals, having concluded that the convention was either hopelessly lost to liberalism or increasingly irrelevant to wider evangelical concerns.[13] Most Southern Baptist conservatives, however, decided to stay and vote with their votes. There is a touch of irony in the fact that the very watchwords of the moderate movement—soul competency, priesthood of all believers, freedom—provided a basis, through the democratic governance of a voluntary association, for the toppling of the moderate regime, a point made well in Arthur Farnsley's chapter.

Thus at precisely the same time as a significant segment of SBC leadership was being drawn into the orbit of mainline concerns, more and more Southern Baptists were beginning to take notice of the common ground they shared with evangelical Christians outside the SBC. This was not an entirely new development. As far back as 1942, Southern Baptist leaders Robert G. Lee and John W. McCall, father of Duke K. McCall, the longtime president of Southern Baptist Theological Seminary in Louisville, were active in the founding of the National Association of Evangelicals. More than anything else, the ministry of Billy Graham made large numbers of Southern Baptists aware of and receptive to the wider world of American evangelicalism. Meanwhile, on college campuses across the nation, thousands of Southern Baptist students were being converted and discipled through the work of Campus Crusade for Christ, Intervarsity Christian Fellowship, the Navigators, and other explicitly evangelical ministries against which the blander Baptist Student Union approach could hardly compete.

Clearly not everyone was pleased with this development. Rather than cultivating closer ties between Southern Baptists and other evangelicals, some moderate leaders responded with a stand-offishness that reinforced old stereotypes of isolation and parochialism. Typical of this perspective was the reaction of an SBC agency head to the press's dubbing of Jimmy Carter as a "Southern Baptist evangelical" during the 1976 presidential campaign: "We are *not* evangelicals. That's a Yankee word. They want to claim us because we are big and successful and growing every year. But we have our own traditions, our own hymns and more students in our seminaries than they have in all of theirs put together.[14] Despite such efforts to equate "Northern" evangelicalism with Yankee imperialism, the 1970s and 1980s were marked by increasing fellowship and cooperation between Southern Baptists and evangelicals.

The writings of inerrantist scholars such as Carl F. H. Henry, Harold Lindsell, John Stott, J. I. Packer, and Francis Schaeffer, among others, began to circulate among Southern Baptist pastors. Such writings served a critical function in focusing the widespread, populist concern over the erosion of scriptural authority, a concern exacerbated by the Elliott controversy in the early sixties, and the Broadman Bible Commentary flap in the early seventies. Schaeffer in particular had an influence on Paige Patterson, one of the principal architects of the conservative movement in the SBC. When the Controversy finally burst into full blaze with the election of Adrian Rogers in 1979, Southern Baptist conservatives, or at least their leaders, were well aware of other recent "battles for the Bible," some won (Lutheran church-Missouri Synod), others lost (Fuller Theological Seminary).

Others have recounted the course of the Controversy itself. In retrospect it appears that the moderates had only one chance to stem the tide. By recognizing and responding pro-actively to the legitimate concerns raised by the conservative movement, rather than by merely reacting defensively to the raucous and sometimes distasteful way in which such concerns were aired, a more balanced and harmonious resolution of the dispute might have been achieved. Later in the Controversy, when in fact something of this approach was tried (e.g., the Glorieta initiative of the seminary presidents in 1986, pledging to seek more balanced faculties, and the SBC Peace Committee report of 1987), it was too little and much too late. As Larry McSwain's chapter in this volume shows, however, the moderate movement itself was deeply divided from the start—between those who saw the conservative resurgence as a benign swinging of the pendulum requiring no vigorous response at all and others who believed it to be a cancerous intrusion that had to be removed root and branch.

What both wings of the moderate movement failed to realize was the deeply ideological character of the conflict. For most conservatives, which is to say for most Southern Baptists, the Controversy *was* about theology, however "political" it may all have seemed to insider moderates and curious onlookers. Students of Christian doctrine who have seen how much rested on a single iota in the fourth-century debates over *homoousios* and *homoiousios* will not be surprised that the future of the SBC came down to whether the miracles in the Bible were really miraculous and the history truly historical. As Richard Condon maintains, "A nuance in an ideological difference is a wide chasm." [15]

Where did this passionate concern for doctrinal integrity come from if, as I argue, the traditional theological consensus had already been worn thin by the "acids of modernity" on the one hand and denominational pragmatism gone to seed on the other? From two sources, primarily: a vestigial memory of and intuitive loyalty to the Baptist heritage, with its reverence for the primary icon of the tradition, the written word of God; and the impetus of the wider evangelical resistance to new cultural values that placed Southern Baptists foursquare at the center of a *Kulturkampf* even larger than their own internal upheaval.

The SBC stands today on the brink of schism. The next several years will likely witness the emergence of a splinter denomination guided by activist moderates who have abandoned their hopes for reforming the SBC in a mainline Protestant direction. Like Landmark Baptists and Independent Baptists who left the convention in earlier generations, these "Free Baptists" (as they might like to be called) will continue to exist side by side with Southern Baptists, offering still another Baptist alternative on the religious landscape— much as the Presbyterian Church in America and the Presbyterian Church (USA) coexist today in most southern cities, representing two distinct variants of the Presbyterian tradition.

The conservative victory in the SBC will prove hollow, however, unless it is accompanied by genuine spiritual and theological renewal and a process of reconciliation with cooperating, Bible-believing moderates. Conservatives can afford to neither gloat in victory nor relax into the halcyon routine of a new establishment. For, as Peter Berger points out, the very social and political successes of evangelical movements are frequently their undoing, as they are sucked into the ambiance of an environing culture inimical to their most basic purpose and ideals. [16] Perhaps the greatest lesson of the past thirty years is this: We are able to understand the present and illuminate the future only to the extent that we do not forsake the warranted wisdom of the past.

Reclaiming Scripture as the Word of God

As we have seen, the Baptist battle for the Bible must be set in the much wider context of the ambivalence that has been inherent in exegetical methodology for more than one hundred years. Johannes Semler (d. 1791), a founder of the modern critical study of the Bible, anticipated the relativizing of both the biblical canon and the classic dogmas of patristic Christianity.

Historic Baptist confessions invariably express unquestioned confidence in the trustworthy character of the Bible, describing it as inspired, infallible, perfect, certain, true, without error, and so forth.[17] For the most part, however, these confessions were drafted in the "pre-Enlightenment" era, prior to the rationalistic assault on the integrity of the biblical materials. We cannot here review the impact of this methodology on the use of the Bible in the life of the church. Suffice it to say that the doctrine of biblical inerrancy as set forth, for example, in the writings of Scottish theologians such as Thomas Chalmers and William Cunningham, and in the Princeton theologians Hodge and Warfield, was a deliberate response to the inroads of destructive biblical criticism. *The Chicago Statements on Biblical Inerrancy* (1978, 1982) are the most recent, and most carefully nuanced, articulations of this position. [18]

The destructive potential of biblical criticism first became a concern among Southern Baptists in the controversy surrounding the pressured resignation of Crawford H. Toy from the faculty of Southern Seminary in 1879. Enamored of advanced theories of "progressive" scholarship, Toy came to deny that many of the events recorded in the Old Testament had actually occurred. He also questioned the christological implications of many messianic prophecies, including Genesis 49:9-10, which the New Testament (Rev. 5:5) specifically applies to Christ.[19] In the wake of the Toy affair, Basil Manly, Jr., one of the seminary's founders, drafted his *Bible Doctrine of Inspiration* (1888) as a deliberate restatement of the historic Protestant doctrine of Scripture. Without naming Toy, he reviewed the impact of "higher criticism," as it was then called, on biblical studies and came to a conclusion that has lost none of its relevance in the intervening century: "We have no need nor disposition to undervalue either the legitimate method or the fairly established results of modern critical research. . . a true 'Higher Criticism' may be just as valuable as a false or misguided attempt at it may be dangerous and delusive."[20]

What is at stake in the present context is not the validity of chastened, "believing" criticism, which responsible conservatives allow, but rather the often uncritical acceptance of postcritical presuppositions concerning the Bible, which some moderates have been reluctant to disavow. The doctrine of inerrancy, as defined by the *Chicago Statements,* precludes neither the recognition of various literary genres within the body of Scripture nor the investigation of sources and forms that were integral to the formation of Scripture in its present canonical shape. It does stand, however, as a check against the evaporation of biblical events and miracles into literary devices or imaginative constructs detached from their specific historical contexts. The account of Jesus' raising of Lazarus in John 11, for instance, is surely about more than the resuscitation of a corpse: it is the manifestation of Jesus as the Resurrection and the Life. But it does not involve anything less than what John says took place in the village of Bethany on a certain day during Jesus' earthly ministry. To interpret this pericope as a post-Easter story interpolated back into the Gospel of John is to do violence to the salvation-historical significance of the Incarnation itself; it is to substitute a Docetic reading of the text for the flesh-and-blood reality of Jesus. What is required of Southern Baptist biblical scholars is not a wholesale rejection of all critical methodologies, but rather an even more rigorous criticism of the underlying assumptions of such approaches, which frequently result in reductionist and antisupernaturalist interpretations of Scripture.

Fortunately Southern Baptist scholars need not start from scratch in this vast undertaking. The wealth of evangelical biblical scholarship over the past generation has largely been ignored in Southern Baptist academic circles until recently. It must now be mined and extended through projects such as the *New American Commentary,* currently in production at Broadman Press. The great heritage of John A. Broadus, A. T. Robertson, and John R. Sampey must be reclaimed, along with the recent contributions of E. Earl Ellis, George R. Beasley-Murray, and Curtis Vaughn, among others. Unnecessary critical concessions that weaken the objective truth and historical factuality of the biblical revelation must be opposed, but an open-minded interaction with promising trends, such as the movement toward canonical theology fostered by Brevard Childs, should be pursued with eagerness. Beyond the classroom, the library, and the word processor, specific steps must be taken to recover the sense of Holy Scripture as the word of God in preaching, evangelism, counseling, education, and missions. Such a process involves not only correct belief about the Bible but also a new and more vibrant place for the Bible in the life of the community of faith.

The Future of Our Religious Past

The conflict of visions in the SBC encompasses not only differing views of the Bible but also diverse claims about relative degrees of fidelity to the Baptist tradition. Sometimes such claims are put forth in exaggerated polemical images—the moderate likens the convention "take-over" to the rape of his mother; the conservative replies that at long last his mother has been rescued from evil molesters! In the heat of the political struggle, both sides have sometimes depicted the conflict as a cosmic battle between the Children of Light and the Children of Darkness. Such apocalyptic language obscures the fact that the Baptist heritage can be described in various ways and that present differences are frequently echoes of earlier contentions. To see how the issue of Baptist identity is shaped by one's reading of the denominational past, we shall look briefly at an issue that has loomed large in recent debates: Are Baptists a creedal people?

On the surface it would seem that such a question is entirely gratuitous. It is like asking whether Baptists sprinkle infants. The statement "Baptists are not a creedal people" has almost become an axiom within our tradition, and yet its meaning is not at all as univocal as some would imply.

Historically Baptists have claimed to be noncreedal for three primary reasons. First, as a protest against state-imposed religious conformity and the attendant civil sanctions. From their earliest emergence in seventeenth-century England, Baptists of all theological persuasions have been ardent supporters of religious liberty. In this vein Roger Williams opposed the Congregationalist ecclesiocracy in New England and John Leland went to prison in Virginia rather than acquiesce to the Anglican state church there. The doctrine of religious liberty required that there be no external political monitoring of the internal religious life of voluntary associations. It was this same cherished tenet, however, that guaranteed the ability of such associations to order their own internal life, their doctrine and discipline, in accordance with their own perception of divine truth.

Second, Baptists declare they are not creedal in that they have never elevated any humanly constructed doctrinal formula above Holy Scripture. As Baptist confessions themselves invariably declare, the Bible alone remains the *norma normans* for all our teaching and instruction, "the supreme standard by which all human conduct, creeds, and religious opinions should be tried." [21]

Lastly, Baptists are not creedal in that no Baptist confession of faith has ever been promulgated as infallible or beyond revision. The multiplicity of Baptist confessions is witness to this distinctive trait. William Lumpkin's anthology, *Baptist Confessions of Faith,* alone lists forty-five separate confessional documents. [22]

Although in these three senses Baptists have never been creedalistic, the idea that voluntary, conscientious adherence to an explicit doctrinal standard is somehow foreign to the Baptist tradition is a peculiar notion not borne out by a careful examination of our heritage. During his lifetime and for many years thence, Andrew Fuller (d. 1815) was doubtless the most influential theologian among Baptists in both England and America. In an essay on "Creeds and Subscriptions" he declared:

> It has been very common among a certain class of writers, to exclaim against creeds on systems in religion as inconsistent with Christian liberty and the rights of conscience; but every well-informed and consistent believer must have a creed—a system which he supposes to contain the leading principles of divine revelation. . . . If the articles of faith be opposed to the authority of Scripture, or substituted in the place of such authority, they become objectionable and injurious; but if they simply express the united judgment of those who voluntarily subscribe them, they are incapable of any such kind of imputation. [23]

In this tradition James P. Boyce and the founders of Southern Seminary set forth the rationale for strict subscription to that institution's Abstract of Principles:

> You will infringe the rights of no man, and you will secure the rights of those who have established here an instrumentality for the production of a sound ministry. It is no hardship to those who teach here, to be called upon to sign the declaration of their principles, for there are

fields of usefulness open elsewhere to every man, and none need accept your call who cannot conscientiously sign your formulary.[24]

Similarly, E. Y. Mullins, the champion of soul liberty, outlined various basic Christian beliefs (e.g., biblical inspiration, the miracles of Christ, the Atonement, bodily Resurrection, a literal Ascension, and an actual Return) and declared before the SBC in 1923: "We believe that adherence to the above truths and facts is a necessary condition of service for teachers in our Baptist schools."[25] This statement served as an impetus for the formulation of the Baptist Faith and Message of 1925, of which Mullins was a principal architect.

The modern aversion to creeds, as opposed to the historic Baptist rejection of creedalism, is related to several developments that have had a profound shaping influence on the contemporary Baptist consciousness. It was Thomas and Alexander Campbell who first raised the cry "No creed but the Bible." The Campbellite campaign against creedalism led one Baptist leader, Robert B. Semple of Virginia, to declare, "Some of your opinions, though true, are pushed to extremes, such as those upon the use of creeds, confessions, . . . in short your views are so contrary to those of Baptist in general, that if a party was to go fully into the practice of your principles I should say a new sect had sprung up, radically different from the Baptists as they now are.[26] Although Alexander Campbell eventually was excluded from the Baptist fellowship, he won a pyrrhic victory when, in time, other Baptists incorporated his anticonfessionalism as their own view and even defended it as the traditional Baptist position!

The Campbellite assimilation was congruent with another trend of major significance, namely, the development of individualism as the governing ethos of American culture. Baptists imbibed freely of the spirit of "rugged individualism," attenuating fixed norms of doctrine to a theology of radical subjectivism. W. S. Hudson, one of the most perceptive interpreters of Baptist history, points to the devastating impact of this development on Baptist ecclesiology:

> To the extent that Baptists were to develop an apologetic for their church life during the early decades of the twentieth century, it was to be on the basis of this highly individualistic principle. It has become increasingly apparent that this principle was derived from the general

> cultural and religious climate of the nineteenth century rather than
> from any serious study of the Bible. . . . The practical effect of the
> stress upon "soul competency" as the cardinal doctrine of Baptists
> was to make every man's hat his own church.[27]

The priesthood of all believers (plural), a historic Reformation principle with corporate implications, devolved into the priesthood of the believer, a lonely, isolated search for truth, the believer's connection to the visible *congregatio sanctorum* being tenuous at best.[28] No doubt this development reflected, in part, a proper Baptist insistence on the personal element in faith against the prevailing sacerdotalism and ritualism of other traditions. Still this emphasis tended toward a religion of "every tub sitting on its own bottom," and accelerated a progressive disengagement from explicit confessional commitments.[29] Among Southern Baptists this mood was reflected in the intense debates surrounding the adoption of the Baptist Faith and Message in 1925. Among Northern Baptists the issue came to a head in 1946, when conservatives failed in their effort to persuade the convention to embrace even a minimal confessional standard.

The struggle for our religious past is apt to continue in the SBC, as disaffected moderates seek historical justification for new initiatives while conservatives look to the heritage for precedents and vindication. How can such a "burned-over district" serve as a basis for dialogue in the quest for a new consensus?

Heritage as a Critical Principle

A better knowledge of the Baptist past will allow a more-informed critique of present trends. What is naïvely assumed as the "historic Baptist view" may be shown to be a development of recent and perhaps questionable vintage. Of course Baptist heritage itself may have been quite wrong at critical points! No one today defends the institution of slavery as did some of the ablest minds among the original founders of the SBC. Likewise, doctrinaire Landmarkism, with its reduction of ecclesiology to the local congregation, is rejected by article seven of the 1963 Baptist Faith and Message, which defines the church as "the body of Christ which includes all of the redeemed of all the ages."[30] Heritage provides a vantage point from which we may gain perspective for evaluating our own theology and practice in the light of Holy Scripture.

Baptist Distinctives and Evangelical Essentials

A careful study of the Baptist past will reveal distinctive features in our denominational history and wide areas of agreement with other evangelical Christians who stand with us as heirs of the Protestant Reformation. Believer's baptism by immersion, congregational polity, the unique contribution Baptists have made to the struggle for religious liberty-these are distinguishing marks of our tradition. On occasion we have stoutly defended our Baptist fences while suffering the foundations to be shaken and destroyed. Robert Wuthnow's analysis of contemporary Protestant church life has led him to conclude that the fundamental religious divide is not among denominations but rather within them.[31]

As Southern Baptists forge a new consensus in the nineties and beyond, we must seek contact and alliances with evangelical believers outside our own tradition, even as we reclaim those elements of special Baptist identity that have shaped and enriched our religious past. With other explicitly evangelical denominations, such as the Assemblies of God and the Lutheran church-Missouri Synod, Southern Baptists can play a major role in leading the wider evangelical community into the next century. To accept this challenge is not to betray our Baptist heritage but rather to enlarge it and share it in the mission of world evangelization.

Common Roots?

Undoubtedly the Baptist heritage has been a source of conflict and polemics in the present controversy. We should not forget, however, that conservatives and moderates still hold much in common, including, presumably, the shared experience of divine grace in salvation. The rhetoric of conflict has frequently overshadowed underlying affinities. Both parties can learn from each other to affirm principles and ideals integral to the Baptist heritage, even though they have become associated with one side or the other in the recent conflict. The doctrine of biblical inerrancy, for example, is embraced by the majority of Baptists, from moderates to conservatives. Similarly, religious liberty and the separation of church and state are valued by nearly everyone, even if there is strong disagreement on how these principles apply to issues of contemporary concern, such as prayer in public schools.

Just as the debate over biblical authority has refocused attention on the central document of the Christian faith, so too the struggle over Baptist heritage can have a healthy effect if it excites a new eagerness to unearth the hidden treasures of our religious past. Historian Walter Shurden puts it well: "To fight over your heritage is not a good way to learn about it; but even that is better than ignoring it altogether."[32]

Theological Renewal: The Recovery of Christian Belief

Throughout their history Baptists have been explicitly orthodox in their continuity with the trinitarian and christological consensus of the early church. Major exceptions to this tradition, such as the General Baptist defection to Unitarianism in the eighteenth century, have been met with swift repudiation. Nevertheless, in recent years accommodationist views of the reality of God, such as those put forth by process theology, have vied for acceptance under the banner of tolerable diversity. Baptist theologians must have the courage to say no to such views, which, if carried to their logical extreme, would undermine the gospel itself.[33]

Southern Baptists must also face squarely the relativizing of the Christian assertion that personal faith in Jesus Christ is the only way of salvation for all peoples everywhere. This presupposition undoubtedly has undergirded the development of the Southern Baptist missionary enterprise from its humble origins to its present status as one of the leading forces of evangelical outreach in the Christian world. Yet it is challenged today by a host of competing ideologies and theories ranging from religious syncretism and unchecked pluralism to "anonymous Christianity" and schemes of "second-chance" salvation. Had such ideas prevailed among Baptists of an earlier era, William

Carey would never have gone to India, nor Lottie Moon to China; or had they done so, they would have merely affirmed the values of the Hindu and Confucian cultures they encountered, rather than calling men and women "out of darkness into the marvelous light." That this topic was hotly debated at a recent meeting of the Evangelical Theological Society is evidence of its growing significance within all sectors of the Christian community.

As Southern Baptists confront these and other explosive issues in our efforts to move toward a renewed framework of theological integrity, it will be helpful to keep in mind several affirmations. First, heresy is a possibility. The earliest Christians found themselves confronted with a pattern of teaching that they could not countenance while remaining faithful to their Lord (Gal. 1:9; 1 John 4:1-3). In the providence of God, heresy has sometimes served a useful purpose by calling forth a clearer definition of the true faith: Marcion's rejection of the Old Testament as Christian Scripture accelerated the formation of the New Testament canon, and Pelagius's merit-based soteriology prompted Augustine's exposition of the doctrines of grace.

In much of contemporary mainline Protestantism, heresy as an operative doctrinal term is beyond the realm of possibility. (Interestingly, the World Council of Churches has declared South African apartheid to be heresy, and certain opponents of fundamentalism have not hesitated to label that movement heretical.) Surely we must be careful to distinguish the heresy from the heretic, and always reject censorious personal attacks against fellow believers, however serious their theological deviations may be. Still, the Church of Jesus Christ must be willing to recognize and to reject perversions of the Gospel when they crop up in its midst. A church that cannot distinguish heresy from truth, or even worse, that no longer thinks this is worth doing, is a church that has lost its right to bear witness to the transforming Gospel of Jesus Christ, who declared himself to be not only the Way and the Life but also the Truth, the only Truth that leads to the Father.

Further, it will be helpful to affirm that theological discrimination is a priority. It is crucial that Southern Baptists learn to distinguish the central declarations of the faith from the peripheral, adiaphorous issues that have become so divisive in our time. Let us consider two issues that have been identified as potentially divisive among Southern Baptists: the revival of interest in Calvinism and women in ministry.

During the past twenty years there has been a growing interest in the

Reformed origins of Southern Baptist life, prompted by the discovery that most early Southern Baptist theologians and church leaders were staunchly Calvinistic concerning the doctrines of grace. One should not overestimate the size of this development; in sociological terms it resembles a special interest group rather than a movement. Still, it has proved controversial in some areas, because "Baptist" and "Calvinistic" are hardly regarded as synonymous, and because the antimissionary struggles of the last century have left deep scars and suspicious attitudes toward topics such as election, predestination, effectual calling, and so forth. Yet most Southern Baptist Calvinists are committed inerrantists; most have been sympathetic to, if not politically active in, the conservative movement. Southern Baptist Calvinists can contribute to the new consensus if they can show their theology to be a legitimate variant within the heritage, and if they can work cooperatively with others who may not "ring all five bells" quite the way they do. Their case for participation will be immensely strengthened if they show themselves to be aggressively evangelistic and missionary minded, thus dispelling the myth that Calvinism is antithetical to the promiscuous preaching of the Gospel and the fulfillment of the Great Commission.

The need to distinguish first- and second-order theological concerns appears even more urgently in the controversy surrounding women in ministry in SBC life. Two entrenched camps have staked out opposing ground on this issue. One group sees any concession to the leadership of women in official church life as a flagrant violation of Scripture, comparable (nearly) to the denial of the Virgin birth or the bodily Resurrection. The other group sees the refusal of such roles to women as a heinous sin comparable to slavery, a matter over which to break fellowship.

One way to refocus this issue would be to separate the question of women in ministry from the theology of feminism, with which it has been largely confused. For evangelicals committed to the authority of Scripture, the question, Should women serve as pastors and/or deacons? must not be answered with, Isn't everyone doing it? but with, What does the Bible say about it? Evangelicals outside of the SBC are divided on the latter question, and two groups, both advocates of biblical inerrancy, have been formed to promote opposing positions: the Council for Biblical Equality and the Council on Biblical Manhood and Womanhood. Regrettably Southern Baptists are only beginning to participate in this wider evangelical discussion.

The incursion of feminist theology into the life of the church is a problem of a different magnitude—one with far greater life-threatening dangers to historic Christian beliefs. The "depatriarchializing" of Scripture; the refusal to call God "Lord" because the word is seen as a term of oppressive domination; the insistence on gender-inclusive language for the Godhead; the quest for female deities to put alongside of, or in place of, Jesus of Nazareth; feminist hermeneutics that relativize the authority of the biblical text—each of these views calls into question the fundamental reality of God and the integrity of his revelation.[34]

This is not to say that all feminist theologies are equally destructive (they are not); nor is it to deny that there are elements of truth in the feminist critique of sexism in both society and the church (there are). It is to claim that the evaluation of feminist theology is a first-order priority that must be distinguished from the intra-evangelical discussion of the proper role of women in the service of the church.

Finally, the cultivation of a holistic orthodoxy is a necessity. In his *Commentary on Daniel* (9:25), John Calvin compared the work of God among his ancient people with the challenge of his own day: "But God still wishes in these days to build his spiritual temple amidst the anxieties of the times. The faithful must still hold the trowel in one hand and the sword in the other, because the building of the church must still be combined with many struggles."[35]

The sword and the trowel—images chosen by one of Calvin's later admirers, Charles H. Spurgeon, to mirror two vital aspects of his own vocation as pastor and theologian. At the heart of biblical faith is the single-minded pursuit of truth, the precise shape of which becomes clear only in confrontation with competing loyalties and affirmations. Polemics cannot be divorced from dogmatics, as Karl Barth's magnum opus abundantly demonstrates in large and small print! Yet both Calvin and Spurgeon were more interested in edifying the faithful than in opposing the naysayers. Without omitting the latter when it is necessary, the task of theological renewal in the SBC must clearly concentrate now on the former.

The cultivation of a holistic orthodoxy embraces not only what is taught in our seminary and college classrooms, as important as that is, but also what is heard from our pulpits, and taught in our Sunday schools, and experienced in our worship, and shared with our neighbors, and passed on to our children. Nothing less than a theological revival, something of more substance than "a happy hour with Jesus," can bring about this kind of transformation in our denominational life. "Ortho-doxy" has the dual connotation of right thinking about God and praise that is worthy of God. The coinherence of warranted wisdom and sincere piety is both the goal and source of theological renewal. *Theologia est scientia vivendo Deo.*

Notes

Parts of this chapter originally appeared as "Conflict and Identity in the Southern Baptist Convention: The Quest for a New Consensus" in *Beyond the Impass?* edited by Robison B. James and David Dockery. © Copyright 1992 Broadman Press. All rights reserved. Used by permission.

1. Throughout this chapter I refer to the two contending parties in the SBC conflict as *moderates* and *conservatives,* the terms of self-description most often used by participants in the struggle. To be sure, conservatives are frequently called *fundamentalists* by moderates, whereas moderates are often dubbed *liberals* by conservatives. As defined historically, both fundamentalism and liberalism may be used validly to describe recent developments in SBC life; however, neither is a value-free term of description in the present context. Both carry pejorative connotations that are eschewed by those so labeled.

2. By "mainline Protestant" I refer to the group of churches and network of leaders that dominated American Protestantism until the 1960s. This coalition constituted a veritable religious establishment among the larger white denominations. Supported by the growing ecumenical movement, leaders of mainline Protestantism enjoyed considerable religious and cultural authority in both church and society in the earlier twentieth century. Although Southern Baptists could certainly boast a regional establishment of their own, until midcentury at least they intentionally held aloof, both theologically and missiologically, from what has been called the "establishment enterprises" of the mainline churches—as did Missouri Synod Lutherans, whose recent denominational travails offer the closest

parallel to SBC trends. Cf. William R. Hutchison, ed., *Between the Times: The Travail of the Protestant Establishment in America, 1900-1960* (Cambridge: Cambridge Univ. Press, 1989), 6.

3. Portions of this chapter have been adapted from my essay, "Conflict and Identity in the SBC: The Quest for a New Consensus," in *Beyond the Impasse: Scripture, Interpretation, and Theology in the SBC,* ed. David S. Dockery and Robison B. James (Nashville, Tenn.: Broadman, 1992). An excerpt from this chapter was also published in the 9 Mar. 1992 issue of *Christianity Today* as "The Southern Baptist Wars: What Can We Learn from the Conservative Victory?"

4. J. M. Frost, ed., *Baptist Why and Why Not* (Nashville, Tenn.: Sunday School Board, 1900), 9.

5. Ibid., 14.

6. Ibid., 12.

7. J. S. Rogers et al., "A Symposium by Southern State Secretaries on the Union Movement," *Southwestern Journal of Theology* 3 (1919): 23. On the role of the ecumenical movement in Southern Baptist life, see Timothy George, "Southern Baptist Relationships with Other Protestants," *Baptist History and Heritage* 25 (1990): 24-34.

8. *Southern Baptist Convention Annual,* 1951, 460.

9. Samuel S. Hill, "The Southern Baptists: Need for Reformation, Redirection," *Christian Century* 9 (Jan. 1963): 40. Apparently this is the first recorded use of the term *moderate* in the context of the SBC conflict. See Bill J. Leonard, *God's Last and Only Hope: The Fragmentation of the Southern Baptist Convention* (Grand Rapids, Mich.: Eerdmans, 1990), 63-64.

10. Nancy Tatom Ammerman, *Baptist Battles: Social Change and Religious Conflict in the Southern Baptist Convention* (New Brunswick, N.J.: Rutgers Univ. Press, 1990), 179. Ammerman states, "Moderate leaders were reluctant to hit the trail in open support of the agenda that had in fact guided their actions. . . . As a result, moderates were reduced to general calls for 'freedom' and to responding to the agenda defined by the fundamentalists."

11. George W. McDaniels, *The People Called Baptists* (Nashville, Tenn.: Sunday School Board, 1919), 8.

12. Peter L. Berger, "Reflections of an Ecclesiastical Expatriate," in *How My Mind Has Changed,* ed. James M. Wall and David Heim (Grand Rapids, Mich.: Eerdmans, 1991), 106-7. Cf. Jeffrey K. Hadden, *The Gathering Storm in the Churches* (Garden City, N.Y.: Doubleday, 1969).

13. Doubtless the incursion of Southern Baptists into the ranks of the Independents contributed to the political coming of age of the latter movement. See Bill J. Leonard, "Independent Baptists: From Sectarian Minority to 'Moral Majority,'" *Church History* 56 (1987).

14. Quoted in Kenneth L. Woodward et al., "Born Again! The Year of the Evangelicals," *Newsweek,* 25 Oct. 1976, 76.

15. Quoted in J. Sears McGee, *The Godly Man in Stuart England* (New Haven, Conn.: Yale Univ. Press, 1976), 1.

16. Berger, "Reflections," 107.

17. See L. Russ Bush and Tom J. Nettles, *Baptists and the Bible* (Chicago: Moody, 1980); and Timothy George, "The Renewal of Baptist Theology," in *Baptist Theologians,* ed. Timothy George and David S. Dockery (Nashville, Tenn.: Broadman, 1990), 20-21.

18. On the Princeton theologians, see Mark A. Noll, *The Princeton Theology, 1812-1921* (Grand Rapids, Mich.: Baker Book House, 1983). On the Scottish inerrantists, see Alec Cheyne, "The Bible and Change in the Nineteenth Century," in *The Bible in Scottish Life and Literature,* ed. David F. Wright (Edinburgh: Saint Andrew Press, 1988), 192-207.

19. On the Toy controversy, see Billy G. Hurt, "Crawford Howell Toy: Interpreter of the Old Testament" (Th.D. diss., Southern Baptist Theological Seminary, 1965); and Pope A. Duncan, "Crawford Howell Toy: Heresy at Louisville," in *American Religious Heretics,* ed. George H. Shriver (Nashville, Tenn.: Abingdon Press, 1966), 56-88.

20. Basil Manly, Jr., *The Bible Doctrine of Inspiration* (Philadelphia: American Baptist Publication Society, 1888), 229.

21. Herschel H. Hobbs, *The Baptist Faith and Message* (Nashville, Tenn.: SBC Convention Press, 1971), 18.

22. William L. Lumpkin, *Baptist Confessions of Faith* (Valley Forge, Pa.: Judson, 1959).

23. Andrew Fuller, *The Complete Works of the Rev. Andrew Fuller* (Philadelphia: American Baptist Publication Society, 1845), 3: 449-51.

24. This quotation is from Boyce's inaugural address before the trustees of Furman University in 1856, "Three Changes in Theological Institutions." The text is printed in full in Timothy George, ed., *James Petigru Boyce: Selected Writings* (Nashville, Tenn.: Broadman, 1989), 30-59. This quotation is found on page 56. Cf. William Cathcart's statement, "The extensive use of a creed in Baptist Churches should be encouraged by earnest Christians who love our Scriptural principles." He also cites with approval this comment from Charles H. Spurgeon: "The pretense that articles of faith fetter the mind, is annihilated by the fact that the boldest thinkers are to be found among men who are not foolhardy to forsake the old landmarks. He who finds his creed a fetter has none at all, for to the true believer a plain statement of his faith is no more a chain than a sword-belt to the soldier, or a girdle to the pilgrim." *The Baptist Encyclopedia* (Philadelphia: Louis H. Everts, 1881), 294.

25. *Southern Baptist Convention Annual, 1923.*

26. Quoted in Robert A. Baker, ed., *A Baptist Source Book* (Nashville, Tenn.: Broadman, 1966), 78. For a recent Southern Baptist exchange on this theme, see both the article by Thomas J. Nettles, "Creedalism, Confessionalism, and the Baptist Faith and Message," and the editor's introduction to it in Robison B. James, ed., *The Unfettered Word: Southern Baptists Confront the Authority-Inerrancy Question* (Waco, Tex.: Word, 1987), 138-54. James cites the writings of John Leland and the fact that the SBC adopted no formal statement at its founding in 1845 as evidence of "noncreedal inclination" among Southern Baptists. In the context of arguing for religious liberty against state-imposed conformity, Leland clearly warned against turning confessional statements into a "Virgin Mary" or "a petty Bible." He too, however, acknowledged confessions as "advantageous" and binding upon those who voluntarily embraced them, as did most Separate Baptists, whose churches and associations adopted numerous confessions and issued disciplinary sanctions against those who violated such commitments. The 293 delegates (as they were called then, rather than "messengers") who gathered in Augusta to organize the SBC in 1845 were thoroughly united in their confessional adherence, the vast majority of them belonging to churches and local associations that embraced the Philadel-

phia Confession of Faith, called the "Century Confession" in the South because of its adoption by Charleston Baptists in 1700, some forty years prior to its promulgation in Philadelphia. See Robert A. Baker and Paul L. Craven, Jr., *Adventure in Faith: The First 300 Years of First Baptist Church, Charleston, South Carolina* (Nashville, Tenn.: Broadman, 1982), 80-83.

27. W. S. Hudson, ed., *Baptist Concepts of the Church* (Chicago: Judson, 1959), 215-16.

28. See Timothy George, "The Priesthood of All Believers and the Quest for Theological Integrity," *Criswell Theological Review* 3 (1989): 284-94.

29. Cf. the statement of Carlyle Marney: "It was a gross perversion of the gospel that inserted a bastard individualism here and taught us that the believer's priesthood meant that 'every tub must set on its own bottom.'" *Priests to Each Other* (Valley Forge, Pa.: Judson, 1974), 12.

30. Hobbs, *Baptist Faith and Message,* 74.

31. Robert Wuthnow, *The Struggle for America's Soul* (Grand Rapids, Mich.: Eerdmans, 1989).

32. Walter B. Shurden, *Not a Silent People* (Nashville, Tenn.: Broadman, 1972), 31.

33. Cf. Karl Barth's ringing challenge: "If we do not have the confidence of *damnamus,* we ought to omit *credimus,* and go back to doing theology as usual." *Church Dogmatics* 1, no. 1 (New York: Harper, 1961), 630.

34. Elizabeth Achtemeier, "Female Language for God: Should the Church Adopt It?" in *The Hermeneutical Quest: Essays in Honor of James Luther Mays,* ed. Donald G. Miller (Allison Park, Pa.: Pickwick, 1986), 114. See also the excellent paper by Roland M. Frye, "Language for God and Feminist Language," distributed by the Center for Theological Inquiry, Princeton Theological Seminary.

35. Commentary on Daniel 9: 25, *Calvin's Commentaries* 13 (Grand Rapids, Mich.: Baker Book House, 1984), 203.

CHAPTER 16

AFTER THE BATTLES: EMERGING ORGANIZATIONAL FORMS
Nancy T. Ammerman

By the summer of 1990, the future direction of presidential politics in the Southern Baptist Convention was no longer in doubt. For years moderates had been declaring each presidential election their final showdown, but this one really was. In 1990 they did not have to face an incumbent. Jerry Vines would be stepping down, and the word on the grapevine was that he would be replaced by Morris Chapman as the fundamentalist standard bearer. Moderates thought Chapman was the weakest opponent they had faced in twelve years. Their choice was Daniel Vestal, a young, attractive, conservative, dynamic preacher. He had many friends, even in the fundamentalist camp, and he had no visible enemies. He had been a declared candidate for more than a year and had stumped the country with the well-oiled political machinery of Baptists Committed supporting him. Moderates had learned from eleven years of defeat and were doing *everything* right.

Everything, that is, except getting enough people to New Orleans to vote. They did not even come close. Chapman's margin of victory was wider than the margin incumbent Jerry Vines had enjoyed over Vestal the year before; and, as Larry McSwain's chapter points out, it was only two percentage points better than the first feeble moderate effort in 1981. The moderate political movement was dead, and for the foreseeable future fundamentalists would be able to elect whomever they chose.

Electing whomever they chose meant, of course, that fundamentalists also would be assured continuing control over the schools and agencies of the denomination. They had already begun the process of changing the policies and personnel in those agencies,[1] but the summer of 1990 brought a series of events that made fundamentalist intentions abundantly clear. At the convention the fundamentalist majority that defeated Vestal also voted to cut the SBC's funding of the Baptist Joint Committee on Public Affairs.[2] Before the month was out, the officers of the Executive Committee had convened in special session (behind doors guarded by armed security officers) to summarily dismiss Dan Martin and Al Shackleford, who had run the denomination's information service, Baptist Press. Meanwhile the board of trustees at the denomination's flagship seminary in Louisville was ready to pursue its house-cleaning agenda. President Roy Honeycutt and three of his faculty members were hanging on by a thread, and the Peace Committee's list of what most Baptists believe (a literal Adam and Eve, literal Jonah, literal miracles, and the like) was adopted as the criterion for all future personnel decisions.

It was during that turning-point summer that Daniel Vestal and Baptists Committed called for a summit conference of sorts. They wanted to gather a hundred or so moderate leaders to talk about what to do. They called representatives of other organizations on the SBC's "left" wing—the Southern Baptist Alliance, Women in Ministry, and the staff of *SBC Today*—and word went out to gather in Atlanta in August. It soon became apparent, however, that the hotel conference room they had rented would not accommodate the crowd that wanted to come. The old-style gathering of leaders was turning into something more broadly participatory. They scrambled to secure convention space, and on 23 August, three thousand "concerned Baptists" gathered at the Inforum in Atlanta.

They sang and worshipped together, listening to the kind of preaching they had been missing at the Pastors' Conference of the SBC. But mostly they talked to each other about the future. For portions of the program, the crowd divided into guided discussion groups of about seventy-five participants each, so that everyone was able to take part. They got to say things they had been wanting to say for ten years. They could express their fears and dreams in an atmosphere of acceptance. Many expressed their amazement at how good it felt to think about the future without worrying about what the fundamentalists would do. They were no longer looking over their shoulders or expecting to be hooted away from a microphone. It was as though in defeat they had found freedom.

Some of those who came brought with them a good deal of skepticism, however. The three thousand who gathered in Atlanta were not the first to occupy this territory along the SBC's frontier. In 1987 the Southern Baptist Alliance (SBA) had been formed by people similarly convinced that the utility of political campaigns was past. In its early days, it was concerned primarily with protesting SBC actions and replacing SBC programs. It provided the same sort of refuge and fellowship this new group had found in Atlanta. The people who formed the SBA were largely the progressives of the SBC. They were the people who fought for civil rights in the sixties and who were the first to champion women ministers in the seventies. Many enjoyed a more liturgical form of worship than did most Southern Baptists, and were more ecumenical in outlook and involvement. They were the "liberals" fundamentalists loved to point out and condemn. It was not surprising that they were among the first to see that the denomination had been lost to their causes. It also was not surprising that the rest of the denomination responded to the new organization's endeavors as the negligible protest of a "fringe" group.

Between 1987 and 1990 the SBA was branded by virtually everyone else in the denomination as too radical for any "normal" Southern Baptist to associate with. And no group was more active in promulgating that image than the moderates, led by Baptists Committed, who were still trying to wage a political battle for control of the convention. They knew that they had to position themselves as centrists if they were to win; distance from extremists of both right (fundamentalists) and left (the SBA) was essential.

For their part, SBA sympathizers grew increasingly disdainful of the moderate quest for power. As they continued to put distance between themselves and the SBC, even the moderate regime of the 1970s no longer looked good to them. After three years of active, mutual distancing, it is little wonder that SBA members arrived in Atlanta dubious, or that Baptist Committed members feared the SBA might taint the effort to draw together a variety of concerned Baptists.

Members of the SBA had not been reassured by the planning process for this meeting. They had been consulted, but only marginally. They were not at all sure that "good old boys" who had only recently held denominational power were ready to think new thoughts and include new people. Women especially were wary, and it was still a very white crowd. When these people talked about inclusion, just who were they willing to include, and for what? There were women ministers on the program (listed with "Rev." in front of their names), but only men preached. The proposed list of directors for a new funding agency looked like a who's who from the "good old days." Progressives who had never been included, even in the good old days, were skeptical at best.

But the experience in Atlanta began to erode that skepticism. When the body decided to create a steering committee to make plans for the future, a vision of broader inclusion began to emerge. The nominees were almost half laity, almost half women, and included four women clergy. The participation of one African American and one Chinese American, and attempts to include a Hispanic American, were evidence that ethnic diversity was at least a conscious goal. The group elected did not look like the old SBC, even in its moderate heyday.

The agenda given this Interim Steering Committee said nothing about regaining control of the SBC. Rather it spoke of promoting community, developing funding proposals and mission statements, communicating a sense of renewal, and planning another meeting. No one could say what those new plans and proposals would be, but the people in Atlanta wanted nothing to do with the way things had been for twelve years. When an occasional voice wondered out loud if some new strategy might bring the fundamentalists to their knees, a chorus of voices declared "No!" These concerned Baptists wanted to do something new. They did not yet know what it would be, but they had turned visibly toward the future. They left Atlanta calling themselves merely "the fellowship," but their "collective effervescence" would soon begin to take more enduring shape.[3]

By the following May, when a larger group—almost six thousand—gathered in Atlanta, there was an official constitution to adopt and concrete missions projects to fund. The group debated a number of official names and settled on "Cooperative Baptist Fellowship." Asked in a survey of the participants if they wanted to fight to regain control of the SBC, less than 4 percent said yes.[4] In a variety of ways the survey revealed a group ready to explore new things. Sixty percent even said they were willing to consider connections outside the SBC, and a similar number said they would recommend something other than an SBC seminary to someone considering a theological education. They ranked alternative ways of doing missions and new materials for Christian education as their highest priorities, but they were nearly as adamant that they needed new avenues for theological education, opportunities for worship and fellowship, and support for confronting ethical issues.

"Are you forming a new denomination?"[5] That was the recurring question from reporters and participants alike, asked of the SBA since 1987 and now asked of the CBF. The difficulty in answering that question reflects the uncertainty of the situation, but it also reflects the uncertainties of Baptist polity and the shifting meaning of denominationalism in American religion.

The Constraints and Opportunities of Baptist Polity

The ambiguities of Baptist polity have emerged in the tension between law and practice, tensions brought to the fore in periods of conflict and change. It has always been the case that the official polity of the Southern Baptist Convention leaves a great deal of room for tenuous connections and creative interpretations. A local church is first a member of a local Baptist association, to which it contributes for local benevolence and mission work and from which it can be "disfellowshipped" for violations of doctrine and practice (recently, ordaining women has been the most common cause). Local associations have no organic connection (no representation or ties of authority) with state and national bodies. A church's membership in one does not determine its membership in any other.

To be a member of the Southern Baptist Convention, a local church must merely declare itself in "friendly cooperation," which is usually taken to mean that the church will contribute to the Cooperative Program. Those contributions usually go through the state convention to national headquarters in Nashville; whether they *must* go to both state and national offices varies by state and is currently being contested. If the church gives more money, they can get more votes at the annual meeting (up to ten), but there is no designated minimum gift—in fact, $2,250 entitles a church to the full ten messengers—nor is there a doctrinal statement to sign or a required pledge of exclusive loyalty to Southern Baptist causes.

This structure of voluntary cooperation was adopted between 1925 and 1931, when the Cooperative Program and the current constitution were put in place. As Samuel Hill, Arthur Farnsley, and David Norsworthy note in their chapters in this volume, those institutions were a clear step toward centralization, a step that did not go unnoticed by the dissidents of that day. Fundamentalists such as J. Frank Norris could not convince many that the SBC of the 1920s was being overrun by liberals, but he got a hearing when he complained about creeping bureaucracy. The centralizers won those battles by *not* writing their desires into law. The constitutional changes they made left room for the local autonomy the skeptics of the time were apparently afraid they would lose. As a result the SBC constitution still leaves room for all the organizational creativity any new group can muster, without requiring official severing of SBC ties.[6]

The centralizers of the 1920s won by establishing practices, not by writing laws. Their eventual authority came both by the sheer weight of their subsequent success and by tying the Cooperative Program to the key symbols and values of Southern Baptists.[7] In the generation that followed they convinced Southern Baptists that the Cooperative Program was biblical—that there were precedents (especially in the Apostle Paul's collection for the church in Jerusalem) for gathering money from scattered churches and giving it through a central authority to those in need. They also convinced Southern Baptists that the Cooperative Program was a necessary tool for evangelism, that it offered them a way to efficiently combine their efforts to spread the Gospel around the world. Although the central authorities of the denomination had no coercive power over local congregations, they achieved high levels of cooperation by linking the means they employed to the common values and goals present among Southern Baptists.

Those common values and goals represented what organizational theorists call the *substantive rationality* of the group—what groups think they want to do together. The organizational structure of the SBC took the particular form it did because of the substance of what Southern Baptists wanted to do and because of the particular technical and cultural materials they had to work with at the time.[8] No one who reads the organizational materials of that era could miss the overriding concern for efficiency that pervades the rhetoric. The dominant models of organization, around which everyone seemed to bc building, were characterized by centralization and hierarchy and increasing specialization—"Fordism." To the extent that Southern Baptist leaders, like other Protestant leaders of the time, had their ears to the national organizational culture, they heard a chorus of voices touting "efficiency."[9]

They were *able* to follow those voices because by the 1920s they had available new material resources. As Southern Baptists became less dependent on a farm economy and more enmeshed in a wage economy, there were regular paychecks to be tithed in the systematic fashion the new bureaucrats advocated. And as the number of college-educated members grew, there were more leaders to staff credential-oriented agencies. That the masses of Southern Baptists were still minimally educated simply meant that denominational leaders gained respect for possessing a credential to which many aspired.

The SBC was able to put a centralized agency system in place because the previous generation of Southern Baptists had already begun to acquire the habit of depending on a centralized agency for accomplishing their local goals. The Sunday School Board, established in 1891, had already begun to supply local churches with materials that went far beyond weekly Bible study lessons. They were already dreaming up programs to help local churches fulfill their evangelistic and educational goals, and they were devising methods of training and certifying local members and pastors that would systematize and standardize what it meant to be an efficient local church.

By the 1950s both the Cooperative Program and the Sunday School Board were in full flower. Without any official authority over local churches they had managed to define the terms of membership. A "good" Southern Baptist church gave at least 10 percent of its budget to the Cooperative Program (and nothing to any non-SBC cause). It got its preacher from an SBC seminary. It purchased all its program support materials from the Sunday School Board and had all the recommended organizations and committees. To measure its accomplishments, it could report each year to "headquarters" on the Uniform Church Letter how many it had enrolled in each of these programs. To ensure proper organizational socialization, it sent its youth to Baptist colleges and its lay leaders to Glorieta and Ridgecrest summer assemblies for training. It would vehemently deny being liturgical but follow the denominational calendar in celebrating everything from Christian Home Sunday to Race Relations Sunday. As one lay person recently remarked, "If we don't have a handbook or a pamphlet from Nashville, we don't know how to do it." And as Richard Groves, president of the SBA replied, "More tellingly, we probably wouldn't even have thought of doing it."

Not only had national structures shaped the life of the local church but associations and state conventions were structured along centralized lines as well. If Nashville created a department for discipleship training, each state convention would have parallel departments, and local associations and churches would have the requisite committees. Each unit would turn to the unit above for training, materials, and guidance. And in most instances, state and local offices received program support funding from their national counterpart. Although money flowed up from the states, it also flowed back down to fund local versions of the programs decreed at the national level.

That a denomination with such a loosely constructed congregational polity could become so functionally centralized makes Southern Baptists a prime example of the organizational form that has come to dominate our thinking about what constitutes a denomination. During this century, *denomination*—regardless of official polity—has come to mean the centralized administration that takes in money from the churches and uses that money to do mission work, create program supports for churches, educate clergy, speak publicly on behalf of the churches, and so on. Polity makes a difference in whether the centralized body owns most of the property, officially appoints the pastors, and presumes to promulgate official doctrine,[10] but the everyday affairs of a denomination's bureaucracies and of the churches connected to it look remarkably similar. The structure resembles a relatively closed system, with all resources, products, and rewards contained within.

Fundamentalist churches in the SBC were never considered really good citizens of the denomination precisely because they refused to play by those rules. They were less likely to support all the denominational programs and more likely to support para-church organizations. They were afraid Nashville was too liberal, so they got help from various fundamentalist publishers; and they *knew* the SBC seminaries were too liberal, so they got their preachers from Mid-America Seminary or Dallas Theological. Moderates tried hard to label them as not "real" Southern Baptists for such behavior, but the official polity (the law, if not the practice) was on the fundamentalists' side.

Now that the fundamentalists have won, some of them are becoming somewhat more cooperative, sending more of their money and program support requests through Nashville. And, not surprisingly, moderates are now rediscovering the advantages of a decentralized official polity over the centralized habits they had praised in the past. If being loyal meant getting pro-life Sunday school lessons, telling missionary teachers they ought to spend their time preaching, and creating fundamentalist training schools out of SBC seminaries, some moderates were not so sure they wanted to send in their money. They began to join the fundamentalists in the para-church market, albeit on the opposite side of the ideological street.[11]

Other moderates still have the disdain for para-church organizations they acquired in all those years of being loyal to the SBC. They remember all the sermons about how the Cooperative Program was a leap forward over the chaotic society method of funding (in which each agency is directly dependent on the churches). Many disgruntled moderates would like to re-create the denominational structure of the old SBC—only with themselves in charge. Some who have served on the leadership boards of the Cooperative Baptist Fellowship like to speak of creating a new "missions delivery system" and asking churches to choose "ours instead of theirs." They are still loyalists to the old structure, just disenchanted with those governing it. If that view of the future wins among those who are creating the CBF, the result will be a clear schism. Churches will be asked to back one comprehensive set of agencies through one central fund; and they will be asked to choose the CBF's plan over the SBC's. That would provide the clearest possible answer to the question about a new denomination, because it would be an answer that accepted all the existing definitions of the word, changing the content, not the structure.

Similar tendencies toward accepting existing definitions of denominational structure exist among those SBA members who are ready to join the American Baptist Churches (ABC, formerly Northern Baptists). The ABC matches the Southern Baptist Alliance's progressive agenda, especially its commitment to civil rights. Healing the North-South split created by slavery strongly appeals to many in the SBA, and an increasing number are seeking dual alignment. Without leaving the SBC, they are also joining the ABC, attempting to create a bridge of reconciliation. Residual regional loyalties (and probably racism) make this an alternative most Southern Baptists, even of the moderate sort, are unwilling to pursue. But for those who do, it represents a straightforward link with existing denominational structures—mission boards, retirement plans, and all. Were these churches (or perhaps the whole SBA) eventually to decide that their SBC affiliation was superfluous, a clear-cut schism could be declared.

Disdain for para-church organizations, wariness toward the ABC, and loyalty to the Cooperative Program function as powerful deterrents to any schismatic movement. People who have learned to think of denominational support as an all-or-nothing affair are reluctant to consider any alternative as long as any small part of the SBC mission effort seems worthy of funding. This reluctance to consider alternatives is often voiced as a fear of "cutting off our missionaries." When, in late 1991, the Foreign Mission Board cut off funding to its seminary in Ruschlikon, Switzerland, because the seminary had hired a liberal professor, many moderates were forced to realize that the missionaries they cared about might be cut off anyway. But even people with grave doubts about the fundamentalist direction of the denomination often see no acceptable alternative. They see no way to avoid sponsoring what they do not like without also cutting off what they do. Such is the strength of the centralized system to which they have pledged their loyalty for three generations.

Other Southern Baptists see no alternatives because they are not looking for them. As I reported in *Baptist Battles*,[12] about half of the denomination appears convinced that what happens at the national level has no effect on their local churches. Taking official polity as reality and ignoring three generations of centralized practice, their habits of participation show no signs of changing. They will keep on buying products and attending meetings as if nothing has happened. The rhetoric of the fundamentalists is convincing to them, and they are reassured to have "Bible believers" in charge. Their unswerving habitual loyalty assures the new regime in the denomination that 80 to 90 percent of existing churches will remain in the fold. The constraints of Southern Baptist habits, then, are very real. They will likely keep the vast majority of the existing denomination intact, with centralized organizational structures under the guidance of fundamentalist leadership.

The opportunities of Baptist polity, however, make room for considerable innovation among those who choose that route. They can invent new programs and link with existing nondenominational agencies, all without officially severing their SBC ties.

Innovation and American Religious Organizations

Those who are finding this a creative moment, who are rediscovering local autonomy and creative cooperation, are joining a movement they often do not see as much bigger than themselves, but it is. Our attempts to define ourselves as dissident Southern Baptists are unfolding within America's rapidly changing religious context, and we will in turn reshape the context by our creations.

Robert Wuthnow, in *The Restructuring of American Religion,* points to the post-World War II growth of the para-church sector of the religious economy.[13] He demonstrates that an enormous array of such organizations already exists—from Campus Crusade to Bread for the World, from the Religious Roundtable to Fuller Seminary, from David C. Cook Publishing to the Sojourners Community. They are organizations that exist outside the structure of official denominations and relate to individuals and churches across a wide range of denominational traditions. These are the organizations Southern Baptists so carefully avoided during their generations of centralized loyalty.

The existence of such specialized religious organizations is made possible in part by advances in technology and by changes in the organizational culture of the late twentieth century. Just as Southern Baptists of the early twentieth century formed their organizational structure out of the values and habits and materials they had at hand, so new technological and cultural resources will make possible new organizational configurations. Already communications technology from conference calls to fax machines to electronic mail make it possible to coordinate the efforts of a broad network of people without requiring that they work in one location. Sophisticated computer software and electronic banking make complicated combinations of payments possible, and desk-top publishing makes huge printing presses unnecessary. It is simply no longer essential to get everybody together under one roof to work or even to vote. It is no longer essential to mass-produce a uniform product to be mass-consumed.

There are other new material resources available to late twentieth-century Baptists, as well. One of the most striking demographic characteristics of the convocation that formed the Cooperative Baptist Fellowship was its high level of education. Even with a median age greater than fifty-five, more than three-quarters of the lay people present had a college degree or more. Virtually all the clergy had seminary degrees. These are the people who have the skills and orientation to become users of information and participants in autonomous, democratic structures. Although they may respect the skills of "experts," they also perceive themselves as capable of discernment.

If high levels of education provide the skill and orientation, high levels of participation by women may provide the innovative passion for these new organizations. After years of struggling to find any place at all in which to minister, Southern Baptist women have had plenty of time to think about how they would do things differently. As they are accepted into leadership roles in the SBA and the CBF, they will undoubtedly change the shape of things. If the technological and organizational climate were not already diminishing the luster of centralized hierarchy, feminist voices would be reminding Baptist organizers to beware of patriarchal structures.

The larger postmodern organizational culture, in fact, does have a much more decentralized and democratic ethos. If *efficiency* was the watchword of the 1920s, *participation* may be today's watchword. The model evolving in business no longer requires that one unified set of goals be divided into minutely specialized tasks and coordinated through one hierarchical order. New organizational structures are allowing each unit more autonomy and more internal democracy.[14] As churches begin to adopt these structures, it will mean that each congregation will assess its own needs and resources, seeking the particular set of organizational connections called for by their sense of mission. Local churches may have active connections with other local churches, with religious and secular associations designed to accomplish their goals, and with denominational and nondenominational agencies through which they choose to work. In turn special-purpose organizations will have to be flexible and responsive to the needs of their "market." Although this echoes the voluntarism of the society method of the nineteenth century, it is distinct because late twentieth-century organizations are able to construct cooperative networks that are dispersed, adaptable, and responsive.

More and more churches are looking to nondenominational agencies to be their mission outreach, their church literature supplier, their voice in Washington, the educator of their clergy. They are leaving the denominations with a crisis that one Nashville executive described as "declining brand loyalty." Although local churches may be nominally Baptist or Lutheran or Presbyterian, they may be less defined by their denomination than by the independent alignments they have to these other organizations.

Those local congregational choices are sometimes constrained by polity—a Catholic parish cannot choose a Presbyterian priest, and a Methodist church had better send its apportionments to the district. But nothing keeps the members of those congregations from working together on a Habitat for Humanity project, buying their advent candles from the same local Christian bookstore, or participating in the Full-Gospel Businessmen's breakfast on Tuesday morning.

Likewise, the members of those congregations are now both more educated and more mobile than ever before. As Wade Clark Roof and William McKinney put it, the old ascriptive loyalties of family, ethnicity, place, and class are less strong.[15] They securely tie us to neither our home communities nor our home churches. And Wuthnow adds that the growth of higher education has introduced an expanding segment of the population to the pluralism of the world they live in. The result is high levels of denominational mobility and a growing no-preference sector of the religious economy. Just as there is increasing choice at the congregational level, even more dramatically there is increasing choice at the individual level.

It is my sense that the denominational maps will simply never look the same again; the choices will never again be so monolithic. For neither individuals nor congregations will the choice of a denomination be the kind of all-encompassing, lifelong commitment that characterized the days of centralized denominational monopolies or the times when land and tradition gave us a secure religious place. For the foreseeable future, the American religious landscape will be occupied by denominations in something like their current form *and* a variety of specialized, entrepreneurial religious organizations that fill specific needs for both diverse denominations and those outside the denominational fold entirely.

Redefining "Denomination" and "Baptist"

As we have seen, for most of this century, the word *denomination* has connoted an identifiable organization to which churches were linked. These organizations collect money and statistics and declare that a "true" member is one on whom they have a record. For several centuries prior to this one, however, denominations primarily took their identity from the theologians who defined the proper boundaries of the faith and from the ethnic groups whose identity was tied to the denomination. Both theology and tradition declared what it meant to be a true member of the body. Taken together, the organizations, the ethnicities, and the theologians produced, over several centuries, widely held images of denominational identity. We all think we know what a Presbyterian is or who is unlikely to belong to an Episcopal church or why we should laugh at a joke about Catholics or Lutherans. Without any visible organizational connection to any religious body, hundreds of individual Americans queried by survey researchers every year are nevertheless able to name their denominational preference. Although this form of membership may be the most tenuous, it has effects that suggest that denominations have a real cultural existence transcending even their own visible structures. [16]

The recent trends in American religious life that we have reviewed—the growth of nondenominational organizations and increasing individual mobility across denominational lines—pose significant questions about our existing definitions. Denomination has long since receded as a significant category for many theologians, so it is not clear we can go to them for answers. Even theologians concerned with ecclesiology (the doctrine of the church) never really developed rationales for the centralized systems most denominations had become. It remains to be seen whether new generations of theologians will take up the task of defining what it means to be a Presbyterian or a Baptist or an Episcopalian and work out theological rationales for our ways of organizing ourselves.

If bureaucratic denominational organizations lose their monopoly, we will also lose our ability to define membership in practical, functional terms. With high individual mobility, and with neither ideologues nor centralized bureaucracies to define the boundaries, existing cultural identities may be expected to erode, as well, at least as this generation gives way to the next.

One of the developments worth watching among new Baptist organizations is how they define what it means to be Baptist. Timothy George's essay calls for renewed attention to that task among the evangelicals who remain in the SBC. Most of the new special-purpose organizations—the Baptist Theological Seminary at Richmond, the Baptist Studies Program at Emory, the Baptist House of Studies at Duke, and the Baptist Center for Ethics—are very self-conscious about their Baptist identity. *None* has used an adjective as a modifier, eschewing regional (ethnic) lines of identification. Even the Southern Baptist Alliance has changed its name to the Alliance of Baptists. All of these organizations represent new efforts at cooperation across Baptist denominational lines and efforts to recover a renewed sense of a Baptist core identity. Although these new agencies are nondenominational in the centralized sense of the word, they are very denominational in the more theological sense of the word. In the coming years, it will be the organizations that can claim legitimate ties to the biblical and evangelistic heritage of Baptists—along with establishing practices that embody Baptist democratic values—that will survive as Baptist into the twenty-first century.

In coming years what it means to be Baptist will be negotiated within a complex organizational and cultural network. Religious agencies will become (if they have not always been) merely one location on a complex denominational map that includes other affiliated organizations, networks of communication, links to various suppliers of ideas and services, and even the interpersonal environment in which denominational identity is defined and passed along.[17] We are in a period of high volatility and creativity in which it is not yet clear what people will mean ten years from now when they tell the General Social Survey, "I am a Baptist." New organizations are being formed; new alliances are being forged; new stories are being told; and new heroes and heroines are being discovered. These new inventions and new relationships will be the social and cultural building blocks out of which a new Baptist identity will be forged.

Notes

1. Larry McSwain's chapter in this volume and chapter 7 of my own *Baptist Battles: Social Change and Religious Conflict in the Southern Baptist Convention* (New Brunswick, N.J.: Rutgers Univ. Press, 1990) offer fuller reviews of this institutional change.
2. See Arthur Farnsley's chapter for a full discussion of this decision.
3. *Collective effervescence* is Durkheim's term (in *The Elementary Forms of the Religious Life* (1915); reprint, New York: Free Press, 1965). The ten-

sions between such "nascent" states and the more stable institutions of churches and denominations is fruitfully explored in Stephen Warner's *New Wine in Old Wineskins* (Berkeley and Los Angeles: Univ. of California Press, 1988).

4. This survey was conducted by the Center for Religious Research at Emory University, and all the survey results reported in this chapter come from our compilation of the data.

5. The press evidently eventually got tired of asking and simply declared it to be so. After the Interim Steering Committee's March meeting in Atlanta, a story went out over the AP wires that a group of disgruntled Baptists had met and formed a new denomination. The story was soon retracted and withdrawn, but not before startled reactions from committee members, who were quite unaware that that was what they did!

6. See Farnsley's chapter for a discussion of fundamentalist explorations of the possibility of changing this definition of membership. It is my hunch that it may eventually be changed, but only if the fundamentalists in charge of writing the bylaws find it useful to declare participation in non-SBC structures a bad influence on churches *they otherwise want to keep*. As long as the only ones leaving are the "liberals" they wish to purge anyway, and as long as funding stays at acceptable levels, there will be no incentive for fundamentalist SBC leaders to change official definitions of membership.

7. The chapters by Samuel Hill and by Farnsley in this volume explore the institutionalizing process in the SBC in more detail. See James Wood's *Leadership in Voluntary Organizations* (New Brunswick, N.J.: Rutgers Univ. Press, 1981) for a full discussion of the links between accepted goals and successful leadership.

8. Stewart R. Clegg, *Modern Organizations: Organization Studies in the Postmodern World* (London: Sage, 1990), esp. chap. 6.

9. See Ben Primer, *Protestants and American Business Methods* (Ann Arbor, Mich.: UMI Press, 1979).

10. On factors affecting parish autonomy, see R. L. Cantrell, J. F. Krile, and G. A. Donohue, "Parish Autonomy: Measuring Denominational Differences," *Journal for the Scientific Study of Religion* 22 (1983): 276-87.

11. Robert Wuthnow argues that special purpose (para-church) groups

tend to cluster around the liberal and conservative poles rather than in the center, thus reflecting the growing divide he sees in American religion. See his *The Restructuring of American Religion: Society and Faith Since World War II* (Princeton, N.J.: Princeton Univ. Press, 1988).

12. Nancy Tatom Ammerman, *Baptist Battles: Social Change and Religious Conflict in the Southern Baptist Convention* (New Brunswick, N.J.: Rutgers Univ. Press, 1990), 258-71.

13. Wuthnow, *Restructuring of American Religion,* esp. chaps. 5 and 6.

14. Clegg, *Modern Organizations,* chap. 7.

15. See Wade Clark Roof and William McKinney, *American Mainline Religion* (New Brunswick, N.J.: Rutgers Univ. Press, 1987).

16. These variations in the definition of *denomination* are explored in my essay "Denominations: Who and What Are We Studying?" (Paper presented at conference on Scholarly Writing of Denominational History, National Humanities Center, Research Triangle Park, N.C., Oct. 1991).

17. This model of the organizational environment follows the ideas developed by Clegg in *Modern Organizations.*

EPILOGUE

■ OBSERVING THE OBSERVERS
Susan Harding

According to most academic and journalistic accounts, the reelection of Charles Stanley as president of the Southern Baptist Convention in 1985 marked "a turning point" in SBC history. The *New York Times* described the presidential election that year as a "showdown between fundamentalists and the more moderate factions" for "control of the appointments to the boards governing an annual budget of $130 million, as well as six seminaries and 7,000 missionaries at home and abroad."[1] The *Times* coverage of the convocation concluded with moderate leader Russell Dilday's summary portrayal of the situation as "a fundamentalist takeover of the denomination's administrative machinery."[2] Most accounts of Stanley's victory, like the *Times'*, cast it in terms that were at once institutional and ideological. But more than money, appointments, programs, policies, and ideas were at stake. The struggle was also representational. Images, value judgments, story lines, points of view, social identities and rank, and "history" itself were also in flux, as fundamentalists contested for control of public representations of themselves, their opponents, and events. Fundamentalist victories in the SBC, and in other arenas, during the 1980s must be measured in terms of increased fundamentalist control of all kinds of resources. But their success must also be gauged in terms of the dramatic transformations in how fundamentalists and their history came to be represented by others, specifically by academics and journalists, the principal professional speakers of the modern discourses constituting "fundamentalism."

Fundamentalists create themselves through their own cultural practices, but not exactly as they please. They are also constituted by modern discursive practices, an apparatus of thought that presents itself in the form of popular stereotypes, media images, and academic "knowledge." Before the 1980s, modern voices, singly and together, unselfconsciously represented fundamentalists and their beliefs as a historical object, a cultural "other," apart from, even antithetical to, all that was modern. Modernity, in turn, emerged as the positive term in an escalating string of oppositions between supernatural belief and unbelief, literal and critical, backward and progressive, bigoted and tolerant. Through polarities such as these between "us" and "them," the modern subject was secured.

From an unreconstructed modern point of view, the word *fundamentalist* conjures up a jumbled and troubling universe of connotations, clichés, images, feelings, poses, and plots. Militant, strident, dogmatic, ignorant, duped, backward, rural, southern, uneducated, antiscientific, anti-intellectual, irrational, absolutist, authoritarian, reactionary, bigoted, racist, sexist, anti-Communist warmongers. You cannot reason with them. They actually believe the Bible is literally true. They are clinging to traditions. They are reacting against rapid social change. They are unfit for modern life. They are dying out. Aren't they dead yet?

The more rhetorically restrained modern academic voice asks: What are the social, politico-economic, and cultural contexts that lead some people to react to modern life by becoming fundamentalists? What is it about the modern world, about late capitalist culture, about the "New South," that enables fundamentalism to survive? How does fundamentalist discourse reproduce the ideological hegemony of the ruling classes even as it appears to reject the modern world those classes rule?

Academic inquiry into fundamentalism is framed by still largely unexamined modern presuppositions that "fundamentalists" is a socially meaningful category of people who are significantly homogeneous in regard to religious belief, interpretive practices, moral compass, and/or socioeconomic conditions, people whose behavior defies reasonable expectations and therefore needs to be—and can be—explained. The explanations, the answers to modern academic questions, tend to pass over or dismiss fundamentalist realities and convert born-again believers into aberrant, usually backward or hoodwinked, versions of modern subjects, who are thereby established as the neutral norm of history. Finally, the voices of modernity—academic, journalistic, literary, and popular—employ the opposition between fundamentalist and

modern in historical time. In the modern historical meta-narrative, "fundamentalist" and "modern" *mean* past and future, and history appears to be the
natural, progressive spread of modern ideas, at times lamentably thwarted by
unnatural outbursts of reactive and reactionary fundamentalist fervor.

This book's authors were assembled, Nancy Ammerman tells us in the
Introduction, because the "fundamentalist take-over" of the Southern Baptist
Convention "challenged many of our pet theories" and was "a phenomenon
to be explained." Even though many of us do not consciously identify ourselves with modernity, and some of us consider ourselves theologically orthodox, insofar as the SBC revolt and related fundamentalist revolts of the 1980s
took us by surprise, we nevertheless articulated—and were articulated by—the
modern point of view. Such revolts simply should not have happened, could
not occur, according to our theories and presuppositions about modern times.
Impossible as these events seemed to us early on, they were not so unthinkable
that we, journalists and academics, could not rally to the occasion, reexamine
"the facts," revise our theories and proliferate new explanations.

But perhaps we have rushed into the intellectual breach produced by
the revolts and filled it up too soon, too much. Perhaps we need to pause
and ponder our passionate, seemingly insatiable, desire to *explain* fundamentalists. Perhaps we need to ask how who "we" are depends on our definitions, our explanations, of "them," and to see our representations of "them"
as major stakes in the struggle. Perhaps we need to make the modern discursive practices that constitute fundamentalism an integral dimension of our
inquiry into it.

Modern interpretive conventions would have us read our academic and
journalistic representations of fundamentalism literally, weighing their truth value
against some hypothetically independent realities. If we do so, we remain cap-
tive to the overarching story line of liberal progress that those representations
reproduce. If we turn our critical attention instead to that modern apparatus of
thought and read the story of fundamentalism as, in part, a modern discursive
invention, then we may ask how fundamentalism was invented, who speaks it,
and what are the categories, assumptions, and trajectories implicit in its narrative representations. Shortly I will try to enlist you as collaborators in such an
interrogation, as I re-narrate the trial of John T. Scopes. Along the way I mean
to impose a series of questions about the fundamentalist revolts of the 1980s,

including the "take-over" of the Southern Baptist Convention: How was fundamentalism "reinvented"—both reproduced and reinscribed—during the revolts? Who voiced the re-representation of fundamentalism, and whom did those voices constitute? What were the categories, assumptions, and trajectories implicit in the narrative representations produced? How, in short, has the modern story of fundamentalism been rewritten through the discursive contests of the 1980s?

The Book of Scopes

The centerpiece of the modern story of fundamentalism as "history" is the Scopes trial of 1925.[3] The terms within which fundamentalism came to be interpreted were not cast in that court battle for the first time, but they were spoken there more vividly, more widely, more sensationally, more disparagingly, more memorably than ever before. The trial produced highly charged, exfoliating representations that cycled, and continue to cycle, through journalistic and academic accounts, high school textbooks, novels, plays, movies, and television dramas. The elements represented, like those of an origin myth, are remarkably stable, invariably zeroing in on the image of two big old white men arguing about the Bible in a courthouse on a sultry southern afternoon. The story may be inflected in various ways, but all accounts concur: the Bible, the old man defending it, and the fundamentalists, "lost," even though they won their case against John Scopes. In histories of the trial, the word "fundamentalist" and all persons and things associated with it are riddled with pejorative connotations, whereas those who interrogated the literal Bible, those who "won" the battle even though they lost their case, merit prestigious associations: educated, scientific, rational, progressive, urbane, tolerant—in a word, modern.

Before the Scopes trial, it was unclear which term of the binary opposition fundamentalist/modern would be the winner and which the loser, which was high and which was low, which term represented the universal and which the residual. During the early 1920s, two loose and fluid Protestant coalitions—most commonly dubbed liberal and conservative—fought for control over doctrinal statements, seminaries, missions, and, effectively as it turned out, the prevailing definition of Protestant Christianity. They were, in other words, struggling to determine which view of Christianity would be hegemonic within American Protestantism. The activists in both camps were minorities who represented themselves as the center, as speaking for the majority, and both tried to stigmatize their opponent as marginal, the infiltrator, the upstart, the violator of order and all that was truly Christian.[4]

Although some of the religious polemics of the period were blunt and deprecatory, most were restrained and even erudite, and overall the tone was one of serious debate about matters of monumental importance. When the Reverend Curtis Lee Laws invented the term "fundamentalist" in 1920, it was embraced as an honorific by his Baptist and Presbyterian colleagues who swore to do "battle royal for the fundamentals of the faith."[5] It and the other, more common labels tagging each side acquired more unsavory connotations in the course of some very heated denominational struggles, but until the Scopes trial, neither liberal nor conservative Protestants succeeded in taking over and tainting their opponents' definition of themselves. Each side was able to sustain its own, dialogically constructed, yet relatively autonomous, version of events, its own "history" of the contest, versions which anticipated winning but could not assume, and did not constitute, victory.

Alongside the intensifying denominational fights that agitated northern cities in the early 1920s, some conservative Protestant ministers allied with politicians in the South to provoke a string of legislative fights over the teaching of evolution and the status of Genesis in public schools. The political debates were more charged, more acrimonious than their religious counterparts, having been taken up on one side by self-declared fundamentalist preachers and laymen under the leadership of William Jennings Bryan, and on the other side by liberal lawyers, scientists, politicians, and journalists in alliance with politically outspoken liberal ministers. The legislative debates produced partial victories for fundamentalists in several states, and in 1925 Tennessee passed a law that represented full victory: evolution was cast as denying the Genesis account, thus as antibiblical and anti-Christian; and its teaching was prohibited, actually criminalized, in schools funded by the state. In July, just a few months after the law was passed, it was challenged in the trial of John T. Scopes.

Even before the Scopes trial began, it was proclaimed the decisive battle that would settle once and for all which side would win the contest between religious liberals and conservatives in both arenas of their struggle, church and state. The remarkable thing is that it did just that. All accounts agree, regardless of the point of view of the author, that the Scopes trial "climaxed" the controversy, which was thereafter known as the fundamentalist (not the conservative Protestant, not the modernist) controversy. They also agree that it was a decisive "defeat" for what then came to be called the fundamentalist movement.[6] Indeed, the Scopes trial was inscribed as the end of the movement, even though the denominational debates and legislative battles persisted for another four or five years.

After the trial a relatively un-nuanced modernist construction of (what was thereafter glossed as) fundamentalism became history—without quotes. It did not abolish fundamentalist—or conservative—versions of events so much as it encapsulated them. Orthodox Protestant constructions of the Scopes trial and the events of the 1920s acquired the double-voicing of the cultural other, a kind of double vision of themselves as at once victims and critics of hegemonic insinuations, and their histories of the period were thereafter marked by an essentially modernist telos, with a sense of the inevitability of their defeat, at least on earth.[7] Insofar as narrative encapsulation is one marker of hegemony, the Scopes trial, in effect, constituted the beginning of liberal Protestant hegemony. How did the trial produce this discursive effect?

The Forces of Representation

The Scopes trial was a representational event—a complex, multi-layered, polyvocal, open-ended discursive process in which participants (including self-appointed observers) created and contested representations of themselves, each other, and the trial.

In the beginning the arena of the trial was the constitutional challenge imagined by the national officers of the ACLU in New York City, who were looking for a test case of the Tennessee law, and the men of Dayton, Tennessee, who concocted the Scopes test. Roger Baldwin, director of the ACLU, described in retrospect what happened to the contours of the case when William Jennings Bryan offered to appear as counsel for the attorney general of Tennessee:

It was immediately apparent what kind of trial it would be: the Good Book against Darwin, bigotry against science, or, as popularly put, God against the monkeys. With Bryan for the prosecution, it was almost inevitable that Clarence Darrow should volunteer for the defense. Darrow was well known as an agnostic; he frequently wrote and lectured on the subject, ridiculing many of the Old Testament myths. . . .

The legal issues faded into obscurity against the vivid advocacies of an unquestioning faith and of a rational and probing common sense. Bryan threw his challenge to the defense lawyers, stating, "These gentlemen . . . did not come here to try this case. They came here to try revealed religion. I am here to defend it. . . . I am simply trying to protect the Word of God against the greatest atheist or agnostic in the United States." And Darrow replied to him, "We have the purpose of preventing bigots and ignoramuses from controlling the education of the United States and you know it, and that is all."[8]

The entry of Bryan, then Darrow, to the Scopes case catapulted it into the arena of national debate over evolution and the Bible, science and religion.

Although Roger Baldwin's prose lightly slurred the pro-Bible camp, it, like virtually all accounts, set up the trial as a fair fight. Each side was represented by a nationally renowned oratorical giant. Both points of view would be articulated at their extremes, and so, it seemed, were nicely balanced and positioned to frame the event, the contest, in the most dramatically mutually exclusive terms. Bryan was prepared to convict evolution as heresy and to defend the Bible as truth; Darrow to convict the Bible as wrong and defend evolution as fact. Finally, neither man would hesitate to deploy against his adversary the powerful contextual associations presented him by the trial. Darrow might—did—use Bryan's rural, populist, southern alliances against him; but Bryan could—would—accuse Darrow and his team of Yankee interventionism and big city, fancy credential elitism.

Everybody had a stake in the trial's looking like a fair fight between Darrow and Bryan, evolution and the Bible, science and religion—or else it could not have produced a winner and a loser; but it was not a fair fight. The sides were not equally represented in the sense that some representations traveled much more widely than others. The representations that circulated in the courtroom seemed to be equally matched; those that traveled around the town and state were tilted toward orthodoxy; but the representations that left the state and spread around the nation and abroad were all but monopolized by the pro-science camp. The case against orthodoxy in the court of national public opinion was therefore just as settled before the fact by this representational imbalance as was the case against Scopes in the court of law.

The Scopes trial was a spectacular media event from the moment Bryan and Darrow signed on and converted it, in Bryan's words, into "a duel to the death" between evolution and Christianity. Radio station WGN, an outlet of the *Chicago Tribune,* made it the occasion of the first national radio hookup, so that news from Dayton, in the courtroom and on the streets, was broadcast live all over the country for two weeks. And then over one hundred, some said two hundred, newspaper reporters and photographers from all the big cities (two from London) descended on Dayton, a town of eighteen hundred in the hills of Tennessee. No doubt many of the journalists considered themselves Christians. Some of them may even have harbored doubts about evolution, and a few wrote with sympathy for the orthodox cause. But none of them identified with the fundamentalist standard, and overall their reportage composed an unrelenting, at times unbridled, rendition of the modern voice.

In the 1920s dozens of orthodox, conservative, fundamental Protestant journals and bulletins had national circulations, but they did not send observers to Dayton. Some did not mention the trial at all, and others described it briefly and belatedly, mainly as another instance of liberals attacking the Bible or as the unfortunate occasion of William Jennings Bryan's death. Thus the trial was constituted for most Americans by the national press, from the modernist point of view. In the "news" read and heard, around the country and abroad, the fundamentalist, even the conservative, point of view, spoken in its own voices, was erased, and then reinscribed within, encapsulated by, the modern meta-narrative.

The Main Frames and Figures

On the eve of the trial, the *New York Times* set the major narrative frame by describing Scopes as "a mere figure over which will joust the forces of evolution and religion, Fundamentalism and Modernism, liberalism and conservatism."[9] Most of the story, however, was not concerned with such lofty issues, but rather with minutely detailed depictions of Bryan preaching "in the hills" to "plain folk" and the "cranks and freaks who flocked to Dayton" for the trial. Subsequent trial coverage bulged with such side stories—some days they seemed like the main stories—which progressively homogenized, stigmatized, and appropriated the voice of fundamentalists, the plain folk, the throngs from the hills.

That the *Times* considered itself fair minded compared to the *Baltimore Evening Sun*'s H. L. Mencken was suggested by a side story entitled "Mencken Epithets Rouse Dayton's Ire."[10] Specifically, the *Times* reported, Daytonians were irked by Mencken's calling them gaping primates, yokels, peasants, hillbillies, Babbits, morons, and mountaineers. Mencken's pieces were indeed excessive, ribald, Rabelaisian parodies of both rural America and Protestant orthodoxy—which were almost indelibly fused in his writing. One of his stories, a rambling account of a healing revival in the hills, peaked with this description of a preacher praying for a penitent:

> Words spouted out from his lips like bullets from a machine gun. . . . Suddenly he rose to his feet, threw back his head and began to speak in tongues—blub-blub-blub, gurgle-gurgle-gurgle. His voice rose to a higher register. The climax was a shrill inarticulate squawk, like that of a man throttled. He fell headlong across the pyramid of supplicants.
>
> A comic scene? Somehow, no. The poor half wits were too horribly in earnest. It was like peeping through a knothole at the writhings of a people in pain.[11]

Back in town, and in court, focusing on the trial, Mencken was not much more restrained, spending much of his verbal excesses on Bryan—the precise details of his dress, his appetite, his corpulence, his somber face, his anxious glaring gaze. Darrow was, in contrast, the unembellished hero of Mencken's stories, a master in court, a source of terror in the town. "All the local sorcerers predict that a bolt from heaven will fetch him in the end."[12] On the day Scopes was found guilty, Mencken summed up the trial like this:

> The Scopes trial, from the start, has been carried on in a manner exactly fitted to the anti-evolution law and the simian imbecility under it. There hasn't been the slightest pretense of decorum. The rustic judge, a candidate for re-election, has postured before the yokels like a clown

in a ten-cent side show, and almost every word he has uttered has been an undisguised appeal to their prejudices and superstitions. . . .

Darrow has lost the case. It was lost long before he came to Dayton. But it seems he has nonetheless performed a great public service by fighting to the finish and in a perfectly serious way. Let no one mistake it for comedy, farcical though it may be in all its details. It serves notice on the country that Neanderthal man is organizing in these forlorn backwaters of the land, led by a fanatic, rid of sense and devoid of conscience.[13]

The circus metaphor evident in Mencken's summation was widespread. It appeared in virtually all secondary accounts, and it is hard to imagine any reporter resisting it. The *New York Times* described Dayton on the eve of the trial as "half circus and half a revival meeting," and the next day as "a carnival in which religion and business had become strangely mixed." [14] In fact, it was not entirely a metaphor. John Scopes recalled in his memoirs that "everybody was doing business" in Dayton during his trial—stores peddled monkey commodities (little cotton apes, a soda drink called Monkey Fizz, a "simian watch fob") and the streets were filled with vendors of hot dogs, lemonade, books and pamphlets, religion and biology: "There was never anything like this. It was a carnival from start to finish. Every Bible-shouting, psalm-singing pulpit hero in the state poured out of the hills . . . and they came from outside the state too. . . . Some professional circus performers, who must have felt at home, brought two chimpanzees. The air was filled with shouting from early morning until late into the night." [15]

John Scopes's reading of the carnivalesque scene in Dayton, like Mencken's and the *Times*', among other readings, constituted a modern voice, the modern point of view. Circus performers did appear and a carnivalesque ambiance did pervade the town, but some were *seen* in the spectacle and others saw it. The journalists, lawyers, scientists and otherwise liberal-minded men who flocked to Dayton were not reckoned inside the carnival, even though they were just as out of place as anyone else. They witnessed it. In their stories, it was as if the trial, the town, happened to *them,* to the observers of, not the participants in, the events. The observers were subjects, the persons around whom events revolve; and the participants were objects in their stories, of this history. The titles of Mencken's dispatches from Dayton went so far as to inscribe explicitly the events on him: "Impossibility of Obtaining Fair Jury Insures Scopes' Conviction, Mencken Says." "Yearning Mountaineers' Souls Need Reconversion Nightly, Mencken Finds."

The Last Day

Although the Tennessee town and countryside seemed to present themselves to the press as a modern nightmare—as the spectacle of premodernity—the trial was more wily, harder to nail down as transparent evidence of modern superiority, at least until the last day. Mencken's final dispatch, a relatively somber meditation on the meaning of Scopes's conviction, was hardly triumphal, but then he wrote it before the last day of the trial. Mencken left early, expecting that the only remaining event was the jury's inevitable guilty verdict. Indeed, part of what made the last day so dramatic was that nobody expected it. Although Darrow and his team obviously had planned for it, they too were galvanized when Bryan accepted Darrow's request that he, Bryan, take the stand as an expert witness on the Bible. Unexpected, it was also the moment everybody had been waiting for, a duel to the death, it turned out quite literally. Or so it seemed. All primary and secondary accounts I have examined, including those written by conservative Protestants, represent the encounter as a decisive moment in which Darrow beat Bryan, and many of the accounts suggest that it was humiliation as much as diabetes that killed Bryan in his sleep five days later. Here, briefly, is how the encounter is generally represented.

The courtroom was so crowded on the last day that the judge, fearing the building might collapse, convened court outdoors. On a platform set up for visiting revivalists, Clarence Darrow interrogated William Jennings Bryan for two hours about the accuracy of well-known Bible stories and about his knowledge of science and history. Bryan did not know that the "big fish" that swallowed Jonah in the Old Testament was called a "whale" in the New Testament. He did not know what would have happened to the earth if "the sun stood still"; where Cain got his wife; that Bishop Ussher's chronology was a calculation, not a quotation, from the Bible; or how the serpent moved before God made it crawl on its belly. Darrow established that (the authors of the Book of) Joshua believed the sun revolved around the earth, yet Bryan acknowledged that he believed the earth revolved around the sun. In what became the most notorious exchange, Darrow led Bryan six times to say that he did not think the six "days" of creation were "necessarily" twenty-four-hour days.

Darrow spliced his biblical thrusts with inquiries that impugned Bryan's knowledge, indeed his intelligence, repeatedly inducing Bryan to confess his ignorance of scholarly knowledge. The interrogation concluded with the following exchange:

> Mr. Bryan—Your Honor, I think I can shorten this testimony. The only purpose Mr. Darrow has is to slur at the Bible, but I will answer his questions. . . . I want the world to know that this man, who does not believe in God, is trying to use a court in Tennessee—
> Mr. Darrow—I object to that.
> Mr. Bryan—To slur at it, and, while it will require time, I am willing to take it.
> Mr. Darrow—I object to your statement. I am examining you on your fool ideas that no intelligent Christian on earth believes.[16]

Mr. Darrow and Mr. Bryan were at this point both standing and shaking their fists at each other; the judge abruptly adjourned court until the next morning. Many spectators, including townspeople who had previously cheered Bryan on, thronged around Darrow to congratulate him on his performance. Bryan, left alone, watched and waited until a few people broke away from the crowd and spoke to him. If Bryan thought Darrow had beaten him, he never admitted it, not even to his wife. Five days later he died during an afternoon nap.

My narrative drift figures the climactic encounter on the courthouse grounds as Bryan's defeat, but it could be re-presented as his victory: as the occasion of a man's standing up publicly for the Bible, for God, taking upon himself the ridicule and scorn of all unbelievers; as an unambiguous demonstration that evolutionary thought was an attack on true Christianity, on Bible believers. Darrow could be cast as a shameless man who "hated" the Bible, a bigot who mocked the common man and persecuted the Great Commoner. Bryan could be etched in our memories as a hero who exposed a villain. At the end of the Scopes trial, and at several points during it, Bryan seemed to be constructing himself and the event in these terms, but no one else took up his story line.[17]

Of course pro-science and pro-religion accounts inflected the events of the last days of the trial differently. Modern voices construed them most literally, as bearing intrinsic, obvious meanings, namely, that Darrow beat Bryan because science is superior to religion; that the truth simply won out; and that Darrow revealed Bryan's ignorance and quite properly found the Bible guilty of not representing reality. Even Bryan admitted, so the modernist story goes, that the Bible could not be, word for word, literally true; and his death proved that he knew he was wrong, profoundly outwitted and outmoded, whether he admitted it or not. The people of Dayton even recognized the truth. The *New York Times* reported:

> These Tennesseans were enjoying a fight. That an ideal of a great man, a biblical scholar, an authority on religion, was being dispelled seemed to make no difference. They grinned with amusement and expectation, until the next blow by one side or the other came, and then they guffawed again. And finally, when Mr. Bryan, pressed harder and harder by Mr. Darrow, confessed he did not believe everything in the Bible should be taken literally, the crowd howled.[18]

Pro-Bible narratives of the interrogation usually passed over the details and discussed the way the encounter was represented in the newspapers and the extent to which journalists, in their stories, converted a bad situation into a rout. According to Reverend R. M. Ramsay, writing for the *Presbyterian and Herald and Presbyter* in August of 1925: "When the trial was over, and everyone saw that the result was just as every sensible, unbiased judge who knew the facts knew it would turn out, then the newspaper reporters raised a great noise of ridicule about the awful scene when Lawyer Darrow questioned Mr. Bryan about his beliefs." Ramsay described Darrow's line of questioning as "repulsive, abusive, ignorant, tiresome twaddle about Bible questions that no true student of God's Holy Word would ever think fit to answer."[19]

Reverend Ramsay's voice was savvy and hostile but nonetheless presupposed Bryan's defeat and thus collaborated in constructing the trial as a modernist victory. Modernist accounts of the Scopes trial, no matter how gloating or unreflexive, could not have by themselves constituted the trial as literally meaning the triumph of modernity. Fundamentalists read the trial, specifically Darrow's interrogation, in essentially the same way, and it was the overlap, the convergence of the two story lines, that produced the sensation that the modern version of events had literally come true. Bryan lost in terms of fundamentalist expectations because he failed to defend the Bible according to code, which required active, aggressive Bible quoting, an ability to parry all "infidel objections" and "standard village atheist questions," and, finally, a willingness to assert that every claim, every word, every jot and tittle, in the Bible is literally true. In each respect Bryan broke the pose of absolute biblical literalism, and that amounted to his publicly betraying fundamentalism as well as the Bible, Christianity, and God.

The point is not that fundamentalists could have interpreted events some other way, but that, given their own narrative constraints, they could not have interpreted events any other way. Certainly not after Bryan said the days of Genesis might not have been literally twenty-four-hour days. With that exchange Darrow robbed Bryan of the very ground upon which he spoke— Bryan, to the amazement of all, was not even a fully formed biblical literalist.

That might well have been enough to have rendered the trial a defeat in fundamentalist eyes, but then Bryan died. His death not only definitively extinguished any residual hope that he might recoup his loss to Darrow but also provided, as deaths do, an ultimate sense of ending. A story takes shape in relation to its ending, the point from which to look back upon events as if they had led up to it. (Imagine, for example, how the story of the Scopes trial would have changed for both sides had Bryan survived and Darrow been struck by lightning on his way home from the trial.) Bryan's death figured as the last event in fundamentalist as well as modernist accounts of the Scopes trial, and most narrators elaborated it as unambiguous evidence of Bryan's loss, his utter humiliation. Darrow's words, it seemed, were deadly; Bryan had, it appeared, internalized the stigma, and it killed him. Insofar as Bryan stood for fundamentalism, his death also marked the definitive end of the movement.

Darrow's interrogation of Bryan was spellbinding and, owing to the narrative fusion that occurred in the wake of Bryan's timely death, positively mythic. It was the moment in which fundamentalists got caught up in the modernist narrative. They were captured by its terms; the modernist story encapsulated their story. In the body of William Jennings Bryan, fundamentalists saw themselves, and were seen, as acting out modernist preconceptions and scenarios. In effect, under the sign "fundamentalist," Protestants who believed the Bible is true were "othered," internally "orientalized," not simply in the numerous accounts of the trial that poured out for years afterward, but in the event itself. Fundamentalists were othered *live* in the Scopes trial; they were present and participated in the event that stigmatized them, cast them out of public life, marked them as a category of inferior persons whose very existence required explanation. The event also constituted, in and after the fact, an apotheosis of the modern gaze, its authorial point of view, its knowing voice, its teleological privilege, its right to exist without explanation.

Modern Times

The yearly battles during the 1980s over the presidency of the Southern Baptist Convention were little Scopes trials in which the William Jennings Bryan "won." That is, they won the elections and gained control of the governing apparatus of the SBC. Did they win the representational struggle? Yes and no. They established their right to be represented and to represent themselves, but they did not achieve narrative hegemony.

The most striking feature of the SBC battles, in vivo and as they were represented after the fact, is their double-voicing.[20] There is no question or confusion about who is on which side, nor that it matters enormously which side a person is on and who won the presidential elections. But there is little agreement about how to characterize the two sides and the conflict between them, about what the stakes were and what difference it made which side won. At one extreme it seems there is only one issue dividing the two sides, so it seems that in every other respect, the two sides are the same—conservative, orthodox, Bible-believing Baptists all. But the two sides do not define themselves, each other, and the issue that divides them in the same way, so at the other extreme, it seems that they have nothing in common, that they do not occupy the same narrative planet. What this situation points to is the failure of either side to establish narrative hegemony, to encapsulate the point of view of the "other." Thus events and texts are marked by double-voicing, that is, by both, or multiple, points of view.

News stories about the 1985 SBC meetings in Dallas in the *New York Times* and *Dallas Morning News* described the election of Charles Stanley as "a fundamentalist take-over," a phrase that betrayed their shaping by modern presuppositions. But the news stories also registered a crisis in the modern point of view by dwelling on disputes over labels and the definition of divisive issues, and by giving space, in the form of direct quotations, to fundamentalist versions of events. In his *New York Times Magazine* story published the Sunday before the election, Michael Berryhill actually concluded his story from inside the fundamentalist point of view: ". . . a loss of belief in the Bible will lead to a loss of the rest of belief, says [Paige] Patterson. Like much of the rest of society that is re-examining its values, fundamentalists are fearful of losing a central core of belief and authority. They see their role not so much as changing something, but as preventing something from happening. And that is a very hard principle to compromise."[21]

It was as if reporters bent over backwards *not* to sound like H. L. Mencken, just as SBC presidential candidates seemed to be refusing to embody or enact Scopes-vintage caricatures of themselves. In particular SBC moderates vociferously resisted their pole of the old fundamentalist/modern opposition (as had their predecessors in the SBC in the 1920s), insisting they were as orthodox as their fundamentalist brethren, only more willing to tolerate diverse views. Unlike the 1920s, the rhetorical mix of orthodoxy and tolerance did not establish the moral high ground for moderates. Instead their declarations of tolerance and fair play made them appear to be drifting toward liberalism, soft, and vulnerable. That vulnerability spilled over into much of the secular/moderate reportage on the 1980s SBC conventions. Thus Nancy Ammerman's fine-grained sociological account of the *Baptist Battles* is so "fair"—I would say double-voiced—that archconservative Paige Patterson claimed it proved the fundamentalist case was true all along.[22]

Of course anyone who tried now to present an unrepentant, unreconstructed modern account of the fundamentalist revolts of the 1980s would be considered wrong as well as unfair. Fundamentalism is far from dead or dying, and modern voices have been humbled, but they have not been muted. The modernity meta-narrative and the point of view it values, if no longer to the exclusion of others, are very much alive. It is difficult to find anyone willing to explicitly declare themselves modern, but the modern point of view is still hard at work implicitly, shaping stories, defining the possibilities of action, thought, and faith, indeed shaping persons, events, and history itself. We can hear the telos, the sense that the future belongs at least to rationalists, in the expectation that the SBC bureaucracy will tame fundamentalists, will teach them tolerance if only through interdependence. We can also hear the modern telos in the tremendous will to explain that motivates the chapters in this volume. We can hear the modern story in the academy's minor publishing and conference boom on fundamentalism. Even when the telos is not articulated, it lies beneath the surface, before it, squirreled away in the desire and the presumption to narrate a secular history.

Moreover, however unstable and fluid the labels are, that secular history is still narrated and experienced in terms of opposed, mutually defining, ranked categories of persons, categories which operate as literal "descriptions," more and less accurate, of freestanding, preexistent people and events "out there."

The point is not to revise, and thereby reproduce, the modernist story of fundamentalism. Nor is it to abolish that story, to pretend it does not exist. We cannot investigate Bible-believing Protestants as if the modern apparatus of thought that makes them an object of investigation had no force. The point is instead to problematize that apparatus, its representations and its constitutive power, as a once- and, probably, still-hegemonic discursive complex that directly defines and dialogically generates its "other." Within that context we can interrogate that which is called fundamentalism as a part of modernism's history, not something outside it. Bible belief is not an invention of modern discourses, but fundamentalism is. And the power of fundamentalists during the 1980s was not a direct, literal, objective expression of their numbers and their actions, but was, like the Scopes trial and the fundamentalist controversy of the 1920s, a modern discursive production. Neither their numbers nor actions had meaning, much less power, apart from how they figured in the modern imaginary.

Notes

Parts of this chapter originally appeared in substantially different form as "Representing Fundamentalism" in *Social Research*, Summer 1991.

1. Michael Berryhill, "The Baptist Schism," *New York Times Magazine*, 9 June 1985.
2. Quoted in "Southern Baptists' Feud Goes on Despite Creation of 'Peace Panel,'" *New York Times*, 13 June 1985.
3. Heave an egg into the academic literature on fundamentalism, and you will hit a "modern" account of the Scopes trial. Even those authored by

evangelical scholars are framed by modernist presuppositions, though, as I suggest, they are double-voiced in the sense that they are also marked by a critique of some modernist presuppositions.

My major sources for this study include: the trial transcript edited and compiled by Leslie Allen; accounts of the trial, its historical context, and principle figures in George Marsden's *Fundamentalism and American Culture: The Shaping of Twentieth-Century Evangelism: 1870-1925* (Oxford: Oxford Univ. Press, 1980); Pete Daniel's *Standing at the Crossroads: Southern Life in the Twentieth Century* (New York: Hill & Wang, 1986); Norman Furniss's *The Fundamentalist Controversy, 1918-1931* (New Haven, Conn.: Yale Univ. Press, 1954); Willard B. Gatewood's *Controversy in the Twenties* (Nashville, Tenn.: Vanderbilt Univ. Press, 1969); Jerry Tompkins's *D-Day at Dayton: Reflections on the Scopes Trial* (Baton Rouge: Louisiana State Univ. Press, 1965); John Scopes and James Presley's *The Center of the Storm: Memoirs of John T. Scopes* (New York: Holt, Rinehart, and Winston, 1967); Eldred C. Vanderlaan, ed., *Fundamentalism Versus Modernism* (New York: H. W. Wilson, 1925); and Lawrence W. Levine's *Defender of the Faith: William Jennings Bryan* (New York: Oxford Univ. Press, 1965); articles in the *New York Times*, the *Baltimore Evening Sun*, the *Moody Bible Institute Monthly*, the *Bible Champion*, the *Presbyterian and Herald and Presbyter*, *Christian Century*; and a variety of modernist and antimodernist theological tracts by figures such as Shailer Mathews, Harry Emerson Fosdick, John Horsch, and John Roach Straton.

4. From the conservative camp, for example, John Horsch wrote in his *Modern Religious Liberalism* (Chicago: Bible Institute Colportage Association, 1920) that "modernist theology discredits and destroys the foundations of Christianity as it has been known in all ages from the time of its origins" (5). From the liberal camp, Shailer Mathews wrote in *The Faith of Modernism* (New York: Macmillan Company, 1925) that "every age has its Modernist movement when Christian life, needing new spiritual support, has outgrown some element of ecclesiastical coercion and incarnated some new freedom of the spirit" (3).

5. From an editorial in *Watchman-Examiner*, 1 July 1920, by Curtis Lee Laws, quoted in a sermon he delivered at the Moody Bible Institute and reprinted in the *Moody Bible Institute Monthly*, Sept. 1922.

6. Norman Furniss, *The Fundamentalist Controversy, 1918-1931* (New Haven, Conn.: Yale Univ. Press, 1954). Furniss states, "The Scopes trial was a part, actually the climax, of the fundamentalist controversy" (3). At the other end of the spectrum, a history of fundamentalism edited by Jerry Falwell in 1981 (with Ed Dobson and Ed Hindson, *The Fundamentalist Phenomenon: The Resurgence of Conservative Christianity* [New York: Doubleday, 1981]) represents the event in virtually the same terms: "The Fundamentalist Movement was brought to an abrupt halt in 1925 at the Scopes trial" (90).

7. Evangelical historian George M. Marsden (*Fundamentalism and American Culture: The Shaping of Twentieth-Century Evangelism: 1870-1925* [Oxford: Oxford Univ. Press, 1980], 184 ff) comes close to destabilizing modernist frames by concentrating on the ways in which the trial and fundamentalists were (mis)interpreted in the press, implicitly calling into question the status of the "events" as such. Marsden also argues that some fundamentalists shortly came to fulfill modernist stereotypes with a vengeance, thus fueling more ridicule and leading moderate orthodox Protestants to fall away. In this way he concedes some "truth" to modern stereotypes, but only after the fact of their invention. See also Ramm, quoted in Louis Gasper, *The Fundamentalist Movement, 1930-1956* (Grand Rapids, Mich.: Baker Book House, 1963) 151 n. 57.

8. Tompkins, *D-Day at Dayton,* 57-58.

9. "Dayton Keyed Up for Opening Today of Trial of Scopes," *New York Times,* 10 July 1925.

10. "Mencken's Epithets Rouse Dayton's Ire," *New York Times,* 17 July 1925.

11. "Yearning Mountaineers' Souls Need Reconversion Nightly, Mencken Finds," *Baltimore Evening Sun,* 14 July 1925.

12. Tompkins, *D-Day at Dayton,* 40.

13. Ibid., 50-51.

14. "Dayton Keyed Up," *New York Times,* 10 July 1925; "Cranks and Freaks Flock to Dayton," *New York Times,* 11 July 1925.

15. Scopes and Presley, *Center of the Storm,* 98-99.

16. Trial transcript, ed. Allen, 156 -57.

17. When I sketched this reframing of Bryan's performance—as it might have been rendered from a fundamentalist point of view that resisted modernist insinuations—it was purely imaginary. Since then the encounter between Bryan and Darrow has been so reinscribed by Gary Wills in *Under God: Religion and Politics in America* (New York: Simon & Schuster, 1990), 97-114. Wills casts Darrow and Mencken as consciously collaborating in a social Darwinist plot to discredit fundamentalism by "diabolizing" Bryan, whom Wills figures as the benign, unassuming, well-intentioned victim. Wills concludes that the Scopes trial did not represent the triumph of evolution. On the contrary, "Just as the lawyers and journalists left Dayton, laughing and congratulating themselves that they had slain fundamentalism, the teaching of evolution was starting its decline in America, one from which it would not recover until the 1960s" (113).

18. "Big Crowd Watches Trial Under Trees," *New York Times,* 21 July 1925.

19. "Tennessee and Evolution," *Presbyterian and Herald and Presbyter,* 6 Aug. 1925, 14.

20. Sources include Nancy Tatom Ammerman's *Baptist Battles: Social Change and Religious Conflict in the Southern Baptist Convention* (New Brunswick, N.J.: Rutgers Univ. Press, 1990); James C. Hefley's *The Truth in Crisis,* vol. 1 (Dallas, Tex.: Criterion, 1986); Joe E. Barnhart's *The Southern Baptist Holy War* (Austin, Tex.: Texas Monthly, 1986); coverage of the 1985 SBC meetings in Dallas in the *New York Times* and the *Dallas Morning News;* stories on the SBC in *Fundamentalist Journal* during the 1980s; *Christianity Today* series on Southern Baptists, 4 Nov. 1988; and early drafts of some of the chapters in this volume. Note: Unlike the Scopes trial, the SBC battles were covered extensively by a national born-again media apparatus.

21. Michael Berryhill, "The Baptist Schism," *New York Times Magazine,* 9 June 1985, 99.

22. "Help for Confused Baptists," *Christianity Today,* 14 Jan. 1991.

■ BIBLIOGRAPHY

Achtemeier, Elizabeth. 1986. "Female Language for God: Should the Church Adopt It?" In *The Hermeneutical Quest: Essays in Honor of James Luther Mays,* ed. Donald G. Miller. Allison Park, Pa.: Pickwick.

Adams, Charles. 1899. *Familiar Letters of John and Abigail Adams.* Boston: Houghton, Mifflin.

Allen, Leslie H., ed. [1925] 1967. *Bryan and Darrow at Dayton: The Record of the "Bible Evolution Trial."* Reprint. New York: Russell and Russell.

Alston, Lee J., and Joseph P. Ferrie. 1985. "Labor Costs, Paternalism and Loyalty in Southern Agriculture: A Constraint on the Growth of the Welfare State." *Journal of Economic History* 45: 95-117.

Ammerman, Nancy Tatom. 1986. "Mobilizing the Messengers: What Brought 45,000 People to Dallas?" Paper presented to the Southern Baptist Researchers Association, Atlanta, June 1986.

———. 1986. "The New South and the New Baptists." *Christian Century* 103, no. 17: 486-88.

———. 1987. *Bible Believers: Fundamentalists in the Modern World.* New Brunswick, N.J.: Rutgers Univ. Press.

———. 1989. "Organizational Conflict in the Southern Baptist Convention." In *Secularization and Fundamentalism Reconsidered,* ed. J. Hadden and A. Shupe. New York: Paragon.

———. 1990. *Baptist Battles: Social Change and Religious Conflict in the Southern Baptist Convention.* New Brunswick, N.J.: Rutgers Univ. Press.

———. 1991. "Denominations: Who and What Are We Studying?" Paper presented at conference, Scholarly Writing of Denominational History. National Humanities Center, Research Triangle Park, N.C., Oct. 1991.

———. 1991. "Southern Baptists and the New Christian Right." *Review of Religious Research* 32, no. 3: 213-36.

Anders, Sarah Frances. 1975. "Changing Responsibilities of Women in the Church." In *Christian Freedom for Women and Other Human Beings,* ed. Harry Hollis. Nashville, Tenn.: Broadman.

——. 1975. "Woman's Role in the Southern Baptist Convention and Its Churches as Compared with Selected Other Denominations." *Review and Expositor* 72, no. 1: 31-39.

——. 1976. "The Role of Women in American Religion." *Southwestern Journal of Theology* 18, no. 2: 51-61.

——. 1983. "Women in Ministry: The Distaff Side of the Church in Action." *Review and Expositor* 80, no. 3: 427-36.

Ashcraft, Morris. 1972. *The Broadman Bible Commentary: Revelation*. Nashville, Tenn.: Broadman.

——. 1975. "Preaching the Apocalyptic Message Today." *Review and Expositor* 72, no. 3: 345-57.

Bailey, Kenneth K. 1964. *Southern White Protestantism in the Twentieth Century*. New York: Harper & Row.w

——. 1977. The "Post-Civil War Racial Separations in Southern Protestantism: Another Look." *Church History* 46, no. 4: 453-73.

Baker, James. T. 1984. "Recent South." In *Encyclopedia of Religion in the South,* ed. Samuel S. Hill. Macon, Ga.: Mercer Univ. Press.

Baker, Robert A. 1958. "Pre-millennial Baptist Groups." *Encyclopedia of Southern Baptists*. Vol. 2. Nashville, Tenn.: Broadman.

——. 1966. *A Baptist Source Book*. Nashville, Tenn.: Broadman.

——. 1974. *The Southern Baptist Convention and Its People, 1607-1972*. Nashville, Tenn.: Broadman.

——, and Paul L. Craven, Jr. 1982. *Adventure in Faith: The First 300 Years of First Baptist Church, Charleston, South Carolina*. Nashville, Tenn.: Broadman.

Barkun, Michael. 1974. *Disaster and the Millennium*. New Haven, Conn.: Yale Univ. Press.

——. 1986. *Crucible of the Millennium: The Burned-Over District of New York in the 1840s*. Syracuse, N.Y.: Syracuse Univ. Press.

Barnes, William. 1954. *The Southern Baptist Convention, 1845-1953*. Nashville, Tenn.: Broadman.

Barnhart, Joe Edward. 1975. *Religion and the Challenge of Philosophy*. Totowa, N.J.: Littlefield, Adams.

——. 1986. *The Southern Baptist Holy War*. Austin: Texas Monthly.

Barth, Karl. 1961. *Church Dogmatics* 1, no. 1. New York: Harper.

Beale, David O. 1985. *S.B.C.: House on the Sand?* Greenville, S.C.: Unusual Publications.

Beasley-Murray, George R. 1972. *Highlights of the Book of Revelation*. Nashville, Tenn.: Broadman.

Bell, Daniel. 1977. "The Return of the Sacred?" *British Journal of Sociology* 28: 419-49.

––––––. 1985. "The Revolt Against Modernity." *Public Interest* 81: 42-63.

Bellah, Robert N. 1972. "Religious Evolution." In *Reader in Comparative Religion,* ed. Lessa and Vogt.wBennett, David H. 1987. *The Party of Fear: From Nativist Movements to the New Right in American History.* Chapel Hill: Univ. of North Carolina Press.

Bensman, Joseph, and Arthur J. Vidich. 1987. *American Society, Revised: The Welfare State and Beyond.* South Hadley, Mass.: Bergin & Garvey.

Berger, Peter L. 1967. *The Sacred Canopy.* Garden City, N.Y.: Doubleday.

––––––. 1991. "Reflections of an Ecclesiastical Expatriate." In *How My Mind Has Changed,* ed. James M. Wall and David Heim. Grand Rapids, Mich.: Eerdmans.

––––––, and Thomas Luckmann. 1966. *The Social Construction of Reality.* Garden City, N.Y.: Doubleday.

Black, Earl, and Merle Black. 1987. *Politics and Society in the South.* Cambridge: Harvard Univ. Press.

Boyce, James Petigru. 1989. *James Petigru Boyce: Selected Writings.* Ed. Timothy George. Nashville, Tenn.: Broadman.

Branch, Taylor. 1988. *Parting the Waters: America in the King Years, 1954-63.* New York: Simon & Schuster.

Burridge, Kenelm. 1969. *New Heaven, New Earth: A Study of Millennarian Activities.* New York: Schocken Books.

Bush, L. Russ, and Tom J. Nettles. 1980. *Baptists and the Bible.* Chicago: Moody.

Calvin, John. 1984. "Commentary on Daniel 9:25." In *Calvin's Commentaries* 13. Grand Rapids, Mich.: Baker Book House.

Campbell, Will D. 1962. *Race and the Renewal of the Church.* Philadelphia: Westminster Press.

––––––. 1986. *Forty Acres and a Goat.* Atlanta: Peachtree.

––––––. 1988. *The Convention: A Parable.* Atlanta: Peachtree.

Cantrell, R. L., J. F. Krile, and G. A. Donohue. 1983. "Parish Autonomy: Measuring Denominational Differences." *Journal for the Scientific Study of Religion* 22: 276-87.

Carroll, Jackson, Barbara Hargrove, and Adair T. Lummis. 1983. *Women of the Cloth: A New Opportunity for the Churches.* San Francisco: Harper & Row.

Cheyne, Alec. 1988. "The Bible and Change in the Nineteenth Century." In *The Bible in Scottish Life and Literature,* ed. David F. Wright. Edinburgh: Saint Andrew Press.

Clegg, Stewart R. 1990. *Modern Organizations: Organization Studies in the Postmodern World*. London: Sage.

Conrad, Charles. 1988. "Communicative Action in Church Decision-Making." *Journal for the Scientific Study of Religion* 27: 345-61.

Criswell, W. A. [1960] 1969. "Pastor's Pen." In *Expository Sermons on Revelation: Five Volumes Complete and Unabridged*. Reprint. Grand Rapids, Mich.: Zondervan.

———. 1969. *Why I Preach that the Bible is Literally True*. Nashville, Tenn.: Broadman.

———. 1972. *Expository Sermons on the Book of Daniel: Four Volumes in One*. Grand Rapids, Mich.: Zondervan.

———, ed. 1979. *The Criswell Study Bible*. Nashville, Tenn.: Thomas Nelson.

Daniel, Pete. 1986. *Standing at the Crossroads: Southern Life in the Twentieth Century*. New York: Hill & Wang.

Davidson, F., ed. 1960. *The New Bible Commentary*. 2d ed. Grand Rapids, Mich.: Eerdmans.

Dockery, David S. 1988. "Biblical Inerrancy: Pro or Con?" *Theological Educator* 37 (Spring): 25.

Draper, James T. 1984. *Authority: The Critical Issue for Southern Baptists*. Old Tappan, N.J.: Fleming H. Revell.

Duncan, Pope A. 1966. "Crawford Howell Toy: Heresy at Louisville." In *American Religious Heretics*, ed. George H. Shriver. Nashville, Tenn.: Abingdon.

Dunteman, George H. 1989. *Principal Components Analysis*. Newbury Park, Calif.: Sage.

Durkheim, Emile. 1965. *The Elementary Forms of the Religious Life*. New York: Free Press.

Edmonson, Munro S., and David R. Norsworthy. 1965. "Industry and Race in the Southern United States." In *Industrialisation and Race Relations*, ed. Guy Hunter. London: Oxford Univ. Press.

Eighmy, John L. 1987. *Churches in Cultural Captivity*. Knoxville: Univ. of Tennessee Press.

Eliade, Mircea. 1963. *Myth and Reality*. New York: Harper & Row.

Elliott, Ralph. 1961. *The Message of Genesis*. Nashville, Tenn.: Broadman.

Erdman, Karen, and Sidney M. Wolfe. 1987. *Poor Health Care for Poor Americans*. Washington, D.C.: Public Citizen Health Research Group.

Fackre, Gabriel J. 1982. *The Religious Right and the Christian Faith*. Grand Rapids, Mich.: Eerdmans.

Falwell, Jerry, with Ed Dobson and Ed Hindson. 1981. *The Fundamentalist Phenomenon: The Resurgence of Conservative Christianity*. Garden City, N.Y.: Doubleday.

Fichter, Joseph, and George L. Maddox. 1965. "Religion in the South, Old and New." In *The South in Continuity and Change,* ed. McKinney and Thompson.

Flynt, J. Wayne. 1979. *Dixie's Forgotten People: The South's Poor Whites.* Bloomington: Indiana Univ. Press.

Frost, J. M. 1900. *Baptist Why and Why Not.* Nashville, Tenn.: Sunday School Board.

Frye, Roland M. N. d. "Language for God and Feminist Language." Paper distributed by the Center for Theological Inquiry, Princeton Theological Seminary.

Fuller, Andrew. 1845. *The Complete Works of the Rev. Andrew Fuller* 3. Philadelphia: American Baptist Society.

Furniss, Norman. 1954. *The Fundamentalist Controversy, 1918-1931.* New Haven: Yale Univ. Press.

Gasper, Louis. 1963. *The Fundamentalist Movement, 1930-1956.* Grand Rapids, Mich.: Baker Book House.

Gatewood, Willard B. 1969. *Controversy in the Twenties.* Nashville, Tenn.: Vanderbilt Univ. Press.

George, Timothy. 1989. "The Priesthood of All Believers and the Quest for Theological Integrity." *Criswell Theological Review* 3: 284-94.

———. 1989. "The Reformation Roots of the Baptist Tradition." *Review and Expositor* 86 (Winter): 9-22.

———. 1990. "The Renewal of Baptist Theology." In *Baptist Theologians,* ed. Timothy George and David S. Dockery. Nashville, Tenn.: Broadman.

———. 1990. "Southern Baptist Relationships with Other Protestants." *Baptist History and Heritage* 25: 24-34.

———. 1992. "Conflict and Identity in the SBC: The Quest for a New Consensus." In *Beyond the Impasse,* ed. David S. Dockery and Robison B. James. Nashville, Tenn.: Broadman.

Gilmore, J. Herbert, Jr. 1972. *They Chose to Live: The Racial Agony of an American Church.* Grand Rapids, Mich.: Eerdmans.

Graham, William Franklin. 1969. *The Challenge: Sermons from Madison Square Garden.* Garden City, N.Y.: Doubleday.

Green, John, and James Guth. 1986. "Faith and Politics: Religion and Ideology among Political Contributors." *American Politics Quarterly* 14: 186-99.

———. 1988. "The Christian Right in the Republican Party: The Case of Pat Robertson's Supporters." *Journal of Politics* 50: 150-65.

Greenhaw, Wayne. 1982. *Elephants in the Cottonfields.* New York: Macmillan.

Greenhouse, Carol. 1986. *Praying for Justice: Faith, Order, and Community in an American Town.* Ithaca, N.Y.: Cornell Univ. Press.

Guth, James. 1983. "The Southern Baptist Clergy: Vanguard of the Christian Right?" In *The New Christian Right*, ed. Liebman and Wuthnow.

———. 1984. "The Politics of Preachers." In *New Christian Politics*, ed. David G. Bromley and Anson D. Shupe. Macon, Ga.: Mercer Univ. Press.

———. 1985-86. "Political Converts: Partisan Realignment among Southern Baptist Ministers." *Election Politics* 3, no. 1: 2-6.

———. 1988. "Southern Baptists and the New Right." In *Religion in American Politics*, ed. Charles W. Dunn. Washington, D.C.: Congressional Quarterly.

———. 1989. *Religion and Political Behavior in the United States*, ed. Ted G. Jelen. New York: Praeger.

———, and John Green. 1989. "God and the GOP." In *Religion and American Political Behavior*, ed. Jelen.

Habermas, Jurgen. 1984. *The Theory of Communicative Action.* Vol. 1, *Reason and the Rationalization of Society.* Trans. Thomas McCarthy. Boston: Beacon.

———. 1987. *The Theory of Communicative Action.* Vol. 2, *Lifeworld and System: A Critique of Functionalist Reason.* Trans. Thomas McCarthy. Boston: Beacon.

Hadden, Jeffrey. 1969. *The Gathering Storm in the Churches.* Garden City, N.Y.: Doubleday.

———, and Charles Swann. 1981. *Prime Time Preachers.* Reading, Mass.: Addison-Wesley.

Harrison, Paul M. 1959. *Authority and Power in the Free Church Tradition.* Princeton, N.J.: Princeton Univ. Press.

Hawkins, O. S. 1989. *Unmasked: Recognizing and Dealing with Impostors in the Church.* Chicago: Moody.

Heck, Fannie E. S. 1913. *In Royal Service: The Mission Work of Southern Baptist Women.* Nashville, Tenn.: Broadman.

Hefley, James C. 1986. *The Truth in Crisis: The Controversy in the Southern Baptist Convention.* Vol. 1. Dallas, Tex.: Criterion.

———. 1987. *The Truth in Crisis: The Controversy in the Southern Baptist Convention.* Vol. 2, *Updating the Controversy.* Hannibal, Mo.: Hannibal Books.

———. 1988. *The Truth in Crisis: Conservative Resurgence or Political Takeover?* Vol. 3. Hannibal, Mo.: Hannibal Books.

Heriot, M. Jean. 1989. "Blessed Assurance: Assessing Religious Beliefs through Actions in a Carolina Baptist Church." Ph.D. diss., Univ. of California, Los Angeles.

Hill, Samuel S. 1963. "The Southern Baptists: Need for Reformation, Redirection." *Christian Century* 9 (Jan.): 39-42.

———. 1966. *Southern Churches in Crisis*. New York: Holt, Rinehart, & Winston.

———. 1972. *Religion and the Solid South*. Nashville, Tenn.: Abingdon.

———. 1980. *The South and the North in American Religion*. Athens: Univ. of Georgia Press.

———. 1986. Fundamentalism and the South. *Perspectives in Religious Studies* 13 (Winter): 62-63.

Hinson, E. Glenn. 1981. "Neo-Fundamentalism: An Interpretation and Critique." *Baptist History and Heritage* 16, no. 2: 33-49.

Hirschman, Charles, and Kim Blankenship. 1981. "The North-South Earnings Gap: Changes During the 1960s and 1970s." *American Journal of Sociology* 84: 388-403.

Hobbs, Herschel H. 1971. *The Baptist Faith and Message*. Nashville, Tenn.: SBC Convention Press.

Hofstadter, Richard, and Walter P. Metzger. 1955. *The Development of Academic Freedom in the United States*. New York: Columbia Univ. Press.

Holmes, Thomas J. 1969. *Ashes for Breakfast: A Diary of Racism in an American Church*. Valley Forge, Pa.: Judson.

Horsch, John. 1920. *Modern Religious Liberalism*. Chicago: Bible Institute Colportage Association.

Huckfeldt, Robert, and Carol Weitzel Kohfeld. 1989. *Race and the Decline of Class in American Politics*. Urbana: Univ. of Illinois Press.

Hudson, W. S., ed. 1959. *Baptist Concepts of the Church*. Chicago: Judson.

Hunt, Alma. 1964. *History of Woman's Missionary Union*. Birmingham, Ala.: Woman's Missionary Union.

Hunter, Allen. 1981. "In the Wings: New Right Ideology and Organization." *Radical America* 15, nos. 1 and 2: 113-38.

Hurt, Billy G. 1965. "Crawford Howell Toy: Interpreter of the Old Testament." Th.D. diss., Southern Baptist Theological Seminary.

Hutchison, William R., ed. 1989. *Between the Times: The Travail of the Protestant Establishment in America, 1900-1960*. Cambridge: Cambridge Univ. Press.wIngram, Larry C. 1986. "Sectarian Colleges and Academic Freedom." *Review of Religious Research* 27: 300-314.

James, Robison B., ed. 1987. *The Unfettered Word: Southern Baptists Confront the Authority-Inerrancy Question*. Waco, Tex.: Word.

———, ed. 1989. *The Takeover in the Southern Baptist Convention*. Decatur, Ga.: SBC Today.

Jelen, Ted G., ed. 1989. *Religion and American Political Behavior*. New York: Praeger.

Johnston, Robert K. 1979. *Evangelicals at an Impasse: Biblical Authority in Practice*. Atlanta: John Knox.

Jones, Phillip B. 1979. "An Examination of the Statistical Growth of the Southern Baptist Convention." In *Understanding Church Growth and Decline, 1950-1978*, ed. Dean R. Hoge and David Roozen. New York: Pilgrim.

Kahlberg, Stephen, 1980. "Max Weber's Types of Rationality: Cornerstones for the Analysis of Rationalization Processes in History." *American Journal of Sociology* 85: 1145-79.

Kamens, David H. 1977. "Legitimating Myths and Educational Organization: The Relationship Between Organizational Ideology and Formal Structure." *American Sociological Review* 42: 208-19.

Keil, C. F., and F. Delitzsch. 1951. *Biblical Commentary on the Old Testament*. Vol. 1, *The Pentateuch*. Trans. James Martin. Grand Rapids, Mich.: Eerdmans.

Kelley, Dean M. 1977. *Why Conservative Churches are Growing*. Rev. ed. New York: Harper & Row.

Knight, Walker. 1969. *Struggle for Integrity*. Waco, Tex.: Word.

Kovacik, Charles F., and John J. Winberry. 1987. *South Carolina: A Geography*. Boulder, Colo.: Westview.

Lechner, Frank. 1985. "Modernity and Its Discontents." In *Neofunctionalism*, ed. Jeffrey Alexander. Beverly Hills, Calif.: Sage.

———. 1989. "Fundamentalism Revisited." *Society* 26 (Jan.-Feb): 51-59.

Lekachman, Robert. 1982. *Greed Is Not Enough*. New York: Pantheon.

Lee, Dallas. 1971. *The Cotton Patch Evidence*. New York: Harper & Row.

Leonard, Bill J. 1981. "Unity, Diversity, or Schism: The SBC at the Crossroads." *Baptist History and Heritage* 16, no. 4: 2-7.

———. 1982. "The Origin and Character of Fundamentalism." *Review and Expositor* 79, no. 1: 5-17.

———. 1985. "Southern Baptists: In Search of a Century." *Christian Century* (17-24 July): 682-84.

———. 1987. "Independent Baptists: From Sectarian Minority to 'Moral Majority.'" *Church History* 56, no. 4: 504-17.

———. 1990. *God's Last and Only Hope: The Fragmentation of the Southern Baptist Convention*. Grand Rapids, Mich.: Eerdmans.

Lessa, W. A., and E. Z. Vogt, eds. 1965. *Reader in Comparative Religion: An Anthropological Approach*. 3d ed. New York: Harper & Row.

Levine, Lawrence W. 1965. *Defender of the Faith: William Jennings Bryan.* New York: Oxford Univ. Press.

Liebman, Robert. 1983. "Mobilizing the Moral Majority." In *The New Christian Right,* ed. Liebman and Wuthnow.

———, and Robert Wuthnow, eds. 1983. *The New Christian Right.* New York: Aldine.

Lindsell, Harold. 1976. *The Battle for the Bible.* Grand Rapids, Mich.: Zondervan.

———. 1978. *The Bible in the Balance.* Grand Rapids, Mich.: Zondervan.

Lumpkin, William L. 1959. *Baptist Confessions of Faith.* Valley Forge, Pa.: Judson.

———. 1973. "The Role of Women in Eighteenth Century Virginia Baptist Life." *Baptist History and Heritage* 8, no. 3: 158-67.

MacDonald, Dennis R. 1983. *The Legend and the Apostle: The Battle for Paul in Story and Canon.* Philadelphia: Westminster.

Manly, Basil, Jr. 1888. *The Bible Doctrine of Inspiration.* Philadelphia: American Baptist Publication Society.

Marney, Carlyle. 1974. *Priests to Each Other.* Valley Forge, Pa.: Judson.

Marsden, George M. 1980. *Fundamentalism and American Culture: The Shaping of Twentieth-Century Evangelism: 1870-1925.* Oxford: Oxford Univ. Press.

Marty, Martin. 1982. "Fundamentalism as a Social Phenomenon." *Review and Expositor* 79 (Winter): 19-30.

Maston, T. B. 1949. *Of One.* Birmingham, Ala.: Woman's Missionary Union.

———. 1959. *The Bible and Race.* Nashville, Tenn.: Broadman.

Mathews, Shailer. 1925. *The Faith of Modernism.* New York: Macmillan Co.

Matthews, Donald. 1977. *Religion in the Old South.* Chicago: Univ. of Chicago Press.

McBeth, Leon. 1979. *Women in Baptist Life.* Nashville, Tenn.: Broadman.w—

———. 1987. *The Baptist Heritage.* Nashville, Tenn.: Broadman.

McDaniels, George W. 1919. *The People Called Baptists.* Nashville, Tenn.: Sunday School Board of the SBC.

McGee, J. Sears. 1976. *The Godly Man in Stuart England.* New Haven, Conn.: Yale Univ. Press.

McKinney, John C., and Edgar T. Thompson, eds. 1965. *The South in Continuity and Change.* Durham, N.C.: Duke Univ. Press.

Metcalf-Whittaker, Marilyn. 1989. "Women in 'Men's Roles': A Case Study of Female Pastors in the Southern Baptist Convention." Master's thesis, Univ. of North Carolina, Chapel Hill.

Moody, Dale. 1975. "The Eschatology of Hal Lindsey." *Review and Expositor* 72, no. 3): 271-78.

Mueller, William A. 1959. *A History of Southern Baptist Theological Seminary.* Nashville, Tenn.: Broadman.

Nathan, Richard P., and Fred C. Doolittle. 1985. "Federal Grants: Giving and Taking Away." *Political Science Quarterly* 100, no. 1: 53-74.

Neil, Ann Thomas, and Virginia Garrett Neely, eds. 1989. *The New Has Come: Emerging Roles for Southern Baptist Women.* Washington, D.C.: Southern Baptist Alliance.

Nettles, Thomas J. 1987. "Creedalism, Confessionalism, and the Baptist Faith and Message." In *The Unfettered Word,* ed. R. B. James.

Noll, Mark A. 1983. *The Princeton Theology, 1812-1921.* Grand Rapids, Mich.: Baker Book House.

Packer, J. I. 1958. *"Fundamentalism" and the Word of God: Some Evangelical Principles.* Grand Rapids, Mich.: Eerdmans.

Palley, Marian. 1984. "Shifts in the Distribution of Aid." In *The Reagan Presidency and the Governing of America,* ed. Salamon and Lund.

Parsons, Talcott. 1951. *The Social System.* Glencoe, Ill.: Free Press.

Patterson, Bob E. 1983. *C. F. H. Henry.* Waco, Tex.: Word.

Popper, Karl R. 1965. *Conjectures and Refutations: The Growth of Scientific Knowledge.* New York: Harper & Row.

Primer, Ben. 1979. *Protestants and American Business Methods.* Ann Arbor: UMI Press.

Pritchard, Linda K. 1976. "Religious Change in Nineteenth-Century America." In *The New Religious Consciousness,* ed. Charles Y. Glock and Robert N. Bellah. Berkeley: Univ. of California Press.

Quinn, Bernard, Herman Anderson, Martin Bradley, Paul Goetting, and Peggy Shriver. 1982. *Churches and Church Membership in the United States in 1980.* Atlanta: Glenmary Research Center.

Rawls, John. 1971. *A Theory of Justice.* Cambridge: Harvard Univ. Press.

Reed, Douglas. 1989. "Politics within the Southern Baptist Convention: A Political Party Analysis." Paper presented at annual meeting of Southern Political Science Association, Memphis, Tenn.

Reed, John Shelton. 1982. *One South: An Ethnic Approach to Regional Culture.* Baton Rouge: Louisiana State Univ. Press.

———. 1983. *Southerners: The Social Psychology of Sectionalism.* Chapel Hill: Univ. of North Carolina Press.

Reichley, James A. 1985. *Religion in American Public Life.* Washington, D.C.: Brookings Institution.

Riker, William H. 1964. *Federalism; Origin, Operation, Significance.* Boston: Little, Brown.

Rogers, J. S., et al. 1919. "A Symposium by Southern State Secretaries on the Union Movement." *Southwestern Journal of Theology* 3.

Roof, Wade Clark, and William McKinney. 1987. *American Mainline Religion.* New Brunswick, N.J.: Rutgers Univ. Press.

Rosenberg, Ellen M. 1989. *The Southern Baptists: A Subculture in Transition.* Knoxville: Univ. of Tennessee Press.

Rosenblatt, Abram, Jeff Greenberg, Sheldon Solomon, Tom Pyszczynski, and Deborah Lyon. 1989. "Evidence for Terror Management Theory: I. The Effects of Mortality Salience on Reactions to Those Who Violate or Uphold Cultural Values." *Journal of Personality and Social Psychology* 57, no. 4): 681-90.

Rothschild-Whitt, Joyce. 1979. "The Collectivist Organization: An Alternative to Rational-Bureaucratic Models." *American Sociological Review* 44 (Aug.): 509-27.

Russell, C. Allyn. 1976. *Voices of American Fundamentalism.* Philadelphia: Westminster.

Salamon, Lester M., and Michael S. Lund, eds. 1984. *The Reagan Presidency and the Governing of America.* Washington, D.C.: Urban Institute Press.

Schluchter, Wolfgang. 1982. "The Future of Religion." In *Religion and America,* ed. Mary Douglas and Steven Tipton. Boston: Beacon.

Scopes, John Thomas, and James Presley. 1967. *The Center of the Storm: Memoirs of John T. Scopes.* New York: Holt, Rinehart, & Winston.

Shurden, Walter B. 1972. *Not a Silent People: Controversies That Have Shaped Southern Baptists.* Nashville, Tenn.: Broadman.

———. 1978. "The Problem of Authority in the Southern Baptist Convention." *Review and Expositor* 75, no. 2 (Spring 1978): 220-33.

———. 1980. "The 1980-1981 Carver-Barnes Lectures," delivered at Southeastern Baptist Theological Seminary, Wake Forest, N.C., 4-5 Nov. 1980. Manuscript circulated by Office of Communications, Southeastern Baptist Theological Seminary.

Simpson, Richard L., and David R. Norsworthy. 1965. "The Changing Occupational Structure of the South." In *The South in Continuity and Change,* ed. McKinney and Thompson.

Smith, Lewis H., and Robert S. Herren. 1987. "Mississippi." In *Reagan and the States,* ed. Richard P. Nathan and Fred C. Doolittle. Princeton, N.J.: Princeton Univ. Press.

Solomon, Sheldon, Jeff Greenberg, and Tom Pyszczynski. 1991. "A Terror

Management Theory of Social Behavior: The Psychological Functions of Self-Esteem and Cultural Worldviews," *Advances in Experimental Social Psychology* 24: 93-159

Spain, Rufus B. 1961. *At Ease in Zion: Social History of Southern Baptists, 1865-1900*. Nashville, Tenn.: Vanderbilt Univ. Press.

Sullivan, Clayton. 1985. *Called to Preach, Condemned to Survive*. Macon, Ga.: Mercer Univ. Press.

Sullivan, James L. 1983. *Baptist Polity as I See It*. Nashville, Tenn.: Broadman.

Swidler, Ann. 1986. "Culture in Action: Symbols and Strategies." *American Sociological Review* 51 (Apr.): 273-86.

Szasz, Ferenc M. 1982. *The Divided Mind of Protestant America*. University: Univ. of Alabama Press.

Talbert, Charles H. 1987. "The Bible's Truth Is Relational." In *The Unfettered Word*, ed. R. B. James.

Talmon, Yonina. 1965. "Pursuit of the Millennium: The Relation Between Religious and Social Change." In *Reader in Comparative Religion*, ed. Lessa and Vogt.wThompson, James J. 1982. *Tried as by Fire: Southern Baptists and the Religious Controversies of the 1920s*. Macon, Ga.: Mercer Univ. Press.

Thompson, John B. 1983. "Rationality and Social Rationalization: An Assessment of Habermas' Theory of Communicative Action." *Sociology* 17 (May): 278-94.

Tindall, George B. 1976. *The Ethnic Southerners*. Baton Rouge: Louisiana State Univ. Press.

Toffler, Alvin. 1980. *The Third Wave*. New York: William Morrow.

Tompkins, Jerry R. 1965. *D-Day at Dayton: Reflections on the Scopes Trial*. Baton Rouge: Louisiana State Univ. Press.

Torbet, Robert G. 1963. *A History of the Baptists*. 3d ed. Valley Forge, Pa.: Judson.

Turner, Helen Lee. 1990. "Fundamentalism in the Southern Baptist Convention: The Crystallization of a Millennialist Movement." Ph.D. diss., Univ. of Virginia.

———. 1990. "Societal Change and Millennialist Visions: Provocateurs of Denominational Strife." *Journal of the South Carolina Baptist Historical Society* 16: 19-30.

———, and James Guth. 1989. "The Politics of Armageddon: Dispensationalism Among Southern Baptist Ministers." In *Religion and American Political Behavior*, ed. Jelen.

Turner, Victor. 1969. *Ritual Process*. Chicago: Univ. of Chicago Press.

Vanderlaan, Eldred C., ed. 1925. *Fundamentalism Versus Modernism*. New York: H. W. Wilson.

Van Til, Cornelius. 1954. *Coming Grace*. Philadelphia: Presbyterian and Reformed.

Wallace, A. F. C. 1956. "Revitalization Movements." *American Anthropologist* 58: 264-81.

Warfield, B. B. 1952. *Biblical and Theological Studies*. Ed. Samuel G. Craig. Philadelphia: Presbyterian and Reformed.

Warner, Stephen. 1988. *New Wine in Old Wineskins*. Berkeley: Univ. of California Press.

Weber, Max. 1958. *The Protestant Ethic and the Spirit of Capitalism*. Trans. Talcott Parsons. New York: Charles Scribner's Sons.

———. 1964. *The Sociology of Religion*. Trans. E. Fischoff. Boston: Beacon.

———. 1978. *Economy and Society: An Outline of Interpretative Sociology*. Ed. Guenther Roth and Claus Wittich. 3 vols. New York: Bedminster.

Wills, Gary. 1990. *Under God: Religion and American Politics*. New York: Simon & Schuster.

Wilson, Charles Reagan. 1980. *Baptized in Blood: The Religion of the Lost Cause, 1865-1920*. Athens: Univ. of Georgia Press.

Wood, James. 1981. *Leadership in Voluntary Organizations*. New Brunswick, N.J.: Rutgers Univ. Press.

Worsley, Peter. 1968. *A Trumpet Shall Sound: A Study of "Cargo" Cults in Melanesia*. New York: Schocken Books.

Wuthnow, Robert. 1976. *The Consciousness Reformation*. Berkeley: Univ. of California Press.

———. 1978. *Experimentation in American Religion: The New Mysticisms and Their Implications for the Churches*. Berkeley: Univ. of California Press.

———. 1987. *Meaning and Moral Order: Explorations in Cultural Analysis*. Berkeley: Univ. of California Press.

———. 1988. *The Restructuring of American Religion*. Princeton, N.J.: Princeton Univ. Press.

———. 1989. *The Struggle for America's Soul*. Grand Rapids, Mich.: Eerdmans.

Yance, Norman A. 1978. *Religion Southern Style: Southern Baptists and Society in Historical Perspective*. Danville, Va.: Association of Baptist Professors of Religion.

Young, Edwin J. 1957. *Thy Word is Truth*. Grand Rapids, Mich.: Eerdmans.

■ CONTRIBUTORS

NANCY T. AMMERMAN, Associate Professor of Sociology of Religion at the Candler School of Theology, Emory University, received her Ph.D. from Yale University in 1983. Having grown up as a Southern Baptist, she began a systematic study of the Southern Baptist Convention in 1985, which resulted in the book *Baptist Battles: Social Change and Religious Conflict in the Southern Baptist Convention* (Rutgers University Press, 1990). It was during the course of that research that she encountered most of the authors in this volume.

SARAH FRANCES ANDERS holds the Herman and Norma Walker Chair of Sociology and is Chair of the Department of Sociology and Social Work at Louisiana College. She has had a lifelong involvement with Southern Baptists, having served on the staffs of two churches and on the faculties of two Baptist colleges. She received her M.Div. degree from Southern Baptist Theological Seminary and her Ph.D. from Florida State University. For the last several years, her research has turned to the status and role of women in the denomination, and her research files on ordained SBC women are the authoritative source on the subject.

JOE E. BARNHART, who received his Ph.D. from Boston University in 1964, is Professor of Philosophy and Religious Studies at the University of North Texas. His reflection on the issues of infallibility and inerrancy inform his book, *The Southern Baptist Holy War* (Texas Monthly Press, 1986). Currently he is completing a novel on the SBC crisis.

ARTHUR E. FARNSLEY II is Associate Director of the Churches in Changing Communities project at the Center for Religious Research at Emory. His area of special interest, Southern Baptists, polity, and types of authority, is the topic of his Ph.D. dissertation, "Majority Rules: The Politicization of the SBC" (Emory University, 1990.)

TIMOTHY GEORGE is the founding dean of Beeson Divinity School, Samford University. He received his M.Div. (1975) and Th.D. (1979) from Harvard Divinity School, and served for ten years as Professor of Church History and Historical Theology at the Southern Baptist Theological Seminary. Among his recent publications are *Theology of the Reformers* (Broadman, 1988), *John Calvin and the Church* (Westminster/John Knox, 1990), *Baptist Theologians* (coedited with David S. Dockery, Broadman, 1990), and *Faithful Witness: The Life and Mission of William Carey* (New Hope, 1991).

JAMES GUTH, who received his Ph.D. from Harvard in 1973, is Professor of Political Science at Furman University. For more than ten years he has studied Southern Baptists, political activism, and realignment among the clergy. He recently published a book with John C. Green, *The Bible and the Ballot Box: Religion and Politics in the 1988 Election* (Westview Press, 1991).

SUSAN HARDING, Professor of Anthropology at the University of California, Santa Cruz, received her Ph.D. from the University of Michigan in 1977. Since 1982 she has been working on an ethnographic study of Jerry Falwell's fundamentalist Baptist community; her book on narrative, rhetoric, and politics in that community is forthcoming.

M. JEAN HERIOT is Visiting Assistant Professor in the Department of Anthropology at Hamilton College. She received her Ph.D. from the University of California at Los Angeles in 1989, and is currently revising her dissertation, "Blessed Assurance: Assessing Religious Beliefs through Actions in a Carolina Baptist Church," for publication. Since 1985 she has been studying Southern Baptists and the nature of religious experience, knowledge, and beliefs.

SAMUEL S. HILL, who received his Ph.D. in 1960 from Duke University, has been studying the history of the Southern Baptist Convention and its role in society since the early 1960s. Professor of Religion at the University of Florida, he is the author of *Southern Churches in Crisis* (Holt, Rinehart, and Winston, 1966), *The South and the North in American Religion* (University of Georgia Press, 1980), and the editor of *The Encyclopedia of Religion in the South* (1984).

LARRY C. INGRAM is Professor of Sociology at the University of Tennessee at Martin; he earned his Ph.D. at the University of Tennessee at Knoxville in 1971. Robert Thornton and Reneé L. Edwards, his coauthors in our volume, were both seniors at the University of Tennessee at Martin when the research was done.

WALKER L. KNIGHT began working as a journalist in 1950 after receiving his B.A. from Baylor University in 1949. He served as the editor of *Missions USA* (formerly *Home Missions*) for more than twenty years. He is now the publisher of *Baptists Today* (formerly *SBC Today*), an independent "moderate" publication for Baptists.

LARRY L. McSWAIN is Provost and Professor of Church and Community at the Southern Baptist Theological Seminary, where he received his S.T.D. in 1970. Since 1984 his observations on the Controversy have focused on the conflict's social dynamics. He is author of "Anatomy of the SBC Institutional Crisis," in *Review and Expositor* and *Conflict Ministry in the Church* (1981).

MARILYN METCALF-WHITTAKER is a graduate student at the University of North Carolina at Chapel Hill; she anticipates receiving her Ph.D. in 1992. Her area of special interest is ordained women as professionals, focusing on the special qualities required for ordained women to function well in a male-dominated profession.

DAVID RAY NORSWORTHY is Professor of Sociology at Whitman College in Washington. During the racial crisis in the late 1950s, he left the Southern Baptist denomination in which he had been reared. He received his Ph.D. from the University of North Carolina at Chapel Hill in 1961. For the last ten years he has studied the inerrancy movement within the SBC from a sociological perspective.

ELLEN M. ROSENBERG is Professor of Anthropology at Western Connecticut State University. At the New School for Social Research in New York, where she received her Ph.D. in 1974, she began studying the intersections of religion, power structure, and cultural expression. While on sabbatical in North Carolina in 1981-82, she began examining sexual conservatism in the Bible Belt. Her most recent publications are *The Southern Baptists: A Subculture in Transition* (University of Tennessee Press, 1989) and "Serving Jesus in the South: Southern Baptist Women Under Assault from the New Right," in *Women in the South: An Anthropological Perspective,* edited by Holly F. Mathews (University of Georgia Press, 1989).

HELEN LEE TURNER is Assistant Professor of Religion at Furman University. Her doctoral dissertation, completed in 1990 at the University of Virginia, was "Fundamentalism in the Southern Baptist Convention: The Crystallization of a Millennialist Movement."

DIANE WINSTON is a graduate student in the Department of Religion at Princeton University; she hopes to receive her Ph.D. by the mid-1990s. She was formerly a reporter with the *Baltimore Sun,* the *Dallas Times Herald,* and the *Raleigh News and Observer*—where she began covering religion and the denominational conflict within the Southern Baptist Convention. She received her M.S. from the Columbia University Graduate School of Journalism in 1982 and her M.T.S. from Harvard Divinity School in 1976.

■ INDEX